T0392768

Global Application of Prescribed Fire

Editors: John R. Weir and J. Derek Scasta

CSIRO

PUBLISHING

CRC Press
Taylor & Francis Group
Boca Raton   London   New York

CRC Press is an imprint of the
Taylor & Francis Group, an **informa** business

A BALKEMA BOOK

Copyright The Authors 2022. All rights reserved.

Except as permitted by applicable copyright laws, no part of this publication may be reproduced, stored in a retrieval system or transmitted in any form or by any means, electronic, mechanical, photocopying, recording, duplicating or otherwise, without the prior permission of the copyright owner. Contact CSIRO Publishing for all permission requests.

The authors and editors assert their moral rights, including the right to be identified as an author or editor.

A catalogue record for this book is available from the National Library of Australia.

ISBN: 9781486312481 (hbk)
ISBN: 9781486312498 (epdf)
ISBN: 9781486312504 (epub)

Published in print in Australia and New Zealand, and in all other formats throughout the world, by CSIRO Publishing.

CSIRO Publishing
Private Bag 10
Clayton South VIC 3169
Australia

Telephone: +61 3 9545 8400
Email: publishing.sales@csiro.au
Website: www.publish.csiro.au
Sign up to our email alerts: publish.csiro.au/earlyalert

Published in print only, throughout the world (except in Australia and New Zealand), by CRC Press/Balkema, with ISBN 9781032137179

CRC Press
6000 Broken Sound Parkway NW, Suite 300, Boca Raton, FL 33487-2742
and
2 Park Square, Milton Park, Abingdon, Oxon, OX14 4RN
Website: www.routledge.com

CRC Press is an imprint of Taylor & Francis Group, LLC

Front cover: (top) Observing a prescribed fire (photo by John Weir); (bottom, left to right) Observing a prescribed fire (photo by Blayr Gourley), stillwater (photo by Stephen L. Winter), a drip torch flame (photo by Todd Johnson).

Set in 10.5/14 Palatino & Optima
Edited by Natalie Korszniak
Cover design by Cath Pirret
Typeset by Envisage Information Technology
Index by Max McMaster
Printed in China by Leo Paper Products Ltd

CSIRO Publishing publishes and distributes scientific, technical and health science books, magazines and journals from Australia to a worldwide audience and conducts these activities autonomously from the research activities of the Commonwealth Scientific and Industrial Research Organisation (CSIRO). The views expressed in this publication are those of the author(s) and do not necessarily represent those of, and should not be attributed to, the publisher or CSIRO. The copyright owner shall not be liable for technical or other errors or omissions contained herein. The reader/user accepts all risks and responsibility for losses, damages, costs and other consequences resulting directly or indirectly from using this information.

CSIRO acknowledges the Traditional Owners of the lands that we live and work on and pays its respect to Elders past and present. CSIRO recognises that Aboriginal and Torres Strait Islander peoples in Australia and other Indigenous peoples around the world have made and will continue to make extraordinary contributions to all aspects of life including culture, economy and science. CSIRO is committed to reconciliation and demonstrating respect for Indigenous knowledge and science. The use of Western science in this publication should not be interpreted as diminishing the knowledge of plants, animals and environment from Indigenous ecological knowledge systems.

The paper this book is printed on is in accordance with the standards of the Forest Stewardship Council® and other controlled material. The FSC® promotes environmentally responsible, socially beneficial and economically viable management of the world's forests.

Oct21_01

CONTENTS

DEDICATION

We dedicate this book to Dr Dave Engle. Dave is an emeritus Regents Professor at Oklahoma State University, a certified Senior Wildland Fire Ecologist and has been active with the Fellowship of Christian Faculty and Faculty Commons. He has spent his career working across the Great Plains and Rocky Mountain regions of the US on topics related to prescribed fire and the restoration of fire in rangeland ecosystems.

Dave has been a sage mentor who has educated many about the importance of prescribed fire over the course of his career, including the editors of this book. He also has continued the lineage of transferring knowledge about prescribed fire over the years. As an undergraduate student in west Texas, Dave worked with the late Dr Henry Wright, the pioneering prescribed fire ecologist and author of the seminal text *Fire Ecology: United States and Southern Canada*, on prescribed burning projects in juniper encroached rangelands.

Interestingly enough, John Weir also had the opportunity to learn from Dr Wright when he was a graduate student at Texas Tech University. The importance of this lineage of prescribed burners cannot be overemphasised because, at some point in all of our careers, a wiser and more experienced person gave us the opportunity to use fire and assured us that it was, indeed, okay to go ahead and strike that match.

Beyond just the technical aspects of prescribed fire, Dave has invested in people and provided tremendous amounts of patience, guidance and encouragement. Our careers, as well as those of others too numerous to list here, have been strongly influenced by Dave and his tutelage about prescribed fire and life in general. We recognise that we stand on the shoulders of those who have come before us, and we are humbled and grateful to Dave for his wisdom, dedication and, most of all, his friendship.

LIST OF CONTRIBUTORS

Davide Ascoli
Department of Agronomy, Forestry and Food Sciences, University of Torino, Italy

Carolyn Baldwin
Agriculture, Natural Resources, and Community Vitality, Kansas State University, Manhattan, Kansas, USA

Vanessa I. Cavanagh
School of Geography and Sustainable Communities, University of Wollongong, Wollongong, New South Wales, Australia

Lars Coleman
Berg-Oliver Associates, Inc. Houston, Texas, USA

Matthew K. Corby
Florida Army National Guard, Camp Blanding Joint Training Center, Starke, Florida, USA

Douglas Cram
Extension Animal Sciences and Natural Resources, New Mexico State University, Las Cruces, New Mexico, USA

Jeff Davidson
Kansas Center for Agriculture Resources and the Environment, Kansas State University, Manhattan, Kansas, USA

G. Matt Davies
School of Environment and Natural Resources, The Ohio State University, Columbus, Ohio, USA

Victoria Donovan
Department of Agronomy and Horticulture, University of Nebraska, Lincoln, Nebraska, USA

David M. Engle
Natural Resource Ecology and Management Department, Oklahoma State University, Stillwater, Oklahoma, USA

Paulo M. Fernandes
Department of Forestry and Landscape Architecture, CITAB – Centre for the Research and Technology of Agro-environmental and Biological Sciences, University of Trás-os-Montes and Alto Douro, Vila Real, Portugal; ForestWISE CoLAB, University of Trás-os-Montes and Alto Douro, Vila Real, Portugal

Alessandra Fidelis
Laboratory of Vegetation Ecology, Instituto de Biociências, Universidade Estadual Paulista, Rio Claro, São Paulo, Brazil

Samuel D. Fuhlendorf
Natural Resource Ecology and Management Department, Oklahoma State University, Stillwater, Oklahoma, USA

Fernando F. Furquim
Grassland Vegetation Research Laboratory, Department of Botany, Universidade Federal do Rio Grande do Sul, Porto Alegre, Rio Grande do Sul, Brazil

Marten Geertsema
British Columbia Ministry of Forests, Lands, Natural Resource Operations and Rural Development, Prince George, British Columbia, Canada

Navashni Govender
Conservation Department, Kruger National Parks, South African National Parks, South Africa

Mercedes Guijarro
INIA, Forest Research Centre, Forest Fires Laboratory, Madrid, Spain; iuFOR, Sustainable Forest Management Research Institute, UVA-INIA, Madrid, Spain

Nuno G. Guiomar
Mediterranean Institute for Agriculture, Environment and Development, University of Évora, Évora, Portugal

Robert G. Hamilton
Joseph H. Williams Tallgrass Prairie Preserve, The Nature Conservancy, Pawhuska, Oklahoma, USA

Carmen Hernando
INIA, Forest Research Centre, Forest Fires Laboratory, Madrid, Spain; iuFOR, Sustainable Forest Management Research Institute, UVA-INIA, Madrid, Spain

Kevin Peter Kirkman
School of Life Sciences, University of KwaZulu-Natal, Pietermaritzburg, South Africa

Asuka Koyama
Forestry and Forest Products Research Institute, Matsunosato, Tsukuba, Ibaraki, Japan

Sonja E.R. Leverkus
Shifting Mosaics Consulting, Northern Fire WoRx Corp., Fort Nelson, British Columbia, Canada; University of Alberta, Fort Nelson, British Columbia, Canada

Javier Madrigal
INIA, Forest Research Centre, Forest Fires Laboratory, Madrid, Spain; ETSI Montes, Polytechnic University of Madrid, Madrid, Spain; iuFOR, University Institute for Sustainable Forest Management, UVA-INIA, Madrid, Spain

Rob Marrs
University of Liverpool, Liverpool, UK

Devan Allen McGranahan
Livestock and Range Research Laboratory, USDA Agricultural Research Service, Miles City, Montana, USA

Steven R. 'Torch' Miller
USDA Forest Service, Fire and Aviation Management, Eastern Region, Milwaukee, Wisconsin, USA

Brett P. Murphy
NESP Threatened Species Recovery Hub, Research Institute for the Environment and Livelihoods, Charles Darwin University, Darwin, Northern Territory, Australia

Toshiya Okuro
The University of Tokyo, Yayoi Campus, Tokyo, Japan

Gerhard E. Overbeck
Grassland Vegetation Research Laboratory, Department of Botany, Universidade Federal do Rio Grande do Sul, Porto Alegre, Rio Grande do Sul, Brazil

Angela M. Reid
Parna Ngururrpa Aboriginal Corporation, Balgo, Western Australia, Australia; Desert Support Services, Perth, Western Australia, Australia

Eric Rigolot
National Research Institute for Agriculture, Food and the Environment (INRAE), Ecology of Mediterranean Forest Research Unit (URFM), Avignon, France

Carlos G. Rossa
School of Technology and Management, Polytechnic of Leiria, and CITAB – Centre for the Research

and Technology of Agro-environmental and Biological Sciences, University of Trás-os-Montes e Alto Douro, Vila Real, Portugal

John Derek Scasta
Ecosystem Science and Management Department, University of Wyoming, Laramie, Wyoming, USA

Isabel B. Schmidt
Pesquisa e Conservação do Cerrado and Ecology Department, Universidade de Brasília, Brasília, Distrito Federal, Brazil

Rheinhardt Scholtz
Department of Agronomy and Horticulture, University of Nebraska, Lincoln, Nebraska, USA

Russell Stevens
Noble Research Institute, Ardmore, Oklahoma, USA

Morgan Treadwell
Texas A&M AgriLife Extension Service, Texas A&M University, San Angelo, Texas, USA

Dirac Twidwell
Department of Agronomy and Horticulture, University of Nebraska, Lincoln, Nebraska, USA

Jamsran Undarmaa
Center for Ecosystem Studies, Mongolian University of Life Sciences, Ulaanbaatar, Mongolia

Vigdis Vandvik
Centre for Sustainable Area Management, Department of Biological Sciences, University of Bergen, Bergen, Norway

Liv Guri Velle
Møreforsking Ålesund, Ålesund, Norway

John R. Weir
Natural Resource Ecology and Management Department, Oklahoma State University, Stillwater, Oklahoma, USA

Yu Yoshihara
Mie University, Tsu, Japan

ACRONYMS

AR	Autonomous region
ATV	All-terrain vehicle (four wheeler, quad bike)
BC	British Columbia; a province in Canada
BRIF	Reinforcement Brigades against Forest Fire (Mediterranean)
CAT	Catalonia
CPBM	Certified Prescribed Burn Manager (US)
DAID	Delayed aerial ignition device
EPA	Environmental Protection Agency (US)
EPRIF	Integral Wildfire Prevention Teams (Spain; Equipos de Prevención Integral de Incendios Forestales)
ERQUA team	Andalusia replicating GRAF teams
EU	European Union
FAO	Food and Agriculture Organization of the United Nations (specialised agency)
FPA	Fire protection associations (Africa)
FR	France
GRAF team	Specialised wildland firefighter teams belonging to the Catalonia Firefighters; started to use prescribed fire to train personnel in the use of fire in 1998 (Catalonia)
HEMMT	Heavy expanded mobility tactical truck (US)
ICONA	Spanish forest service
ICS	Incident command system
IES	Intensive early stocking
IFM	Integrated Fire Management (Brazilian program; Manejo Integrado de Fogo (MIF))
INIA	National Institute for Agricultural and Food Research and Technology (Spain)

IT	Italy
LRMP	Land and Resource Management Plans (Canada)
MODIS	Moderate resolution imaging spectroradiometer (satellite instrument)
NFWRx	Northern Fire WoRx Corporation (Canada)
NGO	Non-governmental agency
NIFC	National Interagency Fire Center (US)
NWCG	National Wildfire Coordinating Group (US)
OPBA	Oklahoma Prescribed Burn Association (US)
PBA	Prescribed Burn Association (US)
PFC	Prescribed Fire Council (US)
PFTC	Prescribed Fire Training Center (US)
PPE	Personal protective equipment
PT	Portugal
RFMP	Regional Fire Management Plan (Italy)
TEK	Traditional ecological knowledge
TNC	The Nature Conservancy
TREX	Prescribed Fire Training Exchanges
UAV	Unmanned aerial vehicle (e.g. drone)
UK	United Kingdom
UNESCO	United Nations Educational, Scientific and Cultural Organization (specialised agency)
USDA	United States Department of Agriculture
UTV	Utility task vehicle (small off-road vehicle, side-by-side)
VFD	Volunteer Fire Department (US)
WUI	Wildland–urban interface

1

Introduction to global application of prescribed fire

John Derek Scasta and John R. Weir

Introduction to prescribed fire

Fire is often viewed as a contradiction. Fire has the power not only to destroy, but also to stimulate. Fire evokes fear in people while at the same stimulating intrigue and fascination. Fire has facilitated the development of cultures, societies and industries, yet, at the same time, it has destroyed infrastructures and lives (Pyne 1997; Brown *et al.* 2009). The importance of fire for ecosystems worldwide has been compared with soils, water and climate and their prominence as ecological drivers (Bond and Keeley 2005). Although the effects of fire are universal on a global scale, they can be quite variable locally and are often strongly influenced by humans from both a suppression and ignition perspective (Parisien *et al.* 2016). Importantly, fire cannot and should not be thought of independently without considering the integrative influence of humans, and particularly human use of fire (Coughlan and Petty 2012). Finally, to begin to untangle the fear and contradictions, it is necessary to distinguish between wildfires and those fires that are intentionally set by humans, fires we call 'prescribed fires'.

The intentional use and application of fire by humans is often referred to as 'prescribed fire', 'controlled fire' or 'cultural fire'. For each term, 'burn' or 'burning' is often used interchangeably with 'fire' (i.e. 'prescribed burn' or 'cultural burning'). Regardless of the terminology or local vernacular, historically these fires were lit with specific objectives and under very certain conditions (Weir 2009), with both objectives and conditions being determined before any ignition. The objectives could be to reduce hazardous fuels or to structure habitat features for a specific organism; the particular conditions could include specific weather, such as low relative humidity or low wind speeds, or could include specific preparations, such as the installation of a certain type of firebreak (e.g. a mowed or ploughed bare soil line). The word 'prescribe' has foundations in the medical terminology and is an indication that an authorised professional advises the application of a treatment in order to achieve some beneficial result (Merriam-Webster 2020). The origin of the word comes from the Latin *praescrībere* (with derivations from late Middle English (*c.* 1425–75)) meaning 'to direct in writing', which is an indication that the recommendation from the authorised professional be explicitly provided in written form (Merriam-Webster 2020). Although the applications of prescribed fire are inherently variable (Figure 1.1), it is the following key features that are consistent: (1) some form of authority indicating fire use; (2) an *a priori* strategy for planned execution; (3) the common practice of some organised and available plan typically expressed verbally and/or in writing; and (4) clearly identified objectives and conditions.

Certainly there are varying opinions about the acceptability and application of prescribed fires. These opinions are influenced by concerns about smoke, risk and competing objectives (Tiedemann *et al.* 2000; Williamson *et al.* 2016). However, whether a region wants prescribed fire may be a moot point because that region very likely has had wildfires burning across the landscape at some point in time, regardless of whether the fires were desired or not. Functionally, the flammability of the landscape and the risk of wildfire must be considered in developing prescribed fire programs. Moreover,

Figure 1.1: Application of prescribed fire under very specific weather, fuel and preparation conditions with a variety of ignition tools, including (a) lighting grassland with a drip torch and a combination of mowed and ploughed lines, (b) lighting brush piles with a drip torch, (c) lighting mountainous terrain with a helitorch and (d) lighting understorey vegetation in a forested system with a terra torch. Photographs courtesy of Derek Scasta (a, b) and Clint W. Dawson, United States Forest Service (c, d).

evidence suggests there may be increasing public support for prescribed fires (Gardner *et al.* 1985).

This book endeavours to provide globally relevant examples of first-hand application, techniques, local issues and methods of prescribed fire use. From lighting fires with sticks to ignition from an unmanned aerial vehicle, or drone, the ways in which fire is applied to the land is as diverse as our many cultures. Each chapter in this book presents a diversity of views and uses of prescribed fire. No other book, to our knowledge, has presented the definitive application of prescribed fire, including why, when and how prescribed fire is used, in ecologically and socially unique regions of the world like this book will. Such a global perspective, particularly with a focus on human applications of prescribed fire, is of utmost importance because, as stated by Bowman *et al.* (2009), *'An Earth system perspective is essential to understanding how fire has developed throughout Earth history, and teasing apart the direct and indirect interactions between humans and fire.'*

Although there are numerous books on the subject of fire ecology that have a global perspective, this book is not focused on the successional impacts of fire in a particular region or ecosystem, but rather the specific logistics, constraints and social dynamics surrounding the intentional human application of fire. Moreover, this book is not a prescribed fire manual intending to instruct on how to burn (if that is what you are seeking, see Weir 2009); rather, this book provides fire practitioners, both neophytes and seasoned veterans, with key ecological and managerial insights into how prescribed fires are conducted around the globe. Such a global assessment and quantification, with the inclusion of the social aspects of prescribed fire application, will allow each reader to discover a new-found knowledge about what is possible with fire relative to a broad spectrum of cultures, constraints and objectives.

Given escalating fire regimes, changing climate patterns, burgeoning human expansion into wild areas and the intensification of land use, such information is extremely timely and needed (Westerling *et al.* 2006). This book will enhance

understanding and knowledge of the application of prescribed fire at a global scale in a way that has not been done before and at a time when such practical application could not be more important. We believe it will be the impetus for a global conversation about how fire as an ecological driver of disturbance, as well as a management tool, can be restored in the Anthropocene (i.e. the current geological age, when human activity has been the dominant influence on climate and the environment) for the benefit of society and the Earth simultaneously.

The editors and authors of this book aspire to accomplish four objectives with this ambitious publication: (1) to explore new techniques, ideas and thoughts on how to apply prescribed fire from a global perspective; (2) to provide regional case studies that present the local nuances and metan-arratives that constrain or enhance prescribed fire projects; (3) to stimulate cross-cultural conversations about how fire should, could or would function in ecosystems with a broad gradient of fire regimes, dependencies and objectives; and (4) to relate prescribed fire with novel wildfire regimes that are emerging globally with implications for the protection of life and property, as well as sustaining unique fire-dependent flora and fauna and fire cultures.

To begin, we establish the current context for prescribed fire globally by highlighting key themes and foci.

Escaped fires and the media

The application of prescribed fire is challenging due to the risk of escapes outside the intentional burn unit. Such escapes are rare, occurring less than 1% of the time (Dether and Black 2006), yet, when such escapes do occur, the media is quick to develop a story. However, when a successful prescribed fire is conducted the public may never hear about it. For a North American example, the 2018 Trail Mountain prescribed fire escaped and became a wildfire on the Manti-La Sal National Forest in Utah in the US, burning thousands of hectares unintentionally

(Pignataro 2018). Such occurrences in other countries are not uncommon either; for example, a recent hazard reduction burn in 2020 in the Sydney Harbour National Park, Australia, jumped over containment lines, leading to evacuations of nearby residents and businesses (Cockburn 2020). Arguably, the public is more likely to see media reports of such escape incidents than media reports of successful prescribed fires, even though the successful fires are critical to sustaining the natural ecosystems and are much more common than fires that escape. For example, in Oklahoma, in the US, between 450 000 and 909 000 ha is burned with prescribed fire annually (Melvin 2018), yet just over 94 000 ha was burned by wildfires each year from 2006 to 2017 (https://www.nifc.gov/fireInfo/fireInfo_statistics.html). Similar disparities have also been shown for the US generally (Hiers *et al.* 2020): even though a greater area is burned intentionally most years with prescribed fire than wildfire, which fires do the public hear about? The catastrophic and scary wildfires. The public likely did not hear about the well-planned and safely executed prescribed fires. This mismatch of media coverage and sensationalism is yet another reason the successful use and need for more prescribed fire needs to be brought to the forefront so that the public can have enhanced awareness of the professional capacity of prescribed burning. The role of the media, sensationalism and the need for education campaigns cannot be overstated (Jacobson *et al.* 2001).

Policies and regulations

How policies and regulations are structured can influence the application of prescribed fire, particularly definitions of liability and negligence (Wonkka *et al.* 2015). Such statutes are established at a variety of scales around the globe, from municipalities to states to national levels, and, depending on the structure and definition, can affect the incentive for conducting prescribed fires. These statutes at the state level in the US can be variable, with at least 10 distinct features that range from how liability is defined, how

negligence is defined and how fuel and wildfire are mismanaged (Yoder *et al.* 2004). In a comparison of areas of the south-eastern US where there have been prescribed fire acts passed and a variety of either *strict negligence*[1] or *gross negligence*[2] statutes with variable requirements, states with simple negligence laws had a fewer number of prescribed burns and a lower total area burned with prescribed fire than states with gross negligence-type laws (Wonkka *et al.* 2015). In contrast to state-level statutes and guidance, Australia has a national-level policy according to the Australian National Position on Prescribed Burning (AFAC 2016). How to best structure prescribed fire policies and regulations is at the leading edge of understanding how to facilitate the optimal use of fire while minimising risk. In addition, local understandings of negligence and liability laws and definitions are necessary for prescribed fire practitioners to effectively do their job.

Fire cultures

The presence of a 'fire culture' today is often the result of the traditional or indigenous use of fire. Examples of fire cultures are available from many people groups around the globe. In the south-eastern US, a fire culture has been maintained because of the more Celtic origins of early settlers, who commonly used fire and whose fire use easily melded with Native American fire use. Similarly, fire cultures have persisted in Aboriginal communities in Australia, Native American communities in North America and indigenous communities in Africa (Hill *et al.* 1999; Gassaway 2009; Sluyter and Duvall 2016; Lake *et al.* 2017). Such persistence is a function of the coevolution between humans and advanced fire use practices (Pyne 1997). In some instances, when indigenous fire use was removed, landscape-level changes were noticed such that questions about the use and effect of indigenous fire were needed (Whitehead *et al.* 2003; Trollope 2011). Areas that have maintained a fire culture have shown the ability to work together. In other words, the notion of a culture that organises around a practice such as prescribed burning emphasises collaboration and the sharing of knowledge and work by its very nature.

Organising around prescribed fire

Not only has fire facilitated the development of fire cultures, but the modern human application of fire brings people together in groups to work together to burn safely and effectively (Figure 1.2). From tribes to community jurisdictions, the unifying role of fire to bring people together has occurred for millennia and around the globe (Gould 1971). Today, in many areas of the US, landowners are trying to reintroduce such fire culture back into areas where it has been missing for decades. These groups, called prescribed burn associations, or cooperatives, have been successfully established in the Great Plains region of the US since the mid-1990s (Weir *et al.* 2015). The success of these local burn associations has been spreading to other parts of the US as well (Riechman *et al.* 2014; Weir *et al.* 2016). Thus, cooperative burning approaches are not unique around the world, but are emerging in areas where fire has been removed from the culture. Being able to bring together the success stories, as well as some of the difficulties these groups have faced in getting fire back on the landscape, is

important to increase the knowledge and use of prescribed fire globally (Toledo *et al.* 2012, 2014).

Indigenous use of fire

The indigenous use of fire cannot be overemphasised when reading this book because humans and fire have been coupled for millennia such that fire was part of the evolutionary process for humans and was a landscape-level driver of plants and animal patterns (Vigilante 2001; Lake *et al.* 2017). For example in the Sierra Nevada region of the US, historical evidence suggests that Native Americans lit more fires than lightning did (Klimaszewski-Patterson *et al.* 2018). In the Cerrado grasslands and savannas of Brazil, the Krahô people intentionally used fire for many reasons, including cultivation, hunting, harvesting natural resources, aesthetic reasons, protection, livestock grazing and to eliminate pests, with many more specific uses within each category (Mistry *et al.* 2005). Similar stories can be told for people groups on other continents with a sophisticated application of highly variable fire regimes, and there is a need for greater introduction of traditional ecological knowledge as it applies to fire management and ecological restoration (Storm and Shebitz 2006; Shaffer 2010). Such efforts are taking place in many countries, and are restoring

Figure 1.2: Prescribed fire serves as an endeavour around which people organise themselves for (a) knowledge sharing and (b) implementation. Photographs courtesy of John Weir.

the social agency needed to effectively restore burning practices (Bird and Nimmo 2018). Today, the spatial pattern of fire ignitions is influenced by access to natural areas as facilitated by roads, with human ignition patterns spatially distinct from natural ignition patterns (Narayanaraj and Wimberly 2012). Although there are debates about the indigenous use of fire in the modern era, particularly in forested ecosystems, it has been noted that such use creates a mosaic of patches on the landscape with varying time since fire and structural characteristics that *'could be used to create firebreaks that reduce the risk of the wildfires that threaten the vulnerable and diverse savanna–forest transition areas'* (Bilbao *et al.* 2010). This approach embraces the heterogeneity or spatial and temporal variation of fire on the landscape. Fundamentally, this is different to a homogeneous perspective of how fire may function in either a system where fire is completely suppressed or where fire is burning under extreme conditions with uniform spread and fuel consumption. Finally, it is important to recognise that indigenous perspectives about the human use of fires can provide innovative approaches and perspectives about how fire is applied from *'well-developed systems of traditional ecological and technological knowledge'* (Lewis 1989).

Need for international information exchange

Another important objective of this book is to accelerate the international exchange of information about prescribed fire. In several chapters, evidence of efforts to accomplish this are noted and include applied training and partnerships. Although each chapter presents unique perspectives about the application of intentional fire, many of the challenges and barriers are similar. Such international exchange can therefore build on the commonalities of overcoming challenges and barriers. A noteworthy example of international exchange is the US National Interagency Prescribed Fire Training Center (PFTC). The PFTC started in 1998 with the objective of providing *'experiential learning through hands on application of prescribed fire'*

(Seamon 2015). The PFTC reached a historic milestone in 2015 when it burned its 454 546 ha. During this period the PFTC trained students from 49 of the 50 US states and from 17 countries outside the US (Seamon 2015). By highlighting these successful international partnerships, creativity and innovation will hopefully continue in this area.

Experiential learning and knowledge transfer

Another aspect of prescribed fire that is critical to sustaining and perpetuating fire cultures is the role of learning and the generational transfer of fire knowledge (Figure 1.3). Because knowledge about fire is attained as much through experience as classroom instruction, it has been considered to be tacit knowledge or *'knowledge that is not easily written down and derives from observing and doing'* (English 2016). In the US, such educational and training systems that produce wildland fire professionals have been slow to organise a modern and collaborative teaching system (Kobziar *et al.* 2009). If learning and transfer do not occur or do not occur effectively, then knowledge can be lost and a fire culture can vanish (Turner *et al.* 2000). This then begs the question, how and when do people learn to safely and effectively burn in our diverse cultures and communities? In many cultures, it was a respected elder who had the experience and guided the decision making. Since the industrial age, gaining access to hands-on burning opportunities seems to have become more and more difficult. Even for students who enrol in a fire ecology program, it has been reported that the most needed training was actual prescribed burning (Godwin and Ferrarese 2014). This hindrance is a disciplinary challenge to the development of competent wildland fire professionals broadly (Sneeuwjagt *et al.* 2013).

Courses that do provide experiential fire training can substantially and positively influence the trajectory of a student's career (Scasta *et al.* 2015). Experience around prescribed fires may also be important for soliciting and building support from the public at large (Loomis *et al.* 2001). Innovation

Figure 1.3: Examples of students engaging in hands-on experiential learning about prescribed fire. (a) Students at Oklahoma State University (Stillwater, OK, USA) in the annual 'spot fire' training practising suppression techniques. (b) Students at the University of Wyoming (Laramie, WY, USA) practising ignition techniques. Photographs courtesy of Derek Scasta.

in this area could also include small fire demonstrations, as shown by Parkinson *et al.* (2003). There are exciting efforts to facilitate more experiential learning, such as the Prescribed Fire Training Exchange (TREX) in the US (https://www.conservationgateway.org/ConservationPractices/FireLandscapes/FireLearningNetwork/Documents/FactSheet_TREX.pdf). TREX claims to provide what no one else is:

> … *a cooperative burning model that services the needs of diverse entities, including federal and state agencies, private landowners and contractors, tribes, academics and international partners – while incorporating local values and issues to build the right kinds of capacity in the right places.*

In 2018, TREX conducted 16 burns on 5643 ha with 569 participants from 8 states and Portugal. In 2018 TREX also hosted a Spanish-language exchange in New Mexico in the US. Harling (2015) effectively described such TREX efforts as 'learning together, burning together'. Such innovation and knowledge sharing about prescribed fire are necessary to avoid losing a fire culture.

Need for prescribed fire research to guide application

If fire is to be effectively restored, current and future fire practitioners will need research to guide such applications of prescribed fire (Figure 1.4; Quinn-Davidson and Varner 2012; Hiers *et al.* 2020). Prescribed fire is often touted as a fuel reduction tool, a wildfire mitigation strategy, an ecological restoration tool and/or a conservation approach. However, the temporal and spatial scales at which prescribed fire should be used to effectively meet the different types of objectives vary across gradients of precipitation and temperature. The biological applicability of prescribed fire varies greatly and there is a highlighted need for more local knowledge and research. Information about local historical and forecasted fire regimes, particularly seasonality, frequency, size, spatial continuity, intensity, type and severity, continues to need to be refined. Then, fire regimes must be contextualised with effects, specifically quantitative assessments of first- and second-order fire effects. First-order fire effects are direct; they occur during or immediately after a fire and are attributed to primarily heat-induced chemical processes. Examples of first-order fire effects

Figure 1.4: Researchers studying how fire moves from the surface of the ground into the canopy of conifers in the Great Plains of North America. Photograph courtesy of Derek Scasta.

include plant injury and mortality, fuel consumption, smoke production and soil heating. Second-order fire effects are indirect and occur over extended periods from days to years after a fire. Examples of second-order fire effects include erosion (both water and wind), hydrophobicity (i.e. soil water repellency), nutrient cycling, plant resprouting or reseeding, physical and structural changes to the plant community, changes to plant productivity, changes to habitat and loss of wildlife species, as well as the attraction of herbivores to the tender regrowth after a fire (termed 'pyric herbivory' or fire-driven grazing). How these fire effects are expressed relative to fire intensity and severity lends to the biological justification and recommendation for prescribed burning, and more research is needed. Broad questions noted nearly three decades ago by Omi and Laven (1982) remain critical questions today, including: how have fire regimes changed and how are they forecast to change; how do fire regimes affect vegetation types; and how does variation in vegetation structure affect fire regimes? Finally, questions persist about the efficacy of prescribed fire for wildfire hazard reduction that emphasise the need for *'more properly designed experiments'* (Fernandes and Botelho 2003).

Fighting fire with fire: call for more prescribed fire during active wildfire years

Momentum for prescribed fire programs can often be linked to extreme events, as articulated in a recent story from the US, which notes *'As wildfires rage across the state, managers are increasingly setting fires to burn the dead timber and ward off catastrophe'* (Little 2018), and in the Overview of Prescribed Burning in Australasia from the Australasian National Burning Project, which states *'There is less general opposition to prescribed burning, in the immediate wake of serious bushfires'* (AFAC 2015). Moreover, evidence suggests that prescribed burning is an underutilised tool for combatting catastrophic wildfires (Kolden 2019; Miller *et al.* 2020). Given the extreme wildfires in Australia and North America in recent years, it has never been more important that we understand how to more effectively apply prescribed fires to avoid such catastrophic events (Vaillant *et al.* 2009; Price 2012; Price *et al.* 2015).

Political geography of fire

As we have illustrated, the political and geographic characteristics of prescribed fire vary greatly as they relate to the persistence, emergence and re-emergence of fire at local and regional levels. In many examples, fire use was a practice that persisted in remote and rural regions for agrarian purposes, either burning for cattle grazing or for clearing crop lands. Certainly Native Americans were known to have many uses for fire, including warfare. In many countries, as politics ebbed and flowed and settlement patterns changed, the use of fire also changed. Specifically, in instances where communal land was traditionally burned for agricultural purposes, the lighting of fires as incendiary protest against authoritarian expropriation emerged. Kuhlken (1999) highlights examples from England, Algeria and the southern US where humans regularly used fire for land management purposes but also *'as an indication of agrarian discontent and a weapon of peasant resistance'*. In Algeria, settlement schemes and establishment of state forests disenfranchised pastoralist enterprises and incendiary protest began (Kuhlken 1999). In the southern US, particularly the states of Alabama, Mississippi and Louisiana, the traditional practice of annually burning and grazing communal lands was challenged when corporate ownership of forests developed, and incendiary protest began (Kuhlken 1999). Tanganyika (formerly a sovereign state in present-day Tanzania) is another example of such rural resistance following the imposition of bans on burning, where a government ban on burning in the 1950s elicited broad-scale burning as 'peasants now openly flaunted authority by firing the hills' (Young and Fosbrooke 1960; Kuhlken 1999). Many other examples from around the world are also readily available, but it is the notion that landowners have the right to burn and a sense of agency to do so. This can be reflected today in 'right to burn' acts for landowners that have global applications (Sun 2006). For example, in Madagascar, agriculturalists burn approximately half the country's grasslands and woodlands each year even though the state has criminalised burning (Kull 2002). However, it is the autonomous use of fire by Madagascar agricultural peasants to maintain pasture and woodlands, prepare fields, control pests and manage wildfires that is at the nexus 'between protest and livelihood practices' (Kull 2002).

Differential policies

In some areas fire policy is dictated by one group that may have a specific use for fire or not see the need for fire, but this decision affects all the other groups that need or want to use fire (Stephens and Ruth 2005). In some cases this may be due to specific ecosystem perspective, such as forests and non-forests. In addition, this can often be seen where the fear of liability completely eliminates or severely limits fire use from management strategies (Stephens and Ruth 2005; Weir et al. 2019). Often, an institution may try to replace fire with chemical and mechanical treatments to appease the masses. These policies may also dictate how the fire is set, the training required to conduct burns and the time of year and conditions under which

the fire may be ignited. All these points lead to one thing: limiting the ability for those who want to implement prescribed fire to actually get fire on the ground. Sometimes the bureaucratic hurdles are so complex or obtuse as to totally discourage the use of prescribed fire. Some agencies require employees to write extensive environmental impact statements on the potential effect of the fire, when they should really be considering why they are not using fire and how the lack of fire is the true degradation of the ecosystem.

Conclusion

This book endeavours to demonstrate how, around the world, there are unique yet similar ways in which humans arrange and organise themselves in order to ignite prescribed fires. Although we point out examples where the types of equipment being used to suppress and control the fire may vary, we also strive to find similarities across fire cultures even though they are separated by great distances. The goals and objectives for prescribed fires are often very specific, but many times they are broad and multifaceted because they have to account for a diversity of stakeholders, policies, ecosystems and more. Moreover, descriptions of fire application on spatial and temporal scales vary greatly, ranging from fires set to manage a few hectares to those burning thousands of hectares in a single day to those attempting to burn something each day in order to restore a functioning fire regime. This inherent diversity should be apparent in this text, and fundamentally embracing this variation in fire applications is necessary in order to restore functional fire regimes that span seasons, weather conditions, fuel types and patterns (Ryan et al. 2013). Yet, as a strategy, it is the unifying themes of prescribed fire practitioners that need additional attention in order to overcome many of the barriers limiting the use of fire. Prescribed fire practitioners around the globe use fire in different seasons of the year, under varying conditions and with different fuel types, but all do it for the same reason … to manage the land they live on and to sustain the

Figure 1.5: Sharing prescribed fire with future generations in a safe and non-threatening situation should be a goal of every prescribed fire user.

land and knowledge for future generations. So, although the application of prescribed fire should be viewed in the context of the biological context of the ecosystem, along with weather and fuel conditions predicting its behaviour, it is the lessons of the humans and their stories that will guide innovation into the future. Thus, the overarching objective of this book is to preserve and share the knowledge of prescribed fire with future generations (Figure 1.5).

Endnotes

1   *Strict negligence* is a breach of legal duty that leads to the harm of another; also known as the tort of failing to perform a legal duty.

2   *Gross negligence* is the extraordinary form of negligence where a person not only fails in the ordinary duty of care, but does so in a manner that such a disregard of care would have been clearly recognised by any reasonable observer in order to prevent injury or harm.

References

AFAC (2105) *Overview of Prescribed Burning in Australasia. Report for the National Burning Project – Subproject 1.* Australasian Fire and Emergency Service Authorities Council Limited, Melbourne, <https://knowledge.aidr.org.au/media/4893/overview-of-prescribed-burning-in-australasia.pdf>.

AFAC (2016) *National Position on Prescribed Burning.* Australasian Fire and Emergency Service Authorities Council Limited, Melbourne, <https://knowledge.aidr.org.au/media/4869/national-position-on-prescribed-burning.pdf>.

Bilbao BA, Leal AV, Méndez CL (2010) Indigenous use of fire and forest loss in Canaima National Park, Venezuela. Assessment of and tools for alternative strategies of fire management in Pemón indigenous lands. *Human Ecology* **38**, 663–673. doi:10.1007/s10745-010-9344-0

Bird RB, Nimmo D (2018) Restore the lost ecological functions of people. *Nature Ecology & Evolution* **2**, 1050–1052. doi:10.1038/s41559-018-0576-5

Bond WJ, Keeley JE (2005) Fire as a global 'herbivore': the ecology and evolution of flammable ecosystems. *Trends in Ecology & Evolution* **20**, 387–394. doi:10.1016/j.tree.2005.04.025

Bowman DM, Balch JK, Artaxo P, Bond WJ, Carlson JM, Cochrane MA, D'Antonio CM, DeFries RS, Doyle JC, Harrison SP, *et al.* (2009) Fire in the Earth system. *Science* **324**, 481–484. doi:10.1126/science.1163886

Brown KS, Marean CW, Herries AI, Jacobs Z, Tribolo C, Braun D, Roberts DL, Meyer MC, Bernatchez J (2009) Fire as an engineering tool of early modern humans. *Science* **325**, 859–862. doi:10.1126/science.1175028

Cockburn P (2020) Hazard reduction burn at Sydney's North Head controlled after blaze jumped containment lines, prompting evacuations. *ABC News*, <https://www.abc.net.au/news/2020-10-17/sydney-north-head-fire-prompts-evacuations/12778726>.

Coughlan MR, Petty AM (2012) Linking humans and fire: a proposal for a transdisciplinary fire ecology. *International Journal of Wildland Fire* **21**, 477–487. doi:10.1071/WF11048

Dether D, Black A (2006) Learning from escaped prescribed fires – lessons for high reliability. *Fire Management Today* **66**, 50–56.

English A (2016) Knowing fire: exploring the scope and management of the tacit fire knowledge of agency staff. *Australian Journal of Emergency Management* **31**, 7–12.

Fernandes PM, Botelho HS (2003) A review of prescribed burning effectiveness in fire hazard reduction. *International Journal of Wildland Fire* **12**, 117–128. doi:10.1071/WF02042

Gardner PD, Cortner HJ, Widaman KF, Stenberg KJ (1985) Forest-user attitudes toward alternative fire management policies. *Environmental Management* **9**, 303–311. doi:10.1007/BF01867302

Gassaway L (2009) Native American fire patterns in Yosemite Valley: archaeology, dendrochronology, subsistence, and culture change in the Sierra Nevada. *Proceedings of the Society for California Archaeology* **22**, 1–19.

Godwin DS, Ferrarese J (2014) Student wildland fire groups: common challenges and shared solutions. *Fire Ecology* **10**, 92–97. doi:10.4996/fireecology.1002092

Gould RA (1971) Uses and effects of fire among the Western Desert Aborigines of Australia. *The Australian Journal of Anthropology* **8**, 14–24. doi:10.1111/j.1835-9310.1971.tb01436.x

Harling W (2015) *Learning Together, Burning Together.* International Association of Wildland Fire, Missoula, <https://www.iawfonline.org/article/learning-together-burning-together/>.

Hiers JK, O'Brien JJ, Varner JM, Butler BW, Dickinson M, Furman J, Gallagher M, Godwin D, Goodrick SL, Hood SM, *et al.* (2020) Prescribed fire science: the case for a refined research agenda. *Fire Ecology* **16**, 11. doi:10.1186/s42408-020-0070-8

Hill R, Baird A, Buchanan D (1999) Aborigines and fire in the Wet Tropics of Queensland, Australia: ecosystem management across cultures. *Society & Natural Resources* **12**, 205–223. doi:10.1080/089419299279704

Jacobson SK, Monroe MC, Marynowski S (2001) Fire at the wildland interface: the influence of experience and mass media on public knowledge, attitudes, and behavioral intentions. *Wildlife Society Bulletin* **29**, 929–937.

Klimaszewski-Patterson A, Weisberg PJ, Mensing SA, Scheller RM (2018) Using paleolandscape modeling to investigate the impact of Native American-set fires on pre-Columbian forests in the Southern Sierra Nevada, California, USA. *Annals of the Association of American Geographers* **108**, 1635–1654. doi:10.1080/24694452.2018.1470922

Kobziar LN, Rocca ME, Dicus CA, Hoffman C, Sugihara N, Thode AE, Varner JM, Morgan P (2009) Challenges to educating the next generation of wildland fire professionals in the United States. *Journal of Forestry* **107**, 339–345.

Kolden CA (2019) We're not doing enough prescribed fire in the western United States to mitigate wildfire risk. *Fire (Basel, Switzerland)* **2**, 30. doi:10.3390/fire2020030

Kuhlken R (1999) Settin' the woods on fire: rural incendiarism as protest. *Geographical Review* **89**, 343–363. doi:10.2307/216155

Kull CA (2002) Madagascar aflame: landscape burning as peasant protest, resistance, or a resource management tool? *Political Geography* **21**, 927–953. doi:10.1016/S0962-6298(02)00054-9

Lake FK, Wright V, Morgan P, McFadzen M, McWethy D, Stevens-Rumann C (2017) Returning fire to the land: celebrating traditional knowledge and fire. *Journal of Forestry* **115**, 343–353. doi:10.5849/jof.2016-043R2

Lewis HT (1989) Ecological and technological knowledge of fire: Aborigines versus park rangers in northern Australia. *American Anthropologist* **91**, 940–961. doi:10.1525/aa.1989.91.4.02a00080

Little J (2018) Fighting fire with fire: California turns to prescribed burning. *Yale Environment 360*, <https://e360.yale.edu/features/fighting-fire-with-fire-california-turns-to-prescribed-burning>.

Loomis JB, Blair LS, González-Cabán A (2001) Prescribed fire and public support: knowledge gained, attitudes changed in Florida. *Journal of Forestry* **99**, 18–22.

Melvin MA (2018) '2018 National Prescribed Fire Use Survey Report'. Coalition of Prescribed Fire Councils, Technical Report 03-18, Newton.

Merriam-Webster (2020) Prescribe. *Merriam-Webster's Unabridged Dictionary*, <https://www.merriam-webster.com/dictionary/prescribe>.

Miller RK, Field CB, Mach KJ (2020) Barriers and enablers for prescribed burns for wildfire management in California. *Nature Sustainability* **3**, 101–109. doi:10.1038/s41893-019-0451-7

Mistry J, Berardi A, Andrade V, Krahô T, Krahô P, Leonardos O (2005) Indigenous fire management in the cerrado of Brazil: the case of the Krahô of Tocantíns. *Human Ecology* **33**, 365–386. doi:10.1007/s10745-005-4143-8

Narayanaraj G, Wimberly MC (2012) Influences of forest roads on the spatial patterns of human-and lightning-caused wildfire ignitions. *Applied Geography (Sevenoaks, England)* **32**, 878–888. doi:10.1016/j.apgeog.2011.09.004

Omi PN, Laven RD (1982) 'Prescribed fire impacts on recreational wildlands: a status review and assessment of research needs'. Eisenhower Consortium Bulletin 11, Eisenhower Consortium for Western Environmental Forestry Research, Fort Collins.

Parisien MA, Miller C, Parks SA, DeLancey ER, Robinne FN, Flannigan MD (2016) The spatially varying influence of humans on fire probability in North America. *Environmental Research Letters* **11**, 075005. doi:10.1088/1748-9326/11/7/075005

Parkinson TM, Force JE, Smith JK (2003) Hands-on learning: its effectiveness in teaching the public about wildland fire. *Journal of Forestry* **101**, 21–26.

Pignataro JR (2018) Trail Mountain Fire update: Utah wildfire reaches 13,710 acres. *Newsweek*, <https://www.newsweek.com/trail-mountain-fire-utah-wildfire-acres-burning-981235>.

Price OF (2012) The drivers of effectiveness of prescribed fire treatment. *Forest Science* **58**, 606–617. doi:10.5849/forsci.11-002

Price OF, Penman TD, Bradstock RA, Boer MM, Clarke H (2015) Biogeographical variation in the potential effectiveness of prescribed fire in south-eastern Australia.

Journal of Biogeography **42**, 2234–2245. doi:10.1111/jbi.12579

Pyne SJ (1997) *World Fire: The Culture of Fire on Earth*. University of Washington Press, Seattle.

Quinn-Davidson LN, Varner JM (2012) Impediments to prescribed fire across agency, landscape and manager: an example from northern California. *International Journal of Wildland Fire* **21**, 210–218. doi:10.1071/WF11017

Riechman JA, Park LO, Ruffner CM, Groninger JW (2014) Challenges and motivations behind sustaining a volunteer-based forest management organization: a case study of the southeastern Illinois Prescribed Burn Association. *Journal of Forestry* **112**, 215–220. doi:10.5849/jof.12-110

Ryan KC, Knapp EE, Varner JM (2013) Prescribed fire in North American forests and woodlands: history, current practice, and challenges. *Frontiers in Ecology and the Environment* **11**(s1), e15–e24. doi:10.1890/120329

Scasta JD, Weir JR, Engle DM (2015) Assessment of experiential education in prescribed burning for current and future natural resource managers. *Fire Ecology* **11**, 88–105. doi:10.4996/fireecology.1101088

Seamon G (2015) Prescribed Fire Training Center reaches burning milestone. *eNews*. Tall Timbers, Tallahassee, <https://talltimbers.org/prescribed-fire-training-center-reaches-burning-milestone/>.

Shaffer LJ (2010) Indigenous fire use to manage savanna landscapes in southern Mozambique. *Fire Ecology* **6**, 43–59. doi:10.4996/fireecology.0602043

Sluyter A, Duvall C (2016) African fire cultures, cattle ranching, and colonial landscape transformations in the neotropics. *Geographical Review* **106**, 294–311. doi:10.1111/j.1931-0846.2015.12138.x

Sneeuwjagt RJ, Kline TS, Stephens SL (2013) Opportunities for improved fire use and management in California: lessons from Western Australia. *Fire Ecology* **9**, 14–25. doi:10.4996/fireecology.0902014

Stephens SL, Ruth LW (2005) Federal forest-fire policy in the United States. *Ecological Applications* **15**, 532–542. doi:10.1890/04-0545

Storm L, Shebitz D (2006) Evaluating the purpose, extent, and ecological restoration applications of indigenous burning practices in southwestern Washington. *Ecological Restoration* **24**, 256–268. doi:10.3368/er.24.4.256

Sun C (2006) State statutory reforms and retention of prescribed fire liability laws on U.S. forest lands. *Forest Policy and Economics* **9**, 392–402. doi:10.1016/j.forpol.2005.10.006

Tiedemann AR, Klemmedson JO, Bull EL (2000) Solution of forest health problems with prescribed fire: are forest productivity and wildlife at risk? *Forest Ecology and Management* **127**, 1–18. doi:10.1016/S0378-1127(99)00114-0

Toledo D, Kreuter UP, Sorice MG, Taylor CA, Jr (2012) To burn or not to burn: ecological restoration, liability concerns, and the role of prescribed burning associations. *Rangelands* **34**, 18–23. doi:10.2111/RANGELANDS-D-11-00037.1

Toledo D, Kreuter UP, Sorice MG, Taylor CA, Jr (2014) The role of prescribed burn associations in the application of prescribed fires in rangeland ecosystems. *Journal of Environmental Management* **132**, 323–328. doi:10.1016/j.jenvman.2013.11.014

Trollope WS (2011) Personal perspectives on commercial versus communal African fire paradigms when using fire to manage rangelands for domestic livestock and wildlife in southern and East African ecosystems. *Fire Ecology* **7**, 57–73. doi:10.4996/fireecology.0701057

Turner NJ, Ignace MB, Ignace R (2000) Traditional ecological knowledge and wisdom of aboriginal peoples in British Columbia. *Ecological Applications* **10**, 1275–1287. doi:10.1890/1051-0761(2000)010[1275:TEKAWO]2.0.CO;2

Vaillant NM, Fites-Kaufman JA, Stephens SL (2009) Effectiveness of prescribed fire as a fuel treatment in Californian coniferous forests. *International Journal of Wildland Fire* **18**, 165–175. doi:10.1071/WF06065

Vigilante T (2001) Analysis of explorers' records of Aboriginal landscape burning in the Kimberley region of Western Australia. *Australian Geographical Studies* **39**, 135–155. doi:10.1111/1467-8470.00136

Weir JR (2009) *Conducting Prescribed Fires: A Comprehensive Manual*. Texas A&M University Press, College Station.

Weir JR, Twidwell D, Wonkka CL (2015) 'Prescribed Burn Association activity, needs, and safety record: a survey of the Great Plains'. Great Plains Fire Science Exchange, Publication 6-19, Manhattan, KS.

Weir JR, Twidwell D, Wonkka CL (2016) From grassroots to national alliance: the emerging trajectory for landowner prescribed burn associations. *Rangelands* **38**, 113–119. doi:10.1016/j.rala.2016.02.005

Weir JR, Kreuter UP, Wonkka CL, Twidwell D, Stroman DA, Russell M, Taylor CA (2019) Liability and prescribed fire: perception and reality. *Rangeland Ecology & Management* **72**(3), 533–538. doi:10.1016/j.rama.2018.11.010

Westerling AL, Hidalgo HG, Cayan DR, Swetnam TW (2006) Warming and earlier spring increase western US forest wildfire activity. *Science* **313**, 940–943. doi:10.1126/science.1128834

Whitehead PJ, Bowman DM, Preece N, Fraser F, Cooke P (2003) Customary use of fire by Indigenous peoples in northern Australia: its contemporary role in savanna management. *International Journal of Wildland Fire* **12**, 415–425. doi:10.1071/WF03027

Williamson GJ, Bowman DMS, Price OF, Henderson SB, Johnston FH (2016) A transdisciplinary approach to understanding the health effects of wildfire and prescribed fire smoke regimes. *Environmental Research Letters* **11**, 125009. doi:10.1088/1748-9326/11/12/125009

Wonkka CL, Rogers WE, Kreuter UP (2015) Legal barriers to effective ecosystem management: exploring linkages between liability, regulations, and prescribed fire. *Ecological Applications* **25**, 2382–2393. doi:10.1890/14-1791.1

Yoder J, Engle D, Fuhlendorf S (2004) Liability, incentives, and prescribed fire for ecosystem management. *Frontiers in Ecology and the Environment* **2**, 361–366. doi:10.1890/1540-9295(2004)002[0361:LIAPFF]2.0.CO;2

Young R, Fosbrooke H (1960) *Smoke in the Hills: Political Tension in the Morogoro District of Tanganyika*. Northwestern University Press, Evanston.

2

Fire in the boreal forest, north-east British Columbia, Canada: putting fire out on the land

Sonja E. R. Leverkus, Samuel D. Fuhlendorf,
Marten Geertsema and David M. Engle

Fire history

The circumboreal forest is the most extensive, intact terrestrial biome on Earth, with an estimated number of more than 100 000 species of plants and animals (Zasada *et al.* 1997; Schmiegelow *et al.* 2006; Burton *et al.* 2008; Flannigan *et al.* 2009). Fire varies across the boreal landscape through space and time, resulting in a shifting mosaic of patches with different fire return intervals, promoting habitat heterogeneity and biodiversity (Christensen 1997; Ostfeld *et al.* 1997; Wiens 1997; Fuhlendorf and Engle 2001; Fuhlendorf *et al.* 2006). The current patchwork mosaic of the boreal ecosystem has been shaped by lightning and anthropogenic fire since the last Ice Age (Rowe and Scotter 1973; Goldammer and Furyaev 1996; Stocks *et al.* 2003). Fire in the boreal forest is evidenced by fire statistics (Johnson 1992), soil profiles containing charcoal (Rowe and Scotter 1973; Larsen and MacDonald 1998), reproductive and morphological traits of boreal plant species (Rowe and Scotter 1973), the oral history of Indigenous people (Lewis and Ferguson 1988; Johnson 1992; Suffling and Speller 1998) and the age-related structural mosaic characteristics of

forest stands (Rowe and Scotter 1973). Prior to European settlement in Canada, large-scale crown fires and high-intensity surface fires occurred across Canadian boreal forests at fire return intervals ranging from 50 to 700 years, with some areas burnt more frequently by humans (Heinselman 1981; Lewis and Ferguson 1988; Peck and Peek 1991; Stocks *et al.* 2003; Leverkus 2015).

Determining a single fire regime or fire return interval for any given location in the boreal forest is virtually impossible because of the variability of climate and the interaction between disturbance agents such as forest fire, geomorphological events, windstorms, insect outbreaks and floods (DeLong *et al.* 2013; Leverkus 2015). The boreal forest is a dynamic system, with fire scars and boundaries from past fires influencing current and future areas burned (Bergeron and Archambault 1993; Johnson *et al.* 1998). In light of the challenges to determine specific return intervals, we do know that the fire return interval of the boreal forest ranges from small frequent burns (annual burning of yards and corridors by First Nations and Indigenous people) to larger wildfire events (Lewis and

Ferguson 1988; Kasischke *et al.* 1995; Larsen and MacDonald 1998; Leverkus 2015).

Species have adapted in the boreal forest in order to withstand the combined pressure of a short but intensive growing season in which fire often occurs followed by a long season of cold temperature and snow cover (Bergeron *et al.* 2004; Burton *et al.* 2006; Leverkus *et al.* 2018a). Adaptations of vegetation to the disturbance of fire include the ability to resprout after the disturbance (e.g. suckering of aspen *Populus tremuloides* Michx; Schier and Campbell 1978), to retain viable seeds in the soil over a long period of time (e.g. seed-banking species such as Bicknell's geranium *Geranium bicknellii* and the corydalis species *Corydalis sempervirens* (L.) Pers. and *Corydalis aurea* Willd.; MacKinnon *et al.* 1999; Catling *et al.* 2001) and cone serotiny (e.g. lodgepole pine *Pinus contorta* var. *latifolia* Douglas ex Loudon; MacKinnon *et al.* 1999; Leverkus 2015; Leverkus *et al.* 2018a). Fire is a critical ecosystem driver across varying spatiotemporal scales in the boreal forest (Leverkus 2015). Plant species composition and structure, the regulation of diseases and insects, the maintenance and promotion of production and the diversity of vegetation types, as well as nutrient cycling and energy fluxes, are all influenced by fire in the boreal forest (Rowe and Scotter 1973; Volney and Hirsch 2005; Leverkus *et al.* 2018a).

North-east British Columbia (BC) provides an example in which fire and disturbance-related processes are primary ecosystem drivers (Parminter 1983). North-east BC is situated within the region encompassed by the Alberta Plateau, Liard Plateau, Liard Plain, Rocky Mountain Foothills and Muskwa Ranges (Holland 1976; DeLong 1990). The forest types in the area include Boreal White and Black Spruce, spruce–willow–birch, sub-boreal spruce and Alpine tundra. Aspen forests, shrubby meadows and grassy slopes, all maintained by fire, are dispersed through the valleys and slopes of the northern Rocky Mountains dominated by conifers (*Picea glauca* (Moench) Voss, *Picea mariana* (Mill.) BSP and *Pinus contorta* Douglas ex Loudon; Raup 1945). A fire avoider with little adaptation to fire

(Agee 1993) in the region is white spruce (*P. glauca*), but it is highly flammable and requires mineral soil where the humus layer and competing vegetation has been consumed by fire (Parminter 1983), suggesting that an interaction with fire may benefit the species. Fire evaders with long-lived propagules stored in the soil or canopy that germinate after fire (Agee 1993) in the region include trembling aspen (root suckers, root collar and stump sprout), tamarack *Larix laricina* (Du Roi) K. Koch (root shoots and layering), balsam poplar *Populus balsamifera* (root suckers and stump sprouts), paper birch *Betula papyrifera* Marsh (stump sprouts), lodgepole pine (serotinous cones), black spruce *P. mariana* (layering), subalpine fir *Abies lasiocarpa* (Hook.) Nutt (layering), highbush cranberry *Viburnum edule* (Michx.) Raf. (20- to 30-cm rhizomes), Labrador tea *Rhododendron groenlandicum* (Oeder) Kron & Judd (15- to 50-cm underground stems), prickly rose *Rosa acicularis* Lindl. (20- to 30-cm underground rhizomes), red-osier dogwood *Cornus stolonifera* Michx. (sprouting from rhizomes and aerial stems) and willows *Salix* sp. (root sprouting; Parminter 1983).

The boreal forest is a pyrogenic ecosystem driven by human and lightning ignitions resulting in a shifting mosaic of vegetation height, composition and distribution (Rowe and Scotter 1973; Goldammer and Furyaev 1996; Fuhlendorf and Engle 2004). Fire plays such an important role in the boreal forest that the type (surface or crown), intensity (amount of energy released), severity (overall effect of fire on the ecosystem), frequency (number of fires) and time since the last fire have significant effects on the distribution and composition of the vegetation present on most sites (Parminter 1983). The number of fires and the number of times a particular area has burned result in differences in vertical structure and species composition that lead to heterogeneity, which has been argued to be the root of biological diversity. The presence of different vegetation types and differences in vegetation structure and distribution are driven by the time since fire (Parminter 1983; Leverkus *et al.* 2017).

Human fire ignitions have affected the spatio-temporal distribution of fire across the boreal forest (Rowe and Scotter 1973; Lewis 1978a, 1978b; Lewis and Ferguson 1988; Gottesfeld 1994; Pyne 2007), and specifically across north-east BC, over the past century (Elliott 1983; Seip and Bunnell 1985; Peck and Peek 1991; Sittler 2013; Plate 1). North-east BC has a long history of wildland and prescribed fire (Figure 2.1). Anthropogenic fire has occurred across the region, with a focus on the rolling hills and mountainous regions for centuries lead by Indigenous people and, in more recent history, by guide outfitters, range tenure holders and the Northeastern BC Wildlife Fund, licenced and permitted by the provincial government to maintain rangelands in their allotted areas. Provincial government staff in north-east BC also contributed to the application of fire on the land from the late

1970s until approximately 2016. For much of the prescribed fire discussed in this chapter, the locations of the prescribed fire units are remote insofar as they are only accessible by boat, plane, helicopter or several days on horseback. It is important to note that this vast area is arguably one of the most intact wilderness places in North America where ecological processes, including fire, occur to support a biologically diverse abundance of wildlife.

The cultural landscape that has resulted over generations of human-caused fires is visible from aerial imagery across north-east BC, where fires were historically ignited for a variety of reasons by the Dene and Cree people, including for hunting and survival, regrowth of vegetation, communication and ceremonial and aesthetic practices. The relationship between fire and the Dene and Cree people of Fort Nelson First Nation is culturally

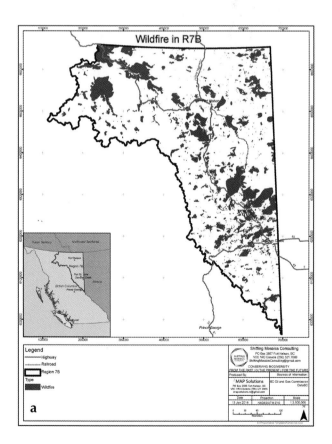
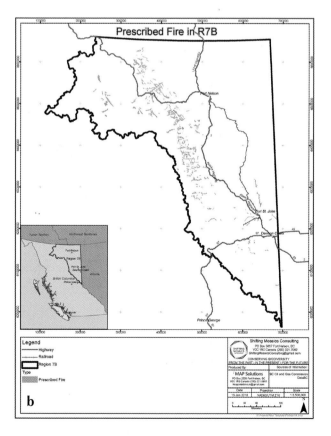

Figure 2.1: (a) Pyrogenic landscape history of documented wildland fire (1922–2018) in north-east British Columbia (Region 7B) compared with (b) the spatial fire history of recorded prescribed fires from 1980 to 2008, adapted from Leverkus *et al.* (2015) and Leverkus *et al.* 2017, 2018a, 2018b, 2018c).

complex and dates back thousands of years (Fort Nelson First Nation and Shifting Mosaics Consulting 2015). The tradition of igniting fires in the spring of each year has since been continued by guide outfitters and range tenure holders across the region (Peck and Peek 1991).

The provincial government operated a prescribed fire program for almost 30 years, beginning in the late 1970s; however, the program has since been discontinued. Indigenous communities have recently started to reconnect with their cultural fire practices, with notable leadership by Fort Nelson First Nation (Dene and Cree) and Blueberry River First Nation (Dunne-za). Although prescribed fire has occurred across the region over the past century, it has become increasingly controversial due to the lack of understanding of the critical ecological role that fire plays across the landscape. There is an inclination by government agencies to reject the notion of fire as an ecological process that interacts with other processes such as herbivory and that, when coupled as pyric herbivory (the fire–grazing interaction; Fuhlendorf et al. 2009), fire drives the ecosystems within the region.

Historical objectives for fire use

Fire regimes become complex when an entire landscape is considered from a broad scale (Wright and Bailey 1982). Different species may require high-frequency and high-intensity disturbances, whereas others may require low disturbance frequency and intensity (Knopf 1996; Fuhlendorf et al. 2012; Figures 2.2, 2.3). Historically, there has been a simplistic view of land management where ecological processes and interactions have not been taken into consideration. The result on large landscapes is that critical patterns derived from these processes are neither comprehensively understood nor accepted (Fuhlendorf et al. 2012).

Rowe and Scotter (1973) suggested that influences that diversify the landscape across space and time will increase the diversity of fauna. They put forward the notion that fire is the main driver that causes this diversity in the resulting mosaic pattern it leaves across the boreal forest. Humans living and depending on the land in the boreal forest have long understood the critical needs for this mosaic pattern, its distribution across the landscape and the importance of putting fire out on the land. Dr Henry Lewis was the first scientist who documented this long-time understanding of the Dene of northern Alberta of prescribed fire in the boreal forest (Lewis 1978a, 1978b; Lewis and Ferguson 1988). Although written documentation of the historical use of fire by First Nations, Indigenous communities, Metis People and long-time residents of the boreal forest in Canada is limited, Dr Lewis and his team provided a foundation for understanding this complex relationship. Efforts have been made by several researchers, in addition to Dr Henry Lewis, to document, incorporate and mobilise traditional and local fire ecological knowledge into fire practices, including Dr Nancy Turner, Dr Richard Suffling and Dr Sonja Leverkus, in partnership with Fort Nelson First Nation and Blueberry River First Nation.

There remains a strong need to document the traditional, cultural and local use of fire in the boreal forest, particularly in north-east BC. Bordering jurisdictions are known to have burned to enhance wildlife and enable the harvest of alpine sweet vetch *Hedysarum alpinum* roots (Hawkes 1983). In his provincial-leading work starting in the early 1980s, Parminter (1983) suggested that if prescribed fire was used by the natives of northern Alberta and the southern Yukon, it could be inferred that it was also part of the Indigenous practices in northern BC. The only study completed to date on this topic in north-east BC was conducted by Fort Nelson First Nation and Shifting Mosaics Consulting. Regional ethnographic information about the traditional use of fires was documented by interviewing Dene and Cree Elders and community members from Fort Nelson First Nation (Fort Nelson First Nation and Shifting Mosaics Consulting 2015). That study documented the importance that fire has always had for Fort Nelson First Nation people and that fire brings people together with the landscape they have been part of

Figure 2.2: Different areas across the boreal, at different times since fire, meet the different resource requirements of wildlife. (a) Wood bison, (b) grouse, (c) fisher and (d) caribou. Photographs courtesy of S. Leverkus (a, b, d) and C. M. Gitscheff (c).

for centuries. The documented use of fire includes grass burning and clearing for the removal of fuel and to support the regrowth of vegetation, to increase the aesthetic and visual quality of the surrounding areas, for spiritual and ceremonial purposes and for hunting. Burning along the rivers produced new growth that enticed the moose and deer, and provided sightlines to make hunting easier. Fort Nelson First Nation people used to burn hillsides, wild hay meadows and around cabins and campsites. In the late 1970s and 1980s, Lewis and Ferguson documented similar practices by

Dene and Metis people in northern Alberta (Lewis 1978a, 1978b; Lewis and Ferguson 1988).

The following are excerpts from the book *Fort Nelson First Nation: Interaction With Fire and Wood Bison* by Fort Nelson First Nation and Shifting Mosaics Consulting (2015); the names of the interviewees are not included:

I was born and raised at Kahntah, and my earliest memory of burning was when I was 10 or 12 years old … They burned in the evening in the early spring for horses, and in August they

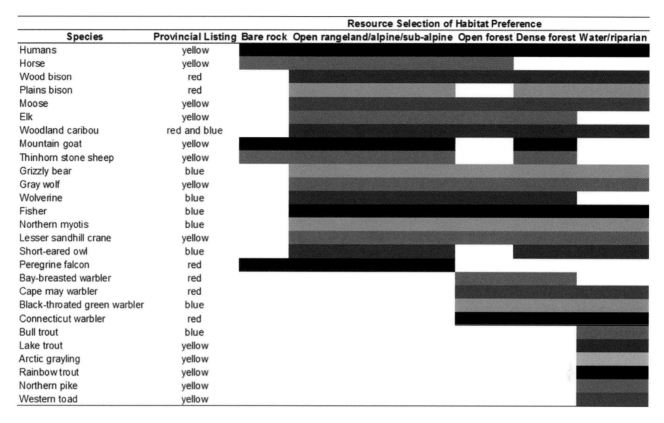

Figure 2.3: Priority wildlife species of the Muskwa-Kechika Management Area and their resource selection of habitat preference. Adapted from Lamprey (1963), Heady (1966) and Leverkus *et al.* (2017).

would cut down the new growth. Deer would eat the new growth too.

I spent most of my childhood in Nelson Forks, and I remember burning every year in the south. We burned to control grass and brush, and it was done mostly for animals, and to make travel much easier within the area. Overgrown brush is a hazard – with build up of brush you could have a big fire and it could burn the cabin. Fire brought in moose and rabbits, and it's been done for centuries. My family has been burning for many generations.

I help burn every year, since I was 5 or 6 years old, and learned it from my grandparents and other elders. Everyone in the family burned because it was the only way to keep the land clear.

My earliest memory is from 1942. They had big fires, forest fires, not just meadows like people are interested in. Fires in the Territories, Alberta, and BC nearly wiped out all the rabbits, and other animals suffered without food. In 1955 people started fighting fire. Tuchodi Lake/Muskwa would burn every year, and it was good for hunting. Today, if you make a small fire for tea, the ranger will charge you a fine. No tea for you.

I burn every year in early Spring. Everyone would burn along creeks and rivers, and around beaver ponds, and around cabins when there was still some snow on the ground. When the willows grow – let them grow and burn the spruce. The usual reasons for burning were for graze for animals. The dead grass that dies off and builds up is the worst to catch fire which is very dangerous. Women would be swatting with their brooms, children would have buckets of water while the men burned. Wet gunny sacks and a *rake were used to smother the fire. Everyone got involved.*

… Lots of rabbits, moose, and bears came to eat the new shoots after burning.

We usually burned to maintain river/mountain corridor … to maintain land for horses, and for safety – to open visual corridors so you're not in a hole peeking through the bush.

I think there should be more fires. There's too much brush and it makes it hard to walk through important areas. The windfall is really bad for animals in the winter. They get in trouble and it's easier for the wolves to get them.

The forestry service should let First Nations people burn in their areas. There are a lot of limitations to burning now, and all the paperwork and permits makes it hard. You can't light a fire in your own yard without being called an arsonist.

Current objectives for fire use

Long-time residents, guide outfitters, transporters and ranchers have continued the practice of igniting fires in the spring of each year in the boreal forest (Peck and Peek 1991). Under the BC *Forest & Range Practices Act*, range tenure holders (guide outfitters, transporters and ranchers) are permitted to manage the rangelands within their tenured areas through the application of fire to provide an improvement to forage quality or quantity on an area. It must be argued that the guide outfitters and range tenure holders in north-east BC have been the strongest leaders in applying fire on the land over many decades in recent history. The shifting mosaic patterns on the landscape are a direct result of their dedication to maintaining and enhancing wildlife habitat and to conserving biodiversity across these broad landscapes. They have been strongly supported by the BC Wildfire Service, which also recognises the important role and process that fire plays in the region.

Weaver and Clements (1938) stated that:

… vegetation is more than the mere grouping of individual plants. It is the result of the interactions of numerous factors. The effects of the plants upon the place in which they live and their influence upon each other are especially significant … A study of vegetation reveals that it is an organic entity and that, like an organism, each part is interdependent upon every other part.

These concepts were applied in the modern-day development of the Peace–Liard Prescribed Fire Program (P-LPFP), founded on the work of the BC government and various stakeholders in the region, including guide outfitters and resident hunters. The previous work on this program included a 5-year plan from 2012 to 2017 (Goddard 2011) and the regional prescribed fire program established in the late 1970s, whereby the Government of British Columbia began a concentrated prescribed fire program in partnership with the northern guide outfitters and range tenure holders. The objectives of this regional prescribed fire program established in the 1970s included the maintenance of rangelands that provide forage for a variety of ungulates and other non-target species through the reduction of woody vegetation encroachment and the promotion of optimal forage plants, the maintenance of ecosystem diversity through biodiversity and the maintenance of winter ranges for ungulates to minimise conflict in agricultural areas

The P-LPFP (Leverkus *et al.* 2018b, 2018c) incorporated past discussions and plans into several modernised documents, including implementation plans, operational plans, strategic plans, a geographic information system (GIS) database, monitoring plans, public outreach and engagement and the incorporation of a multispecies and multiobjective program. Although the first and foremost objective for prescribed fire use in the boreal by First Nations, Indigenous communities, Metis People and long-time residents like guide outfitters and cattlemen has been maintaining and increasing the availability, productivity, access and quality of forage and browse for wildlife and livestock, there are many supporting objectives for prescribed fire in north-east BC, including:

> … *vegetation composition, structure, integrity and distribution as it relates to fire behaviour (as a fuel type), carrying capacity and animal unit months (as forage, browse and other sources of nutrition), habitat (as structural components and required resources for species survival), anthropogenic economic production (as timber and other features to sell, non-timber forest products), spiritual, cultural and recreational practices (medicinal plants and berries, peaceful enjoyment and sacred places), and carbon storage amongst others. (Leverkus et al. 2018b, 2018c)*

Rationales for putting fire on the land include reducing fuel load and fuel continuity, removing logging debris, silviculture preparation, reducing vegetation competition, controlling insects and disease, increasing heterogeneity, supporting fire-dependent species, reducing woody shrub encroachment onto boreal rangelands, visual quality and aesthetic enhancement, access for forestry workers, recreational users and livestock, increasing safe passage along transportation corridors such as the Alaska Highway, nutrient cycling, enhancing and maintaining wildlife habitat to support a biologically diverse abundance of species, supporting species and ecosystems at risk and respecting cultural and traditional values (Leverkus *et al.* 2018b, 2018c).

There are two additional considerations to acknowledge when discussing human interactions with fire in this region. Anthropogenic history of fire across north-east BC includes the unique relationship that many long-time residents and First Nations have as members of wildland firefighting crews. Many members of Indigenous communities have served on wildland firefighting crews across the north and across the province over the past six decades and beyond. It is of urgent importance to document the knowledge and experiences of these fires, how they were actioned, what the fire effects were and the need to integrate fire in a good way from here forward. This knowledge and wisdom are also present in many local ecological knowledge holders in the region, and attempts have been made to integrate and incorporate this information into natural resource planning and management in the region; however, this has met much resistance under the current management regime.

The second consideration is the interaction between predator and prey species and the influence that varied time since fire has on this relationship. Elliott (1986) reported a decline in ungulate herds attributed to high predation by wolves *Canis lupus*. Although there is a lack of regional scientific information for large carnivore use of prescribed fire, it has been anecdotally noted that wolves and bears (*Ursus* sp.) use recently burned areas and lynx *Lynx canadensis* have been documented to use burned areas in response to an increase in snowshoe hare *Lepus americanus* abundance (Fisher and Wilkinson 2005).

Fuels and distribution of fire

In the boreal forest, the typical fuels targeted for prescribed fire include deciduous (D-1, leafless aspen), mixedwood (M-1, boreal mixedwood-leafless) and grass (O-1a, matted grass; O-1b, standing grass; Canadian Forest Fire Behaviour Prediction System Fuel Types; Taylor *et al.* 1996). These fuels are often found in an assemblage of aspen-dominated rangelands existing throughout the region, derived from previous disturbance and recent time since fire.

The application of fire in certain areas across north-east BC has had a significant effect on the current distribution, abundance, access and quality of vegetation. Over 3.5 million ha (30% of the regional area of 11.7 million ha) has been burned by wildfire between 1922 and 2012, and more than 260 000 ha (2% of the regional area) was burned by prescribed fire from 1980 to 2008 (Parminter 1983; Leverkus 2015; Leverkus *et al.* 2017, Leverkus *et al.* 2018a, 2018b, 2018c; Figure 2.4). In all, 3204 fires were recorded from 1922 to 2012, but earlier records may not represent the complete area burned and

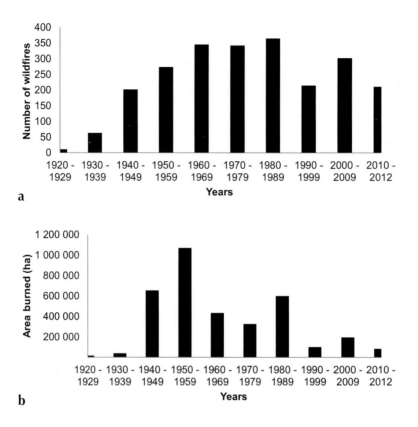

Figure 2.4: (a) Number of wildfires in north-east British Columbia from 1922 to 2012 and (b) the area burned, in hectares, per decade (Leverkus 2015).

the number of fires given the remoteness and lack of satellite imagery to confirm. However, written documentation, the mosaic nature of forest stands and their age structure, the presence of charcoal in the soil profile and the distribution of wildlife demonstrate the strong influence of fire in the region (Parminter 1983).

Leverkus (2015) and Leverkus *et al.* (2017) studied the fire history over the past century to determine the spatiotemporal distribution of wildland fire (1922–2015) and prescribed fire (1980–2008) across the north-east BC region (Figure 2.5; Table 2.1). Until 2014, the largest fires in the recorded history of the province were located in north-east BC, and included the Wisp fire in 1950 (1 400 000 ha), the Kech fire in 1958 (225 000–244 027 ha), the Tee fire in 1971 (98 899–110 419 ha) and the Eg fire in 1982 (166 698–182 725 ha; Parminter 1983; Leverkus 2015; Leverkus *et al.* 2017, 2018a, 2018b, 2018c; BC Wildfire Service 2020).

A fire history was also completed for seven select watersheds, ranging in size from 1.2 million ha (Kechika) to 295 000 ha (Halfway), presented in Table 2.2 (Leverkus 2015). The area burned by wildfire ranges from 15 847 ha (5% of the burnable area in the Halfway watershed) to 205 991 ha (50% of the burnable area in the Liard watershed). When the same analysis was conducted for prescribed fire, the results show that the prescribed fire area burned varies across watersheds from 26 633 ha (2% of the burnable area in the Kechika watershed) to 92 811 ha (12% of the burnable area in the Fort Nelson watershed) and 49 543 ha (15% of the Toad watershed). It is important to note that data are limited given the remote setting of these watersheds, the complex arrangement of numerous fire overlapping areas and the potential for ignition source (lightning or human) to be under-represented. Even though there may be an under-representation of the area burned by wildfire and prescribed fire, the results

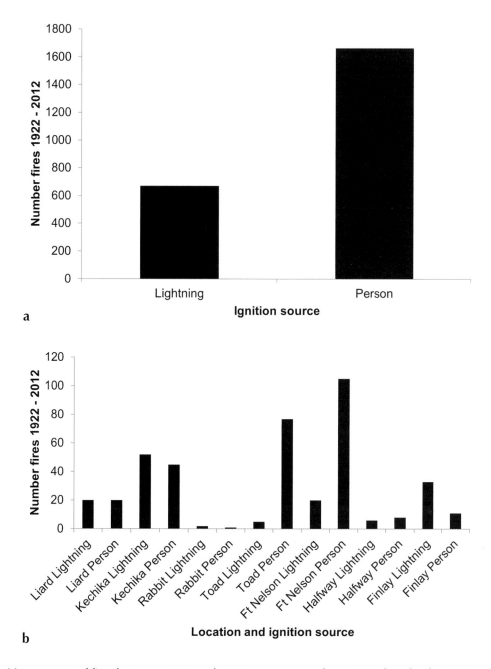

Figure 2.5: Ignition sources of fires between 1922 and 2012 across (a) north-east British Columbia (BC) and the Muskwa-Kechika Management Area and (b) seven watersheds within north-east BC based on the historical wildfire polygon dataset from the BC Wildfire Service (Leverkus 2015). Although all attempts are made to spatially document all fires in the region, it is possible that fires may have gone undetected before the availability of high-quality remotely sensed data.

of these studies suggest that the number of prescribed fires has dramatically declined over the past two decades to the point where there have not been any approved prescribed fires for several years.

Requirements and barriers to fire application: cultural and social issues

Ethnographic information about the traditional use of fires that has been documented by Fort

Table 2.1. Fire history across two spatial scales in British Columbia (BC), Canada: regional north-east BC and the subregional Muskwa-Kechika Management Area (M-KMA)

The mean per year of wildfire (Wild) was calculated from 1922 to 2012 (= 91 years), whereas the mean per year of prescribed fire (Rx) was calculated from 1980 to 2008 (= 29 years). The historical fire return interval is considered from Stocks and Kauffmann (1994), who suggest a fire return interval for the boreal of 50–150 years, whereas Johnson et al. (1998) found that every 300–400 years almost all of the areas will have burned in the western boreal, boreal montane and near-boreal forest. The years required to burn all burnable area are considered to be an estimation due to limitations in the data. Values are in hectares and numbers in parentheses represent the percentage of the total burnable area

	North-east BC	M-KMA
Total area (ha)	19 091 797	6 386 094
Burnable area (ha)	11 736 663	4 843 839
Unburnable land cover: cloud cover (ha)	2 205 926	268 458
Unburnable land cover: shadow cover (ha)	412 403	127 233
Area burned 1922–2012 (Wild) (ha)	3 539 814 (30.2)	926 663 (19.1)
Area burned 1980–2008 (Rx) (ha)	261 766 (2.2)	203 236 (4.2)
Mean per year Wild 1922–2012 (ha)	38 899 (0.3)	10 183 (0.2)
Mean per year Rx 1980–2008 (ha)	9026 (0.1)	7008 (0.1)
Average size Wild 1922–2012 (ha)	1517	2322
Average size Rx 1980–2008 (ha)	442	469
Maximum size Wild 1922–2012 (ha)	244 027	244 027
Maximum size Rx 1980–2008 (ha)	6100	6100
Years required to burn all (Wild + Rx)	281	390
Historical fire return interval (years)	50–400	50–400

Nelson First Nation, from interviews with Dene Elders and community members, was used to evaluate the role of the Dene in developing and maintaining a cultural landscape (Lewis 1978a, 1978b). Oral history is important to consider when identifying the role of Indigenous people in shaping a landscape (Nolan and Turner 2011). The interviews were conducted in English and Dene or Cree where appropriate (Gottesfeld 1994). These interviews reveal that, together, the Dene and other First Nations and Indigenous Communities, along with the guide outfitters, ranchers and the government of north-east BC, have used fire to shape the landscape. Fires were historically ignited for various reasons, including hunting and survival, regrowth of vegetation, communication and ceremonial and aesthetic practices (Fort Nelson First Nation and Shifting Mosaics Consulting 2015). The tradition of igniting fires in the spring of each year has since been continued by guide outfitters and range tenure holders across the region (Peck and

Peek 1991). The resulting cultural landscape can be seen from the air across mountainous valleys and rolling hills.

Many have argued that the provincial parks established in north-east BC are located in watersheds where cultural fire has shaped the landscape. Several provincial parks are located in areas that have been historically treated with prescribed fire (e.g. Toad River, Fort Nelson and Kechika watersheds). These areas have high visual quality and increased aesthetic values resulting from the diversity in fire-driven vegetation structure and composition, but they are at risk of significant encroachment due to the lack of recent fire across the landscape. In addition, increases in hunting pressure (minimal fire across the land results in concentrated areas of availability of certain vegetation and habitat types of huntable species) and localised areas of use are rising, which may result in complex human interactions between hunting parties and increased potential for environmental degradation.

Table 2.2.   Fire history across seven watersheds in north-east British Columbia, Canada (Leverkus 2015)

The mean per year of wildfire (Wild) was calculated from 1922 to 2012 (= 91 years), whereas the mean per year of prescribed fire (Rx) was calculated from 1980 to 2008 (= 29 years). The historical fire return interval is considered from Stocks and Kauffmann (1994), who suggest a fire return interval for the boreal of 50–150 years, whereas Johnson et al. (1998) found that every 300–400 years almost all of the areas will have burned in the western boreal, boreal montane and near-boreal forest. The years required to burn all burnable area are considered to be an estimation due to limitations in the data. Values are in hectares and numbers in parentheses represent the percentage of the total burnable area

	Watershed						
	Liard	Kechika	Rabbit	Toad	Ft Nelson	Halfway	Finlay
Total area (ha)	671 988	1 965 538	370 533	712 011	1 295 040	336 903	875 794
Burnable area (ha)	409 626	1 282 879	156 649	341 804	781 882	294 728	610 461
Unburnable land cover: cloud cover (ha)	198 861	198 885	185 088	108 337	163 049	979	47 877
Unburnable land cover: shadow cover (ha)	3646	25 901	1084	28 293	36 419	1965	25 693
Area burned 1922–2012 (Wild) (ha)	205 991 (50.3)	413 050 (32.2)	16 616 (10.6)	86 460 (25.3)	113 910 (14.6)	15 847 (5.4)	64 862 (10.6)
Area burned 1980–2008 (Rx) (ha)	20 655 (5.0)	26 633 (2.1)	0 (0)	49 543 (14.5)	92 811 (11.9)	12 405 (4.2)	0 (0)
Mean per year Wild 1922–2012 (ha)	2264 (0.6)	4539 (0.4)	183 (0.1)	950 (0.3)	1252 (0.2)	174 (0.1)	713 (0.1)
Mean per year Rx 1980–2008 (ha)	712 (0.2)	918 (0.1)	0 (0)	1708 (0.5)	3200 (0.4)	428 (0.1)	0 (0)
Average size Wild 1922–2012 (ha)	5150	4258	5539	1054	911	1132	1474
Average size Rx 1980–2008 (ha)	383	2049	0	522	393	288	0
Maximum size Wild 1922–2012 (ha)	50 784	232 389	11 637	28 952	15 401	7223	17 871
Maximum size Rx 1980–2008 (ha)	4480	6100	0	3549	3864	2018	0
Years required to burn all (Wild + Rx)	164	266	858	229	344	949	856
Historical Fire Return Interval (years)	50–400	50–400	50–400	50–400	50–400	50–400	50–400

The biggest issue with putting fire on the land is the lack of approvals and the resulting inability to implement prescribed fire burn plans. In Canada, Crown land is governed by each province and territory in a variety of ways. Over the past 5 years in particular, there has been a marked management shift away from prescribed fire throughout northeast BC towards single-species management. The current system does not recognise the urgent need for varied time since fire to support multiple landscape objectives and values. Rather, current management relies on forest-centric plans that focus on seral stages and static vegetative communities that do not allow for disturbance. These forest-centric plans were rejected by all stakeholders, First Nations and Indigenous Communities and the public in the region when they were first drafted almost a decade ago, but they appear to be the direction chosen by decision makers in recent years. Although we have produced documentation of traditional and local knowledge stating that fire is integral to maintaining and promoting wildlife populations and their habitat in this region, which includes species at risk, and we have demonstrated in peer-reviewed science that fire is important, there remains a reluctance by decision makers to approve current prescribed fire burn plans.

Requirements and barriers to fire application: laws and policies governing the use of fire

Laws and policies that govern the use of fire are found in the Wildfire Acts and Regulations for each province and territory in Canada. In BC, various pieces of legislation govern the use of 'resource management open fire' (BC Wildfire Regulation), including:

- the BC *Wildfire Act* and associated regulations, which legislate prescribed fire in BC
- the 2010 BC Wildland Fire Management Strategy (BC Wildfire Service 2010)
- *Environmental Management Act*
- Open Burning Smoke Control Regulation

- *Muskwa-Kechika Management Area Act* and Muskwa-Kechika Wildlife Management Plan Parts A and B
- *Forest and Range Practices Act* and regulations, which legislate prescribed fire as a range development
- *Park Act*
- *Forest Act*
- *Range Act*
- Range Planning and Practices Regulation
- *Wildlife Act*
- the 1981 Memorandum of Understanding between the Ministry of Environment and the Ministry of Forests regarding the use of prescribed fire for wildlife habitat
- the 1997 Protocol Agreement between the Ministry of Forests and Ministry of Environment, Lands and Parks – BC Parks regarding the administration and management of *Range Act* agreements in provincial parks and protected areas
- land and resource management plans (1997–99).

Several provincial and regional leading documents and publications have been released over the past two decades calling for increased knowledge, training, support and application of prescribed fire, including The Northern Fire Ecology Project (Parminter 1983), Firestorm 2003: Provincial Review (Filmon 2004), the 2010 BC Wildland Fire Management Strategy (BC Wildfire Service 2010), Addressing the New Normal: 21st Century Disaster Management in British Columbia (a report and findings of the BC flood and wildfire review, an independent review that examined the 2017 flood and wildfire seasons; Abbott and Chapman 2018) and the P-LPFP (Leverkus et al. 2018b, 2018c). Over the past three decades, peer-reviewed publications and government reports have been published based on scientific and cultural knowledge of fire in the region, including Brink et al. (1972), Lord and Luckhurst (1974), Elliott (1983, 1986), Parminter (1983), Seip and Bunnell (1985), Haber (1988), Peck and Peek (1991), Pyne (2007), Lousier et al. (2009), Leverkus (2015), Fort Nelson First

Nation and Shifting Mosaics Consulting (2015), Leverkus *et al.* (2017, 2018a, 2018b) and Sittler *et al.* (2019).

Parminter (1983) states that:

… the ultimate goal of the [Fire Ecology] project is to establish an ecological basis for fire management activities in northern British Columbia based on a knowledge of fire–ecological relationships within specific ecosystem types. This will permit the development of fire management policies, guidelines and procedures which support multiple resource management objectives and recognise the historical relationships between fire and the existing vegetation. The fire–ecological component of the project therefore provides needed information which will be incorporated into the overall fire and land management planning process.

Almost 40 years later, debate and heated controversy continue over the critical ecological need for prescribed fire, yet there is considerably increased resistance to approving the application of fire on the land. We are continually asked to incorporate different measures into operational prescribed fire burn plans without any acknowledgement that two strategic documents already exist, funded by the tax payers of BC, that are the appropriate documents to bring forward the science and ecological knowledge to address current government requirements, including (but not limited to): buffers on creeks and rivers where only slow-moving backing surface fires would occur; to conduct pre-fire surveys in remote settings for bird nests and bat roosting; to detail and mitigate prevention measures for soil stability; and to delineate multiple escape routes in mountainous terrain and remote access locations.

The laws and policies in BC allow for the application of prescribed fire, and we have much more supporting documentation to rely on thanks to Parminter's leadership and the BC Wildfire Service. However, now more than ever, this cultural landscape that has resulted from decades of applying fire to the land with recently evolved strategies and plans for future implementation remains without meaningful prescribed fire. The greatest challenge is that the law has not changed, but the decision makers and regional management personnel have. With these changes in personnel over the past 6 years, there has been a shift from prescribed fire as a rangeland management practice, wildlife habitat maintenance program and ecological process to a heavily scrutinised project similar to that of an industrial development project, like a mine or an oil and gas pipeline or a hydroelectric dam on a major river system. What were once simple plans, prescribed fire burn plans are now subject to the same kind of extensive environmental impact reviews as major resource extraction projects in the region.

Requirements and barriers to fire application: regulatory requirements

The regulatory requirements when conducting a prescribed fire on Crown land in BC include the development and submission of a prescribed fire burn plan, signed off by a registered forest professional (Association of BC Forest Professionals), to the local Natural Resource District or BC Parks and then to the BC Wildfire Service. If the plan is approved, a registration number is issued that grants permission for the fire. Apart from completing all logistical arrangements for the safe implementation of the prescribed fire burn plan, the proponent must also advise the local fire centre when they plan to conduct their ignition. Prescribed fire must also be included in the Range Use Plan as part of the range tenure agreement between a range tenure holder and the BC government. Currently in BC, there appears to be significant confusion around requirements for prescribed fire burn plans in different locations within the province. Although the BC Wildfire Service offers a provincial template, there are new questions being asked, with new information being required to be included in these plans, without clear guidance or direction. Over the past 6 years, more than 40 prescribed fire burn plans have been developed and submitted, yet only three have been approved in the region. The prescribed fire burn plans have been subjected to in-depth reviews similar to those of special projects such as pipelines and dam construction. This process and the types of questions being asked by government agencies demonstrate a lack of understanding that prescribed fire has occurred throughout the region over the past century, that prescribed fire is an integral process in this pyrogenic ecosystem and that there are multiple objectives across the landscape that rely on varied time since fire for proper functioning. At this time, the process required to complete a prescribed fire burn plan for a provincial park remains unclear. The level of detail required in prescribed fire burn plans for the region in order that the plans be accepted and approved by provincial government decision makers is also unclear.

Requirements and barriers to fire application: current and past issues

Fire suppression has been active across BC, yet fire remains a dominant process driving the ecosystems of north-east BC. Fire suppression has been actively implemented across BC: in 2011–20, the Government of BC spent an average of CAD 145.5 million on fire suppression efforts over 1352 fires that burned, on average, 348 917 ha per year (BC Wildfire Service 2021). However, the application of repeated prescribed fire in certain areas has had a greater effect on the current state of vegetation cover in north-east BC than have fire suppression activities (Parminter 1983).

Typical historical prescribed fires were ignited in the spring while snow was still present, before soil thawing during the spring dip (when foliar moisture content is low). South-facing slopes were most often targeted for ignition, with natural features (snow, rock, ice) providing firebreaks (Peck and Peek 1991). South-facing aspects are first to be snow free in the spring, and they provide significant forage value and quantity for wildlife and livestock throughout the year. North-facing aspects

Table 2.3. Distribution of wildfire (Wild) and prescribed fire (Rx) across aspect classes in British Columbia, Canada, over the Muskwa-Kechika Management Area (M-KMA)

Values are in hectares, with numbers in parentheses representing the percentage of total burnable area. North (Class 1) = 315°–45°; East (Class 2), 45°–135°; South (Class 3), 135°–225°; West (Class 4), 225°–315°; Flat (Class 5), –1°. Data ranged from –1° to 359°. In the absence of fire on certain aspects and slopes, closed forests develop that burn in high-intensity fire similar to eucalypt fires in the Mediterranean basin and other brush fires in California and Australia

Aspect	M-KMA Wild (ha)	Rx (ha)
North	250 231 (5.2)	20 733 (0.4)
East	153 393 (3.2)	27 859 (0.6)
South	260 416 (5.4)	116 406 (2.4)
West	138 445 (2.9)	37 912 (0.8)
Flat	6959 (0.1)	53 (0.0)

are cooler and wetter than south-facing aspects. Our results show that south-facing slopes burned 95 000 ha more than north-facing slopes largely due to anthropogenic ignitions (Tables 2.3, 2.4; Leverkus 2015; Leverkus et al. 2017, 2018a). It is important to note that there is a lack of recorded data over the past century, resulting in an underestimation of the number of total fires, the number of times burned and area burned across the region.

The primary rationale provided for the closure of the prescribed fire program in north-east BC is due to concern about the interaction between fire and caribou. There is urgent need for a collaborative approach to discuss and resolve the issues that have arisen from the closure of the prescribed fire program. In 2018, the Northeast BC Prescribed Fire Council was struck to provide leadership and support for prescribed fire in the region with the intention of supporting and proactively facilitating the necessary discussions to resolve the discrepancies around prescribed fire in the region, to understand where prescribed fire is acceptable and not acceptable and to move forward with collaboration and cooperation among all prescribed fire practitioners in the region. This leadership and support is extremely important in light of the significant work completed on the evolved prescribed fire program for the region, paid for by the taxpayers of BC, where the science that was produced and integrated

Table 2.4. Distribution of wildfire (Wild) and prescribed fire (Rx) across aspect classes in British Columbia, Canada, over seven watersheds

Values are in hectares, with numbers in parentheses representing the percentage of total burnable area. North (Class 1) = 315°–45°; East (Class 2), 45°–135°; South (Class 3), 135°–225°; West (Class 4), 225°–315°; Flat (Class 5), –1°. Data ranged from –1° to 359°. In the absence of fire on certain aspects and slopes, closed forests develop that burn in high-intensity fire similar to eucalypt fires in the Mediterranean basin and other brush fires in California and Australia

Watershed	Liard		Kechika		Rabbit		Toad		Fort Nelson		Halfway		Finlay	
Aspect	Wild (ha)	Rx (ha)	Wild (ha)	Rx (ha)	Wild (ha)	Rx (ha)	Wild (ha)	Rx (ha)	Wild (ha)	Rx (ha)	Wild (ha)	Rx (ha)	Wild (ha)	Rx (ha)
North	64 248 (15.7)	2200 (0.5)	110 077 (8.6)	4409 (0.3)	7535 (4.8)	0 (0.0)	25 458 (7.4)	5141 (1.5)	28 777 (3.7)	9067 (1.2)	4455 (1.5)	438 (0.1)	20 142 (3.3)	0 (0.0)
East	35 692 (8.7)	2758 (0.7)	58 827 (4.6)	3549 (0.3)	4077 (2.6)	0 (0.0)	16 936 (5.0)	5966 (1.7)	23 777 (3.0)	14 690 (1.9)	3303 (1.1)	1648 (0.6)	9243 (1.5)	0 (0.0)
South	50 127 (12.2)	12 132 (3.0)	107 421 (8.4)	14 594 (1.1)	3491 (2.2)	0 (0.0)	28 330 (8.3)	28 288 (8.3)	38 190 (4.9)	52 347 (6.7)	5896 (2.0)	9834 (3.3)	23 298 (3.8)	0 (0.0)
West	21 902 (5.3)	3528 (0.9)	73 129 (5.7)	6071 (0.5)	1364 (0.9)	0 (0.0)	10 980 (3.2)	10 087 (3.0)	16 970 (2.2)	16 602 (2.1)	1796 (0.6)	1650 (0.6)	9282 (1.5)	0 (0.0)
Flat	1284 (0.3)	4 (0.0)	4696 (0.4)	40 (0.0)	102 (0.1)	0 (0.0)	51 (0.0)	0 (0.0)	77 (0.0)	9 (0.0)	1 (0.0)	0 (0.0)	732 (0.1)	0 (0.0)

into the strategic prescribed fire program was rejected by regional managers. The millions of dollars spent on habitat enhancement and maintenance over the past 50 years has not been a good investment because the time since fire and the area burned continue to decrease, with the wildlife and their habitat being the biggest losers of all.

Getting fire on the ground

Prescriptions: weather, season and other conditions

Prescribed fire burn plans have evolved over the past 50 years throughout the region. Sometimes, in times past, plans were verbal or written on a note or the back of a small photocopy of a map. This has evolved into the integration of the BC Wildfire Service Prescribed Fire Burn Plan Template referenced by and integrated in a Range Use Plan, the management document each range tenure holder is required to prepare and submit to demonstrate their stewardship of the land. The BC Prescribed Fire Burn Plan Template requires that information be provided regarding objectives, fuel description, burn prescription (which outlines the desired effects, values at risk, weather, ignition, suppression and patrol plans), budget, monitoring and public relations and information strategies. Additional schedules in the Template include fuel description maps, a prescribed fire complexity worksheet and rating guide, an organisation chart, communications plan, medical operations plan, safe work procedures, information plans, traffic plans, security plans, a 'Go-No-Go' checklist and a map of the prescribed fire unit and ignition operations. Depending on the complexities of the surrounding landscape, the plans can be as short as 12–15 pages or as long as 40–50 pages.

Historically in north-east BC, prescribed fires were primarily lit in the early spring while snow was still in the bush. The snow provided a natural fireguard, allowing people to burn safely into the bush. This practice of spring burning has been documented by two scientists, Dr Henry Lewis in his film Fires of Spring (Lewis 1978a) and

publication A Time for Burning (Lewis 1982) and Dr Sonja Leverkus with the CBC The National's documentary Imagine the Fire (CBC *et al.* 2013) and the recent Georama TV Productions documentary Megafires: Investigating A Global Threat (Dannoritzer and Koutsikas 2020).

Anecdotal observations made consistently across the region over the past 3–6 years suggests that there are changes in the moisture regime and post-winter thaw in the boreal. Prescribed fire practitioners have noted that the snow and moisture that were typically relied upon and trusted to act as a fuel break in the past have not been present at the same time of year. This change is attributed to rapidly higher temperatures in the spring after the long winter, resulting in what appears to be sublimation of the snow within 48–72 h in some locations.

Typical burn unit: determination, size and topography

A typical prescribed fire unit in north-east BC has historically ranged from 2500 ha to upwards of 15 000 ha. Most units used to be determined by topography and natural features acting as boundaries that would prevent the further spread of fire once ignited. The location of the prescribed fire units typically targeted south-facing slopes and areas of importance for forage and browse for horses and ungulates, and were most often topographically bounded by the rock on the ridgelines of mountains.

Common firebreaks or boundaries

The people of north-east BC who have conducted prescribed fires throughout their life have used naturally occurring fuel-free zones as firebreaks and boundaries. Natural boundaries for prescribed fire units include rock, rivers and creeks, snow, ice, non-vegetated mountain tops and previous fire scars.

Equipment used to ignite and extinguish fires

Creativity, efficacy and industriousness led to many ignitions throughout north-east BC over the past century. Ignition devices have included propane torches, drip torches, plastic sphere dispensers, matches, diamond willow, folded grass, hot coals in a bucket and other resourceful tools. Tools to extinguish fire included damp blankets, water buckets, back-burning, snow, rakes, shovels and firefighting pumps and hoses. Most guide outfitters in the region have access to aerial ignition opportunities to help implement their prescribed fire burn plans in remote locations.

People: training needs and opportunities and cultural knowledge

Northern Fire WoRx Corporation (NFWRx; https://northernfireworx.com) and Shifting Mosaics Consulting (https://shiftingmosaics.com) have spent the past 6 years developing fire training opportunities that incorporate fire science mobilised with traditional and local ecological knowledge and operational capacity. The resulting fire schools are taught on an annual basis across BC and incorporate wildfire suppression certification for Type 2 and Type 3 wildland firefighters. There is a considerable need to increase this capacity across the province and throughout the country. NFWRx, Shifting Mosaics Consulting, Oklahoma State University and the University of Alberta are working collaboratively to produce Canadian training material to support the advancement of prescribed fire practitioners and knowledge in Canada.

Fire behaviour: how fire typically burns

Typically, prescribed fires throughout the region are surface fires with occasional crowning. Fire intensity may range from a Fire Weather Index (FWI) of 0 to an FWI of 20 depending on the location and strength of the prescribed fire unit boundaries. Although most prescribed fire occurs in the spring, there are occasional fires in the autumn. Springtime prescribed fire usually occurs while soils are still frozen, therefore the depth of the burn into the soil and the potential for root damage and erosion are minimal.

Future of fire in the region

At this time it is unknown whether fire will continue in a prescribed and strategic manner across the region. North-east BC is an area where there are few people, minimal infrastructure and much area to allow fire to move to natural features. This region has the strongest history of prescribed fire in the province of BC, and arguably in Canada, insofar as area burned and the number of prescribed fires across a broad landscape to meet multiple objectives. However, as of July 2019, all prescribed fire has been disallowed as further information or clarification is required according to response letters received from government officials by range tenure holders.

In 2017–19, an updated evolved version of the P-LPFP was developed in consultation and engagement with hundreds of participants across the region. A structured decision-making process was developed, along with a mapping tool and database. These documents were intended to provide the overarching structure and strategy for the implementation of prescribed fire in the region. Unfortunately, changes in management led to the rejection of this work and the reliance on draft management plans that suggested forest-centric and successional phases to be the targeted priorities for land management.

This direction is in opposition to the desire and concerns expressed by Indigenous Communities, guide outfitters, ranchers, resident hunters, wildlife conservationists and long-time residents, who expressed significant concern about the lack of fire in the region. This concern for the need and shared responsibility to take care of the wildlife and their habitat has brought together many people from varied backgrounds in letter-writing campaigns, meetings with senior government officials, town hall meetings, conferences and public presentations, and has now reached political levels in the province.

What are future issues?

Future issues faced by prescribed fire practitioners include challenges for social licence and acceptance, air quality and interactions with pandemics, management regimes around changing climate and single-species management (i.e. boreal and northern mountain caribou) and loss of key personnel in critical management positions. Over the past 20 years, and more specifically over the past decade, there have been significant changes in the region from retiring biologists to changes in government mandates involving single-species management to an intense restriction in allowable area to be burned in each prescribed fire unit (currently between 100 and 200 ha).

North-east BC is home to many Indigenous communities, some of whom are part of Treaty 8. There are rights and privileges under the provisions of the Treaty that include access to and benefit of the resources for as long as the sun shines, the grass grows and the rivers flow. A future issue that many people are currently discussing is the right to cultural fire practices. It has yet to be determined in the provincial court system in BC and in the federal court system of Canada whether applying fire to the land is part of a Treaty right and cultural practice. Although there are First Nations and Indigenous communities across the province with firekeepers who practice traditional law and who exercise their rights to apply fire to the land, the process remains heavily influenced by provincial government approvals and permissions.

What will stop the use of prescribed fire?

There are several challenges that have persisted in north-east BC for the past several decades around the application of fire on the land, including: (1) a lack of scientific knowledge local to the area; (2) personal understanding and bias either for or against fire on the land; (3) broad management statements and policies that can have different interpretations depending on the land manager and statutory decision maker at the time; and (4) the general misunderstanding of the fire–grazing interaction and its importance for wildlife, livestock and vegetation on northern Canadian rangelands.

At the core of these challenges, which have been attempted to be addressed numerous times over the past several decades, is the need to determine how much fire is wanted across the landscape,

where fire is unwanted and what the holistic vision of the landscape, incorporating ecological, cultural, social and economic values and objectives, is. One of the forefathers of the prescribed fire program, Dr John Elliott, worked collaboratively with local guide outfitters, range tenure holders, the Northeast BC Wildlife Fund and others to implement a program that would support ungulate enhancement on the east side of the Rocky Mountain slope in north-east BC. This program (run from the late 1970s to early 2000s) was immensely successful, and many wildlife enthusiasts, hunters and people out on the land have reported an increase in ungulates following this prescribed fire program. At the time, this program followed what guide outfitters, range tenure holders and First Nations had already been practising across the land: burning south-facing slopes in the spring, and sometimes in the autumn, to promote access to and the quality and production of forage and browse. Many staff members of the BC Wildfire Service and the BC Range Program participated in the prescribed fires throughout their time serving in the Fort Nelson, Fort St. John and Dawson Creek district offices. The one constant factor throughout this time has been the pressure and leadership applied by the guide outfitters, range tenure holders and backcountry enthusiasts. Without their support (donations of both time and money resulting from annual fundraisers, sponsorship and donated hunts in-kind), prescribed fire in north-east BC would not have been possible.

The biggest challenge that we face in northeast BC currently and into the future is collaboration. We urgently need to stand side by side, standing on the shoulders of the giants before us, to work together. We need to refine our strategic prescribed fire burn plans and operational treatment plans so that we can ensure there is sufficient spatiotemporal distribution of fire across this pyrogenic and fire-maintained ecosystem. There needs to be an agreement that heterogeneity resulting from the distribution of time since fire across the landscape not only supports multiple species and the conservation of biodiversity, but that it also influences recreational values and reduces wildfire risk to communities. The application of fire across the landscape allows for continued aesthetic enjoyment (the provincial parks in this area were designated in these locations because of their high aesthetic and wildlife values, all resulting from interactions with fire through space and time) and decreased negative interactions between hunters, who are currently centralised on the few remaining places to harvest wildlife in light of the minimal time since fire. Fire applied in the region will provide for fire-absorbent landscapes, where wildfires can still stretch broadly but will eventually run into a recent prescribed fire and be absorbed rather than continuing to gain energy and potentially becoming a megafire.

How will prescribed fire continue to be used?

Because vegetation structure, composition and distribution are driven by time since disturbance across the region, it is integral to include disturbance into landscape management planning (Leverkus *et al.* 2017). A paradigm of landscape management and models to promote the conservation of biodiversity needs to be applied in the region (Leverkus *et al.* 2017, 2018b, 2018c). Not only will this allow time since fire to be diversified across the landscape, but it will also allow land managers to view fire in a new way as an ecological process that maintains and promotes resilience in the boreal ecosystem. Landscape pattern, heterogeneity and resources required by herbivores are important contributing factors to the longevity and function of an ecosystem (Turner *et al.* 1993).

However, the pendulum of prescribed fire decision making has swung from one that supports the strategic application of fire to the land (Goddard 2011; Leverkus *et al.* 2018a, 2018b, 2018c) to one that is buried in bureaucracy and processes that are complex and not understood. Across north-east BC there is a tension between the historical and natural range of variability contrasted with landscape disturbance matrices that incorporate historical, current and future spatiotemporal distributions of

fire to support multiple species' resource selection (Leverkus *et al.* 2017). There is great need to recognise that the interaction of fire with other disturbance processes is a pattern-driving process that contributes to heterogeneity and is of global significance for conserving biodiversity and cultures (Fuhlendorf *et al.* 2012).

Shifting mosaics realised through the distribution of fire across the landscape through space and time are critical for species requiring varied habitat types and structure throughout their life cycle (Leverkus *et al.* 2017). The practice of applying fire to the land is such an accepted and fundamental process in north-east BC that it is simply part of life in the north. Spring fires have always been ignited when fuels are available for consumption, when the weather is warm, dry and sunny, with a slight breeze and while snow, rock and ice act as natural fuel breaks.

Over the past decade, we have conducted research on prescribed fire in north-east BC. We have documented traditional, cultural and local practices of applying fire to the land. We have continued to integrate these practices in the planning and implementation of prescribed fire. We have also combined this knowledge with our research on the largest mammalian herbivores in the region (bison and horses) to gain a better understanding of the fire–grazing interaction and the important role it plays across this landscape. We have observed post-fire effects through on-the-ground research plots and aerial surveys. We know that strategically planned and collaboratively implemented prescribed fire will continue to be beneficial for many species and people. We have developed training and certified wildland fire crews and the capacity to put fire out on the land in a good way. In 2019, we conducted the first prescribed fires for an oil and gas company in Canada. The objectives of that prescribed fire were to integrate an ecological process in the recovery of an industrially disturbed site in north-east BC. While currently confidential, the results from that fire far surpassed the anticipated objectives such that some companies are considering prescribed fire as an effective component of decommissioning industrially disturbed sites.

In this era of megafires and concern for other features and landscape objectives, we confidently state and argue that it is even more integral to continue applying fire to the land in a way that increases fire absorbency and heterogeneity through changes in vegetation structure, distribution and abundance. Both scientific and traditional, cultural and local knowledge prove that this is the right path to follow and that this is not new science, but rather these are practices based on generations of knowledge and wisdom, on listening and observing responses to fire by wildlife and vegetation and by talking the talk and walking the walk. This region is argued to be one of the last intact wilderness settings in the world, similar to the Serengeti in Africa, where fire also dances through space and time. Putting fire out on the land is more than a practice, treaty right and permitted activity; it is a responsibility that we owe to the current and next seven generations of all living beings as we humans are part of this ecosystem.

Acknowledgements

The authors acknowledge the range tenure holders, Northern Guides Association of BC, Northeast BC Wildlife Fund, Fort Nelson First Nation, Prophet River First Nation, Blueberry River First Nation, Esk'etemc, the cattlemen of north-east BC and the many trappers, hunters and backcountry enthusiasts who have spent much time over the past decade sharing stories and knowledge of fire, the land and the way that life has been over the recent century. The authors thank the BC Wildfire Service and the BC Fish and Wildlife Branch for providing the fire datasets integral to this chapter. The authors also thank M. Gregory and Natural Resource Ecology and Management graduate students of Oklahoma State University and Roberto Concepcion for technical support associated with spatial analyses, and Dr Gillian Leverkus, Trevor Scott and Sejer Meyhoff for their critical review, feedback and support. Finally, we thank our families and all the people in northern Canada who have taught us what it means to be good stewards of the land and wildlife, who stand strong by our side to conserve what we know is the right thing to do and who join us as a voice for fire.

References

Abbott G, Chapman M (2018) 'Addressing the new normal: 21st century disaster management in British Columbia'. BC Flood and Wildfire Review, Victoria, <https://www2.gov.bc.ca/assets/gov/public-safety-and-emergency-services/emergency-preparedness-response-recovery/embc/bc-flood-and-wildfire-review-addressing-the-new-normal-21st-century-disaster-management-in-bc-web.pdf>.

Agee JK (1993) *Fire Ecology of Pacific Northwest Forests*. Island Press, Washington, DC.

BC Wildfire Service (2010) *Wildland Fire Management Strategy: Achieving Global Excellence in Fire Management*. Government of British Columbia, Victoria, <https://www2.gov.bc.ca/assets/gov/public-safety-and-emergency-services/wildfire-status/governance/bcws_wildland_fire_mngmt_strategy.pdf>.

BC Wildfire Service (2020) *Major Historical Wildfires*. Government of British Columbia, Victoria, <https://www2.gov.bc.ca/gov/content/safety/wildfire-status/about-bcws/wildfire-history/major-historical-wildfires>.

BC Wildfire Service (2021) *Wildfire Averages*. Government of British Columbia, Victoria, <https://www2.gov.bc.ca/gov/content/safety/wildfire-status/about-bcws/wildfire-statistics/wildfire-averages>.

Bergeron Y, Archambault S (1993) Decreasing frequency of forest fires in the southern boreal zone of Québec and its relation to global warming since the end of the 'Little Ice Age'. *The Holocene* **3**(3), 255–259. doi:10.1177/095968369300300307

Bergeron Y, Flannigan M, Gauthier S, Leduc A, Lefort P (2004) Past, current and future fire frequency in the Canadian boreal forest: implications for sustainable forest management. *Ambio* **33**(6), 356–360. doi:10.1579/0044-7447-33.6.356

Brink VC, Luckhurst A, Morrison D (1972) Productivity estimates from alpine tundra in British Columbia. *Canadian Journal of Plant Science* **52**, 321–323. doi:10.4141/cjps72-051

Burton PJ, Messier C, Adamowicz WL, Kuuluvainen T (2006) Sustainable management of Canada's boreal forests: progress and prospects. *Ecoscience* **13**(2), 234–248. doi:10.2980/i1195-6860-13-2-234.1

Burton PJ, Parisien MA, Hicke JA, Hall RJ, Freeburn JT (2008) Large fires as agents of ecological diversity in the North American boreal forest. *International Journal of Wildland Fire* **17**, 754–767. doi:10.1071/WF07149

Catling PM, Sinclair A, Cuddy D (2001) Vascular plants of a successional alvar burn 100 days after a severe fire and their mechanisms of re-establishment. *Canadian Field Naturalist* **115**, 214–222.

CBC, The National, McCue D (2021) *Imagine the Fire*. CBC, Toronto, <https://shiftingmosaics.com/imaginethefire/>.

Christensen NL (1997) Managing for heterogeneity and complexity on dynamic landscapes. In *The Ecological Basis for Conservation: Heterogeneity, Ecosystems, and Biodiversity*. (Eds SA Pickett, RS Ostfeld, M Shachak and GE Likens) pp. 167–186. Chapman and Hall, New York.

Dannoritzer C (Producer), Koutsikas N (Author) (2020) *Megafires: Investigating a Global Threat*. Georama TV Productions, Toulouse, <https://shiftingmosaics.com/megafires/>.

DeLong C (1990) 'A field guide for the identification and interpretation of ecosystems of the northeast portion of the Prince George Forest Region'. British Columbia Ministry of Forests, Victoria.

DeLong C, Burton P, Geertsema M (2013). Natural disturbance processes. In *Encyclopedia of Environmetrics*, 2nd edn. (Eds AH El-Shaarawi and W Piegorsch) pp. 1–5. John Wiley and Sons, Chichester.

Elliott JP (1983) 'Northeastern British Columbia 1982–1983 elk enhancement program'. BC Fish and Wildlife Branch, Victoria.

Elliott JP (1986) 'Kechika enhancement project of northeastern British Columbia wolf/ungulate management'. Ministry of Environment and Parks, Wildlife Working Report No. WR-20, Fort St. John.

Filmon G (2004) 'Firestorm 2003 – provincial review'. Government of British Columbia, Victoria.

Fisher JT, Wilkinson L (2005) The response of mammals to forest fire and timber harvest in the North American boreal forest. *Mammal Review* **35**(1), 51–81. doi:10.1111/j.1365-2907.2005.00053.x

Flannigan M, Stocks BJ, Turetsky M, Wotton M (2009) Impacts of climate change on fire activity and fire management in the circumboreal forest. *Global Change Biology* **15**, 549–560. doi:10.1111/j.1365-2486.2008.01660.x

Fort Nelson First Nation and Shifting Mosaics Consulting (2015) *Fort Nelson First Nation Interaction with Fire and Wood Bison*. Fort Nelson First Nation and Shifting Mosaics Consulting, Fort Nelson, <https://shiftingmosaics.com/fireandwoodbison/>.

Fuhlendorf SD, Engle DM (2001) Restoring heterogeneity on rangelands: ecosystem management based on evolutionary grazing patterns. *Bioscience* **51**, 625–632. doi:10.1641/0006-3568(2001)051[0625:RHOREM]2.0.CO;2

Fuhlendorf SD, Engle DM (2004) Application of the fire-grazing interaction to restore a shifting mosaic on tallgrass prairie. *Journal of Applied Ecology* **41**, 604–614. doi:10.1111/j.0021-8901.2004.00937.x

Fuhlendorf SD, Harrell WC, Engle DM, Hamilton RG, Davis CA, Leslie DM (2006) Should heterogeneity be the basis for conservation? Grassland bird response to fire and grazing. *Ecological Applications* **16**(5), 1706–1716. doi:10.1890/1051-0761(2006)016[1706:SHBTBF]2.0.CO;2

Fuhlendorf SD, Engle DM, Kerby J, Hamilton R (2009) Pyric herbivory: rewilding landscapes through the recoupling of fire and grazing. *Conservation Biology* **23**(3), 588–598. doi:10.1111/j.1523-1739.2008.01139.x

Fuhlendorf SD, Engle DM, Elmore RD, Limb RF, Bidwell TG (2012) Conservation of pattern and process: developing an alternative paradigm of rangeland management. *Rangeland Ecology and Management* **65**, 579–589. doi:10.2111/REM-D-11-00109.1

Goddard A (2011) 'Peace–Liard burn program: five-year burn plan 2012–2017'. BC Ministry of Forests, Lands and Natural Resource Operations, Peace Region Technical Report, Fort St. John.

Goldammer JG, Furyaev VV (1996) Fire in ecosystems of boreal Eurasia: ecological impacts and links to the global system. In *Fire in Ecosystems of Boreal Eurasia*. (Eds JG Goldammer and VV Furyaev) pp. 1–20. Kluwer Academic Publishers, Dordrecht.

Gottesfeld LJ (1994) Aboriginal burning for vegetation management in northwest British Columbia. *Human Ecology* **22**(2), 171–188. doi:10.1007/BF02169038

Haber GC (1988) 'Wildlife management in northern British Columbia: Kechika-Muskwa wolf control and related issues'. Wolf Haven International, Tenino, WA.

Hawkes BC (1983) 'Fire history and management study of Kluane National Park'. Canadian Forestry Service, Victoria.

Heady HF (1966) Influence of grazing on the composition of Themeda Triandra grassland, East Africa. *Journal of Ecology* **54**(3), 705–727.

Heinselman ML (1981) Fire intensity and frequency as factors in the distribution and structure of northern ecosystems. In *Proceedings of the Conference Fire Regimes and Ecosystem Properties*. 11–15 December, Honolulu. General Technical Report WO-26. (Eds HA Mooney, TM Bonnicksen, NL Christensen, JE Lotan and WA Reiners) pp. 7–57. USDA Forest Service, Washington, DC.

Holland SS (1976) 'Landforms of British Columbia. A physiographic outline'. BC Department of Mines and Mineral Resources, Bulletin No. 48, Victoria.

Johnson EA (1992) *Fire and Vegetation Dynamics: Studies From the North American Boreal Forest*. Cambridge University Press, Cambridge.

Johnson EA, Miyanishi K, Weir JH (1998) Wildfires in the western Canadian boreal forest: landscape patterns and ecosystem management. *Journal of Vegetation Science* **9**, 603–610. doi:10.2307/3237276

Kasischke ES, Christensen NL, Stocks BJ (1995) Fire, global warming, and the carbon balance of boreal forests. *Ecological Applications* **5**(2), 437–451. doi:10.2307/1942034

Knopf FL (1996) Prairie legacies – birds. In *Prairie Conservation: Preserving North America's Most Endangered Ecosystem.* (Eds FB Samson and FL Knopf) pp. 135–148. Island Press, Washington, DC.

Lamprey HF (1963) Ecological separation of the large mammal species in the Tarangire Game Reserve, Tanganyika. PhD thesis. University of Oxford, UK.

Larsen CS, MacDonald GM (1998) An 840-year record of fire and vegetation in a boreal white spruce forest. *Ecology* **79**(1), 106–118. doi:10.1890/0012-9658(1998)079[0106: AYROFA]2.0.CO;2

Leverkus SER (2015) Conservation of biodiversity in northern Canada through ecological processes and cultural landscapes. PhD thesis. Oklahoma State University, USA.

Leverkus SER, Fuhlendorf SD, Geertsema M, Elmore RD, Engle DM, Baum KA (2017) A landscape disturbance matrix for conserving biodiversity. *Journal of Ecosystems and Management* **17**(1), 1–26.

Leverkus SER, Fuhlendorf SD, Geertsema M, Allred BW, Gregory M, Bevington AR, Engle DM, Scasta JD (2018a) Resource selection of free-ranging horses influenced by fire in northern Canada. *Human-Wildlife Interactions* **12**(1), 85–101.

Leverkus SER, Scasta JD, Concepcion RL, Lavallée M, White K (2018b) 'Peace–Liard Prescribed Fire Program: part A – rationale'. BC Ministry of Forests, Lands, Natural Resource Operations, and Rural Development, Fort Nelson.

Leverkus SER, Scasta JD, Concepcion RL, Lavallée M, White K (2018c) 'Peace–Liard Prescribed Fire Program: part B – operational plan'. BC Ministry of Forests, Lands, Natural Resource Operations, and Rural Development, Fort Nelson.

Lewis HT (1978a) *Fires of Spring.* Department of Anthropology, University of Alberta, Edmonton, <https://shiftingmosaics.com/firesofspring/>

Lewis HT (1978b) Traditional uses of fire by Indians in northern Alberta. *Current Anthropology* **19**(2), 401–402. doi:10.1086/202098

Lewis HT (1982) 'A time for burning'. Occasional Publication No. 17, Boreal Institute for Northern Studies, The University of Alberta, Alberta.

Lewis HT, Ferguson TA (1988) Yards, corridors, and mosaics: how to burn a boreal forest. *Human Ecology* **16**(1), 57–77. doi:10.1007/BF01262026

Lord TM, Luckhurst AJ (1974) Alpine soils and plant communities of a stone sheep habitat in northeastern British Columbia. *Northwest Science* **48**(1), 38–51.

Lousier JD, Voller J, McNay RS, Sulyma R, Brumovsky V (2009) 'Response of wildlife to prescribed fire in the Peace Region of British Columbia: a problem analysis'. Wildlife Infometrics Inc., Report No. 316a, Mackenzie.

MacKinnon A, Pojar J, Coupé R (1999) *Plants of Northern British Columbia.* Lone Pine Publishing, Vancouver.

Nolan J, Turner NJ (2011) Ethnobotany, the study of people–plant relationships. In *Textbook for Ethnobiology.* (Eds EN Anderson, D Pearsall, E Hunn and N Turner) pp. 133–148. John Wiley & Sons, Hoboken.

Ostfeld RS, Pickett SA, Shachak M, Likens GE (1997) Defining scientific issues. In *The Ecological Basis for Conservation: Heterogeneity, Ecosystems, and Biodiversity.* (Eds SA Pickett, RS Ostfeld, M Shachak and GE Likens) pp. 167–186. Chapman and Hall, New York.

Parminter J (1983) 'Fire–ecological relationships for the biogeoclimatic zones and subzones of the Fort Nelson timber supply area'. BC Ministry of Forests, Northern Fire Ecology Project, Victoria.

Peck VR, Peek JM (1991) Elk, *Cervus elaphus*, habitat use related to prescribed fire, Tuchodi River, British Columbia. *Canadian Field Naturalist* **105**(3), 354–362.

Pyne SJ (2007) *Awful Splendour: A Fire History of Canada.* University of British Columbia Press, Vancouver.

Raup HM (1945) Forests and gardens along the Alaska Highway. *Geographical Review* **35**(1), 22–48. doi:10.2307/210930

Rowe JS, Scotter GW (1973) Fire in the boreal forest. *Quaternary Research* **3**, 444–464. doi:10.1016/0033-5894(73)90008-2

Schier GA, Campbell RB (1978) Aspen sucker regeneration following burning and clearcutting on two sites in the Rocky Mountains. *Forest Science* **24**, 303–308.

Schmiegelow FA, Stepnisky DP, Stambaugh CA, Koivula M (2006) Reconciling salvage logging of boreal forests with a natural-disturbance management model. *Conservation Biology* **20**(4), 971–983. doi:10.1111/j.1523-1739.2006.00496.x

Seip DR, Bunnell FL (1985) Species composition and herbage production of mountain rangelands in northern British Columbia. *Canadian Journal of Botany* **63**, 2077–2080. doi:10.1139/b85-291

Sittler KL (2013) Influence of prescribed fire on Stone's sheep and Rocky Mountain elk: forage characteristics and resource separation. MSc thesis. University of Northern British Columbia, Canada.

Sittler KL, Parker KL, Gillingham MP (2019) Vegetation and prescribed fire: implications for Stone's sheep and elk. *The Journal of Wildlife Management* **83**(2), 393–409. doi:10.1002/jwmg.21591

Stocks BJ, Kauffmann JB (1994) Biomass consumption and behavior of wildland fires in boreal, temperate and tropical ecosystems: parameters necessary to interpret historic fire regimes and future fire scenarios. In *Sediment Records of Biomass Burning and Global Change Series 1: Global Environmental Change*. (Eds JS Clark, H Cachier, JG Goldammer and B Stocks) pp. 169–188. Springer-Verlag, Heidelberg.

Stocks BJ, Mason JA, Todd JB, Bosch EM, Wotton BM, Amiro BD, Flannigan MD, Hirsch KG, Logan KA, Martell DL, Skinner WR (2003) Large forest fires in Canada, 1959–1997. *Journal of Geophysical Research* **107**, 1–12.

Suffling R, Speller D (1998) The fire roller coaster in Canadian boreal forests. In *Proceedings of the Workshop on Decoding Canada's Environmental Past: Climate Variations and Biodiversity Change During the Last Millennium*. (Eds DC MacIver and RE Meyer) pp. 1–20. Environment Canada Atmospheric Service, Ontario.

Taylor SW, Pike RG, Alexander ME (1996) 'Field guide to the Canadian forest fire behaviour prediction (FBP) system'. Natural Resources Canada, Canadian Forest Service, Northern Forestry Service, Special Report 11, Edmonton.

Turner MG, Romme WH, Gardner RH, O'Neil RV, Kratz TK (1993) A revised concept of landscape equilibrium: disturbance and stability on scaled landscapes. *Landscape Ecology* **8**(3), 213–227. doi:10.1007/BF00125352

Volney JA, Hirsch KG (2005) Disturbing forest disturbances. *Forestry Chronicle* **81**(5), 662–668. doi:10.5558/tfc81662-5

Weaver JE, Clements FE (1938) *Plant Ecology*. McGraw-Hill Book Company, New York.

Wiens JA (1997) The emerging role of patchiness in conservation biology. In *The Ecological Basis for Conservation: Heterogeneity, Ecosystems, and Biodiversity*. (Eds SA Pickett, RS Ostfeld, M Shachak and GE Likens) pp. 167–186. Chapman and Hall, New York.

Wright HA, Bailey AW (1982) Douglas fir and associated communities. In *Fire Ecology: United States and Southern Canada*. (Eds HA Wright and AW Bailey) pp. 238–311. John Wiley and Sons, New York.

Zasada JC, Gordon AG, Slaughter CW, Duchesne LC (1997) 'Ecological considerations for the sustainable management of the North American boreal forests'. International Institute for Applied Systems Analysis, Interim Report IR-97-024, Laxenburg.

3

Burning in the Pampa and Cerrado in Brazil

Alessandra Fidelis, Isabel B. Schmidt,
Fernando F. Furquim and Gerhard E. Overbeck

Introduction to fire in the region

In large parts of Brazil, fire is an extremely problematic and controversial issue. In the Amazon region, fires are linked to both deforestation to clear pastures and to extreme drought events, as in 2005 and 2010 (Aragão *et al.* 2018; Brando *et al.* 2020), with feedback loops between different drivers (Nepstad *et al.* 2001). Moreover, fire events may increase in frequency and intensity due to climate change (specifically under drier and hotter climate conditions), and are expected to contribute substantially to carbon emissions to the atmosphere, and thus to climate change, in coming decades (Brando *et al.* 2020). The Amazon forest is a fire-sensitive ecosystem with low flammability and ignition (Pivello 2011) that may burn during short-term dry windows when local people burn areas for agricultural practices (Barlow *et al.* 2020). Most Amazon plant species are poorly fire adapted; thus, even low-intensity fires can lead to tree mortality and canopy exposure, altering the forest microclimate and favouring invasion by exotic species (Barlow and Peres 2008; Silvério *et al.* 2013).

However, in Brazil's open ecosystems, such as the Cerrado, the central Brazilian savanna system, and the Campos Sulinos, the southern Brazilian grasslands (see Box 3.1), fire is an important factor for the maintenance of typical vegetation types and biodiversity (Fidelis and Pivello 2011). Thus, these ecosystems have been considered fire-dependent, or at least fire-influenced or fire-tolerant, in contrast with the fire-sensitive moist forests of the Amazon (Pivello 2011; Figure 3.1). Palaeoecological studies assessing charcoal particles give clear evidence of the presence of fire in the Cerrado and in the southern Brazilian grasslands for the past 30–40 thousand years (Salgado-Labouriau *et al.* 1997; Behling *et al.* 2004). In the Cerrado, fire is known to have played a role shaping ecosystems since at least 4 million years ago, when there was a diversification of plant species likely in response to fire (Simon *et al.* 2009). In the southern Brazilian grasslands, a similarly important role of fire through vegetation history has been suggested, even though fewer studies are available (Overbeck *et al.* 2018b).

Box 3.1: Defining the Cerrado and Campos Sulinos

Cerrado

'Cerrado' is the Brazilian term for the country's tropical savannas, originally extending over 2 million square kilometres and located in the centre of the country under a typical savanna climate (Köppen's Aw). The Cerrado consists of a variety of vegetation physiognomies, including open grasslands, savannas and forests (riparian and non-riparian), in addition to vegetation associated with specific topographic, drainage or soil conditions, such as wetlands and rock outcrops (Ribeiro and Walter 2008). The Cerrado is one of the world's biodiversity hotspots. Plant species diversity amounts to over 12 000 plant species (Joly *et al.* 2019).

Campos Sulinos

The Campos Sulinos, or southern Brazilian grasslands, include the grassland vegetation in the three southernmost states of Brazil. At present, the remaining grasslands are almost entirely used for cattle grazing. The region is under a temperate climate without a dry season, with hot or warm summers (Köppen's Cfa and Cfb). The Campos Sulinos includes the Brazilian Pampa, in the south, as well as grassland enclaves located in the southern part of the Atlantic Forest biome. The southern Brazilian grasslands hold around 3000 plant species (Overbeck *et al.* 2007).

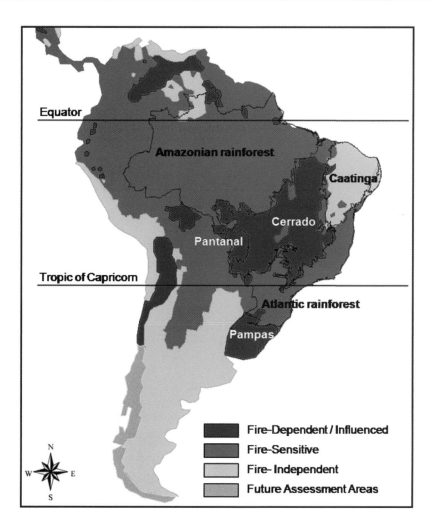

Figure 3.1: Brazilian biomes and their relationship to fire. From Pivello (2011), based on Hardesty *et al.* (2005). Reproduced with permission from Springer Nature.

Fires in the Cerrado and southern Brazilian grasslands are surface fires that mostly consume the biomass of the herbaceous layer (Fidelis *et al.* 2010; Rissi *et al.* 2017; Rodrigues *et al.* 2021). In the Cerrado, natural fires are ignited by lightning strikes that occur more frequently at the beginning and end of the wet season (Ramos-Neto and Pivello 2000), with fire frequencies of approximately 3–8 years (Coutinho 1982; Pivello 2011). There are no studies on natural fire regimes in the southern Brazilian grasslands, but we can assume that natural fires will mostly occur during the summer months, when thunderstorms are frequent (http://queimadas.dgi.inpe.br/queimadas/) and when sufficient biomass is available. Overall, the current climatic conditions in southern Brazil imply a much lower risk of fire than in the Cerrado (Silva *et al.* 2016).

Human activity has increased the frequency of fire in both regions, as it is applied, often annually or biannually, in the management of natural and planted pastures or agricultural areas. Planted pastures in the Cerrado are commonly burned during the mid or late dry season (July–October) to stimulate resprouting of forage grasses. In contrast, the fire management of native grasslands and savannas for cattle ranching traditionally involves an intricate system of wet season burnings (October–November), as well as early (April–June), mid (June–July) and late (August–October) dry season burns (Eloy *et al.* 2019b). In southern Brazil, where the climate is temperate (Köppen's Cfa and Cfb) and governed by a large variation in mean temperatures throughout the year, and not by the presence of rainy and dry seasons, fires are set at the end of winter (i.e. from July to September, with a peak in August) to remove accumulated dead grass biomass and stimulate resprouting (Overbeck *et al.* 2007). Thus, human-set fires differ considerably from natural fires and, especially in the Cerrado, where dry season wildfires are more intense than natural wet season fires, they bring about the risk of spreading to adjacent areas, including fire-sensitive riparian forests. Conversely, a 'zero-fire' policy has prevailed for a long

time in protected areas in Brazil, likely because of the problematic role of fire in Brazil's moist forests, which, for a long time, have been at the centre of conservation debates and efforts (Moura *et al.* 2019). In other words, fire in general has been considered a degrading factor (Durigan and Ratter 2016; Fidelis 2020). In addition, a misunderstanding of the ecology of open ecosystems such as grasslands, particularly with regard to the role of fire, had led to the (obviously erroneous) perception that savannas and grasslands could be the consequence of former deforestation (see also Veldman *et al.* 2015).

Consequently, there have been considerable efforts over a long period of time to avoid the occurrence of any fires in protected areas throughout the country. However, as is known from other regions throughout the world, the suppression of fire in fire-prone ecosystems leads to increased fuel loads, thus increasing the probability of more intense wildfires, as well as the severity of fire effects (Starns *et al.* 2019), just like the fires experienced in Brazil in 2017 (Fidelis *et al.* 2018). In other situations, fire suppression may lead to severe changes in biodiversity and ecosystem processes by woody species encroachment (e.g. Abreu *et al.* 2017; Rosan *et al.* 2019). In past years, Brazilian vegetation ecologists and environmental managers have increasingly called for the development of active fire management strategies for those ecosystems where fires are, and have been, a natural factor (Fidelis and Pivello 2011; Pivello 2011; Durigan and Ratter 2016; Overbeck *et al.* 2018b; Schmidt *et al.* 2018). The basis for these calls is an increasing number of studies from projects on the effects of fire based on experimental burns, such as the 'Fire Project' conducted in the Cerrado, more specifically in Brasília (1992–2012), in which 4- and 10-ha plots of three different vegetation types (grasslands, typical savanna and forests (*cerradão*)) were experimentally burned at two different fire intervals (biennial and quadrennial) and in three fire seasons, namely the early (June), mid (August) and late (September) dry season (Miranda 2010). A long-term fire experiment established in Central

Brazil (Reserva Natural Serra do Tombador (RNST), Goiás; 13°35′–38′S, 47°45′–51′W) in 2013 aims to evaluate the effects of fire season (early, mid and late dry season) and frequency (fire exclusion, annual and biennial fires) mostly on the herbaceous layer of open savannas (Rissi *et al.* 2017; Rodrigues *et al.* 2021). Four replicates for each fire treatment were established in the area (30-m × 30-m plots) and all fire parameters are evaluated during prescribed burns. Moreover, within each plot, 10 subplots (1-m × 1-m) were established to analyse plant community composition twice a year, once each during the wet and dry seasons. Finally, fuel load, productivity, plant traits (above- and belowground), plant community phenology (Zirondi *et al.* 2021) and carbon dynamics are also being sampled in the different treatments. Other experimental fire studies have been established in other areas of the Cerrado since 2003, focusing on the effects of fire season and frequency on native vegetation (e.g. Schmidt *et al.* 2016, 2017), as well as in southern Brazil.

Characteristics of fire in the Cerrado and southern Brazilian grasslands

Although a reasonable number of studies are available on the effects of fire on vegetation composition and dynamics, as well as ecosystem processes, in the Cerrado (e.g. Miranda *et al.* 2002; Gomes *et al.* 2018, 2020) and the southern Brazilian grasslands (e.g. Overbeck *et al.* 2006; Fidelis *et al.* 2012), fire management as such has not been a topic of much scientific work thus far (but see, for example,

Pivello and Norton (1996), and the review by Gomes *et al.* (2020), which includes fire effects). Overall knowledge of fire behaviour in Brazilian grassland and savanna ecosystems is still much lower than for other fire-prone ecosystems of the world (18 studies analysed in Gomes *et al.* 2020). Because most biomass is herbaceous and fine fuels (i.e. grasses) prevail at least in open systems, fires in Brazilian grassland and savanna ecosystems are mostly fast, of rather low intensity and characterised by rather low temperatures (Table 3.1; see also Gomes *et al.* 2020). Rissi *et al.* (2017) showed that the higher the quantity of dead material and the lower its moisture content, the higher the fire intensity and flame height in savanna burns. These fire behaviours also suggest that fire severity will vary within a given year. It also has been shown that the presence of an invasive grass, such as *Urochloa brizantha* (a C_4 grass native to Africa), with vigorous growth, increases fuel quantities, and thus fire intensity (Gorgone-Barbosa *et al.* 2015).

Fuel availability is also a consequence of fire return intervals and fire season. In subtropical Campos grasslands, Fidelis *et al.* (2010) showed that after fire exclusion for longer periods (in this case, 6 years) fuel loads increased by 40%, and thus led to fires with higher flames, higher temperatures and higher fire residence time than areas with more frequent burns (every 2–4 years). In the Cerrado, fires at the end of the dry season can be more intense (Rissi *et al.* 2017; Schmidt *et al.* 2017). In wet Cerrado grasslands, mean (±s.e.m.) fire intensity at the beginning of the rainy season was 470 ± 236 kW m^{-1}, compared

Table 3.1.   Characteristics of fire in different Brazilian grasslands and savannas from selected studies

Vegetation type	Total fuel load (kg m^{-2})	Velocity of fire spread (m s^{-1})	Fire intensity (kW m^{-1})
Subtropical Campos grassland (Fidelis *et al.* 2010)	0.39–1.44	0.01–0.02	93.52–179.04
Subtropical Campos grassland (F. Furquim, unpubl. data)	1.10–1.15	0.03–0.05	359–598
Tropical wet savanna (Schmidt *et al.* 2017)	0.52–1.32	0.03–0.16	240–1083
Tropical open savanna (Rissi *et al.* 2017)	0.65–0.75	0.05–0.35	503–3009
Tropical savanna invaded by *Urochloa brizantha* (Gorgone-Barbosa *et al.* 2015)	0.35–0.62	–	140–1611
Tropical savanna (Miranda *et al.* 1993)	0.67–0.99	0.13–0.42	2842–16 394

with 750 ± 147 kW m⁻¹ at the end of the rainy season (Schmidt *et al.* 2017). In a study of open savannas, Rissi *et al.* (2017) showed that fire intensity increased with increasing time in drought during the dry season. In that study, fire intensity was low in May, at the beginning of the dry season (<1000 kW m⁻¹) and reached values four-fold higher at the end of the dry season, in October (Rissi *et al.* 2017; Figure 3.2).

Fire temperature is an important parameter to define the mortality of plant tissues (Bova and Dickinson 2005), as well as seed germination after fire (Moreira *et al.* 2010). The evaluation of fire residence time is important, because it shows how long plant tissues will be exposed to high temperatures, which is another determinant of plant survival. For the subtropical grasslands in southern Brazil studied by Fidelis *et al.* (2010), maximum temperatures varied from 48°C to 537°C at the soil surface. However, the highest residence time of 360s (at temperatures >60°C) was measured 50 cm above the soil surface, where large amounts of biomass were accumulated (Fidelis *et al.* 2010). In wet grasslands, where the maximum temperature varied from 57°C to 442°C, fire residence time did not exceed 180s, with few exceptions (Figure 3.3; Schmidt *et al.* 2017). However, in the study of Rissi *et al.* (2017) in open savanna,

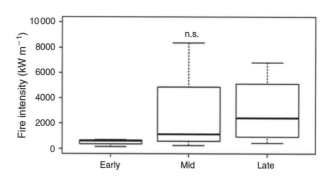

Figure 3.2: Box plots showing fire intensity in open savannas in the Cerrado at the beginning (Early; May), middle (Mid; July) and end (Late; October) of the dry season. The boxes show the interquartile range, with the median value indicated by the horizontal line; whiskers show the range. Although the differences between fire seasons were not significant, there is a tendency for an increase in fire intensity as the dry season progresses (Rissi *et al.* 2017). Reproduced with permission from CSIRO Publishing.

maximum temperatures at 50 cm above the soil surface were >600°C in all seasons, and at the end of the dry season were never <120°C.

In their analysis of six experiments that evaluated, based on prescribed fires, fire behaviour and its drivers in a systemic perspective, Gomes *et al.* (2020) found vapour pressure deficit (a microclimate variable) to be the most important predictor variable for fire behaviour. Fine fuel load, in

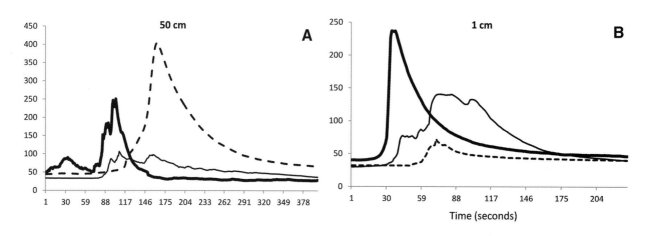

Figure 3.3: Fire temperatures (°C) over time in fire experiments in wet grasslands in central Brazil (a) 50 and (b) 1 cm above the soil surface. Each line represents a sensor measuring fire temperature every 2 s (Schmidt *et al.* 2017). Reproduced with permission from Springer Nature.

contrast, was important for the prediction of heat released, fine fuel consumption, combustion factor or carbon emissions. Consequently, Gomes *et al.* (2020) recommend that vapour pressure deficit, together with wind speed, is considered an important variable in applying prescribed burns.

Requirements and barriers for fire use

The first Brazilian nature conservation law, the 1934 Forest Code, totally prohibited the use of fire in ecosystem management. This changed with the 1965 Forest Code, in which fire remained prohibited, but with one exception: the use of fire for agricultural or silvicultural practices where the circumstances justified it and under appropriate authorisation. In 1998, a decree (Decreto 2661) specified this provision and included the term 'controlled fire'. An important change came about in 2012, when the Law for the Protection of Native Vegetation (Lei da Proteção da Vegetação Nativa, lei 12.651), which superseded the former Forest Code, allowed, for the first time, the use of fire in protected areas, as long as it was in accordance with the management plans of the area and if fire had been an important factor in the evolution of the ecosystem in question. This change finally opened the possibility of using fire in protected areas, even though it required the development of institutional capacities and experience with fire management, which take time to develop. From the perspective of scientists working with Cerrado ecology, this was a welcome and important change in policy in light of the clear evidence that a zero-fire policy can lead to catastrophic fire events in protected areas in these fire-dependent ecosystems, especially in years with extreme climate conditions that can lead to so-called megafires (Fidelis *et al.* 2018). In 2014, the national Integrated Fire Management (IFM) program (in Portuguese, Manejo Integrado de Fogo (MIF)) was started in three protected areas in Brazil (Schmidt *et al.* 2018) and then expanded (Eloy *et al.* 2019a; Schmidt and Eloy 2020).

The three first protected areas to implement IFM were located in the northern Cerrado, where the largest protected areas and best conserved Cerrado areas are found but where, to date, less research has been performed: Jalapão State Park (158 000 ha) and Serra Geral do Tocantins Ecological Station (713 000 ha), in the State of Tocantins and both established in 2001, and Chapada das Mesas National Park (161 000 ha), in Maranhão State, established in 2005. Although these three areas are protected areas of restricted use, where no human settlements are allowed in theory, local communities have existed in all three for at least a century (Schmidt *et al.* 2016). As all other local communities in the Cerrado, those dwelling in these three protected areas traditionally used fire for cattle raising, subsistence agriculture and landscape management, including to prevent wildfires (Eloy *et al.* 2019b; Moura *et al.* 2019). After many years of fire prohibition and conflicts between the managers of these protected areas and local inhabitants, in 2011 local agreements started to be built and established between local communities and the managers of the protected areas to allow for the use of fire. These agreements recognised the presence of the local communities and their right to use and manage the territories they had lived in for generations. They also helped establish honest communication between conservation managers and local communities, reducing conflicts. This is important because fire prohibition has, in fact, never been effective in preventing the use of fire, which is necessary for the survival of the cattle raised on native vegetation. In the Jalapão region, fire is also used to manage wet grasslands where *Syngonanthus nitens* (Eriocaulaceae) flower stalks are harvested. This species is harvested to produce handicrafts that represent one of the main sources of income of the local communities (Schmidt *et al.* 2007; Schmidt and Ticktin 2012). After the first years of discussion to establish local agreements on fire use, the implementation of the IFM program helped institutionalise community burning calendars, whereby managers of protected area and local inhabitants discussed which types of fire were necessary and when and how areas could be burnt for achieve the different management goals.

The application of the IFM program, including prescribed burns at the beginning of the dry season and community burns according to the burning calendars, led to a reduction in the total areas burned, and thus reduced the risk of uncontrolled wildfires (Schmidt *et al.* 2018). Importantly, fire management significantly reduced emissions from late dry season fires. This reduction has become strategic for the Brazilian government and was included in the country's 2016 National Emissions Inventory (Mistry *et al.* 2019).

In order to advance the use of fire for conservation, or even within pastoral/agricultural activities, the objectives of vegetation management should be the guiding principals (see also Durigan and Ratter 2016). Because Brazil's non-forest systems usually consist of mosaics of different vegetation types, it probably makes sense to use fire strategically to maintain these mosaics (e.g. apply fire at different frequencies and in different seasons). It has been argued that despite the evident need to get better and more monitoring data, existing data, including that obtained from knowledge of fire management by Indigenous people, is sufficient to develop fire management plans for protected areas (Pivello 2011; Durigan and Ratter 2016). Although some general recommendations have been made (e.g. Pivello 2011), it is clear that fire management across different regions of Brazil's non-forest ecosystems will have to be applied variably and allowed to differ in terms of fire frequency and season depending on the specific objectives of fire management and the ecological characteristics of each region.

Getting fire on the ground

Because fire management in savannas and grasslands is recent in Brazil, no general procedures or guidelines have yet been developed. Nonetheless, in the course of the IFM program much experience has been developed and, throughout the country, fires are today being used applying the same general principles, but respecting specific features of the regions or locations in question. In general, management strategies do not try to simulate natural fire regimes (where they are known) because the landscapes are considerably altered and fragmented. Often, fire management aims to include knowledge of Indigenous or Traditional peoples, especially in Indigenous Territories (Eloy *et al.* 2019b). However, given that climate and other factors have already greatly changed some systems and their fire dynamics, there is a strong need to include recent scientific knowledge.

Local communities in the Cerrado are very diverse and include communities of Indigenous people who have inhabited the area for thousands of years, communities of African descendent (quilombola communities that have been in the region for several centuries) and small farming communities. People from these distinct communities have developed different traditions and ways of using the Cerrado in past centuries (Lúcio *et al.* 2014; Borges *et al.* 2016; Eloy *et al.* 2016; Moura *et al.* 2019). The most common use of fire among non-Indigenous communities is to raise cattle. Usually, fire is applied at different times of the year (from the early dry season to the early rainy season) in different vegetation types, including dry grasslands and savannas, as well as wet grasslands. Across the landscape, this promotes mosaics of areas with different fire histories (0 to 3 or 4 years since last fire). Although cattle grazing is the principal land use, fire is also used to prevent wildfires in fire-sensitive vegetation (e.g. riparian forests) and agricultural areas (Eloy *et al.* 2019b). At a smaller scale, fire is also used for slash and burn agriculture and hunting, especially by Indigenous communities (Mistry *et al.* 2005; Melo and Saito 2011; Mistry and Bizerril 2011; Lúcio 2019; Welch and Coimbra 2019).

One important aspect at the beginning of fire management in Brazil was to work with very safe fires to help gain acceptance in society. When prescribed fires started to be used in 2014, fires were set at the beginning of the dry season and under climatic conditions that would allow the fires to extinguish themselves at the end of the day, as dictated by diurnal temperature and humidity rhythms. The first prescribed fires rarely exceeded 100 ha individually. These fires needed little management and few resources, including in terms of people. This cautious use of fire at the beginning of fire management in Brazil was important for managers to gain experience and an understanding of fire characteristics and the factors that influence them, as well as the effects and risks of fires. Once areas had been under fire management for longer periods, fires were also set in the middle and at the end of the dry season, with older fire scars (from early dry season burns) serving as firebreaks, conferring safety.

One important objective at the start of fire management in Brazil had been the change in fire season by the use of prescribed fires (as opposed to controlled fires that were used by local people as more production-oriented tools in land management; Eloy *et al*. 2019b) to reduce the risk of late season burns and thus damage to fire-sensitive ecosystems. Fire-sensitive vegetation (e.g. riparian forests) was typically used as a natural firebreak, at least for early dry season fires. Roads can also be used as firebreaks. In many protected areas, specific conservation targets (e.g. nesting areas of endangered species, areas under restoration) are protected from fire, just as infrastructure and housing are protected. In some cases, fire management is specifically adapted to manage vegetation so that certain conservation goals can be met. One such example is fire management for *S. nitens*, the species used to make handicrafts, as noted earlier; indeed, these handicrafts have become a symbol of the Jalapão region and even of the state of Tocantins. *S. nitens* occurs in wet grasslands and the adult plants form 3- to 4-cm rosettes that flower massively 1 year after an area has been burnt (Schmidt *et al*. 2007; Schmidt and Ticktin 2012). These wet grasslands are therefore managed with fire every 2–3 years, during the dry season (especially June–August) to promote grass resprouting just after the fire for cattle and to stimulate *S. nitens* flowering the following year (Schmidt *et al*. 2007).

Fire management in Brazil is typically conducted using simple and easily available equipment, such as drip torches, backpack hand pumps and portable or hand-held fire blowers. Fuel load maps are used to delineate burn units. In past years, thousands of people have been trained in fire management, mostly within the IFM program in Brazil's network of national protected areas. In regions where federal and state fire brigades are hired to work in protected areas, training in applying prescribed fires has been incorporated into the annual training of fire brigade candidates. This training is free of charge, lasts 1 week (~40 h) and consists of both theoretical classes and practical tests to select those who will be hired by the fire brigades. The fire brigades hired to work in protected areas are also accompanied and further trained by the government agency responsible for their hiring, either federal institutions or state environmental agencies responsible for the management of the protected areas.

Future of fire in the region

Fire in Brazil will remain a complicated issue, and one that requires very distinct strategies for distinct ecosystems. In the Amazon region, the development of policy that effectively reduces fire occurrence and fire risk is of utmost importance, not only for the protection of Amazon biodiversity itself, but also because to its considerable importance in continental and global ecological processes (e.g. Lovejoy and Nobre 2018). Current predictions point to increased risks of drought and heat waves, which will increase the risks of fires and resulting degradation (De Faria *et al*. 2017; Brando *et al*. 2020). There is a dire need for ecosystem and landscape management strategies that reduce fire risk, and thus the risk of further degradation of the Amazon forest. Unfortunately, recent reductions in government spending in the field of conservation and the political discourse regarding biodiversity conservation could add to an already difficult situation for conservation sciences and practice in Brazil, as seen in the 2019 Amazon burns (Bernard *et al*. 2014;

Fernandes *et al.* 2017; Overbeck *et al.* 2018a; Schmidt and Eloy 2020).

Conversely, the role of fire is very different in Brazil's natural grassland and savannas, as discussed at the beginning of this chapter and highlighted by Fidelis (2020). Although the need for fire management for biodiversity and landscape conservation and management has been recognised by scientists and environmental managers, this perspective often encounters resistance from different stakeholders involved in biodiversity and landscape management, including some scientists and people in both the conservation and agricultural sectors (Eloy *et al.* 2019a). One problem is cultural: the debate regarding the use of fire even in savannas and grasslands (i.e. fire-dependent systems) is still often conducted from forest-focused perspectives, where fire is a disturbance that needs to be avoided. This is especially true in regions with forest–grassland mosaics, which have very different conservation objectives (see, for example, Luza *et al.* 2014; Overbeck *et al.* 2016). Overall, however, as demonstrated in this chapter, fire management has been established as an important part of conservation policy, at least in federal protected areas and Indigenous areas in Brazil's non-forest regions.

Despite the success of the IFM program, considerable capacity building is still needed to develop and implement larger-scale fire management programs and to work with prescribed burns in protected areas throughout the Cerrado and southern Brazilian grassland regions. This will also require increased and well-coordinated interactions among conservation authorities, stakeholders and scientists, with a need to also develop adequate and relevant monitoring (for more details on governance questions, see Eloy *et al.* (2019a). Permanent plots for research and participant monitoring are essential for researchers, fire brigades and environmental agents to gain knowledge and exchange experiences. There are currently around 130 permanent plots used to monitor vegetation in four protected areas in the Cerrado (Jalapão State Park, Chapada das Mesas National Park, Serra Geral do Tocantins Ecological Station and Chapada dos Veadeiros National Park) that will help with this process. The federal biodiversity monitoring program (MONITORA), managed by ICMBio (the Chico Mendes Institute for Biodiversity Conservation, the agency responsible for national protected areas), will also enable data to be collected over time in areas subjected to fire management.

Fire will remain an important topic not only in the management of protected areas, but also in those regions, especially in southern Brazil, where fire is used as a management tool: the experiences of farmers, even though not formally documented so far, are highly relevant, and assistance by extension agencies should be developed. A topic that is becoming increasingly relevant in the Brazilian conservation debate is ecological restoration, and this is especially highly relevant for the Cerrado and the Campos Sulinos, where there are high rates of land use change (Overbeck *et al.* 2015), threatening biodiversity and ecosystem services. Although, as in conservation, a forest bias remains frequent in the restoration debate, the use of fire in the restoration of the Cerrado or southern Brazilian grasslands (e.g. Buisson *et al.* 2019) may turn out to be an important way in which to shift the public perspective of fire in non-forest grassland from a disturbance with negative effects to an interesting conservation tool.

References

Abreu RCR, Hoffmann WA, Vasconcelos HL, Pilon NA, Rossatto DR, Durigan G (2017) The biodiversity cost of carbon sequestration in tropical savanna. *Science Advances* 3, e1701284. doi:10.1126/sciadv.1701284

Aragão LEOC, Anderson LO, Fonseca MG, Rosan TM, Vedovato LB, Wagner FH, Silva CVJ, Silva Junior CHL, Arai E, Aguiar AP, *et al.* (2018) 21st Century drought-related fires counteract the decline of Amazon deforestation carbon emissions. *Nature Communications* 9, 536. doi:10.1038/s41467-017-02771-y

Barlow J, Peres CA (2008) Fire-mediated dieback and compositional cascade in an Amazonian forest. *Philosophical Transactions of the Royal Society of London. Series B, Biological Sciences* 363, 1787–1794. doi:10.1098/rstb.2007.0013

Barlow J, Berenguer E, Carmenta R, França F (2020) Clarifying Amazonia's burning crisis. *Global Change Biology* 26, 319–321. doi:10.1111/gcb.14872

Behling H, Pillar VD, Orlóci L, Bauermann SG. (2004) Late Quaternary Araucaria forest, grassland (Campos), fire and climate dynamics, studied by high-resolution pollen, charcoal and multivariate analysis of the Cambará do Sul core in southern Brazil. *Palaeogeography, Palaeoclimatology, Palaeoecology* **203**, 277–297. doi:10.1016/S0031-0182(03)00687-4

Bernard E, Penna LAO, Araújo E (2014) Downgrading, downsizing, degazettement, and reclassification of protected areas in Brazil. *Conservation Biology* **28**, 939–950. doi:10.1111/cobi.12298

Borges SL, Eloy L, Schmidt IB, Barradas ACS, Dos Santos IA (2016) Manejo do fogo em veredas: novas perspectivas a partir dos sistemas agrícolas tradicionais no Jalapão. *Ambiente & Sociedade* **19**, 275–300.

Bova AS, Dickinson MB (2005) Linking surface-fire behavior, stem heating, and tissue necrosis. *Canadian Journal of Forest Research* **35**, 814–822. doi:10.1139/x05-004

Brando PM, Soares-Filho B, Rodrigues L, Assunção A, Morton D, Tuchschneider D, Fernandes ECM, Macedo MN, Oliveira U, Coe MT (2020) The gathering firestorm in southern Amazonia. *Science Advances* **6**, eaay1632. doi:10.1126/sciadv.aay1632

Buisson E, Le Stradic S, Silveira FAO, Durigan G, Overbeck GE, Fidelis A, Fernandes GW, Bond WJ, Hermann J-M, Mahy G *et al.* (2019) Resilience and restoration of tropical and subtropical grasslands, savannas, and grassy woodlands. *Biological Reviews of the Cambridge Philosophical Society* **94**, 590–609. doi:10.1111/brv.12470

Coutinho LM (1982) Ecological effects of fire in the Brazilian Cerrado. In *Ecology of Tropical Savannas*. (Eds JB Huntley and BH Walker) pp. 273–291. Springer, New York.

De Faria BL, Brando PM, Macedo MN, Panday PK, Soares-Filho BS, Coe MT (2017) Current and future patterns of fire-induced forest degradation in Amazonia. *Environmental Research Letters* **12**, 95005. doi:10.1088/1748-9326/aa69ce

Durigan G, Ratter JA (2016) The need for a consistent fire policy for Cerrado conservation. *Journal of Applied Ecology* **53**, 11–15. doi:10.1111/1365-2664.12559

Eloy L, Aubertin C, Toni F, Lúcio SLB, Bosgiraud M (2016) On the margins of soy farms: traditional populations and selective environmental policies in the Brazilian Cerrado. *The Journal of Peasant Studies* **43**, 494–516. doi:10.1080/03066150.2015.1013099

Eloy L, Bilbao BA, Mistry J, Schmidt IB (2019a) From fire suppression to fire management: advances and resistances to changes in fire policy in the savannas of Brazil and Venezuela. *The Geographical Journal* **185**, 10–22. doi:10.1111/geoj.12245

Eloy L, Schmidt IB, Borges SL, Ferreira MC, dos Santos TA (2019b) Seasonal fire management by traditional cattle ranchers prevents the spread of wildfire in the Brazilian Cerrado. *Ambio* **48**, 890–899. doi:10.1007/s13280-018-1118-8

Fernandes GW, Vale MM, Overbeck GE, Bustamante MMC, Grelle CEV, Bergallo HG, Magnusson WE, Akama A, Alves SS, Amorim A, *et al.* (2017) Dismantling Brazil's science threatens global biodiversity heritage. *Perspectives in Ecology and Conservation* **15**, 239–243. doi:10.1016/j.pecon.2017.07.004

Fidelis A (2020) Is fire always the 'bad guy'? *Flora* **268**, 151611. doi:10.1016/j.flora.2020.151611

Fidelis A, Pivello VR (2011) Deve-se usar o fogo como instrumento de manejo no Cerrado e Campos Sulinos? *Biodiversidade Brasileira* **1**, 12–25.

Fidelis A, Delgado-Cartay MD, Blanco CC, Müller SC, Pillar VD, Pfadenhauer J (2010) Fire intensity and severity in Brazilian Campos grasslands. *Interciencia* **35**, 739–745.

Fidelis A, Blanco C, Müller S, Pillar VD, Pfadenhauer J (2012) Short-term changes caused by fire and mowing in Brazilian Campos grasslands with different long-term fire histories. *Journal of Vegetation Science* **23**, 552–562. doi:10.1111/j.1654-1103.2011.01364.x

Fidelis A, Alvarado S, Barradas A, Pivello V (2018) The Year 2017: megafires and management in the Cerrado. *Fire (Basel, Switzerland)* **1**, 49. doi:10.3390/fire1030049

Gomes L, Miranda HS, Bustamante MMC (2018) How can we advance the knowledge on the behavior and effects of fire in the Cerrado biome? *Forest Ecology and Management* **417**, 281–290. doi:10.1016/j.foreco.2018.02.032

Gomes L, Miranda HS, Silvério DV, Bustamante MMC (2020) Effects and behaviour of experimental fires in grasslands, savannas, and forests of the Brazilian Cerrado. *Forest Ecology and Management* **458**, 117804. doi:10.1016/j.foreco.2019.117804

Gorgone-Barbosa E, Pivello VR, Bautista S, Zupo T, Rissi MN, Fidelis A (2015) How can an invasive grass affect fire behavior in a tropical savanna? A community and individual plant level approach. *Biological Invasions* **17**, 423–431. doi:10.1007/s10530-014-0740-z

Hardesty J, Myers R, Fulks W (2005) Fire, ecosystems and people: a preliminary assessment of fire as a global conservation issue. *Fire Management* **22**, 78–87. doi:10.2307/43597968

Joly CA, Padgurschi MCG, Pires APF, Agostinho AA, Marques AC, Amaral AG, Cervone COFO, Adams C, Baccaro FB, Sparovek G *et al.* (2019) Capítulo 1: Apresentando o Diagnóstico Brasileiro de Biodiversidade e Serviços Ecossistêmicos. In *1° Diagnóstico Brasileiro de Biodiversidade e Serviços Ecossistêmicos*. (Eds CA Joly, FR Scarano, CS Seixas, JP Metzger, JP Ometto, MCM Bustamante, MCG Padgurschi, APF Pires, PFD Castro, T Gadda *et al.*) pp. 6–33. Editora Cubo, São Carlos.

Lovejoy TE, Nobre C (2018) Amazon tipping point. *Science Advances* **4**, eaat2340. doi:10.1126/sciadv.aat2340

Lúcio SLB (2019) Foice, machado, fogo e enxada: práticas de cultivo e sucessão secundária em matas de galeria inundáveis do Cerrado após agricultura itinerante. PhD thesis. University of Brasilia, Brazil.

Lúcio SLB, Eloy L, Ludewigs T (2014) O gado que circulava: desafios da gestão participativa de unidades de conservação nos gerais do norte de Minas. *Biodiversidade Brasileira* **1**, 130–156.

Luza AL, Carlucci MB, Hartz SM, Duarte LDS (2014) Moving from forest vs. grassland perspectives to an integrated view towards the conservation of forest–grassland mosaics. *Natureza & Conservação* **12**, 166–169.

Melo MM, Saito CH (2011) Regime de queima das caçadas com uso do fogo realizadas pelos Xavante no cerrado. *Biodiversidade Brasileira* **2**, 97–109.

Miranda HS (2010) 'Efeitos do regime de fogo sobre a estrutura de comunidades de cerrado: resultados do Projeto Fogo'. Ministério do Meio Ambiente, Brasília.

Miranda AC, Miranda HS, De Fátima Oliveira Dias I, De Souza Dias BF, Dias IFPO, Dias BFS (1993) Soil and air temperatures during prescribed cerrado fires in Central Brazil. *Journal of Tropical Ecology* **9**, 313–320. doi:10.1017/S0266467400007367

Miranda HS, Bustamante MMC, Miranda AC (2002) The fire factor. In *The Cerrados of Brazil*. (Eds PS Oliveira and RJ Marquis) pp. 51–68. Columbia University Press, New York.

Mistry J, Bizerril M (2011) Why it is important to understand the relationship between people, fire and protected areas. *Biodiversidade Brasileira* **1**, 40–49.

Mistry J, Berardi A, Andrade V, Krahô T, Krahô P, Leonardos O (2005) Indigenous fire management in the Cerrado of Brazil: the case of the Krahô of Tocantíns. *Human Ecology* **33**, 365–386. doi:10.1007/s10745-005-4143-8

Mistry J, Schmidt IB, Eloy L, Bilbao B (2019) New perspectives in fire management in South American savannas: the importance of intercultural governance. *Ambio* **48**, 172–179. doi:10.1007/s13280-018-1054-7

Moreira B, Tormo J, Estrelles E, Pausas JG (2010) Disentangling the role of heat and smoke as germination cues in Mediterranean Basin flora. *Annals of Botany* **105**, 627–635. doi:10.1093/aob/mcq017

Moura LC, Scariot AO, Schmidt IB, Beatty R, Russell-Smith J (2019) The legacy of colonial fire management policies on traditional livelihoods and ecological sustainability in savannas: impacts, consequences, new directions. *Journal of Environmental Management* **232**, 600–606. doi:10.1016/j.jenvman.2018.11.057

Nepstad D, Carvalho G, Cristina Barros A, Alencar A, Paulo Capobianco J, Bishop J, Moutinho P, Lefebvre P, Lopes Silva U Jr, Prins E (2001) Road paving, fire regime feedbacks, and the future of Amazon forests. *Forest Ecology and Management* **154**, 395–407. doi:10.1016/S0378-1127(01)00511-4

Overbeck GE, Müller SC, Pillar VD, Pfadenhauer J (2006) Floristic composition, environmental variation and species distribution patterns in burned grassland in southern Brazil. *Brazilian Journal of Biology* **66**, 1073–1090.

Overbeck GE, Muller S, Fidelis A, Pfadenhauer J, Pillar V, Blanco C, Boldrini II, Both R, Forneck ED (2007) Brazil's neglected biome: the south Brazilian Campos. *Perspectives in Plant Ecology, Evolution and Systematics* **9**, 101–116. doi:10.1016/j.ppees.2007.07.005

Overbeck GE, Vélez-Martin E, Scarano FR, Lewinsohn TM, Fonseca CR, Meyer ST, Müller SC, Ceotto P, Dadalt L, Durigan G, *et al.* (2015) Conservation in Brazil needs to include non-forest ecosystems. *Diversity and Distributions* **21**, 1455–1460. doi:10.1111/ddi.12380

Overbeck GE, Ferreira PMA, Pillar VD (2016) Conservation of mosaics calls for a perspective that considers all types of mosaic-patches. Reply to Luza *et al. Natureza & Conservação* **14**, 152–154.

Overbeck GE, Bergallo HG, Grelle CEV, Akama A, Bravo F, Colli GR, Magnusson WE, Tomas WM, Fernandes GW (2018a) Global biodiversity threatened by science budget cuts in Brazil. *Bioscience* **68**, 11–12. doi:10.1093/biosci/bix130

Overbeck GE, Scasta JD, Furquim FF, Boldrini II, Weir JR (2018b) The south Brazilian grasslands – a South American tallgrass prairie? Parallels and implications of fire dependency. *Perspectives in Ecology and Conservation* **16**, 24–30. doi:10.1016/j.pecon.2017.11.002

Pivello VR (2011) The use of fire in the Cerrado and Amazonian rainforests of Brazil: past and present. *Fire Ecology* **7**, 24–39. doi:10.4996/fireecology.0701024

Pivello VR, Norton GA (1996) FIRETOOL: an expert system for the use of prescribed fires in Brazilian savannas. *Journal of Applied Ecology* **33**, 348. doi:10.2307/2404756

Ramos-Neto MB, Pivello VR (2000) Lightning fires in a Brazilian savanna national park: rethinking management strategies. *Environmental Management* **26**, 675–684. doi:10.1007/s002670010124

Ribeiro JF, Walter BMT (2008) As principais fitofisionomias do bioma Cerrado. In *Cerrado: ecologia e flora*. (Eds SM Sano, SP Almeida, JF Ribeiro) pp. 151–212. EMBRAPA, Brasília.

Rissi MN, Baeza MJ, Gorgone-Barbosa E, Zupo T, Fidelis A (2017) Does season affect fire behaviour in the Cerrado? *International Journal of Wildland Fire* **26**, 427–433. doi:10.1071/WF14210

Rodrigues CA, Zirondi HL, Fidelis A (2021) Fire frequency affects fire behavior in open savannas of the Cerrado. *Forest Ecology and Management* **482**, 118850. doi:10.1016/j.foreco.2020.118850

Rosan TM, Aragão LEOC, Oliveras I, Phillips OL, Malhi Y, Gloor E, Wagner FH (2019) Extensive 21st-century woody encroachment in South America's savanna. *Geophysical Research Letters* **46**, 6594–6603. doi:10.1029/2019GL082327

Salgado-Labouriau ML, Casseti V, Ferraz-Vicentini KR, Martin L, Soubiès F, Suguio K, Turcq B (1997) Late Quaternary vegetational and climatic changes in Cerrado and palm swamp from central Brazil. *Palaeogeography, Palaeoclimatology, Palaeoecology* **128**, 215–226. doi:10.1016/S0031-0182(96)00018-1

Schmidt IB, Eloy L (2020) Fire regime in the Brazilian savanna: recent changes, policy and management. *Flora* **268**, 151613. doi:10.1016/j.flora.2020.151613

Schmidt IB, Ticktin T (2012) When lessons from population models and local ecological knowledge coincide – effects of flower stalk harvesting in the Brazilian savanna. *Biological Conservation* **152**, 187–195.

Schmidt IB, Figueiredo IB, Scariot A (2007) Ethnobotany and effects of harvesting on the population ecology of *Syngonanthus nitens* (Bong.) Ruhland (Eriocaulaceae), a NTFP from Jalapão Region, Central Brazil. *Economic Botany* **61**, 73–85.

Schmidt IB, Fonseca CB, Ferreira MC, Sato MN (2016) Experiências Internacionais de Manejo Integrado do Fogo em Áreas Protegidas – Recomendações para Implementação de Manejo Integrado de Fogo no Cerrado. *Biodiversidade Brasileira* **6**, 41–54.

Schmidt IB, Fidelis A, Miranda HS, Ticktin T (2017) How do the wets burn? Fire behavior and intensity in wet grasslands in the Brazilian savanna. *Brazilian Journal of Botany* **40**, 167–175. doi:10.1007/s40415-016-0330-7

Schmidt IB, Moura LC, Ferreira MC, Eloy L, Sampaio AB, Dias PA, Berlinck CN (2018) Fire management in the Brazilian savanna: first steps and the way forward. *Journal of Applied Ecology* **55**, 2094–2101.

Silva P, Bastos A, DaCamara CC, Libonati R (2016) Future projections of fire occurrence in Brazil using EC-Earth climate model. *Revista Brasileira de Meteorologia* **31**, 288–297. doi:10.1590/0102-778631320150142

Silvério DV, Brando PM, Balch JK, Putz FE, Nepstad DC, Oliveira-Santos C, Bustamante MM (2013) Testing the Amazon savannization hypothesis: fire effects on invasion of a neotropical forest by native Cerrado and exotic pasture grasses. *Philosophical Transactions of the Royal Society of London. Series B, Biological Sciences* **368**, 20120427. doi:10.1098/rstb.2012.0427

Simon MF, Grether R, de Queiroz LP, Skema C, Pennington RT, Hughes CE (2009) Recent assembly of the Cerrado, a Neotropical plant diversity hotspot, by in situ evolution of adaptations to fire. *Proceedings of the National Academy of Sciences* **106**, 20359–20364.

Starns HD, Fuhlendorf SD, Elmore RD, Twidwell D, Thacker ET, Hovick TJ, Luttbeg B (2019) Recoupling fire and grazing reduces wildland fuel loads on rangelands. *Ecosphere* **10**, e02578. doi:10.1002/ecs2.2578

Veldman JW, Overbeck GE, Negreiros D, Mahy G, Le Stradic S, Fernandes GW, Durigan G, Buisson E, Putz FE, Bond WJ (2015) Where tree planting and forest expansion are bad for biodiversity and ecosystem services. *Bioscience* **65**, 1011–1018. doi:10.1093/biosci/biv118

Welch JR, Coimbra CEA (2019) Indigenous fire ecologies, restoration, and territorial sovereignty in the Brazilian Cerrado: the case of two Xavante reserves. *Land Use Policy* **104**, 104055. doi:10.1016/j.landusepol.2019.104055

Zirondi HL, Ooi MKJ, Fidelis A (2021) Fire-triggered flowering is the dominant post-fire strategy in a tropical savanna. *Journal of Vegetation Science* **32**, e12995. doi:10.1111/jvs.12995

4

Sanctioned burning in sub-Saharan Africa

Devan Allen McGranahan, Navashni Govender,
Rheinhardt Scholtz and Kevin Kirkman

Fire regimes south of the Sahara

Africa is widely understood to be a continent of fire. Europeans noted the prevalence of smoke as they first approached sub-Saharan portions of the continent by sea. Geological evidence confirms an extensive fire history extending at least 170 000 years into the past (Daniau *et al.* 2013), and remote sensing technology reminds us that fire remains a fundamental component of ecosystems across the continent today.

Extant burning

The majority of Africa below the Sahara burns frequently, with fire only excluded from the wet equatorial Guineo-Congolian rainforests and fuel-sparse deserts (Plate 2). Although infrequent in deserts, fire does shape plant population dynamics when it occurs, such as in the Kalahari (Seymour and Huyser 2008). Ericaceous shrublands from the Cape Floristic Region to the Ethiopian Highlands are as fire prone and as fire adapted as any such ecosystems on Earth (Wesche *et al.* 2000; Pooley 2012). Nearly everywhere else, expansive C_4-dominated grassland and grassy savanna ecosystems (e.g. rangelands, or veld) evolved with fire, which helps maintain the open structure (Bond 2008). Many areas with the climatic potential for woody vegetation remain open through high-frequency fires (Devine *et al.* 2017), often driven by winds such as South Africa's föhn-like berg winds or West Africa's seasonal Harmattan (Dobson 1781; Geldenhuys 1994).

Combustion across the African continent drives regional and global biogeochemical processes. Sub-Saharan Africa contributes approximately half the global gas and particle emissions from biomass burning, 60% of which is attributable to wildland fire (e.g. wildfire and agricultural burning; Scholes *et al.* 2011). Burning vegetation biomass mostly affects short-term carbon cycles, as opposed to fossil fuel combustion, which reintroduces 'forgotten' carbon into biological and atmospheric cycles. Greater albedo following fires in Africa affects the energy budget of the entire Earth system (Saha *et al.* 2019).

Fire on the continent includes all fire types. Given the preponderance of grass-dominated fuel types, most fires are surface fires that consume most aboveground grass and shrub biomass. Ground fires also occur in wetlands with high levels of soil organic matter, such as Botswana's Okavango Delta (Ellery *et al.* 1989; Gumbricht *et al.* 2002); indigenous forests also burn, such as those around Mount Kenya (Poletti *et al.* 2019).

Common across the breadth of African fire regimes is the signature of humans. Despite their frequency, most fires in Africa are small and, owing to the prevalence of human ignitions, often purposeful (Archibald *et al.* 2010); medium-sized fires are limited to areas with lower human population densities in Central Africa (Dwyer *et al.* 2000). Most regions also have short fire seasons of 4–6 months or less across much of the continent; however, grassland ecosystems can have fire seasons as long as 12 months (Chuvieco *et al.* 2008). Because of the high proportion of human ignitions, Africa has followed the recent global trend in decreasing burned area (Andela *et al.* 2017). Detailed analysis of sub-Saharan regions indicates that most of the decline in burned area in Africa has occurred in croplands north of the equator, consistent with changing trends in agricultural practices, human settlement and recent decades of high precipitation (Zubkova *et al.* 2019).

Indigenous burning

As the cradle of mankind, Africa is also the cradle of humanity's relationship with fire. The earliest evidence for controlled, intentional use of fire by human ancestors in Africa extends as far back as 1.5 million years ago; similar evidence does not appear in Europe until 400 000 years ago (Bentsen 2014). It is likely that early hominins interacted intentionally with landscape fire long before using it in the hearth in a manner that leaves an archaeological record (Gowlett and Wrangham 2013). For example, a spike in fire incidence 400 000 years ago has been attributed to increased human ignitions across sub-Saharan Africa (Bird and Cali 1998). Feder and Noronha (1987) describe pre-colonial land tenure in some regions of sub-Saharan Africa beginning with the 'master of fire' and continuing through his descendants, highlighting the ubiquity and importance of fire in land development.

In any case, the close relationship between fire and African peoples was well established by the time European observers arrived on the continent. In fact, a key term in modern ecology – 'regime' – was first used as a condescending reference to the indigenous burning practices encountered by early Europeans in Africa. French observers used the word *régime* to describe wasteful burning in the justification of the pogroms that became European colonisation (Krebs *et al.* 2010). *Régime*, with the accent retained, likely migrated to English in the course of colonial administration and forestry science; a typically disparaging use appeared in a missive from India about how local fire practices interfered with colonial attempts at industrial forestry (Hearle 1888).

Colonial fire policies and their legacies

European colonial administrations generally held a negative view of fire, appreciating only its potential benefit for improving crop yield under what they called 'primitive agriculture' (Figure 4.1). From early on, they sought to restrict intentional burning for land clearing or other agricultural purposes. For example, Botha (1924) described provisions in a 1687 law in the Cape Colony that imposed death by hanging for a citizen's second conviction for burning a pasture, field or forest without what we would refer to today as a burn permit. Such policies created tension between local populations and colonial administrations throughout the colonial period (e.g. Kull 2002).

An inherent bias towards forests as valuable resources requiring protection led colonial administrators to view savannas, and the fires that maintain them, as evidence of human-caused environmental degradation (Jones 1938; MacDonald 1944; Laris 2004), often through the lens of Clementsian succession (Phillips 1930; Mentis and Bailey 1990). Aubréville (1947) blamed forest recession on anthropogenic fires pushing into forests from grasslands and creating a transition zone referred to by many Europeans at the time as 'derived savanna'.

Growing awareness that rural landscapes would inevitably burn prompted a turn to the emerging

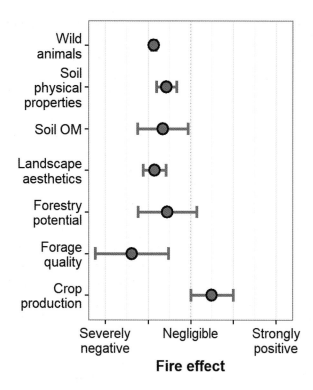

Figure 4.1: A snapshot of perceptions towards wildland fire in the mid-20th century. This figure illustrates an attempt to summarise the effect of fire across 10 ecosystem types found throughout 'trans-Saharan Africa', in which Phillips (1968) categorised the strength of each response and noted whether the effect was 'helpful' or caused 'harm'. Data in the figure are effect size estimates and 95% confidence intervals based on statistical simulations of scores (Phillips 1968, table 2). Among experts in each field, many of these perceptions have changed in subsequent decades. OM, organic matter.

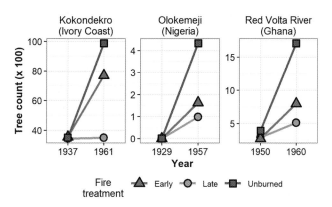

Figure 4.2: Results from three late colonial-era savanna fire studies in West Africa, as summarised by Innes (1972). These and other contemporary studies created a simplistic view of fire and savanna dynamics that strongly affected colonial and post-colonial fire policies in West Africa (Laris and Wardell 2006). The Olokemeji plots were cleared of trees at the beginning of the study. To compensate for differences in initial tree count and plot sizes, Kokondekro and Red Volta River data are plotted as per hectare tree density. No trials were replicated.

science of field ecology for management alternatives to fire exclusion. A series of studies was initiated to compare the effects of fires conducted early in the dry season with those that burn later in the dry season, when thoroughly cured fuels carry intense fires (Figure 4.2). Fire was still regarded as a force of environmental degradation, but early season fires were accepted as a 'necessary evil' that reduced fuel loads and reduced tree mortality from late season fires (Dundas 1944; Fairhead and Leach 2000).

The results of studies in West Africa on the savanna fire triad (i.e. early season burns, late season burns and fire exclusion) had a strong and lasting effect on colonial fire policy that continues today (Laris and Wardell 2006). Unfortunately, the studies were substantially flawed from their inception. The plots were large but unreplicated and were thus subject to considerable variability within treatments (Louppe *et al.* 1995). Furthermore, the seasonality treatment creates a false dichotomy: the strict comparison of early versus late dry season fires ignored the reality of local human ignitions, which begin early in the dry season and continue within a fragmented patchwork that limits the spread of high-intensity fires later in the season (Bucini and Lambin 2002; Butz 2009; Laris *et al.* 2017).

Distressingly, many post-colonial governments reverted to anti-fire policies more reminiscent of early colonial attitudes than late colonial concessions to the inevitability of human fire use. For example, Guinea implemented a total ban on forest burning in 1972 that carried death penalties (Fairhead and Leach 1995). Post-independence regimes in Madagascar continued to criminalise human ignitions through the 1970s and 1990s, and setting vegetation ablaze became a popular act of protest (Kull 2002). Although the post-colonial revival of fire exclusion gave way to *restricted inclusion* in fire management (Laris and Wardell 2006), post-colonial forestry policies still tend to be restrictive, requiring site preparation and permitting akin to formal prescribed fire in the West (Bassett and Zuéli 2000; Goldammer and De Ronde 2004; Pooley 2018).

Fire in sub-Saharan Africa

As with many regions in which rural human populations pursue subsistence livelihoods, Africa defies the Western dichotomy between prescribed burning and wildfire. In many Western countries, *prescribed burning* refers to fire that has been intentionally set or allowed to burn under a specific set of conditions, or prescription. Such prescriptions or burn plans are often written to meet legal criteria regarding outcomes, risk management and liability, and intentional ignitions without approved documentation would be considered unlawful.

Sanctioned versus unsanctioned fire

The above dichotomy fails to capture the diversity of fire in sub-Saharan Africa. Human ignitions in Africa constitute a complex political ecology (Kepe 2005; Laris *et al.* 2015). Most of Africa's anthropogenic fire occurs outside of formal policy and practice but is no less purposeful; even those critical of burning in land use have long distinguished between accidental and intentional fire (e.g. MacDonald 1944). As such, rather than rely on the Western typology of prescribed burning versus wildfire, we distinguish here between *sanctioned* and *unsanctioned fire* (McGranahan and Wonkka 2021). In this typology, sanctioned fire is that intentionally set and managed under any cultural or political authority, regardless of whether it occurs outside of, or even counter to, national legislation.

Conversely, unsanctioned fire consists of arson and undesired natural or accidental ignitions, including most fire requiring suppression activity. Arson is not a negligible category of anthropogenic ignitions in the complex political ecology of wildland fire in Africa. Fire is 'the weapon of the weak',

and *rural incendiarism* refers to the use of fire by local populations to protest or resist political or economic authorities across Africa and beyond (Goody 1980; Onyeka Nwanunobi 1990; Kuhlken 1999; Kepe 2005).

Diversity of authority

Unlike many Western countries in which the authority to regulate fire rests primarily with government, control over sanctioned fire in much of Africa is decentralised and often at odds between levels and types of authorities. Most countries have national legislation providing environmental, conservation and natural resource policy that often provides authority over wildland fire use and emergency fire services, but the impact of national-level legislation on fire occurrence is often quite limited (Mbow *et al.* 2000). Rather, many rural jurisdictions are administered by local authorities whose economically and culturally motivated natural resource management priorities can run counter to national policy. For example, in areas under traditional control around Zambia's Kasanka National Park, a local Chief orders a late dry season burning period that begins weeks after the Department of Forestry's legal burning season (Eriksen 2007).

Fire administration has rarely been confined to a single level through either the colonial or post-colonial periods. Recognising the failure of fire exclusion, some colonial authorities sought to transfer control to local forest departments who could encourage early burning (Dundas 1944). In post-colonial Madagascar, the 'state' consisted of two levels: the anti-fire central government and the officials charged with enforcement. Locals mostly interacted with the latter, who were more likely to use their own discretion in enforcing legislation (Kull 2002).

Land use and cultural norms affect the timing and type of sanctioned fire. Along the border of Botswana and South Africa, conservation areas, commercial farms and communal grazing areas each show contrasting spatial patterns of fire (Hudak *et al.* 2004). Around the Kasanka National

Park in Zambia, locally sanctioned fire occurs in at least two periods, with savanna burning at the end of the rainy season and burning crop residue in a swidden agriculture system once the rainy season begins (Eriksen 2007). Indeed, at a continental scale, agricultural fire seasons are offset from periods of 'natural' burning (Magi *et al.* 2012). Cultural differences within broad fire seasons appear in which days of the week Africans burn agricultural plots: fire activity is lowest on Sundays in Christian-dominated areas and lowest on Fridays in Muslim-dominated areas (Pereira *et al.* 2015).

Sanctioned fire and natural resources

Fire is used intentionally for natural resource management throughout sub-Saharan Africa. Here we review the application of fire in the control of woody plant encroachment, several components of agricultural productivity and conservation of biodiversity.

Woody encroachment

Fire is used widely in sub-Saharan Africa to control or eliminate woody plants. Many ecosystems have the climatic potential to support dense trees but for millennia have been maintained as open, grassy ecosystems in which fire is a major driver (Bond *et al.* 2003; Bond 2008). Across Africa, fire exclusion results in substantial increases in woody vegetation at the expense of graminoids and herbaceous vegetation (Harrington 1974; Swaine *et al.* 1992; de Villiers and O'Connor 2011; Devine *et al.* 2017).

Considerable research attention is given to which aspects of fire regime best maximise fire effects on woody vegetation. Because many woody savanna species are *resprouters* (i.e. plants recover aboveground material lost to fire by growing back from belowground meristems and stored energy reserves), managers often burn frequently to maintain low woody cover (Kinyamario 1985; Higgins *et al.* 2000; Nyazika *et al.* 2017). But frequent fires can also shift the height and structure of woody vegetation without necessarily substantially

reducing overall woody canopy cover (Higgins *et al.* 2007; Gandiwa 2011; Mudongo *et al.* 2016). High-intensity fires might be more effective in substantially reducing the woody component of savanna vegetation (Ryan and Williams 2011; Smit *et al.* 2016). High fire intensities are achieved by burning during winter, when fine fuels are cured, and under longer fire return intervals, which allow greater fuel accumulation (Govender *et al.* 2006).

Agricultural productivity and soils

Whether for purposes of grazing or farming, improving agricultural productivity is a primary purpose of anthropogenic ignitions across sub-Saharan Africa. Observers of indigenous fire regimes have long noted the intention of farmers and pastoralists to improve the nutrient value of soil and forage alike, as well as to clear moribund vegetation (Pillans 1924; Meiklejohn 1955; Kemmis *et al.* 1967; Egunjobi 1970; Innes 1972). Concerns about negative soil impacts predate even these early observations of fire use.

Cropping

Sanctioned burning is an integral part of *swidden* agricultural systems, colloquially known as 'slash and burn', which support rural livelihoods across sub-Saharan Africa (Figure 4.3). Cutting, piling and burning secondary growth from fallow plots releases nutrients in plant-available forms and increases crop yields (Ando *et al.* 2014). The ubiquity of anthropogenic ignitions for agricultural burning drives a continent-wide pattern of relatively small fires that often occur outside of natural, weather-controlled seasons of natural burning (Archibald *et al.* 2010; Magi *et al.* 2012). Burning crop fields is seasonally distinct from savanna burning in Zambia (Eriksen 2007). In Tanzania, farm preparation is the largest source (34%) of fires spreading through miombo woodlands (Katani *et al.* 2014).

Grazing

Fire has long been recognised for increasing the quality of the grass sward for livestock. In contrast

can act as a physical barrier to herbivory and generally reduces the proportional crude protein content of the average feeding station (Figure 4.4). Conversely, succulent post-fire regrowth is high in crude protein and other nutrients, and its dominance in a feeding station increases the quality of forage available to livestock (Mes 1958; Tainton *et al.* 1977; Van de Vijver *et al.* 1999). Although these patterns have been routinely demonstrated in mesic veld, fire also increases the crude protein and phosphorous content in unfertilised semi-arid veld

Figure 4.3: Two views of agricultural plots following slash–burning in western Ethiopia. Fire after fallow maintains soil organic and total soil nitrogen pools in this shifting agricultural system (Terefe and Kim 2020). Photographs courtesy of Dong-Gill Kim.

to the forestry mindset in West Africa, early researchers in South Africa recognised the role of fire in maintaining productive grasslands (Phillips 1919; Glover 1938). Subsequently, similar patterns have been observed across sub-Saharan Africa: spatially discrete, occasional burns late in the dry season promoted tiller development and increased grass basal area in Nigerian savanna (Afolayan 1979) and greater grass production followed fires in the Kalahari desert (Skarpe 1980).

Fire improves forage quality through both direct and indirect mechanisms. Directly, fire removes low-quality litter and standing dead material that

Figure 4.4: Cattle in Pondoland, eastern South Africa, focus their grazing in recently burned patches with short but succulent green regrowth that contrasts against the tall, less-nutritious and less-palatable areas with longer time since fire. The political ecology of local fire regimes in Pondoland is complex (Kepe 2005). Photographs courtesy of Kevin Kirkman.

on the edge of South Africa's Karoo (Mbatha and Ward 2010).

Indirect effects of fire on grazing resources relate to sward composition, which varies with fire regime. Different fire frequencies and burn seasons favour different species assemblages. In South Africa, *Themeda triandra* (red grass or *rooigras*) is a desirable forage grass and responds favourably to annual burning (Figure 4.5); *T. triandra* also increases with increasing fire frequency in Uganda, but there it is considered less desirable (Harrington 1974). However, disturbances at too great a frequency can diminish grass responses in even resilient, high-rainfall veld; for example, annual fire and high grazing intensity caused degradation of grassland plant communities in eastern South Africa (Little *et al.* 2015). In the Kruger National Park, frequent burning improves rangeland condition in high-rainfall veld, but is associated with degradation in drier areas (Trollope *et al.* 2014).

Burners can also manipulate the season of fire to optimise forage responses, although it can be difficult to parse whether seasonality differences are attributable to different fire characteristics or plant phenology (N'Dri *et al.* 2018). Harrington

(1974) concluded that late dry season fires provided the best grazing resources in Uganda; likewise, late burning increased the basal area of perennial grasses in Nigeria (Afolayan 1979). Conversely, growing season fires, attempted primarily to introduce diversity to fire regimes, were found to reduce primary production and reduce the abundance of desirable species in montane grasslands in South Africa, and the practice was subsequently discontinued (Scotcher and Clarke 1981). Trollope (1987) also found growing season burns occurring after spring rains were deleterious to grass productivity in the Eastern Cape.

Soils

One of the most controversial environmental issues related to fire is the effect of burning on abiotic and biotic soil properties. In addition to tree mortality, soil exposure, organic matter loss, 'desiccation' and subsequent erosion were major motivations behind colonial fire exclusion policies (Kanthack 1930; Phillips 1930, 1936; Jones 1938).

It can be challenging to interpret experimental results on the effects of fire on soil; some direct, short-term losses, such as nitrogen volatilisation and organic matter combustion, can be mitigated over the long term by indirect benefits of fire to the plant community. For example, despite greater levels of plant-available forms of four macronutrients, the immediate declines in carbon and nitrogen prompt some authors to caution against burning veld (e.g. Materechera *et al.* 1998; Snyman 2002). However, an evaluation of soils under the 50-year fire experiment at Ukulinga in KwaZulu-Natal, South Africa, found that fire stimulated fine root growth and turnover, which compensated for losses of soil organic matter in the upper layers of the soil (Fynn *et al.* 2003). As Cook (1939) concluded, the minor reductions in soil organic matter from grassland fires do not offset the substantial productivity declines of veld left unburned. And in cropping systems, cultivation practices appear to override burning in terms of residue management effects on soil organic matter (Kotzé and du Preez 2007).

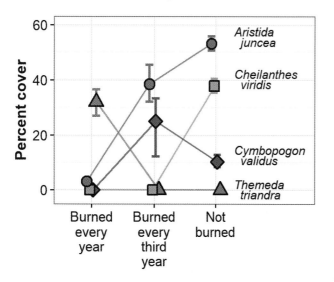

Figure 4.5: Grass community composition in the Ukulinga plots in KwaZulu-Natal, South Africa, varies considerably with different fire regimes (Kirkman *et al.* 2014).

Biodiversity conservation

Many ecosystems throughout sub-Saharan Africa evolved with fire, and plant and animal species in those ecosystems have adapted to the emergent fire regimes. Thus, sanctioned burning plays a critical role in conserving biodiversity in fire-dependent ecosystems. But ensuring managed fire regimes meet the needs of fire-adapted species and protect fire-sensitive species is challenging.

Burning issues

Two issues about using sanctioned fire for biodiversity conservation in Africa relate to fire regime characteristics: (1) patchiness and variability; and (2) the similarity of fire behaviour and fire effects between prescribed and 'natural' fire regimes. In both cases, the primary concern is negative effects on species more sensitive to fire.

As with livestock, wildlife have a strong attraction to recently burned areas throughout sub-Saharan Africa (Wilsey 1996; Archibald *et al.* 2005; Klop *et al.* 2007). Populations of some antelope species of conservation concern are supported by burned areas within their ranges (Gureja and Owen-Smith 2002; Parrini and Owen-Smith 2010). Burned areas increase prey sight distances for predator avoidance; patchy burns that leave sufficient unburned cover in the area ensure predator fitness does not decline under active fire management (Eby *et al.* 2013).

However, many organisms are sensitive to fire, from pipits on the South African Highveld to black rhinos in the Serengeti (Little *et al.* 2013; Anderson *et al.* 2020). More broadly, there is concern that burning too frequently and too extensively will deplete natural resources otherwise sustained by moderate fire regimes. A joint report between the US Forest Service and Zambia Forestry Department found that nearly 20% of Zambia's Eastern Province burns annually, under a fire regime that threatens environmental quality; the report concluded that fire return intervals should be lengthened and burning shifted to the early dry season (Hollingsworth *et al.* 2015). To the west, rural residents around the Kasanka National Park themselves report to be concerned that the economically motivated, high-frequency, late dry season fire regime advocated by their local leaders causes long-term harm to the savanna resources that such fires are intended to stimulate (Eriksen 2007).

Conversely, the moderate fire intensities that result from prudent fire management can harm local biodiversity by depriving species of the high-intensity fire under which they evolved. In the fynbos of South Africa, an indigenous vegetation type dominated by ericaceous shrubs that is prone to wildfire, much was made about the 'devastation' wrought by veld fire in early ecological accounts (Levyns 1924; Pillans 1924; Adamson 1927). Scholars have since recovered the lost history of fire in the fynbos (Pooley 2012; Kraaij *et al.* 2013), and prescribed burning was reintroduced to manage fire in the ecosystem (van Wilgen 2009). However, the effectiveness of these burns has been called into question. First, only a small proportion of the fynbos receives prescribed fire, and it is thus ineffective in reducing wildfire (van Wilgen *et al.* 2010). Second, 'the failure of safe prescribed burning' is evident in the assumed extinction of the indigenous Proteaceae species *Mimetes stokoei* in an area subject to prescribed fire until 24 seedlings emerged after 'an uncontrollable blaze' (van Wilgen 2013). The situation is further complicated by the costs of controlling alien species in the wake of wildfire (van Wilgen 2009).

Pyrodiversity

Clearly, there is no one-size-fits-all approach to fire and ecosystem management. 'Pyrodiversity' refers to the natural variability within fire regimes (Martin and Sapsis 1992). As a management principle, pyrodiversity uses landscape ecology to understand the spatial and temporal dynamics that create a broad gradient of fire effects and successional stages and enhance biodiversity conservation.

Based on the premise that diversity of the fire pattern in a landscape enhances biodiversity, the original strategy in several of South Africa's protected areas was patch-mosaic burning, in which managers limited annual burned area through the tactical placement of point ignitions, rather than homogeneous block burning (Parr and Brockett 1999). Initially, patch mosaic burning was implemented through an adaptive management framework that calculated the number of point ignitions to set based on fuel load data and expected extent of individual fires (Brockett *et al.* 2001). The point ignition system increased variability in fire regime and increased the influence of sanctioned fire over arson in conservation areas (Mulqueeny *et al.* 2010).

Pyrodiversity has been critiqued for not considering the appropriate fire regime for species of conservation concern, and evidence suggests some taxa do not respond to arbitrary point ignition burns (Parr *et al.* 2004; Parr and Andersen 2006). An alternative approach is heterogeneity-based management, in which managers adapt the spatial pattern of fire to interact with other landscape-level processes to increase the spatial contrast between patches, and stabilise this contrast within and among seasons (Fuhlendorf *et al.* 2017). In African rangelands, primary considerations include pyric herbivory (i.e. the interaction between fire and herbivory) and maintaining a diversity of patches with different time since fire (McGranahan and Kirkman 2013). Wild herbivores across sub-Saharan Africa demonstrate pyric herbivory (Trollope 1974; Wilsey 1996; Archibald and Bond 2004; Archibald *et al.* 2005; Klop *et al.* 2007), but examples of heterogeneity-based management targeting patch contrast with time-since-fire gradients are scant (but see Mentis and Rowe-Rowe 1979; Bernard *et al.* 2015; for research on the spatial extent of burns, see Donaldson *et al.* 2018). There are, however, examples of functionally heterogeneous landscape mosaics maintained with traditional fire use throughout sub-Saharan Africa (Laris 2002; Johansson and Granström 2014).

Wildland fire science and management

Africa has a long tradition of wildland fire research, with much of it aimed at understanding the effects of intentional burning on natural resources. Throughout the past century, field studies have been implemented to study the long-term effects of repeated fire; several from throughout sub-Saharan Africa are described in the peer-reviewed literature (Table 4.1). Results from other studies are limited to local reports (the so-called 'grey literature'; Swift *et al.* 1994), many of which are cited in Schrige and Penderis (1978) and O'Connor (1985). Information gained from even the oldest studies can still be useful today, although results must be considered within their historical context (Laris *et al.* 2017). Scale is a timeless issue: Swift *et al.* (1994) contrasted the average plot size in 16 long-term African fire experiments (0.46 ha) against the average size of wildfires in Hwange National Park, Zimbabwe (18 300 ha).

Trends in fire research

We delineate three broad periods of wildland fire research in sub-Saharan Africa: the imperial, empirical and inclusive periods.

The imperial period

As discussed above, early colonial managers and naturalists generally held a negative view of anthropogenic fire use (Figure 4.1) and sought to restrict sanctioned burning. The natural sciences of this era were largely descriptive (e.g. Adamson 1927; Levyns 1929); several papers available from a 1924 symposium on veld burning in South Africa exemplify the scientific discourse of the day (Botha 1924; Levyns 1924; Pillans 1924). Field studies seem to have been designed more to demonstrate conventional wisdom than to test falsifiable hypotheses (Figure 4.2). Nonetheless, these studies were translated into colonial policies that began to sanction early dry season burning as a 'necessary evil', which remained influential in the decades after African countries became independent (Laris and Wardell 2006).

The empirical period

By the mid-20th century, fire ecology was well established as a global discipline and research in Africa was starting to become more experimental. The 1971 Tall Timbers Fire Ecology Conference in

Table 4.1.   Summary of several long-term wildland fire research studies in sub-Saharan Africa reported in the literature

Asterisks (*) behind study period endpoints indicate the last year of data found in our literature review for studies where a definite endpoint or explicit statement that the study is ongoing was not found. *a.n., ad nunc* (up to now), for trials ongoing as of printing

Location (name)	Vegetation type	Study period	Pertinent references
Hilton, South Africa	Wattle plantation	1928–48*	Beard and Darby (1951)
Nigeria (Olokemeji)	Transitional savanna	1929–62*	Hopkins and Jenkin (1962)
Ndola, Zambia	Miombo woodland	1933–82*	Trapnell (1959), Chidumayo (1988)
Cote d'Ivoire (Aubréville's Kokondékro plots)	Transitional savanna	1936–95*	Louppe *et al.* (1995)
Zimbabwe (Matopos)	Thornveld, sandveld	1947–63*	Kennan (1972)
North-east Ghana (Red Volta River)	Transitional savanna	1949–77*	Brookman-Amissah *et al.* (1980)
KwaZulu-Natal, South Africa (Ukulinga)	Mesic grassland	1950–*a.n.*	Tainton *et al.* (1978), Kirkman *et al.* (2014)
Zimbabwe (Marondera)	Miombo woodland	1953–91, 2007	Furley *et al.* (2008)
KwaZulu-Natal, South Africa (Cathedral Peak catchments)	Mesic grassland	1954–*a.n.*	Everson and Tainton (1984), Uys *et al.* (2004)
North-east South Africa (Kruger National Park)	Fine- and broad-leaf savanna	1954–*a.n.*	van Wilgen *et al.* (2007)
Eastern Cape, South Africa (Camp 32, Fort Hare)	Semi-arid grassland	1973–99*	Uys *et al.* (2004)
KwaZulu-Natal, South Africa (Brotherton trials)	Mesic grassland	1980–*a.n.*	Uys *et al.* (2004), Short (2007)
Eastern Cape, South Africa	Semi-arid savanna	1980–2008*	Mopipi (2012)

Tallahassee (FL, USA), which was devoted to 'Fire in Africa', illustrated the transition in wildland fire science: in addition to colonial-era data discussing the threat of anthropogenic fire to the *preservation* of forest resources (Innes 1972), papers also reported research on using fire for the *conservation* of Africa's biodiversity and ecosystems (Gillon 1972a, 1972b; Skovlin 1972; van Wyk 1972).

Unfortunately, the scientific standards of the empirical approach did not include human dimensions of African fire regimes. In the 'Fire in Africa' symposium, Komarek (1972) elaborated on the role of lightning as an ignition source in sub-Saharan Africa, identified vegetative fuel load and condition as the main drivers of fire occurrence and downplayed the role of humans as only capable of amplifying natural conditions necessary for burning. A panel of experts convened to identify fire ecology knowledge gaps and research priorities in South Africa articulated eight thematic areas, none of which referenced humans or their activities in any capacity (Huntley 1978); nor did Trollope's (1981) delineation of standard fire ecology terminology like 'fire regime' make any reference to human dimensions in wildland fire.

An inclusive period?

Managers, researchers and policy makers have begun to consider the human dimensions of natural resource management in the early 21st century. As fire ecology has improved its understanding of variability within the fire environment and fire regimes, the science is increasingly influenced by landscape ecology and social sciences like political ecology and human geography (Laris 2002, 2011; Kepe 2005; Laris and Dembele 2012). Non-equilibrium theories of ecosystem dynamics make it possible to consider multiple alternative outcomes under interacting social and environmental scenarios (Laris *et al.* 2016).

Including human dimensions in the study of sanctioned fire regimes is critical to addressing

21st century problems in sub-Saharan Africa. 'Robust wildland fire science' refers to research that collects and reports data on fuels and fire behaviour, and communicates results within the socioecological understanding of wildland fire regimes (McGranahan and Wonkka 2018). We have already reviewed several examples of how researchers from political ecology and geography have made substantial contributions to understanding the role of humans and human systems in modulating the spatial and temporal pattern of ignitions across Africa. Below, we highlight two more components of wildland fire science and management that make fire ecology in sub-Saharan Africa more inclusive, namely the connection of fire behaviour to fire effects and understanding the wildland–urban interface.

Connecting fire behaviour and effects

Transferability of results from wildland fire research is enhanced when mechanistic understandings of the underlying processes of fire behaviour can be used to predict whether similar patterns in fire effects will be observed in a repeated application of the effort. When fire behaviour measurements are not feasible, researchers are encouraged to collect and report data on fuels and fire weather and, if possible, use published models to predict fire behaviour and direct effects. Studies should test responses along environmental gradients instead of relying on categorical group mean comparisons, or use a dose–response framework (McGranahan and Wonkka 2018).

There is a growing body of literature from sub-Saharan Africa that informs ecological understanding of sanctioned fire use. Decades of research from South Africa break the fire environment into fuels, weather and seasonality to understand impacts on fire behaviour and fire effects (Trollope 1978, 1984, 1987; Everson *et al.* 1985; Trollope and Potgieter 1985; Govender *et al.* 2006). Other studies use fuel moisture data collected over space and time to parameterise fire behaviour models that simulate wildland fire effectiveness, seasonality and the impact of invasive species (van Wilgen and

Richardson 1985; Sow *et al.* 2013; McGranahan *et al.* 2016, 2018).

Wildland–urban interface

The zone where natural vegetation abuts the built human environment is known as the wildland–urban interface. In flammable landscapes, the interface creates challenges to fire managers that are unique from either context alone. As rural emigration causes human development to spread around urban centres, often in an informal manner, fire in the wildland–urban interface is of increasing concern in sub-Saharan Africa (van Niekerk 2014). Similarly, an increasing urban population, being less familiar with rural livelihoods, is more likely to critique the use of sanctioned fire, whether in conservation areas or working landscapes.

South Africa has several examples of the wildland–urban interface. The city of Cape Town encircles Table Mountain National Park, a series of steep geological features covered by fynbos (Figure 4.6). Fires in the fynbos were recorded by the earliest European visitors (Joubert 1977), and

Figure 4.6: A wildfire on Signal Hill put smoke into the skies over Cape Town, South Africa, on 15 March 2020. Such fires have been a concern since the Cape was settled by Europeans; in the same frame is an area that burned in February 1919 (Michell 1922). The fynbos around the iconic geological features of Table Mountain National Park creates a wildland–urban interface, and prescribed burning programs are inadequate in preventing wildfire (van Wilgen *et al.* 2010). Photograph courtesy of Matthew Knight.

wildfires have been a specific challenge in Cape Town for over a century (Michell 1922). Ironically, prescribed fire programs have proven inadequate for both wildfire risk reduction and the conservation of highly fire-adapted biodiversity (van Wilgen et al. 2010; van Wilgen 2013). These issues, combined with proximity to human settlements and invasive species issues, complicate natural resource management throughout the fynbos (Kraaij et al. 2011; van Wilgen et al. 2012). After severe fires around Cape Town in 2000, a public–private partnership called Ukuvuka: Operation Firestop formed to reduce the fire threat in the wildland–urban interface and simultaneously create jobs through education and vegetation management (Kruger 2001).

Other challenges related to human settlement patterns and drought can send fire from the built environment into surrounding wildlands, a pattern unique among wildland–urban interface issues worldwide. Initially urban fires in informal peri-urban settlements are deadly, difficult for fire brigades to fight and can spread into forest stands (Kahanji et al. 2019). The tactics of fighting such conflagrations raise sustainability questions for municipalities with stressed water supplies (Mac Bean and Ilemobade 2019).

Wildland fire policy

As described above, fire policy across sub-Saharan Africa through both the colonial and post-colonial eras has followed a cyclical pattern of harsh restrictions aimed at fire prevention followed by prescriptions for burning aimed at fire management, constituting negative and positive legislation respectively (Dundas 1944). Despite these cycles, the general arc of formal policy through the past century has followed basic forest protection–fire prevention principles. Many African governments identify their forestry departments as having the primary control over wildland fire management (e.g. Benin, Ethiopia, Kenya, Namibia, Sénégal and South Africa; Goldammer 2001). Instances of positive legislation to promote 'safe' fire use remain

ineffective because many local populations conduct sanctioned burning under traditional authority.

South Africa: a case study in sanctioned burning

To review issues in wildland fire policy in sub-Saharan Africa, we highlight South Africa as a case study in sanctioned burning. We review some barriers to ecologically motivated fire in a typical post-colonial, forestry-focused policy environment, highlight opportunities for fire in biodiversity conservation and job creation and consider the developments and challenges that make up the future of sanctioned fire in South Africa and beyond.

Wildland fire use: policy and operations

Together, indigenous forests and tree plantations cover less than 3% of South Africa's land area, but nonetheless fire prevention legislation controlled by forestry departments has been the primary wildland fire policy in South Africa (de Ronde and Goldammer 2001). Despite long traditions of burning grassland, and accumulating evidence for the value of sanctioned fire in these ecosystems, veld management remains at odds with forestry-oriented policy. The Department of Forestry, which has undergone several name changes, adopted a formal policy for prescribed fire in the *Mountain Catchment Areas Act 63* of 1970, but the conditions under which it could proceed were strict and all but guaranteed low-intensity burns (Pooley 2018). According to Pooley (2018), a primary lesson from the fire ecology research by South Africa's Winston Trollope and others during the 1980s is the ecological importance of high-intensity fire, the opposite of what forestry programs around Africa had been advocating since the colonial era.

Wildland fire in South Africa is currently regulated primarily under the *National Veld and Forest Fire Act No. 101* of 1998, the purpose of which is to prevent and combat veld, forest and mountain fires throughout South Africa. The Act mainly focuses on fire prevention through the establishment of firebreaks and a national fire danger index, and fire suppression through firefighting standards and requirements. The key administrative mechanism for implementation is through Fire Protection Associations, whose objective is to improve communication, awareness, training, standards and skills within the different wildland land uses affected by fire to advance safer and more effective fire practices. Current amendments to the *National Veld and Forest Fire Act* seek to promote the use of sanctioned (prescribed) fire for ecological benefits and fire risk reduction.

In South Africa, fire is used in each of three broad realms of wildland land uses: conservation areas, commercial forest plantations and rural agricultural areas that are primarily rangeland (veld). There are myriad objectives for sanctioned burning: to reduce wildfire risk, maintain habitat, improve forage resources, stimulate primary productivity, manage stand composition, control pests and diseases and manage watersheds (de Ronde *et al.* 2004b).

Prescribed fire use in several of South Africa's conservation areas has generally been progressive and has yielded insight into the role of fire in open, grassy ecosystems (Figure 4.7). For example, the uKhahlamba Drakensberg Park has used long rotational block burning to maintain heterogeneous but grassland-dominated landscapes (Nänni 1969; Mentis *et al.* 1974). The Kruger National Park in particular is a complex socioecological landscape that serves as a microcosm of many natural resource issues in sub-Saharan Africa, including: land claims, subsistence poaching, ecotourism and rural livelihoods; climate change, biodiversity conservation and the integrity of broad-scale animal migrations; and international conservation efforts and illicit trade in animal products (Venter *et al.* 2008).

Very broadly, the Kruger National Park adopted a fire suppression policy in 1948 and transitioned to wildland fire use in 1957, when it implemented spring block burning on a 3-year fire return interval; in 1992, sanctioned ignitions were limited to lightning; in 2002, Park management sought to mimic the natural fire regime, first with adaptive management of point ignitions (until 2011) and then using targeted ecological criteria (van Wilgen *et al.* 2014; Attorre *et al.* 2015). The lightning-only policy reflected a laissez faire wilderness-based philosophy in which the strict block burning was seen as contrary to the variability understood to characterise natural ecosystems (Bond and

Figure 4.7: The Kruger National Park has conducted leading research in the effects of different fire regimes on fire behaviour and fire effects at landscape scales, including point (left) and perimeter (right) ignitions. Note tracer lines surrounding the burn unit in photograph on the left (see also Figure 4.8). Photograph courtesy of South African National Parks.

Archibald 2003). The 2001 patch mosaic system used vegetation parameters to determine how many point ignitions would be required to achieve a target extent of annual burned area within biophysically defined large fire management units (Parr and Brockett 1999; van Wilgen *et al.* 2014).

Outside of conservation areas, rangelands are primarily either communal or commercial. The majority of communal rangelands are located in former 'homelands' or other areas set aside for Black South Africans by White-minority governments between the *Natives' Land Act* of 1913 and the end of Apartheid in 1994. Management is controlled by local authorities, typically under a traditional governance system. Commercial rangelands are delineated as farm tracts registered with the government and are privately owned and managed, either independently or in coordination with neighbours as part of a conservancy. Commercial farms have historically been owned and operated by White South Africans, although an increasing number of landowners are Black South Africans who have purchased farms or have had access to land restored through land reform programs.

Prescribed burning proceeds quite similarly across all three realms of wildland land use (with the possible exception of communal areas, where fire-specific equipment is less common and burners depend on natural and human-built landscape features to limit fire spread). Standard operations include external fire protection, which involves maintaining a firebreak on the perimeter of a property to prevent the spread of wildfires (either coming onto the property from neighbouring land or escaping to neighbouring land), and internal fire protection, which involves the division of a property into burn blocks (de Ronde *et al.* 2004a). When natural features or roads are unavailable or too narrow to provide adequate defence against fire spread, establishing firebreaks along property boundaries and internal block divisions begins well before the fire season with tracer lines, created by mowing or spraying a chemical desiccant along narrow strips of vegetation to create a cured fuel bed bound by live vegetation (de Ronde *et al.* 2004b).

The green, high-moisture vegetation helps prevent fire from spreading beyond the tracer line because it is burned out and all potential fuel removed (Figure 4.8).

As currently applied, much of the utility of these firebreaks stops with their installation: once the surrounding vegetation goes dormant and cures, the burned-out tracer lines provide defensible space from which to widen firebreaks as part of fire suppression operations. However, these same practices can be used to support safe, ecologically motivated burning fire by containing sanctioned fire in a unit, or to protect a unit from which burning is to be seasonally deferred.

South Africa implemented a program to develop skilled wildland firefighters to address national needs for wildland fire control and economic development. An expanded public works program called Working on Fire was launched in 2003 as a government-funded job creation program focused on implementing integrated fire management in South Africa (Figure 4.9). Working on Fire employs more than 5000 young men and women from marginalised communities, 94% of whom are youth,

Figure 4.8: An interior firebreak between blocks begins with a tracer line through green grassland in Mpumalanga, South Africa. Cutting the grass within the tracer line and burning the dried biomass while the surrounding vegetation remains green makes burning out wider firebreaks later in the season easier and safer to manage. Photograph courtesy of Colleen Rabothata.

Figure 4.9: South Africa's Working on Fire program has created thousands of jobs while protecting natural resources and expanding prescribed fire operations across the country. Photograph courtesy of South African National Parks.

31% are women (which is the highest level in any comparable fire service in the world) and 3% are disabled. All are fully trained as wildfire firefighters and conduct fire prevention, prescribed burning and fire awareness and education from more than 200 stations across South Africa.

Future of sanctioned burning

In this section we highlight several key topics relevant to the future of sanctioned burning in South Africa with implications for the utility and effectiveness of sanctioned fire throughout sub-Saharan Africa.

Fire management and mapping technology. Fire management and mapping technology includes fire detection and early warning systems supported by remotely sensed Earth observation data, such as the Advanced Fire Information System (https://www.afis.co.za/), which helps resource managers determine the proximity of ignitions to infrastructure such as power transmission lines and plantations. The South African Weather Service and commercial weather networks such as iLeaf (www.ileaf.co.za) provide fire weather data used to formulate the National Fire Danger Index and are available for sanctioned fire planning. Fire

managers at the Kruger National Park have developed several systems related to decision support and thresholds of potential concerns.

Climate variability. The 2015–16 drought in the Kruger National Park had nearly twice as many days above 35°C and four times as many days above 40°C than the previous worst drought on record (1991–92). Extended periods of high temperatures increase vegetation desiccation and increase the frequency of days with high fire danger, both of which contribute to burns with higher severity and greater extent.

Woody vegetation. Bond *et al.* (2019) describe a new iteration in the colonial/Clementsian critique of Africa's 'degraded' rangelands, namely the African Forest Landscape Restoration Initiative (https://afr100.org), which seeks to 'restore' 100 million ha in Africa by 2030 by planting trees that might reduce global atmospheric carbon dioxide emissions. However, decades of research from sub-Saharan Africa describe the structure and function of grasslands and savannas as non-equilibrium states maintained by frequent fire. Increasing tree and shrub cover in these ecosystems is a primary threat to their sustainability and their delivery of essential ecosystem services, including the provision of drinking water. Active burning is key to maintaining these ecosystems and their function, and the importance of sanctioned fire, which is literally ancient in sub-Saharan Africa, must not be forgotten even when international organisations offer millions of dollars to plant trees and protect them from fire.

Conclusion

'Sanctioned fire' refers to burning conducted under the authority of governments and cultures, and better describes the breadth of anthropogenic ignitions across sub-Saharan Africa than the Western wildfire-prescribed fire dichotomy. African ecosystems have evolved with fire and African peoples have set fires for eons; the patterns of these ignitions create uniquely African signatures of fire regimes and fire use when considered at a global scale.

Intentions behind ignitions range widely, from using 'the weapon of the weak' as a form of protest to enhancing agricultural productivity to managing biodiversity. Social and environmental factors have long challenged fire management and will continue to do so in the future. Although perceptions of fire use have varied widely through time as political eras and social norms have changed, the presence of fire across sub-Saharan Africa has been, and will continue to be, persistent.

References

Adamson RS (1927) The plant communities of Table Mountain: preliminary account. *Journal of Ecology* **15**, 278–309. doi:10.2307/2255992

Afolayan TA (1979) Change in percentage ground cover of perennial grasses under different burning regimes. *Vegetatio* **39**, 35–41. doi:10.1007/BF00055326

Andela N, Morton DC, Giglio L, Chen Y, van der Werf GR, Kasibhatla PS, DeFries RS, Collatz GJ, Hantson S, Kloster S, *et al.* (2017) A human-driven decline in global burned area. *Science* **356**, 1356–1362. doi:10.1126/science.aal4108

Anderson TM, Ngoti PM, Nzunda ML, Griffith DM, Speed JDM, Fossøy F, Røskaft E, Graae BJ (2020) The burning question: does fire affect habitat selection and forage preference of the black rhinoceros *Diceros bicornis* in East African savannahs? *Oryx* **54**, 234–243. doi:10.1017/S0030605318000388

Ando K, Shinjo H, Noro Y, Takenaka S, Miura R, Sokotela SB, Funakawa S (2014) Short-term effects of fire intensity on soil organic matter and nutrient release after slash-and-burn in Eastern Province, Zambia. *Soil Science and Plant Nutrition* **60**, 173–182. doi:10.1080/00380768.2014.883487

Archibald S, Bond WJ (2004) Grazer movements: spatial and temporal responses to burning in a tall-grass African savanna. *International Journal of Wildland Fire* **13**, 377–385. doi:10.1071/WF03070

Archibald S, Bond WJ, Stock WD, Fairbanks DHK (2005) Shaping the landscape: fire–grazer interactions on an African savanna. *Ecological Applications* **15**, 96–109. doi:10.1890/03-5210

Archibald S, Scholes RJ, Roy DP, Roberts G, Boschetti L (2010) Southern African fire regimes as revealed by remote sensing. *International Journal of Wildland Fire* **19**, 861–878. doi:10.1071/WF10008

Attorre F, Govender N, Hausmann A, Farcomeni A, Guillet A, Scepi E, Smit IPJ, Vitale M (2015) Assessing the effect of management changes and environmental features on the spatio-temporal pattern of fire in an African savanna. *Journal for Nature Conservation* **28**, 1–10. doi:10.1016/j.jnc.2015.07.001

Aubréville A (1947) The disappearance of the tropical forests of Africa. *Unasylva* **1**, 5–11.

Bassett TJ, Zuéli KB (2000) Environmental discourses and the Ivorian savanna. *Annals of the Association of American Geographers* **90**, 67–95. doi:10.1111/0004-5608.00184

Beard J, Darby G (1951) An experiment on burning in wattle silviculture. *Journal of the South African Forestry Association* **20**, 53–77. doi:10.1080/03759873.1951.9631068

Bentsen SE (2014) Using pyrotechnology: fire-related features and activities with a focus on the African Middle Stone Age. *Journal of Archaeological Research* **22**, 141–175. doi:10.1007/s10814-013-9069-x

Bernard M, Menz A, Booth L (2015) The longevity of the magnet effect: fire–herbivory interactions in central Kenya. *Consilience: The Journal of Sustainable Development* **14**, 207–213.

Bird MI, Cali JA (1998) A million-year record of fire in sub-Saharan Africa. *Nature* **394**, 767–769. doi:10.1038/29507

Bond WJ (2008) What limits trees in C$_4$ grasslands and savannas? *Annual Review of Ecology, Evolution, and Systematics* **39**, 641–659. doi:10.1146/annurev.ecolsys.39.110707.173411

Bond WJ, Archibald S (2003) Confronting complexity: fire policy choices in South African savanna parks. *International Journal of Wildland Fire* **12**, 381–389. doi:10.1071/WF03024

Bond WJ, Midgley GF, Woodward FI, Hoffman MT, Cowling RM (2003) What controls South African vegetation – climate or fire? *South African Journal of Botany* **69**, 79–91. doi:10.1016/S0254-6299(15)30362-8

Bond WJ, Stevens N, Midgley GF, Lehmann CER (2019) The trouble with trees: afforestation plans for Africa. *Trends in Ecology & Evolution* **34**, 963–965 doi:10.1016/j.tree.2019.08.003.

Botha CG (1924) Note on early veld burning in the Cape Colony. *South African Journal of Science* **21**, 351–352.

Brockett B, Biggs H, Van Wilgen B (2001) A patch mosaic burning system for conservation areas in southern African savannas. *International Journal of Wildland Fire* **10**, 169–183. doi:10.1071/WF01024

Brookman-Amissah J, Hall JB, Swaine MD, Attakorah JY (1980) A re-assessment of a fire protection experiment in north-eastern Ghana savanna. *Journal of Applied Ecology* **17**, 85–99. doi:10.2307/2402965

Bucini G, Lambin EF (2002) Fire impacts on vegetation in Central Africa: a remote-sensing-based statistical analysis. *Applied Geography (Sevenoaks, England)* **22**, 27–48. doi:10.1016/S0143-6228(01)00020-0

Butz RJ (2009) Traditional fire management: historical fire regimes and land use change in pastoral East Africa.

International Journal of Wildland Fire **18**, 442. doi:10.1071/WF07067

Chidumayo EN (1988) A re-assessment of effects of fire on miombo regeneration in the Zambian Copperbelt. *Journal of Tropical Ecology* **4**, 361–372. doi:10.1017/S0266467400003011

Chuvieco E, Giglio L, Justice C (2008) Global characterization of fire activity: toward defining fire regimes from Earth observation data. *Global Change Biology* **14**, 1488–1502. doi:10.1111/j.1365-2486.2008.01585.x

Cook L (1939) A contribution to our information on grass burning. *South African Journal of Science* **36**, 270–282.

Daniau AL, Goñi MFS, Martinez P, Urrego DH, Bout-Roumazeilles V, Desprat S, Marlon JR (2013) Orbital-scale climate forcing of grassland burning in southern Africa. *Proceedings of the National Academy of Sciences of the United States of America* **110**, 5069–5073.

de Ronde C, Goldammer JG (2001) *Fire Situation in South Africa (IFFN No. 25).* Joint FAO/ECE/ILO Committee on Forest Technology, Management and Training, Geneva, <https://gfmc.online/iffn/country/za/za_19.html>.

de Ronde C, Everson TM, Everson CS (2004a) Fire management in rural areas and industrial forestry plantations. In *Wildland Fire Management Handbook for Sub-Saharan Africa.* (Eds JG Goldammer and C de Ronde) pp. 144–157. Global Fire Monitoring Center, Freiburg.

de Ronde C, Trollope WSW, Bailey AB, Brockett BH, Everson TM, Everson CS (2004b) Application of prescribed burning. In *Wildland Fire Management Handbook for Sub-Saharan Africa.* (Eds JG Goldammer and C de Ronde) pp. 285–323. Global Fire Monitoring Center, Freiburg.

de Villiers A, O'Connor T (2011) Effect of a single fire on woody vegetation in Catchment IX, Cathedral Peak, KwaZulu-Natal Drakensberg, following extended partial exclusion of fire. *African Journal of Range & Forage Science* **28**, 111–120. doi:10.2989/10220119.2011.642074

Devine AP, McDonald RA, Quaife T, Maclean IMD (2017) Determinants of woody encroachment and cover in African savannas. *Oecologia* **183**, 939–951. doi:10.1007/s00442-017-3807-6

Dobson M (1781) IV. An account of the Harmattan, a singular African wind. *Philosophical Transactions of the Royal Society of London* **71**, 46–57.

Donaldson JE, Archibald S, Govender N, Pollard D, Luhdo Z, Parr CL (2018) Ecological engineering through fire–herbivory feedbacks drives the formation of savanna grazing lawns. *Journal of Applied Ecology* **55**, 225–235 doi:10.1111/1365-2664.12956.

Dundas J (1944) Bush burning in tropical Africa. *Empire Forestry Journal* **23**, 122–125.

Dwyer E, Pereira JMC, Gregoire J-M, DaCamara CC (2000) Characterization of the spatio-temporal patterns of global fire activity using satellite imagery for the period April 1992 to March 1993. *Journal of Biogeography* **27**, 57–69 doi:10.1046/j.1365-2699.2000.00339.x.

Eby S, Mosser A, Packer C, Ritchie M, Swanson A (2013) The impact of burning on lion *Panthera leo* habitat choice in an African savanna. *Current Zoology* **59**, 335–339. doi:10.1093/czoolo/59.3.335

Egunjobi J (1970) Savanna burning, soil fertility and herbage productivity in the derived savanna zone of Nigeria. In *Wildlife Conservation in West Africa.* (Ed. DCD Happold) pp. 52–58. International Union for Conservation of Nature and Natural Resources, Morges.

Ellery WN, Ellery K, McCarthy TS, Cairncross B, Oelofse R (1989) A peat fire in the Okavango Delta, Botswana, and its importance as an ecosystem process. *African Journal of Ecology* **27**, 7–21. doi:10.1111/j.1365-2028.1989.tb00924.x

Eriksen C (2007) Why do they burn the 'bush'? Fire, rural livelihoods, and conservation in Zambia. *The Geographical Journal* **173**, 242–256. doi:10.1111/j.1475-4959.2007.00239.x

Everson C, Tainton N (1984) The effect of thirty years of burning on the highland sourveld of Natal. *Journal of the Grassland Society of Southern Africa* **1**, 15–20. doi:10.1080/02566702.1984.9647976

Everson TM, Smith FR, Everson CS (1985) Characteristics of fire behaviour in the montane grasslands of Natal. *Journal of the Grassland Society of Southern Africa* **2**, 13–21. doi:10.1080/02566702.1985.9648006

Fairhead J, Leach M (1995) Reading forest history backwards: the interaction of policy and local land use in Guinea's forest–savanna mosaic, 1893–1993. *Environment and History* **1**, 55–91. doi:10.3197/096734095779522708

Fairhead J, Leach M (2000) Desiccation and domination: science and struggles over environment and development in colonial Guinea. *Journal of African History* **41**, 35–54. doi:10.1017/S0021853799007641

Feder G, Noronha R (1987) Land rights systems and agricultural development in sub-Saharan Africa. *The World Bank Research Observer* **2**, 143–169. doi:10.1093/wbro/2.2.143

Fuhlendorf SD, Fynn RWS, McGranahan DA, Twidwell D (2017) Heterogeneity as the basis for rangeland management. In *Rangeland Systems: Processes, Management and Challenges.* Springer Series on Environmental Management. (Ed DD Briske) pp. 169–196. Springer International Publishing, <https://link.springer.com/chapter/10.1007/978-3-319-46709-2_5>.

Furley PA, Rees RM, Ryan CM, Saiz G (2008) Savanna burning and the assessment of long-term fire experiments with particular reference to Zimbabwe. *Progress in Physical Geography* **32**, 611–634 doi:10.1177/0309133308101383.

Fynn RWS, Haynes RJ, O'Connor TG (2003) Burning causes long-term changes in soil organic matter content of a South African grassland. *Soil Biology & Biochemistry* **35**, 677–687. doi:10.1016/S0038-0717(03)00054-3

Gandiwa E (2011) Effects of repeated burning on woody vegetation structure and composition in a semiarid southern African savanna. *International Journal of Environmental Sciences* **2**, 458–471.

Geldenhuys C (1994) Bergwind fires and the location pattern of forest patches in the southern Cape landscape, South Africa. *Journal of Biogeography* **21**, 49–62. doi:10.2307/2845603

Gillon D (1972a) The effect of bush fire on the principal pentatomid bugs (Hemiptera) of an Ivory Coast savanna. In *Fire Ecology Conference Proceedings*, Vol. 11. Tall Timbers, Tallahassee Research Station, <https://talltimbers.org/wp-content/uploads/2018/09/377-GillonD1971_op.pdf>.

Gillon Y (1972b) The effect of bush fire on the principal acridid species of an Ivory Coast savanna. In *Fire Ecology Conference Proceedings*, Vol. 11. Tall Timbers Research Station, Tallahassee, <https://talltimbers.org/wp-content/uploads/2018/09/419-GillonY1971_op.pdf>.

Glover H (1938) A contribution to the ecology of the high-veld grassland at Frankenwald, in relation to grazing and burning. *South African Journal of Science* **35**, 274–279.

Goldammer JG (2001) *Africa Fire Special (IFFN No. 25)*. Joint FAO/ECE/ILO Committee on Forest Technology, Management and Training, Geneva, <https://gfmc.online/iffn/iffn_25/content25.html>.

Goldammer JG, De Ronde C (2004) *Wildland Fire Management Handbook for Sub-Sahara Africa*. Global Fire Monitoring Center, Freiburg, <http://www.africanminds.co.za/wp-content/uploads/2012/05/Wildland%20Fire%20Management%20Handbook%20for%20Sub-Sahara%20Africa.pdf>.

Goody J (1980) Rice-burning and the green revolution in northern Ghana. *The Journal of Development Studies* **16**, 136–155 doi:10.1080/00220388008421752.

Govender N, Trollope WSW, Van Wilgen BW (2006) The effect of fire season, fire frequency, rainfall and management on fire intensity in savanna vegetation in South Africa. *Journal of Applied Ecology* **43**, 748–758 doi:10.1111/j.1365-2664.2006.01184.x.

Gowlett JAJ, Wrangham RW (2013) Earliest fire in Africa: towards the convergence of archaeological evidence and the cooking hypothesis. *Azania* **48**, 5–30 doi:10.1080/0067270X.2012.756754.

Gumbricht T, McCarthy TS, McCarthy J, Roy D, Frost PE, Wessels K (2002) Remote sensing to detect sub-surface peat fires and peat fire scars in the Okavango Delta, Botswana. *South African Journal of Science* **98**, 351–358.

Gureja N, Owen-Smith N (2002) Comparative use of burnt grassland by rare antelope species in a lowveld game ranch, South Africa. *South African Journal of Wildlife Research* **32**, 31–38.

Harrington G (1974) Fire effects on a Ugandan savanna grassland. *Tropical Grasslands* **8**, 87–101.

Hearle N (1888) The grazing question in Jaunsar. *Indian Forester* **14**, 243–250.

Higgins SI, Bond WJ, Trollope WS (2000) Fire, resprouting and variability: a recipe for grass–tree coexistence in savanna. *Journal of Ecology* **88**, 213–229. doi:10.1046/j.1365-2745.2000.00435.x

Higgins SI, Bond WJ, February EC, Bronn A, Euston-Brown DIW, Enslin B, Govender N, Rademan L, O'Regan S, Potgieter ALF, *et al.* (2007) Effects of four decades of fire manipulation on woody vegetation structure in savanna. *Ecology* **88**, 1119–1125 doi:10.1890/06-1664.

Hollingsworth L, Johnson D, Sikaundi G, Siame S (2015) *Fire Management Assessment of Eastern Province, Zambia*. Technical report, USDA Forest Service, International Programs, Washington, DC. <https://www.fs.fed.us/rm/pubs_journals/2015/rmrs_2015_hollingsworth_l001.pdf>.

Hopkins B, Jenkin RN (1962) Vegetation of the Olokemeji Forest Reserve, Nigeria: I. General features of the reserve and the research sites. *Journal of Ecology* **50**, 559–598 doi:10.2307/2257471.

Hudak AT, Fairbanks DHK, Brockett BH (2004) Trends in fire patterns in a southern African savanna under alternative land use practices. *Agriculture, Ecosystems & Environment* **101**, 307–325. doi:10.1016/j.agee.2003.09.010

Huntley BJ (1978) *South African Programme for the SCOPE Mid-term Project on the Ecological Effects of Fire*. National Scientific Programmes Unit, CSIR, Pretoria, <https://researchspace.csir.co.za/dspace/bitstream/handle/10204/2302/SANSP%20032.pdf?sequence=1&isAllowed=y>.

Innes RR (1972) Fire in west African vegetation. In *Fire Ecology Conference Proceedings*, Vol. 11. Tall Timbers Research Station, Tallahassee, <https://talltimbers.org/wp-content/uploads/2018/09/147-Innes1971_op.pdf>.

Johansson MU, Granström A (2014) Fuel, fire and cattle in African highlands: traditional management maintains a mosaic heathland landscape. *Journal of Applied Ecology* **51**, 1396–1405. doi:10.1111/1365-2664.12291

Jones B (1938) Desiccation and the West African colonies. *The Geographical Journal* **91**, 401–423. doi:10.2307/1787502

Joubert D (1977) Ecological effects of fire: an overview. *South African Journal of Science* **73**, 166–169.

Kahanji C, Walls RS, Cicione A (2019) Fire spread analysis for the 2017 Imizamo Yethu informal settlement conflagration in South Africa. *International Journal of Disaster Risk Reduction* **39**, 101146. doi:10.1016/j.ijdrr.2019.101146

Kanthack FE (1930) The alleged desiccation of South Africa. *The Geographical Journal* **76**, 516–521. doi:10.2307/1783696

Katani J, Madoffe S, Amanzi N, Amanzi N, Rija A, Midtgaard F, Mbeyale G, Zahabu E, Tarimo B (2014) Assessment of fire prevalence and reduction strategies in miombo woodlands of eastern Tanzania. *Tanzania Journal of Forestry and Nature Conservation* **84**, 24–37.

Kemmis EL, McCrillis CP, Dubois JMF, DeLano HR (1967) 'Land management study of Northern Nigeria'. US Department of Interior, Bureau of Land Management, Washington, DC.

Kennan TCD (1972) The effects of fire on two vegetation types at Matopos, Rhodesia. In *Fire Ecology Conference Proceedings*, Vol. 11. Tall Timbers Research Station, Tallahassee, <https://talltimbers.org/wp-content/uploads/2018/09/53-Kennan1971_op.pdf>.

Kepe T (2005) Grasslands ablaze: vegetation burning by rural people in Pondoland, South Africa. *The South African Geographical Journal* **87**, 10–17. doi:10.1080/03736245.2005.9713821

Kinyamario J (1985) Effects of prescribed dry season burn on a bushed East African grassland at Kiboko, Kenya. *East African Agricultural and Forestry Journal* **51**, 113–115. doi:10.1080/00128325.1985.11663473

Kirkman KP, Collins SL, Smith MD, Knapp AK, Burkepile DE, Burns CE, Fynn RWS, *et al.* (2014) Responses to fire differ between South African and North American grassland communities. *Journal of Vegetation Science* **25**, 793–804. doi:10.1111/jvs.12130

Klop E, van Goethem J, de Iongh HH (2007) Resource selection by grazing herbivores on post-fire regrowth in a West African woodland savanna. *Wildlife Research* **34**, 77–83. doi:10.1071/WR06052

Komarek EV (1972) Lightning and fire ecology in Africa. In *Fire Ecology Conference Proceedings*, Vol. 11. Tall Timbers Research Station, Tallahassee, <https://talltimbers.org/wp-content/uploads/2018/09/473-Komarek1971_op.pdf>.

Kotzé E, du Preez CC (2007) Influence of long-term wheat residue management on organic matter in an Avalon soil. *South African Journal of Plant and Soil* **24**, 114–119. doi:10.1080/02571862.2007.10634791

Kraaij T, Cowling RM, Van Wilgen BW (2011) Past approaches and future challenges to the management of fire and invasive alien plants in the new Garden Route National Park. *South African Journal of Science* **107**, 633. doi:10.4102/sajs.v107i9/10.633

Kraaij T, Baard JA, Cowling RM, van Wilgen BW, Das S (2013) Historical fire regimes in a poorly understood, fire-prone ecosystem: eastern coastal fynbos. *International Journal of Wildland Fire* **22**, 277. doi:10.1071/WF11163

Krebs P, Pezzatti GB, Mazzoleni S, Talbot LM, Conedera M (2010) Fire regime: history and definition of a key concept in disturbance ecology. *Theory in Biosciences* **129**, 53–69. doi:10.1007/s12064-010-0082-z

Kruger T (2001) *Santam/Cape Argus Ukuvuka Operation Firestop (IFFN No. 25)*. Joint FAO/ECE/ILO Committee on Forest Technology, Management and Training, Geneva, <https://gfmc.online/iffn/country/za/za_20.html>.

Kuhlken R (1999) Settin' the woods on fire: rural incendiarism as protest. *Geographical Review* **89**, 343–363. doi:10.2307/216155

Kull CA (2002) Madagascar aflame: landscape burning as peasant protest, resistance, or a resource management tool? *Political Geography* **21**, 927–953. doi:10.1016/S0962-6298(02)00054-9

Laris P (2002) Burning the seasonal mosaic: preventative burning strategies in the wooded savanna of southern Mali. *Human Ecology* **30**, 155–186.

Laris P (2004) Grounding environmental narratives: the impact of a century of fighting against fire in Mali. In *African Environment and Development: Rhetoric, Programs, Realities*. (Eds WG Moseley and BI Logan) pp. 63–85. Ashgate Publishing, London.

Laris P (2011) Humanizing savanna biogeography: linking human practices with ecological patterns in a frequently burned savanna of southern Mali. *Annals of the Association of American Geographers* **101**, 1067–1088 doi:10.1080/00045608.2011.560063.

Laris P, Dembele F (2012) Humanizing savanna models: integrating natural factors and anthropogenic disturbance regimes to determine tree–grass dynamics in savannas. *Journal of Land Use Science* **7**, 459–482 doi:10.1080/1747423X.2011.597444.

Laris P, Wardell DA (2006) Good, bad or 'necessary evil'? Reinterpreting the colonial burning experiments in the savanna landscapes of West Africa. *The Geographical Journal* **172**, 271–290. doi:10.1111/j.1475-4959.2006.00215.x

Laris P, Caillault S, Dadashi S, Jo A (2015) The human ecology and geography of burning in an unstable savanna environment. *Journal of Ethnobiology* **35**, 111 doi:10.2993/0278-0771-35.1.111.

Laris P, Dadashi S, Jo A, Wechsler S (2016) Buffering the savanna: fire regimes and disequilibrium ecology in West Africa. *Plant Ecology* **217**, 583–596 doi:10.1007/s11258-016-0602-0.

Laris P, Koné M, Dadashi S, Dembele F (2017) The early/late fire dichotomy: time for a reassessment of Aubréville's savanna fire experiments. *Progress in Physical Geography* **41**, 68–94 doi:10.1177/0309133316665570.

Levyns M (1924) Some observations on the effects of bush fires on the vegetation of the Cape Peninsula. *South African Journal of Science* **21**, 346–347.

Levyns MR (1929) Veld-burning experiments at Ida's Valley, Stellenbosch. *Transactions of the Royal Society of South Africa* **17**, 61–92. doi:10.1080/00359192909518772

Little IT, Hockey PAR, Jansen R (2013) A burning issue: fire overrides grazing as a disturbance driver for South African grassland bird and arthropod assemblage structure and diversity. *Biological Conservation* **158**, 258–270 doi:10.1016/j.biocon.2012.09.017.

Little IT, Jansen R, Hockey PAR (2015) Impacts of fire and grazing management on South Africa's moist highland grasslands: a case study of the Steenkampsberg Plateau, Mpumalanga, South Africa. *Bothalia* **45**, a1786. doi:10.4102/abc.v45i1.1786

Louppe D, Oattara N, Coulibaly A (1995) The effects of brush fires on vegetation: the Aubreville fire plots after 60 years. *Commonwealth Forestry Review* **74**, 288–292.

Mac Bean CB, Ilemobade AA (2019) An evaluation of the primary South African standard and guideline for the provision of water for firefighting. *Water SA* **45**, 691–699 doi:10.17159/wsa/2019.v45.i4.7551.

MacDonald KR (1944) The devastation of Africa by fire. *Farm and Forest* **5**, 23–25.

Magi BI, Rabin S, Shevliakova E, Pacala S (2012) Separating agricultural and non-agricultural fire seasonality at regional scales. *Biogeosciences* **9**, 3003–3012 doi:10.5194/bg-9-3003-2012.

Martin RE, Sapsis DB (1992) Fires as agents of biodiversity: pyrodiversity promotes biodiversity. In *Proceedings of the Symposium on Biodiversity of Northwestern California*. 28–30 October 1991, Santa Rosa. pp. 150–157. Cooperative Extension, University of California-Berkeley, Berkeley, <https://www.sierraforestlegacy.org/Resources/Conservation/FireForestEcology/FireScienceResearch/FireEcology/FireEcology-Martin91.pdf>.

Materechera SA, Mandiringana OT, Mbokodi PM, Nyamapfene K (1998) Organic matter, pH and nutrient distribution in soil layers of a savanna Thornveld subjected to different burning frequencies at Alice in the Eastern Cape. *South African Journal of Plant and Soil* **15**, 109–115 doi:10.1080/02571862.1998.10635127.

Mbatha KR, Ward D (2010) The effects of grazing, fire, nitrogen and water availability on nutritional quality of grass in semi-arid savanna, South Africa. *Journal of Arid Environments* **74**, 1294–1301 doi:10.1016/j.jaridenv.2010.06.004.

Mbow C, Nielsen TT, Rasmussen K (2000) Savanna fires in east-central Senegal: distribution patterns, resource management and perceptions. *Human Ecology* **28**, 561–583. doi:10.1023/A:1026487730947

McGranahan D, Kirkman K (2013) Multifunctional rangeland in southern Africa: managing for production, conservation, and resilience with fire and grazing. *Land (Basel)* **2**, 176–193 doi:10.3390/land2020176.

McGranahan D, Wonkka C (2018) Wildland fire science literacy: education, creation, and application. *Fire (Basel, Switzerland)* **1**, 52. doi:10.3390/fire1030052

McGranahan DA, Wonkka CL (2021) *The Ecology of Fire-Dependent Ecosystems: Wildland Fire Science, Policy, and Management*. CRC Press, Boca Raton.

McGranahan DA, Ramaano R, Tedder MJ, Kirkman KP (2016) Variation in grassland fuel curing in South Africa. *Fire Ecology* **12**, 40–52. doi:10.4996/fireecology.1203040

McGranahan DA, Archibald S, Kirkman KP, O'Connor TG (2018) A native C_3 grass alters fuels and fire spread in montane grassland of South Africa. *Plant Ecology* **219**, 621–632 doi:10.1007/s11258-018-0822-6.

Meiklejohn J (1955) The effect of bush burning on the microflora of a Kenya upland soil. *Journal of Soil Science* **6**, 111–118 doi:10.1111/j.1365-2389.1955.tb00835.x.

Mentis M, Bailey A (1990) Changing perceptions of fire management in savanna parks. *Journal of the Grassland Society of Southern Africa* **7**, 81–85. doi:10.1080/02566702.1990.9648211

Mentis MT, Rowe-Rowe DT (1979) Fire and faunal abundance and diversity in the Natal Drakensberg. *Proceedings of the Annual Congresses of the Grassland Society of Southern Africa* **14**, 75–77 doi:10.1080/00725560.1979.9648863.

Mentis MT, Meiklejohn MJ, Scotcher JSB (1974) Veld burning in Giant's Castle Game Reserve, Natal Drakensberg. *Proceedings of the Annual Congresses of the Grassland Society of Southern Africa* **9**, 26–31 doi:10.1080/00725560.1974.9648716.

Mes MG (1958) The influence of veld burning or mowing on the water, nitrogen and ash content of grasses. *South African Journal of Science* **54**, 83–86.

Michell MR (1922) Some observations on the effects of a bush fire on the vegetation of Signal Hill. *Transactions of the Royal Society of South Africa* **10**, 213–232. doi:10.1080/00359192209519281

Mopipi K (2012) The roles of competition, disturbance and nutrients on species composition, light interception and biomass production in a South African semi-arid savanna. PhD thesis. University of KwaZulu-Natal, South Africa, <http://researchspace.ukzn.ac.za/handle/10413/10003>.

Mudongo E, Fynn R, Bonyongo MC (2016) Influence of fire on woody vegetation density, cover and structure at Tiisa Kalahari Ranch in western Botswana. *Grassland Science* **62**, 3–11 doi:10.1111/grs.12110.

Mulqueeny CM, Goodman PS, O'Connor TG (2010) Landscape-level differences in fire regime between block and patch-mosaic burning strategies in Mkuzi Game Reserve, South Africa. *African Journal of Range & Forage Science* **27**, 143–150 doi:10.2989/10220119.2010.527300.

N'Dri AB, Soro TD, Gignoux J, Dosso K, Koné M, N'Dri JK, Koné NA, Barot S (2018) Season affects fire behavior in annually burned humid savanna of West Africa. *Fire Ecology* **14**, 5 doi:10.1186/s42408-018-0005-9.

Nänni UW (1969) Veld management in the Natal Drakensberg. *South African Forestry Journal* **68**, 5–15. doi:10.1080/00382167.1969.9629203

Nyazika TP, Zisadza-Gandiwa P, Chanyandura A, Gandiwa NME (2017) Influence of fire frequency on woody vegetation structure and composition in Lake Chivero Recreational Park, northern Zimbabwe. *Tropical Ecology* **58**, 583–589.

O'Connor TG (1985) *Synthesis of Field Experiments Concerning the Grass Layer in the Savanna Regions of Southern Africa.* National Scientific Programmes Unit, CSIR, Pretoria, <https://researchspace.csir.co.za/dspace/bitstream/handle/ 10204/2393/SANSP%20114.pdf?sequence=1& isAllowed=y>.

Onyeka Nwanunobi C (1990) Incendiarism and other fires in nineteenth-century Lagos (1863–88). *Africa* **60**, 111–120 doi:10.2307/1160429.

Parr CL, Andersen AN (2006) Patch mosaic burning for biodiversity conservation: a critique of the pyrodiversity paradigm. *Conservation Biology* **20**, 1610–1619 doi:10.1111/j.1523-1739.2006.00492.x.

Parr C, Brockett B (1999) Patch-mosaic burning: a new paradigm for savanna fire management in protected areas? *Koedoe* **42**, 117–130. doi:10.4102/koedoe.v42i2.237

Parr CL, Robertson HG, Biggs HC, Chown SL (2004) Response of African savanna ants to long-term fire regimes. *Journal of Applied Ecology* **41**, 630–642. doi:10.1111/j.0021-8901.2004.00920.x

Parrini F, Owen-Smith N (2010) The importance of post-fire regrowth for sable antelope in a Southern African savanna. *African Journal of Ecology* **48**, 526–534. doi:10.1111/j.1365-2028.2009.01143.x

Pereira JMC, Oom D, Pereira P, Turkman AA, Turkman KF (2015) Religious affiliation modulates weekly cycles of cropland burning in sub-Saharan Africa. *PLoS One* **10**, e0139189. doi:10.1371/journal.pone.0139189

Phillips E (1919) A preliminary report on the veld burning experiments at Groenkloof, Pretoria. *South African Journal of Science* **16**, 286–299.

Phillips JFV (1930) Fire: its influence on biotic communities and physical factors in South and East Africa. *South African Journal of Science* **27**, 352–367.

Phillips J (1936) Fire in vegetation: a bad master, a good servant, and a national problem. *Journal of South African Botany* **2**, 35–45.

Phillips JFV (1968) Influence of fire in trans-Saharan Africa. In *Conservation of Vegetation in Africa South of the Sahara. Proceedings of a Symposium Held at the 6th Plenary Meeting of the AETFAT*, 12–16 September 1966, Uppsala (Eds I Hedberg and O Hedberg) pp. 13–20. Acta Phytogeographica Suecica, Uppsala.

Pillans N (1924) Destruction of indigenous vegetation by burning on the Cape Peninsula. *South African Journal of Science* **21**, 348–350.

Poletti C, Dioszegi G, Nyongesa KW, Vacik H, Barbujani M, Kigomo JN (2019) Characterization of forest fires to support monitoring and management of Mount Kenya Forest. *Mountain Research and Development* **39**, doi:10.1659/MRD-JOURNAL-D-18-00104.1.

Pooley S (2012) Recovering the lost history of fire in South Africa's fynbos. *Environmental History* **17**, 55–83 doi:10.1093/envhis/emr117.

Pooley S (2018) Fire, smoke, and expertise in South Africa's grasslands. *Environmental History* **23**, 28–55 doi:10.1093/envhis/emx094.

Ryan CM, Williams M (2011) How does fire intensity and frequency affect miombo woodland tree populations and biomass? *Ecological Applications* **21**, 48–60. doi:10.1890/09-1489.1

Saha MV, D'Odorico P, Scanlon TM (2019) Kalahari wildfires drive continental post-fire brightening in sub-Saharan Africa. *Remote Sensing* **11**, 1090 doi:10.3390/rs11091090.

Scholes RJ, Archibald S, von Maltitz G (2011) Emissions from fire in sub-Saharan Africa: the magnitude of sources, their variability and uncertainty. *Global Environmental Research* **15**, 53–63.

Schrige GU, Penderis AH (1978) 'Fire in South African ecosystems: an annotated bibliography'. National Scientific Programmes Unit, CSIR, Pretoria.

Scotcher J, Clarke J (1981) Effects of certain burning treatments on veld condition in Giant's Castle Game Reserve. *Proceedings of the Annual Congresses of the Grassland Society of Southern Africa* **16**, 121–127. doi:10.1080/00725560.1981.9648934

Seymour CL, Huyser O (2008) Fire and the demography of camelthorn (*Acacia erioloba* Meyer) in the southern Kalahari – evidence for a bonfire effect? *African Journal of Ecology* **46**, 594–601 doi:10.1111/j.1365-2028.2007.00909.x.

Short A (2007) Special feature: revisiting the Brotherton burning trial. *African Journal of Range & Forage Science* **24**, iii–v. doi:10.2989/102201107780178186

Skarpe C (1980) Observations on two bushfires in the western Kalahari, Botswana. *Acta Phytogeographica Suecica* **68**, 131–140.

Skovlin J (1972) The influence of fire on important range grasses of East Africa. In *Fire Ecology Conference Proceedings*, Vol. 11. Tall Timbers Research Station, Tallahassee, <https://talltimbers.org/wp-content/uploads/2018/09/201-Skovlin1971_op.pdf>.

Smit IPJ, Asner GP, Govender N, Vaughn NR, van Wilgen BW (2016) An examination of the potential efficacy of high-intensity fires for reversing woody encroachment in savannas. *Journal of Applied Ecology* **53**, 1623–1633 doi:10.1111/1365-2664.12738.

Snyman HA (2002) Fire and the dynamics of a semi-arid grassland: influence on soil characteristics. *African Journal of Range & Forage Science* **19**, 137–145 doi:10.2989/10220110209485786.

Sow M, Hély C, Mbow C, Sambou B (2013) Fuel and fire behavior analysis for early-season prescribed fire planning in Sudanian and Sahelian savannas. *Journal of*

Arid Environments **89**, 84–93 doi:10.1016/j.jaridenv.2012.09.007.

Swaine MD, Hawthorne WD, Orgle TK (1992) The effects of fire exclusion on savanna vegetation at Kpong, Ghana. *Biotropica* **24**, 166–172 doi:10.2307/2388670.

Swift M, Seward P, Frost P, Qureshi J, Muchena F (1994) Long-term experiments in Africa: developing a database for sustainable land use under global change. In *Long-Term Experiments in Agricultural and Ecological Sciences*. (Eds R Leigh and A Johnston) pp. 229–251. CAB International, Wallingford.

Tainton NM, Groves RH, Nash R (1977) Time of mowing and burning veld : short term effects on production and tiller development. *Proceedings of the Annual Congresses of the Grassland Society of Southern Africa* **12**, 59–64 doi:10.1080/00725560.1977.9648806.

Tainton NM, Booysen P de V, Bransby DI, Nash RC (1978) Long term effects of burning and mowing on tall grass-veld in natal: dry matter production. *Proceedings of the Annual Congresses of the Grassland Society of Southern Africa* **13**, 41–44 doi:10.1080/00725560.1978.9648831.

Terefe B, Kim D-G (2020) Shifting cultivation maintains but its conversion to mono-cropping decreases soil carbon and nitrogen stocks compared to natural forest in western Ethiopia. *Plant and Soil* **453**, 105–117. doi:10.1007/s11104-019-03942-0

Trapnell CG (1959) Ecological results of woodland and burning experiments in northern Rhodesia. *Journal of Ecology* **47**, 129–168 doi:10.2307/2257252.

Trollope WSW (1974) Role of fire in preventing bush encroachment in the Eastern Cape. *Proceedings of the Annual Congresses of the Grassland Society of Southern Africa* **9**, 67–72 doi:10.1080/00725560.1974.9648722.

Trollope WSW (1978) Fire behaviour – a preliminary study. *Proceedings of the Annual Congresses of the Grassland Society of Southern Africa* **13**, 123–128 doi:10.1080/00725560.1978.9648846.

Trollope WSW (1981) Recommended terms, definitions and units to be used in fire ecology in South Africa. *Proceedings of the Annual Congresses of the Grassland Society of Southern Africa* **16**, 107–109 doi:10.1080/00725560.1981.9648931.

Trollope WSW (1984) Fire behaviour. In *Ecological Effects of Fire in South African Ecosystems*. Ecological Studies 48. (Eds PV Booysen and NM Tainton) pp. 199–218. Springer, Berlin.

Trollope W (1987) Effect of season of burning on grass recovery in the false thornveld of the eastern Cape. *Journal of the Grassland Society of Southern Africa* **4**, 74–77. doi:10.1080/02566702.1987.9648074

Trollope WSW, Potgieter ALF (1985) Fire behaviour in the Kruger National Park. *Journal of the Grassland Society of Southern Africa* **2**, 17–22 doi:10.1080/02566702.1985.9648000.

Trollope W, van Wilgen B, Trollope LA, Govender N, Potgieter AL (2014) The long-term effect of fire and grazing by wildlife on range condition in moist and arid savannas in the Kruger National Park. *African Journal of Range & Forage Science* **31**, 199–208 doi:10.2989/10220119.2014.884511.

Uys RG, Bond WJ, Everson TM (2004) The effect of different fire regimes on plant diversity in southern African grasslands. *Biological Conservation* **118**, 489–499 doi:10.1016/j.biocon.2003.09.024.

Van de Vijver C, Poot P, Prins H (1999) Causes of increased nutrient concentrations in post-fire regrowth in an East African savanna. *Plant and Soil* **214**, 173–185. doi:10.1023/A:1004753406424

van Niekerk D (2014) From burning to learning: adaptive governance to wildfires in the north-west province of South Africa. *Journal of Human Ecology (Delhi, India)* **48**, 329–339 doi:10.1080/09709274.2014.11906802.

van Wilgen BW (2009) The evolution of fire and invasive alien plant management practices in fynbos. *South African Journal of Science* **105**, 335 doi:10.4102/sajs.v105i9/10.106.

van Wilgen BW (2013) Fire management in species-rich Cape fynbos shrublands. *Frontiers in Ecology and the Environment* **11**, e35–e44 doi:10.1890/120137.

van Wilgen BW, Richardson DM (1985) The effects of alien shrub invasions on vegetation structure and fire behaviour in South African fynbos shrublands: a simulation study. *Journal of Applied Ecology* **22**, 955–966. doi:10.2307/2403243

van Wilgen BW, Govender N, Biggs HC (2007) The contribution of fire research to fire management: a critical review of a long-term experiment in the Kruger National Park, South Africa. *International Journal of Wildland Fire* **16**, 519–530. doi:10.1071/WF06115

van Wilgen BW, Forsyth GG, Klerk HD, Das S, Khuluse S, Schmitz P (2010) Fire management in Mediterranean-climate shrublands: a case study from the Cape fynbos, South Africa. *Journal of Applied Ecology* **47**, 631–638 doi:10.1111/j.1365-2664.2010.01800.x.

van Wilgen BW, Forsyth GG, Prins P (2012) The management of fire-adapted ecosystems in an urban setting: the case of Table Mountain National Park, South Africa. *Ecology and Society* **17**, art8 doi:10.5751/ES-04526-170108.

van Wilgen BW, Govender N, Smit IPJ, MacFadyen S (2014) The ongoing development of a pragmatic and adaptive fire management policy in a large African savanna protected area. *Journal of Environmental Management* **132**, 358–368 doi:10.1016/j.jenvman.2013.11.003.

van Wyk P (1972) Veld burning in the Kruger National Park: an interim report of some aspects of research. In *Fire Ecology Conference Proceedings*, Vol. 11. Tall Timbers Research Station, Tallahassee, <https://talltimbers.org/wp-content/uploads/2018/09/9-VanWyk1971_op.pdf>.

Venter FJ, Naiman RJ, Biggs HC, Pienaar DJ (2008) The evolution of conservation management philosophy: science, environmental change and social adjustments in Kruger National Park. *Ecosystems* **11**, 173–192 doi:10.1007/s10021-007-9116-x.

Wesche K, Miehe G, Kaeppeli M (2000) The significance of fire for afroalpine ericaceous vegetation. *Mountain Research and Development* **20**, 340–347 doi:10.1659/0276-4741(2000)020[0340:TSOFFA]2.0.CO;2.

Wilsey BJ (1996) Variation in use of green flushes following burns among African ungulate species: the importance of body size. *African Journal of Ecology* **34**, 32–38 doi:10.1111/j.1365-2028.1996.tb00591.x.

Zubkova M, Boschetti L, Abatzoglou JT, Giglio L (2019) Changes in fire activity in Africa from 2002 to 2016 and their potential drivers. *Geophysical Research Letters* **46**, 7643–7653 doi:10.1029/2019GL083469.

5

Forged by fire: burning the Australian tropical savannas

Angela M. Reid and Brett P. Murphy

Australia is often reported to be the most fire-prone continent, with most of the continent experiencing regular fire and having a biota that is highly adapted to surviving, and possibly even promoting, landscape fires. Within Australia, fire activity is strongly concentrated in the tropical savannas, which cover the northern 17% of the continent (Russell-Smith *et al.* 2007; Murphy *et al.* 2013, 2019; Department of Agriculture, Water and the Environment 2015). The lowland mesic savannas (mean annual rainfall >1000 mm) along the northern coast typically burn every 1–3 years, making them among the most frequently burnt landscapes on Earth. In this chapter, we describe the broad patterns of fire, and the history of fire management, in the tropical savannas of northern Australia, identifying key challenges and opportunities in the use of fire for the sustainable development of these landscapes. In discussing such a large geographic area, we attempt to cover information relevant to the whole region, but what we present is most relevant to north-western tropical savannas falling within Western Australia and the Northern Territory.

Tropical savannas of northern Australia

Northern Australian tropical savannas cover over 1.3 million square kilometres of mainland Australia and represent nearly one-third of the relatively intact and unconverted tropical savannas remaining on Earth, including the largest expanses (Woinarski *et al.* 2007). Australia's tropical savannas overlay a matrix of infertile sandy soils and relatively fertile volcanic soils and are dominated by an open canopy of fire-adapted eucalypts (*Eucalyptus* and *Corymbia* spp.) and a C_4 grassy understorey (Plate 3a; Mott *et al.* 1985). Most dominant woody plant species resprout vigorously after fire (Lacey *et al.* 1982; Andersen *et al.* 2005). Flat to rolling hills are common, often interspersed by rugged escarpment country. The growth of the grassy understorey is largely seasonal, with over 90% of annual biomass accumulating during the wet season (December–April; Mott *et al.* 1985). Average fine fuel (diameter <6 mm) loads vary with soil type, time since fire, season and amount of rainfall in the preceding wet season, and are typically in the range of 2–10 t ha^{-1} (commonly 2–5 t ha^{-1}; Figure 5.1; Mott *et al.* 1985; Bowman and Wilson 1988; Andersen

Figure 5.1: Dominant fuel structure of canopy trees, fire-suppressed seedlings and grassy understorey in (a) low (500 mm)-, (b) medium (1000 mm)- and (c) high (1500 mm)-rainfall savanna. Photographs courtesy of Angela M. Reid (a) and Brett P. Murphy (b, c).

et al. 2003; Bowman *et al.* 2007b; Reid 2019). Although grasses make up the majority of the fine fuel load early in the dry season, leaf and twig litter can contribute a significant proportion (up to 70% in areas with high tree density), especially after seasonal leaf flushing, which peaks late in the dry season, thus substantially increasing the overall fine fuel load in some areas (Williams *et al.* 1997; Andersen *et al.* 2003). Large native grazers (kangaroos and wallabies in the marsupial family Macropodidae) and introduced grazers (e.g. cattle (*Bos* spp.), water buffalo *Bubalus bubalis*, horse *Equus caballus* and donkey *Equus asinus*) occur in various

combinations across northern Australia and can significantly impact fuel loads, potentially altering fire patterns on the landscape (~20–70% fine fuel reduction in northern Western Australia and Northern Territory; Petty *et al.* 2007; Reid 2019).

Mean annual rainfall varies greatly across the tropical savannas (400–1800 mm, decreasing from north to south; Plate 3a; Mott *et al.* 1985) and occurs primarily during the wet season (November–March), after which the fine fuels rapidly desiccate as the dry season progresses, making the monsoonal climate an important driver of the extremely high seasonal flammability of the biome. Fire return intervals are typically 1–5 years, with the longer intervals more common in areas with lower rainfall (Plate 3b; Vigilante *et al.* 2004; Fensham 2012; Murphy *et al.* 2013; Legge *et al.* 2015c). Most vegetation in the high-rainfall savannas will burn within 2 years without active fire management (Legge *et al.* 2015b), so strategic fire management (primarily using prescribed burning) is required to maintain long unburnt patches of vegetation that many species of flora and fauna rely on. Prescribed burning tends not to shift fire return intervals markedly (because these tend to be driven largely by rainfall in the preceding wet seasons; Legge *et al.* 2015b); thus, prescribed burning primarily serves to adjust season of burn rather than frequency (Price *et al.* 2012).

Human-induced changes to the fire regime

Northern Australia's fire history and management have undergone tremendous change over time and can be divided into three historical periods: pre-human, traditional Aboriginal fire use (pre-European) and post-European settlement (Plate 4).

Pre-human fire history

The monsoon climate was established in the late Tertiary, setting up ideal circumstances for frequent landscape fire, whereby several months of rain are followed by intense seasonal drought, leaving a dry, well-aerated fuel source, plus dry lightning storms occurring in advance of the wet season to provide a regular ignition source (Bowman 2002). With both ample fuel and ignition sources, the region can burn regularly, even annually in higher-rainfall areas. The pre-human wildfire regime of late dry season, high-intensity fires was changed by the Australian Aboriginal people who arrived in northern Australia at least 65 000 years ago (Bowman 1998; Clarkson *et al.* 2017).

Traditional Aboriginal fire use

With the arrival of a human population, the season, if not the frequency, of fire was altered in accordance with diverse objectives. Aboriginal people have traditionally managed fire for many reasons, including food gathering (foraging and hunting), providing high-quality forage for wildlife, protection of sacred sites and plant resources, managing wildfire and ease of travel (Lewis 1985, 1989; Head *et al.* 1992; Head 1994; Saint and Russell-Smith 1997; Bowman *et al.* 2001; Vigilante 2004; Walsh and Cross 2004). Often referred to as 'fire-stick farming' (Jones 1969), the complex use of fire by Aboriginal people resulted in a diverse and patchily burned landscape dissimilar to the previous regime of large wildfires, strongly concentrated in the late dry season when dry lightning is common. Although the dominant fire season varied across the north with some areas focusing on late dry season burning, ethnographic records and traditional ecological knowledge (TEK) widely characterise fire regimes under the management of Aboriginal people as having frequent, small fires of low intensity throughout the dry season (starting as early as March through to December) with high spatial and temporal heterogeneity (Thomson 1939; Braithwaite 1991; Crowley and Garnett 2000; Bowman and Vigilante 2001; Vigilante 2001; Bowman *et al.* 2004). Substantial proportions of the landscape burned each year (Thomson 1939), with fire refugia protecting habitats such as rainforest patches, which are very sensitive to recurrent fire (Mangglamarra *et al.* 1991; Garde 2009; Ondei *et al.* 2017b). The fire return interval was likely similar under Aboriginal fire management to that during the pre-human fire regime, although this is highly uncertain given the inherent difficulty of inferring fire frequency from charcoal records (Bowman 1998), as well as a lack of charcoal records in the tropical savannas (Mooney *et al.* 2011).

Post-European settlement fire regime

Fire regimes underwent a further drastic change following European colonisation in the 19th century. Aboriginal burning practices were disrupted in many regions as Aboriginal populations declined due to conflict and disease or people moved away to permanent settlements either voluntarily or, in many cases, forcibly (Crawford 1982;

Russell-Smith 2001; Vigilante 2001; Edwards *et al.* 2003; Fisher *et al.* 2003; Russell-Smith *et al.* 2003b; Legge *et al.* 2011). Depopulated Aboriginal lands were taken up as pastoral leases and other tenures, such as national parks (Plate 3c). Pastoralism became a dominant land use across the region as European settlers established pastoral leases. Prescribed burning on pastoral land during this period was largely motivated by wildfire mitigation as well as to increase forage quality and control cattle movements (Crowley and Garnett 2000). Pastoralists tended to burn less often and favoured burning in the early dry season to avoid catastrophic losses to their pasture (Stanton 1992; Crowley and Garnett 2000; Russell-Smith *et al.* 2003b; Petty and Bowman 2007; Skroblin *et al.* 2014). Storm-burning (lighting fires following the first rains of the wet season) was practised less frequently and predominantly on flood plains (Russell-Smith *et al.* 1997a; Crowley and Garnett 2000). Similarly, managers of conservation areas pre-emptively burned to eliminate late dry season wildfires and create patchiness but, in areas where Aboriginal people had typically burned with low-intensity, late dry season fires, this resulted in a seasonal shift in dominant fire management (Press 1987; Bowman *et al.* 2007a).

Other lands, less suitable for pastoralism or more remote from settlement, remained undeveloped. Some of these lands were set aside as Aboriginal reserves, but government policies aimed at concentrating human populations in communities meant that many of these areas were sparsely populated. Unallocated crown lands and other reserves often had little or no deliberate burning. By the 1950s, large, high-intensity wildfires burned predominantly in the late dry season and came to characterise the fire regime of unmanaged landscapes across northern Australia for many decades (Russell-Smith *et al.* 1997b; Vigilante 2001).

A cascade of ecological repercussions has been linked to the alteration of traditional Aboriginal fire regimes, including increased tree mortality, reduced production of tree fruit, reduced landscape-scale fire patchiness and damage to rainforest patches and populations of obligate-seeding trees and shrubs (McKenzie and Belbin 1991; Russell-Smith and Bowman 1992; Bowman and Panton 1993; Williams 1995, 1997; Setterfield 1997; Legge *et al.* 2015b; Trauernicht *et al.* 2015). There is also evidence that the loss of traditional Aboriginal fire management across much of northern Australia has contributed to the decline of small native mammals (Woinarski *et al.* 2011; Lawes *et al.* 2015) and granivorous birds (Franklin 1999; Legge *et al.* 2015a).

A new era of Aboriginal burning

As ecological repercussions are being realised and large tracts of land are being returned to the care and management of Aboriginal Traditional Owners (under the *Native Title Act 1993*), a new period is being ushered in where TEK and western scientific methods are being used together to meet traditional and contemporary fire management objectives. Using landscape fire in a culturally and ecologically appropriate way is an important management focus for Aboriginal Traditional Owners who now own and/or manage a large portion of the northern savannas (Plate 3c; Geoscience Australia 2004), and is being variously termed 'Right Way Fire' (Wunambal Gaambera Aboriginal Corporation 2010) and Aboriginal or Indigenous cultural burning (Steffensen 2020). Therefore, fire management programs that better replicate pre-European Aboriginal fire regimes are becoming increasingly important across much of northern Australia (as well as other regions) on Aboriginal land and places of joint management (e.g. Kakadu National Park), and are integral to incorporating greater spatial and temporal variation than an unchecked wildfire regime (Vigilante *et al.* 2004, 2017; Bliege Bird *et al.* 2008; Legge *et al.* 2015b; Kakadu Board of Management 2016). Such an approach is also becoming critically important for the management of Australia's conservation reserves, given that a large and increasing proportion of Australia's National Reserve System is owned and managed by Aboriginal people (mainly as Indigenous Protected Areas).

The past two decades roughly correspond to the transition from unmanaged wildfire regimes to active fire management and the handing over of land management rights to Aboriginal groups. This transition has been characterised by an increase in the frequency of fires, predominantly during the early dry season (Plate 5), but more than halving the annual maximum fire size and mean fire size (Table 5.1). In addition, by the late 1990s and early 2000s, advances in remote sensing enabled better documentation of the extent of wildfires (Maier and Russell-Smith 2012) and novel ways to provide information to fire managers to make broad-scale fire management more feasible (e.g. the North Australia and Rangelands Fire Information website; https://firenorth.org.au/nafi3/).

Requirements and barriers for fire use

Whether an area will be burnt by humans is dictated by a wide range of factors, including accessibility, land tenure, public safety and perception

Table 5.1. Number of fires, area burnt, maximum fire size, mean (±s.e.m.) fire size and the total percentage area burnt across northern Australian tropical savannas from 2000 to 2019

The periods of 2000–2009 and 2010–2019 are summarised (± standard error) and the difference between the periods are calculated at the bottom as these time periods roughly mark the transition between wildfire driven fire regimes and the use of 'right way fire'. Data obtained from North Australia and Rangelands Fire Information (https://firenorth.org.au/nafi3/)

Year	No. fires	Area burnt (km²)	Maximum fire size (km²)	Mean fire size (km²)	% Area burnt
2000	11 356	312 299	7291	27.5 ± 1.8	23.7
2001	14 131	428 874	14 443	30.3 ± 2.2	32.6
2002	9359	227 156	11 447	24.3 ± 2.0	17.3
2003	11 856	185 413	20 130	15.6 ± 2.1	14.1
2004	13 047	444 385	24 739	34.1 ± 3.3	33.8
2005	11 281	172 980	6350	15.3 ± 1.1	13.1
2006	19 452	346 405	15 499	17.8 ± 1.4	26.3
2007	15 731	314 277	16 275	20 ± 2	23.9
2008	13 147	204 019	18 192	15.5 ± 1.7	15.5
2009	10 417	283 132	20 287	27.2 ± 2.7	21.5
Mean (±s.e.m.) 2000–09	12 978 ± 927	291 894 ± 30 437	15 465 ± 1844	22.7 ± 2.0	22.2 ± 2.3
2010	10 787	114 027	4595	10.6 ± 0.7	8.7
2011	14 895	282 299	19 815	19.0 ± 1.7	21.5
2012	14 861	343 639	15 767	23.1 ± 1.8	26.1
2013	27 720	151 132	1899	5.5 ± 0.2	11.5
2014	41 826	266 520	5548	6.4 ± 0.3	20.3
2015	28 006	172 218	2283	6.1 ± 0.3	13.1
2016	18 595	144 800	5482	7.8 ± 0.5	11.0
2017	27 506	189 545	3923	6.9 ± 0.4	14.4
2018	27 797	205 322	4708	7.4 ± 0.3	15.6
2019	21 549	146 948	2866	6.8 ± 0.3	11.2
Mean (±s.e.m.) 2010–19	23 354 ± 2880	201 645 ± 23 179	6688 ± 1916	9.9 ± 0.6	15.3 ± 1.8
Difference	–10 376	90 249	8777	12.8	6.9

and Aboriginal cultural law, which dictates who can burn certain areas and how and when it is done (Bowman and Vigilante 2001). In the past, Aboriginal people burnt the country as they traversed it on foot, but now access is a serious issue given the largely depopulated and mostly remote area that covers 1.3 million square kilometres. Limited road networks, inaccessibility following wet season flooding and rugged sandstone country make aerial burning techniques the most economically feasible for large-scale fire management.

The growing tourism industry in remote northern Australia can influence fire management, sometimes creating a barrier to burning. Public safety and perceptions become an issue when tourists, unaccustomed to seeing landscape fires (particularly those deliberately lit), travel through remote regions. The public frequently has strong negative perceptions of prescribed burning, lacking the understanding of the history and importance of Aboriginal fire use (Bowman and Vigilante 2001). Undoubtedly, arriving to a national park and seeing the landscape recently burnt can negatively affect tourist satisfaction, which can then impact fire management decisions. There is a need for greater public education regarding wildland fire to adjust tourist expectations and understanding of fire ecology.

There is a suite of other barriers to the reinstatement of fire regimes similar to those before the colonial disruption of Aboriginal fire management. Fire is regulated by state fire laws (Northern Territory *Bushfires Management Act 2016*, Western Australia *Bushfires Act 1954*, Queensland *Fire and Emergency Services Act 1990*) that have wildfire prevention and public safety as primary goals, but there is considerable uncertainty in the interpretation of these and other legislation as to whether Aboriginal people have the right to apply traditional fire management (Preece 2007). Burn permits are required from respective state governing bodies and can sometimes be difficult to obtain in the latter half of the dry season due to intensifying fire danger weather patterns. Consequently, this legislation can act to limit burning to the early dry

season, reducing opportunities for fire managers to burn under appropriate conditions later in the season (Vigilante *et al.* 2004).

Carbon credit programs (*Carbon Credits (Carbon Farming Initiative—Emissions Abatement through Savanna Fire Management) Methodology Determination 2015*), which are extensive throughout the tropical savannas (Plate 3d), may also influence seasonality of burning by economically incentivising the avoidance of late dry season wildfires. It is important to note that these programs aimed at wildfire abatement, which award carbon credits to landowners for reducing greenhouse gas emissions on their land by reducing the extent of late dry season wildfires (which tend to burn more fuel and produce more greenhouse gas emissions than low-intensity fires in the early dry season), have played a major role in ending the previous wildfire regime and funding ongoing fire management but are an influencing factor potentially limiting the seasonal diversity of fire use. Currently, a cut-off date of 1 August applies across the ecosystem to separate early and late dry season burning, but new methodologies are proposed to adopt fire severity measures rather than seasonality. Although groups participating in carbon projects can continue to burn during the late dry season, the economic risk of income loss can influence the decisions more than ecological objectives.

Burning the bush: getting fire on the ground

At the peak of the monsoon season (January–March), vegetation is unlikely to burn. Early dry season burning (May–June) tends to be preferred by government and conservation agencies because fire weather conditions are relatively mild (Andersen *et al.* 2003). Late dry season (August onwards) is typically considered wildfire season, although some traditional Aboriginal fire regimes used progressive burning throughout the dry season as different areas of the landscape dried out (Lewis 1989; Braithwaite 1991) and customary burning is still practiced in some areas where Aboriginal people reside on Country at outstations (very small communities, typically consisting of a single extended family; e.g. parts of Arnhem Land, Northern Territory). Fine fuel moisture is higher during the early dry season, with live grass fuel moisture remaining much higher than dead fine fuel even at the end of the dry season (mean (±s.e.m.) 53.1 ± 1.2% and 6.3 ± 0.9% respectively, as measured in Western Australia); dead moisture ranged from 0–44% and live from 29–84% for mid- to late dry season (late June–early November; Reid, unpubl. data; Andersen et al. 2003; Reid 2019). In addition to drier fuels, late season fires are generally under conditions of higher wind speed and air temperature and lower humidity (Andersen et al. 2003).

Typical fire sizes are normally large, with most of the north being burned by fires exceeding 1000 km^2 (including wildfires; Russell-Smith 2016). Fire is sometimes managed on a property scale, but is also commonly managed on a landscape or regional scale under collaborative projects (e.g. West Arnhem Land Fire Abatement Project (28 000 km^2)). The size of a fire is typically determined by the presence of firebreaks, such as watercourses, areas burnt earlier in the dry season, roads and tracks. As mentioned previously, the network of roads is limited and, although there are many tracks in some parts of northern Australia, they are not always an effective firebreak given the amount of grass growth each wet season. There are many ephemeral but few perennial watercourses, which is another reason people burn early in the dry season when the presence of intermittent streams is highest and they can be used as natural firebreaks.

Ignition techniques vary, but dropping aerial incendiaries out of light aircraft is most common, especially in the early dry season when road access is still limited by wet season flooding. Patterns of aerial ignition can be variable, with incendiaries dropped in a spatially random pattern or along creek lines and other linear firebreaks, such as roads and tracks (Legge et al. 2015b), or along fixed transects to create patchiness (e.g. systematic ignition). When vehicle access improves with the progression of the dry season, lighting from vehicles often occurs as well. Drip torches or long-burn matches are used for on-foot ignition around infrastructure and key assets or to replicate traditional Aboriginal burning. Many Aboriginal groups undertake extended multiday 'fire walks', where Traditional Owners walk through remote areas lighting spot fires with long-burn matches in order to incorporate more traditional ignition patterns (Figure 5.2).

Fire intensity in the savannas varies greatly depending on conditions, but is generally of low intensity (e.g. compared with southern Australian eucalypt forests) and is restricted to surface fires because the open canopy cannot sustain a crown fire; torching of individual trees is not uncommon (Gillon 1983; Williams et al. 1998). The intensity of late dry season fires (4000–7700 kW m^{-1}) can be an order of magnitude greater than that of early dry season fires (500–2000 kW m^{-1}), which are generally patchy and limited in extent (Haynes 1985; Unwin et al. 1985; Braithwaite 1987; White 1997; Andersen et al. 2003; Russell-Smith et al. 2003a), and the proportion of fine fuels burnt inside fire scars is higher for late than early dry season fires (99% and 75% respectively; Legge et al. 2015b). The rates of fire spread have been measured to range from <0.1 to 1.8 ms^{-1} during experimental head fires, with the rate of spread for early dry season fires approximately half that of late dry season rates (Williams et al. 1998).

Fires are often allowed to burn themselves out, especially in the early dry season when fine fuel moisture is high and fires self-extinguish overnight as humidity increases and the dew point is reached. Remote fire suppression techniques have been developed by land managers, such as fire teams being dropped into remote locations and using petrol-driven leaf blowers to create bare earth breaks to back-burn off to halt wildfires during cooler parts of the day or night. If a fire is heading towards a structure or fire protection area, back-burning from the area is employed. State fire services will be called in if a fire continues jumping containment lines. Leaf blowers and light-vehicle-mounted water tanks are commonly

Figure 5.2: Traditional Owners from Wunambal Gaambera Aboriginal Corporation in northern Western Australia burning their lands on an annual fire walk aimed at applying fire to the landscape replicating traditional methods of ground-based spot ignitions while travelling. Participants use long-burn matches to light spot fires as they travel across the landscape during a week-long camping trip. This kind of ignition technique, although better replicating traditional burning, is time consuming and expensive, and not feasible property-wide. Pictured: Jason Adams and Neil Waina. Photograph courtesy of Angela M. Reid.

used for firefighting on the ground and helicopter-mounted water buckets are common for aerial firefighting.

Both Aboriginal and non-Aboriginal land managers in northern savannas possess considerable knowledge about the use of landscape fire based on experience and/or formal training. For example, Aboriginal Rangers throughout the Kimberley, a region in north-western Australia, typically complete certificates in Conservation and Land Management with 'hands-on' training before participating in formal fire operations. Hence, formalised fire training is complementing invaluable TEK of fire management across northern Australia. However, an overarching issue is the lack of cross-cultural exchange between Aboriginal and Western practitioners. There is a pressing need to incorporate educational exchange into fire management across all of Australia's fire-prone biomes.

The future of fire in Australia's tropical savannas

Regardless of future fire management decisions, fire will continue to play a central ecological role in Australia's tropical savannas. As Aboriginal people take on increasing land management responsibilities over large tracts of savanna, where 'right way fire' is prioritised, managed fire will become more prevalent than the wildfire regime seen in the recent past. Hence, prescribed burning is increasingly replacing wildfire, although with little reduction in annual area burnt (Gill *et al.* 2000; Edwards *et al.* 2001). Fire will continue to be used for both wildfire mitigation and as a land management tool to maintain biodiversity and improve forage quality, yet there are several issues to consider in future management.

Climate change projections for northern Australia suggest an increasing average temperature and more hot days and warm periods, but future changes to the timing and amount of rainfall are still very uncertain (Whetton *et al.* 2015). More extreme heat may lead to increasingly severe fire weather conditions in the dry season, providing fewer days to safely burn, and may increase fire frequency, intensity and extent. There is already concern over high fire frequencies in some areas and loss of long unburnt areas for conservation of fire-sensitive flora and fauna (Andersen *et al.* 2005; Ondei *et al.* 2017a). Evidence of a native grass–fire cycle, where frequent burning leads to the dominance of annual grasses and increased fire frequencies, only adds to these concerns (Russell-Smith *et al.* 2003a; Elliott *et al.* 2009). Furthermore, the introduction of invasive grass species (e.g. gamba grass *Andropogon gayanus* and mission grass *Cenchrus polystachios* and *Cenchrus pedicellatus*) has increased fine fuel loads more than fourfold that of non-invaded savannas (Rossiter *et al.* 2003), leading to marked increases in fire intensities. This rapidly leads to a decline in the tree canopy (Bowman *et al.* 2014), and continuing management and control will be required to reduce the spread of these grasses.

Up until 2010 many landowners lacked the funds and resources to undertake effective fire management and limit the wildfires that dominated the fire regime. Carbon abatement introduced new economic and business decisions to fire management (Russell-Smith 2016) that enabled landowners to fund fire management programs and mitigate wildfires on their lands, but the schemes are limited to wildfire mitigation and do not yet incentivise co-benefits (natural or sociocultural) or other fire-related services, such as biodiversity management (Perry *et al.* 2016). Designing fire management for carbon abatement alone can potentially lead to undesirable biodiversity outcomes (Reside *et al.* 2017; Corey *et al.* 2020), but many landowners are using carbon abatement to fund fire management for more than just economic objectives, including environmental, social and cultural objectives (Ansell *et al.* 2020). Therefore, it is important to balance the economic incentive to uniformly burn during the early dry season with biodiversity and seasonal fire diversity objectives.

Most importantly, it is imperative that the next period of fire management in Australia is characterised by shared knowledge and collaboration between Aboriginal and non-Aboriginal land managers and fire ecologists. As northern Australian savannas move beyond the unmanaged wildfire regimes prevalent since European colonisation, the emerging fire management has been characterised by applying modern technology and equipment to traditional Aboriginal knowledge.

Acknowledgements

The authors thank and acknowledge the Traditional Owners of the lands that we work on within the north Australian tropical savanna conservation management zone for sharing their knowledge and experience. Specifically, the authors thank the Uunguu Rangers and other members of the Wunambal Gaambera Aboriginal Corporation in Western Australia, and Wesley Campion and Joshua Rostron and family from the Northern Territory who assisted Angela M. Reid with research. Brett Murphy was supported by a fellowship from the Australian Research Council (FT170100004).

References

Andersen AN, Cook GD, Williams RJ (2003) *Fire in Tropical Savannas: The Kapalga Experiment*. Springer Science & Business Media, Berlin.

Andersen AN, Cook GD, Corbett LK, Douglas MM, Eager RW, Russell-Smith J, Setterfield SA, Williams RJ, Woinarski JCZ (2005) Fire frequency and biodiversity conservation in Australian tropical savannas: implications from the Kapalga fire experiment. *Austral Ecology* **30**, 155–167. doi:10.1111/j.1442-9993.2005.01441.x

Ansell J, Evans J, Adjumarllarl Rangers, Arafura Swamp Rangers, Djelk Rangers, Jawoyn Rangers, Mimal Rangers, Numbulwar Numburindi Rangers, Warddeken Rangers, Yirralka Rangers, Yugul Mangi Rangers (2020) Contemporary Aboriginal savanna burning projects in Arnhem Land: a regional description and analysis of the fire management aspirations of Traditional Owners. *International Journal of Wildland Fire* **29**, 371–385. doi:10.1071/WF18152

Bliege Bird R, Bird DW, Codding BF, Parker CH, Jones JH (2008) The 'fire stick farming' hypothesis: Australian Aboriginal foraging strategies, biodiversity, and anthropogenic fire mosaics. *Proceedings of the National Academy of Sciences of the United States of America* **105**(39), 14796–14801. doi:10.1073/pnas.0804757105

Bowman DMJS (1998) The impact of Aboriginal landscape burning on the Australian biota. *New Phytologist* **140**, 385–410. doi:10.1046/j.1469-8137.1998.00289.x

Bowman DMJS (2002) The Australian summer monsoon: a biogeographic perspective. *Australian Geographical Studies* **40**, 261–277. doi:10.1111/1467-8470.00179

Bowman DMJS, Panton WJ (1993) Decline of *Callitris intratropica* R. T. Baker & H. G. Smith in the Northern Territory: implications for pre- and post-European colonization fire regimes. *Journal of Biogeography* **20**, 373–381. doi:10.2307/2845586

Bowman D, Vigilante T (2001) Conflagrations: the culture, ecology and politics of landscape burning in the north Kimberley. *Ngoonjook* **20**, 97–103.

Bowman DMJS, Wilson BA (1988) Fuel characteristics of coastal monsoon forests, Northern Territory, Australia. *Journal of Biogeography* **15**, 807–817. doi:10.2307/2845341

Bowman D, Garde M, Saulwick A (2001) Kunj-ken makka man-wurrk Fire is for kangaroos: interpreting Aboriginal accounts of landscape burning in Central Arnhem Land. In *Histories of Old Ages: Essays in Honour of Rhys Jones*. (Eds A Anderson, I Lilley and S O'Connor) pp. 61–78. Pandanus Books, Canberra.

Bowman DMJS, Walsh A, Prior LD (2004) Landscape analysis of Aboriginal fire management in Central Arnhem Land, north Australia. *Journal of Biogeography* **31**, 207–223. doi:10.1046/j.0305-0270.2003.00997.x

Bowman DMJS, Dingle JK, Johnston FH, Parry D, Foley M (2007a) Seasonal patterns in biomass smoke pollution and the mid 20th-century transition from Aboriginal to European fire management in northern Australia. *Global Ecology and Biogeography* **16**, 246–256. doi:10.1111/j.1466-8238.2006.00271.x

Bowman DMJS, Franklin DC, Price OF, Brook BW (2007b) Land management affects grass biomass in the *Eucalyptus tetrodonta* savannas of monsoonal Australia. *Austral Ecology* **32**, 446–452. doi:10.1111/j.1442-9993.2007.01713.x

Bowman DMJS, MacDermott HJ, Nichols SC, Murphy BP (2014) A grass–fire cycle eliminates an obligate-seeding tree in a tropical savanna. *Ecology and Evolution* **4**, 4185–4194. doi:10.1002/ece3.1285

Braithwaite RW (1987) Effects of fire regimes on lizards in the wet–dry tropics of Australia. *Journal of Tropical Ecology* **3**, 265–275. doi:10.1017/S0266467400002145

Braithwaite RW (1991) Aboriginal fire regimes of monsoonal Australia in the 19th century. *Search* **22**, 247–249.

Clarkson C, Jacobs Z, Marwick B, Fullagar R, Wallis L, Smith M, Roberts RG, Hayes E, Lowe K, Carah X, *et al.* (2017) Human occupation of northern Australia by 65,000 years ago. *Nature* **547**, 306–310. doi:10.1038/nature22968

Clean Energy Regulator (2019) *Project Mapping Files*. Australian Government, Canberra, <http://www.cleanenergyregulator.gov.au/ERF/project-and-contracts-registers/project-register/project-mapping-files>.

Corey B, Andersen AN, Legge S, Woinarski JCZ, Radford IJ, Perry JJ (2020) Better biodiversity accounting is needed to prevent bioperversity and maximize co-benefits from savanna burning. *Conservation Letters* **13**, e12685. doi:10.1111/conl.12685

Crawford IM (1982) Traditional Aboriginal plant resources in the Kalumburu Area: aspects in ethno-economics. *Records of the Western Australian Museum* (Supplement 15), <http://museum.wa.gov.au/sites/default/files/1.Crawford.pdf>.

Crowley GM, Garnett ST (2000) Changing fire management in the pastoral lands of Cape York Peninsula of northeast Australia, 1623 to 1996. *Australian Geographical Studies* **38**, 10–26. doi:10.1111/1467-8470.00097

Department of Agriculture, Water and the Environment (2015) *Conservation Management Zones of Australia*. Australian Government, Canberra, <https://www.environment.gov.au/biodiversity/conservation-management-zones>.

Edwards A, Hauser P, Anderson M, McCartney J, Armstrong M, Thackway R, Allan G, Hempel C, Russell-Smith J (2001) A tale of two parks: contemporary fire regimes of Litchfield and Nitmiluk National Parks, monsoonal northern Australia. *International Journal of Wildland Fire* **10**, 79–89. doi:10.1071/WF01002

Edwards A, Kennett R, Price O, Russell-Smith J, Spiers G, Woinarski J (2003) Monitoring the impacts of fire regimes on vegetation in northern Australia: an example from Kakadu National Park. *International Journal of Wildland Fire* **12**, 427–440. doi:10.1071/WF03031

Elliott LP, Franklin DC, Bowman DMJS (2009) Frequency and season of fires varies with distance from settlement and grass composition in *Eucalyptus miniata* savannas of the Darwin region of northern Australia. *International Journal of Wildland Fire* **18**, 61–70. doi:10.1071/WF06158

Fensham R (2012) Fire regimes in Australian tropical savanna: perspectives, paradigms and paradoxes. In *Flammable Australia: Fire Regimes, Biodiversity and Ecosystems in a Changing World*. (Eds RA Bradstock, AM Gill and RJ Williams) pp. 173–193. CSIRO Publishing, Melbourne.

Fick SE, Hijmans RJ (2017) WorldClim 2: new 1-km spatial resolution climate surfaces for global land areas. *International Journal of Climatology* **37**, 4302–4315. doi:10.1002/joc.5086

Fisher R, Vigilante T, Yates C, Russell-Smith J (2003) Patterns of landscape fire and predicted vegetation response in the North Kimberley region of Western Australia. *International Journal of Wildland Fire* **12**, 369–379. doi:10.1071/WF03021

Franklin DC (1999) Evidence of disarray amongst granivorous bird assemblages in the savannas of northern Australia, a region of sparse human settlement. *Biological Conservation* **90**, 53–68. doi:10.1016/S0006-3207(99)00010-5

Garde M (2009) The language of fire: seasonality, resources and landscape burning on the Arnhem Land Plateau. In *Culture, Ecology and Economy of Fire Management in North Australian Savannas: Rekindling the Wurrk Tradition*. (Eds J Russell-Smith, P Whitehead and P Cooke) pp. 85–164. CSIRO Publishing, Melbourne.

Geoscience Australia (2004) *Australian Land Tenure 1993 – Geoscience Australia. Bioregional Assessment Source Dataset*. Australian Government, Canberra, <https://data.gov.au/data/dataset/d51a641a-df86-4b10-985a-8714b570386a>.

Gill A, Ryan P, Moore P, Gibson M (2000) Fire regimes of World Heritage Kakadu National Park, Australia. *Austral Ecology* **25**, 616–625.

Gillon D (1983) The fire problem in tropical savannas. In *Ecosystems of the World*. Vol. 13. (Ed. F Bourliere) pp. 617–642. Elsevier, Amsterdam.

Haynes CD (1985) The pattern and ecology of munwag: traditional Aboriginal fire regimes in north-central Arnhemland [Northern Territory]. In *Proceedings of a joint symposium with the Australian Mammal Society in association with the Darwin Institute of Technology*. 15–17 May 1983, Darwin. (Eds MG Ridpath and LK Corbett) pp. 203–214. Darwin Institute of Technology, Darwin.

Head L (1994) Landscapes socialised by fire: post-contact changes in Aboriginal fire use in northern Australia, and implications for prehistory. *Archaeology in Oceania* **29**, 172–181. doi:10.1002/arco.1994.29.3.172

Head L, O'Neill A, Marthick J, Fullagar R (1992) A comparison of Aboriginal and pastoral fires in the north-west Northern Territory. In *Conservation and Development Issues in Northern Australia*. (Eds I Moffatt and A Webb) pp. 130–144. Australian National University, Canberra.

Jones R (1969) Fire-stick farming. *Australian Natural History* **16**, 224–228.

Kakadu Board of Management (2016) *Kakadu National Park Management Plan 2016–2026*. Parks Australia, Canberra, <https://www.environment.gov.au/system/files/resources/1f88c5a3-409c-4ed9-9129-ea0aaddd4f33/files/kakadu-management-plan-2016-2026.pdf>.

Lacey C, Walker J, Noble I (1982) Fire in Australian tropical savannas. In: *Ecology of Tropical Savannas*. (Eds BJ Huntley and BH Walker) pp. 246–272. Springer, New York.

Lawes MJ, Murphy BP, Fisher A, Woinarski JCZ, Edwards AC, Russell-Smith J (2015) Small mammals decline with increasing fire extent in northern Australia: evidence from long-term monitoring in Kakadu National Park. *International Journal of Wildland Fire* **24**, 712–722. doi:10.1071/WF14163

Legge S, Murphy S, Kingswood R, Maher B, Swan D (2011) EcoFire: restoring the biodiversity values of the Kimberley region by managing fire. *Ecological Management & Restoration* **12**, 84–92. doi:10.1111/j.1442-8903.2011.00595.x

Legge S, Garnett S, Maute K, Heathcote J, Murphy S, Woinarski JCZ, Astheimer L (2015a) A landscape-scale, applied fire management experiment promotes recovery of a population of the threatened Gouldian finch, *Erythrura gouldiae*, in Australia's tropical savannas. *PLoS One* **10**, e0137997. doi:10.1371/journal.pone.0137997

Legge S, Webb T, Cooper T, Lewis F, Swan D, Maher W, Barton T (2015b) 'EcoFire – Part 1: Kimberley regional fire pattern analysis (2000 to 2014)'. Australian Wildlife Conservancy, Perth.

Legge S, Webb T, Cooper T, Swan D, Maher B, Barton T, Smith J, McGregor H (2015c) 'EcoFire 2014 project report'. Australian Wildlife Conservancy, Perth.

Lewis HT (1985) Burning the 'Top End': kangaroos and cattle. In *Proceedings of the Fire Ecology and Management of Western Australian Ecosystems Symposium*. 10–11 May, Perth. (Ed. JR Ford) pp. 21–31. Environmental Studies Group, Report No. 14, Western Australian Institute of Technology, Perth.

Lewis HT (1989) Ecological and technological knowledge of fire: Aborigines versus park rangers in Northern Australia. *American Anthropologist* **91**, 940–961. doi:10.1525/aa.1989.91.4.02a00080

Maier SW, Russell-Smith J (2012) Measuring and monitoring of contemporary fire regimes in Australia using satellite remote sensing. In *Flammable Australia: Fire Regimes, Biodiversity and Ecosystems in a Changing World*. (Eds RJ Williams, AM Gill and RA Bradstock) pp. 79–95. CSIRO Publishing, Melbourne.

Mangglamarra G, Burbidge AA, Fuller PJ (1991) Wunambal words for rainforest and other Kimberley plants and animals. In *Kimberley Rainforests of Australia*. (Eds NL McKenzie, RB Johnston and PG Kendrick) pp. 413–421. Department of Conservation and Land Management, Perth and Department of Arts, Heritage and Environment, Canberra.

McKenzie N, Belbin L (1991) Kimberley rainforest communities: reserve recommendations and management considerations. In *Kimberley Rainforests of Australia*. (Eds NL McKenzie, RB Johnston and PG Kendrick) pp. 453–468. Department of Conservation and Land Management, Perth and Department of Arts, Heritage and Environment, Canberra.

Mooney S, Harrison S, Bartlein P, Daniau AL, Stevenson J, Brownlie K, Buckman S, Cupper M, Luly J, Black M (2011) Late Quaternary fire regimes of Australasia. *Quaternary Science Reviews* **30**, 28–46. doi:10.1016/j.quascirev.2010.10.010

Mott J, Williams J, Andrew M, Gillison A (1985) Australian savanna ecosystems. In *Ecology and Management of the World's Savannas*. (Eds JC Tothill and JJ Mott) pp. 56–82. Australian Academy of Science, Canberra.

Murphy BP, Bradstock RA, Boer MM, Carter J, Cary GJ, Cochrane MA, Fensham RJ, Russell-Smith J, Williamson GJ, Bowman DMJS (2013) Fire regimes of Australia: a pyrogeographic model system. *Journal of Biogeography* **40**, 1048–1058. doi:10.1111/jbi.12065

Murphy BP, Prior LD, Cochrane MA, Williamson GJ, Bowman DMJS (2019) Biomass consumption by surface fires across Earth's most fire-prone continent. *Global Change Biology* **25**, 254–268.

Ondei S, Prior LD, Vigilante T, Bowman DMJS (2017a) Fire and cattle disturbance affects vegetation structure and rain forest expansion into savanna in the Australian monsoon tropics. *Journal of Biogeography* **44**, 2331–2342. doi:10.1111/jbi.13039

Ondei S, Prior LD, Williamson GJ, Vigilante T, Bowman D (2017b) Water, land, fire, and forest: multi-scale determinants of rainforests in the Australian monsoon tropics. *Ecology and Evolution* **7**, 1592–1604. doi:10.1002/ece3.2734

Perry JJ, Vanderduys EP, Kutt AS (2016) Shifting fire regimes from late to early dry-season fires to abate greenhouse emissions does not completely equate with terrestrial vertebrate biodiversity co-benefits on Cape York Peninsula, Australia. *International Journal of Wildland Fire* **25**, 742–752. doi:10.1071/WF15133

Petty A, Bowman D (2007) A satellite analysis of contrasting fire patterns in Aboriginal- and European-managed lands in tropical north Australia. *Fire Ecology* **3**, 32–47. doi:10.4996/fireecology.0301032

Petty AM, Werner PA, Lehmann CER, Riley JE, Banfai DS, Elliott LP (2007) Savanna responses to feral buffalo in Kakadu National Park, Australia. *Ecological Monographs* **77**, 441–463. doi:10.1890/06-1599.1

Preece N (2007) Traditional and ecological fires and effects of bushfire laws in north Australian savannas. *International Journal of Wildland Fire* **16**, 378–389. doi:10.1071/WF05079

Press AJ (1987) Fire management in Kakadu National Park: the ecological basis for the active use of fire. *Search* **18**, 244–248.

Price OF, Russell-Smith J, Watt F (2012) The influence of prescribed fire on the extent of wildfire in savanna landscapes of western Arnhem Land, Australia. *International Journal of Wildland Fire* **21**, 297–305. doi:10.1071/WF10079

Reid AM (2019) Grass, fire, kangaroos and cattle: the nexus between fire and herbivory in northern Australia. PhD thesis. Univeristy of Tasmania, Australia.

Reside AE, VanDerWal J, Moran C (2017) Trade-offs in carbon storage and biodiversity conservation under climate change reveal risk to endemic species. *Biological Conservation* **207**, 9–16. doi:10.1016/j.biocon.2017.01.004

Rossiter NA, Setterfield SA, Douglas MM, Hutley LB (2003) Testing the grass–fire cycle: alien grass invasion in the tropical savannas of northern Australia. *Diversity & Distributions* **9**, 169–176. doi:10.1046/j.1472-4642.2003.00020.x

Russell-Smith J (2001) Pre-contact Aboriginal, and contemporary fire regimes of the savanna landscapes of northern Australia: patterns, changes and ecological responses. *Ngoonjook* **20**, 6–32.

Russell-Smith J (2016) Fire management business in Australia's tropical savannas: lighting the way for a new ecosystem services model for the north? *Ecological Management & Restoration* **17**, 4–7. doi:10.1111/emr.12201

Russell-Smith J, Bowman D (1992) Conservation of monsoon rainforest isolates in the Northern Territory, Australia. *Biological Conservation* **59**, 51–63. doi:10.1016/0006-3207(92)90713-W

Russell-Smith J, Lucas D, Gapindi M, Gunbunuka B, Kapirigi N, Namingum G, Lucas K, Giuliani P, Chaloupka G (1997a) Aboriginal resource utilization and fire management practice in western Arnhem Land, monsoonal Northern Australia: notes for prehistory, lessons for the future. *Human Ecology* **25**, 159–195. doi:10.1023/A:1021970021670

Russell-Smith J, Ryan PG, Durieu R (1997b) A LANDSAT MSS-derived fire history of Kakadu National Park, monsoonal northern Australia, 1980–94: seasonal extent, frequency and patchiness. *Journal of Applied Ecology* **34**, 748–766. doi:10.2307/2404920

Russell-Smith J, Whitehead PJ, Cook GD, Hoare JL (2003a) Response of *Eucalyptus*-dominated savanna to frequent fires: lessons from Munmarlary, 1973–1996. *Ecological Monographs* **73**, 349–375. doi:10.1890/01-4021

Russell-Smith J, Yates C, Edwards A, Allan GE, Cook GD, Cooke P, Craig R, Heath B, Smith R (2003b) Contemporary fire regimes of northern Australia, 1997–2001: change since Aboriginal occupancy, challenges for sustrainable management. *International Journal of Wildland Fire* **12**, 283–297. doi:10.1071/WF03015

Russell-Smith J, Yates C, Whitehead PJ, Smith R, Craig R, Allan GE, Thackway R, Frakes I, Cridland S, Meyer MC, Gill AM (2007) Bushfires 'down under': patterns and implications of contemporary Australian landscape burning. *International Journal of Wildland Fire* **16**(4), 361–377.

Saint P, Russell-Smith J (Eds) (1997) *Malgarra: Burning the Bush.* Gordon Reid Foundation, Perth; Bush Fires Board of WA, Perth; Cooperative Research Centre for Tropical Savannas, Darwin.

Setterfield SA (1997) The impact of experimental fire regimes on seed production in two tropical eucalypt species in northern Australia. *Australian Journal of Ecology* **22**, 279–287. doi:10.1111/j.1442-9993.1997.tb00673.x

Skroblin A, Legge S, Webb T, Hunt LP (2014) EcoFire: regional-scale prescribed burning increases the annual carrying capacity of livestock on pastoral properties by reducing pasture loss from wildfire. *The Rangeland Journal* **36**, 133–142. doi:10.1071/RJ13095

Stanton J (1992) JP Thompson oration: the neglected lands: recent changes in the ecosystems of Cape York Peninsula and the challenge of their management. *Queensland Geographical Journal* **7**, 1–18.

Steffensen V (2020) *Fire Country: How Indigenous Fire Management Could Help Save Australia.* Hardie Grant Travel, Melbourne.

Thomson DF (1939) The seasonal factor in human culture illustrated from the life of a contemporary nomadic group. *Proceedings of the Prehistoric Society* **5**, 209–221.

Trauernicht C, Brook BW, Murphy BP, Williamson GJ, Bowman DM (2015) Local and global pyrogeographic evidence that indigenous fire management creates pyrodiversity. *Ecology and Evolution* **5**, 1908–1918. doi:10.1002/ece3.1494

Unwin G, Stocker G, Sanderson K (1985) Fire and the forest ecotone in the Herberton highland, north Queensland. In *Ecology of the Wet–Dry Tropics: Proceedings of a Joint Symposium With the Australian Mammal Society in Association With the Darwin Institute of Technology.* 15–17 May 1983, Darwin. (Eds MG Ridpath and LK Corbett) pp. 215–224. Ecological Society of Australia, Darwin.

Vigilante T (2001) Analysis of explorers' records of Aboriginal landscape burning in the Kimberley Region of Western Australia. *Australian Geographical Studies* **39**, 135–155. doi:10.1111/1467-8470.00136

Vigilante T (2004) The ethnoecology of landscape burning around Kalumburu Aboriginal Community, North Kimberley Region, Western Australia: an examination of the ecological and cultural significance of Aboriginal landscape burning in the North Kimberley using experimental, ethnographic and historical approaches. PhD thesis. Charles Darwin University, Australia, <https://ris.cdu.edu.au/ws/portalfiles/portal/22706036/Thesis_CDU_6477_Vigilante_T_Abstract.pdf>.

Vigilante T, Bowman DMJS, Fisher R, Russell-Smith J, Yates C (2004) Contemporary landscape burning patterns in the far North Kimberley region of north-west Australia: human influence and environmental determinants. *Journal of Biogeography* **31**, 1317–1333. doi:10.1111/j.1365-2699.2004.01104.x

Vigilante T, Ondei S, Goonack C, Williams D, Young P, Bowman D (2017) Collaborative research on the ecology and management of the 'Wulo' monsoon rainforest in Wunambal Gaambera Country, North Kimberley, Australia. *Land (Basel)* **6**, 68 doi:10.3390/land6040068.

Walsh F, Cross B (2004) *Bushfires and Burning: Aspects of Aboriginal Knowledge and Practice in Areas of the Kimberley.* Kimberley Regional Fire Management Project, Natural Heritage Trust, Canberra.

Whetton P, Ekström M, Gerbing C, Grose M, Bhend J, Webb L, Risbey J (2015) 'Climate change in Australia. Projections for Australia's NRM regions'. CSIRO, Canberra.

White K (1997) Fire behaviour and on ground evidence of fire intensity for remote sensing evaluation. In *Malgarra: Burning the Bush: Report of the Fourth North Australian Fire Management Workshop, Kalumburu, North Kimberley, Western Australia.* (Eds P Saint and J Russell-Smith) pp. 20–25. Cooperative Research Centre for Tropical Savannas, Darwin.

Williams R (1995) Tree mortality in relation to fire intensity in a tropical savanna of the Kakadu region, Northern Territory, Australia. *CALMscience* **4**(Supplement), 77–82.

Williams R (1997) Fire and floral phenology in a humid tropical savanna at Kapalga, Kakadu National Park, northern Australia. In *Proceedings of the Australian Bushfire Conference.* 8–10 July, Darwin. (Eds BJ McKaige, RJ Williams and WM Waggitt) pp. 54–59. CSIRO Tropical Ecosystems Research Centre, Darwin.

Williams R, Myers B, Muller W, Duff G, Eamus D (1997) Leaf phenology of woody species in a north Australian tropical savanna. *Ecology* **78**, 2542–2558. doi:10.1890/0012-9658(1997)078[2542:LPOWSI]2.0.CO;2

Williams R, Gill A, Moore P (1998) Seasonal changes in fire behaviour in a tropical savanna in northern Australia. *International Journal of Wildland Fire* **8**, 227–239. doi:10.1071/WF9980227

Woinarski J, Mackey B, Nix H, Traill B (2007) *The Nature of Northern Australia: Its Natural Values, Ecological Processes and Future Prospects.* Australian National University Press, Canberra.

Woinarski JCZ, Legge S, Fitzsimons JA, Traill BJ, Burbidge AA, Fisher A, Firth RSC, Gordon IJ, Griffiths AD, Johnson CN, *et al.* (2011) The disappearing mammal fauna of northern Australia: context, cause, and response. *Conservation Letters* **4**, 192–201. doi:10.1111/j.1755-263X.2011.00164.x

Wunambal Gaambera Aboriginal Corporation (WGAC) (2010) *Wunambal Gaambera Healthy Country Plan – Looking After Wunambal Gaambera Country 2010–2020.* WGAC, <https://wunambalgaambera.org.au/wp-content/uploads/2020/06/Healthy-Country-Plan.pdf>

6

The (re)emergence of Aboriginal women and cultural burning in New South Wales, Australia

Vanessa Cavanagh

Interviewer: Do you think it's important for Aboriginal women to be involved in cultural burning, and why?

Participant: Yeah, I do. I think that it is for two reasons, particularly it reinforces that our cultural rites of passage as Aboriginal women in a matriarchal society and it's a practice we would have traditionally have done, and, you know, we all know through colonisation that patriarchal line has taken some of our rites of passage away, but I also think it's important for Aboriginal women to be involved in cultural burning because they're the ones who we're going to rely on to pass that down to their children and their grandchildren and that, to me, is more important – that's the most important part of having women involved because traditionally our women are teachers.[1]

In January 2020, Australia saw in the new decade with an unprecedented bushfire crisis unfolding, particularly in the south-east of the continent. (Note, in this article the word 'bushfire' is used to denote what may be referred to in other locations as 'wildfire'.) The phrase 'unprecedented bushfire' is becoming commonplace in Australia, as we experience the reality of global increasing fire frequency and intensity (Bowman *et al.* 2016; Clarke *et al.* 2020). In the search for potential responses to the ongoing crisis, growing attention has turned to focus on Aboriginal[2] peoples'[3] caring for Country knowledge, in particular how fire has shaped Australia (Gammage 2011; Fletcher *et al.* 2021) and how Aboriginal fire knowledge may mitigate future fire events (Steffensen 2020). This chapter presents an overview of Australian Aboriginal peoples' fire practice in New South Wales (NSW), with particular emphasis on Aboriginal women.

Before delving into fire and women, the concepts of connection to Country and caring for Country deserve attention. The landscapes of the landmass now known as Australia have been articulately and actively curated for millennia (Gammage 2011; Steffensen 2020; Fletcher *et al.* 2021). Western science evidences Aboriginal occupation in Australia to at least 65 000 years (Clarkson *et al.* 2017; McNiven *et al.* 2018). Indigenous peoples of this continent are deeply related to the places from which our identities and heritages are borne (Arabena 2020). Simply, this relatedness is perceived as 'connection to Country'. This connection is nurtured via actions of caring for Country that enact these deep relationships, responsibilities and knowledge systems in complex and comprehensive ways. Caring for Country is defined by Arabena (2020) *'as having knowledge, a sense of responsibility and an inherent right to be involved in the management of traditional lands … with the objective of promoting ecological and human health'*. Caring for Country involves not only the caring of and for landscapes, but also the kin of that landscape, the peoples who belong to it and exist with it, a process of nurturing our connections to place, people and spirit (Weir *et al.* 2011; Arabena 2020). There is a strong correlation between healthy Country and the health and well being of people (Burgess *et al.* 2009; Weir *et al.* 2011; Jones *et al.* 2018; Arabena 2020). Changes in the land and climate directly affect emotional health and well being, particularly of Indigenous peoples (Cunsolo Willox *et al.* 2013; Arabena 2020) and particularly where fire affects Aboriginal heritage and resources (Cavanagh 2020a; Williamson *et al.* 2020). In recent decades, the concept of caring for Country has been a developing factor within scholarship on Indigenous land management relationships (Pleshet 2018). The phrase 'caring for Country' has since gained traction in the national vernacular as the mainstream population try to understand Indigenous cultures and the landscapes of Australia (Goddard 2020).

Western science has started to acknowledge Indigenous Australian peoples' specialised knowledge of and for Country (e.g. Ward-Fear *et al.* 2019). However, this is married to a noticeable concentration of research located in the less-inhabited regions of the Australian continent (Smith *et al.* 2019), particularly the north, central and north-west. These regions coincide with large areas of Indigenous-owned lands, Indigenous Protected Areas and shorter periods of European invasion, which suggest less fragmentation of Indigenous

precolonial knowledge given that Indigenous culture is inherently woven with Country (Carpentaria Land Council Aboriginal Corporation 2020; Cary and McKemey 2020). Although much of this activity is well documented, recently research has started to explore Aboriginal peoples' interaction with fire in the south-east (Maclean *et al.* 2018; McKemey *et al.* 2019, 2020a; Neale *et al.* 2019; Weir and Freeman 2019; Feary 2020; Freeman 2020). This attention is paralleled by an energising of Aboriginal peoples' (re)engagement with fire, as a caring for Country process, in the region. This engagement with fire is commonly referred to as 'cultural burning'.

Cultural burning is an embodied practice, led by local Aboriginal people with cultural authority and one in which people situated within Country are responsive to Country's needs and articulations (to learn more about cultural burning, go to firesticks.org.au). Aboriginal fire facilitator Oliver Costello (2020) says, *'Caring for Country can be understood as maintaining the interconnected relationships (kinships) between all elements and beings'*. Cultural burning practitioners are physically present on the ground, feeling the air, the temperature and the wind and examining the grasses, the ground cover and the ground itself. They are walking through Country before and with the fire to witness and respond to its intimate requirements. Cultural burning can be undertaken for a range of reasons. Indigenous burning, inextricably embedded in Indigenous worldviews, has many purposes and meanings. It can be undertaken to protect sacred sites, stimulate the growth of bush foods and medicines, clear Country for hunting and reduce debris, as well as to protect Country from intense wildfires (firesticks.com.au; Steffensen 2020). Smoke is as important as flame for ceremony and cultural activities. In precolonial times, fire and smoke were used to communicate with other groups at a physical distance. Smoking ceremonies, where people bathe in smoke from a designated ceremonial fire, feature regularly in modern-day Indigenous gathering and welcoming ceremonies. Families may welcome a newborn child through a smoking ceremony, and new buildings may be smoked as part of the official opening of the building.

Cultural burning activities themselves are diverse, from the way that the fires are lit, to the areas that are intended to be burnt, to who is involved and what preparations and equipment are used. Generally, in the south-east of the continent, cultural burning is distinct from mainstream hazard reduction fires that are undertaken by formal fire agencies. Cultural burning follows an Indigenous-led approach, where local Aboriginal people lead the burn and process. This leadership may result in limitations placed on who is involved and how it is undertaken. Although cultural burning in the south-east may be led by Aboriginal people, it is still regulated by policy and permit systems. Thus, there are fires that are undertaken as cultural burns that, due to the local conditions and environment (e.g. being close to residential areas), may also involve local fire agencies and processes, including the presence of fire trucks and the engagement of containment lines such as roads, rivers or the physical removal of combustible materials to create a burn edge. But, distinctively, cultural burns usually opt for more organic approaches that involve minimal mechanical intervention.

Features of cultural burns include lighting from a small ignition point, sometimes one match starting the burn at one single point. The fire then undertakes its own burn path, often creating a mosaic by burning some areas while leaving other parts unburnt (Steffensen 2020). By removing debris at a tree base before the flames arrive, or by subduing the flames as they climb a tree trunk, people may interact in the fire's burn path to reduce the occurrence of fire burning up tree trunks and entering the canopy. In addition, people may get involved in the fire's burn path to intervene if the energy and heat of the fire become excessive, or to protect other assets. The fires of cultural burns are often self-extinguishing, and this occurrence is the result of burning at the right time and in the right way (Steffensen 2020). The equipment used by Indigenous people to apply fire to the landscape varies depending on the intention and approaches

being used. There is a range of perspectives on what should be involved in a cultural burn. Aboriginal cultural burning can involve a range of equipment. Some cultural burns are lit using only locally acquired resources. These fires are often started by drilling one stick into another (firesticks), creating friction until heat and a fire ember appear, the ember catching alight the dry aerated bundle of fibrous bark, grass or leaves placed near the drill hole. Similarly, flint stones may be used to strike sparks into the dry materials. With these fires, no foreign or non-organic materials are being used to initiate the fire, and this appeals to some people's desires for fire processes that adhere closely to precolonial approaches. Some cultural burns in the south-east are lit with matches or (cigarette) lighters; these burns also fulfil cultural burning goals of Aboriginal communities by essentially reviving burning relationships between people and Country making use of appropriate or accessible tools. For this to occur, people have to be present in the landscape to undertake the cultural burn. They are not able to undertake a cultural burn without walking Country first, to be able to respond to the characteristics and needs of Country. As a result, it is unlikely that cultural burns in the south-east involve lighting the fire using helicopters and aerial incendiaries.

Cultural burning differs from mainstream fire management

Mainstream hazard reduction burns that are undertaken by agencies are often prioritised in relation to life and property, and the protection of assets. Mainstream hazard reduction burns are applied to the landscape in response to the assets, and they are measured in terms of hectares or total area burned. Fires that are lit by fire agencies or using a mainstream hazard reduction approach are typically lit from a distinct edge, such as a road, waterway or where combustible materials have been physically removed to create a containment edge. These fires are ignited along the edge in a continuous line or with numerous ignition points.

Some of these fires are lit using helicopters and aerial incendiaries or drip torches and their petroleum-based fuels, and garden blowers are used to forcefully increase the flames. There is less concern with the characteristics of the biota present other than its flammability and potential response to being burnt at a given date. Fuel moisture, air temperature and wind speed are the factors influencing each fire.

Cultural burning involves people of all ages and demographics of the local community. Cultural burns will often aim to be inclusive of Aboriginal Elders, children and genders. There may be cultural burn events that are gender specific or that are guided by other sensitivities. In contrast, for mainstream agency fires, participants are trained firefighters aged upwards from their mid- to late teens, all are wearing the required personal protective equipment and they are predominantly male.

Examples of the gendered dimensions of fire

Statistically, firefighting in NSW is a predominantly male activity. In 2011, female membership in the NSW Rural Fire Service (RFS) was 20% (NSW RFS 2011). The NSW RFS has a stated workplace diversity target of 50% women, but in 2017, 2018 and 2019 the proportion of women in the RFS hovered at around 34% (NSW RFS 2019). In July 2019, a hazard reduction burn in Scheyville National Park, north-western Sydney, was undertaken for the first time with an all-female crew (DPIE 2019). However, this is not the first collective of female firefighters in Australian colonial history. The Armidale Amazons of 1901–03 (Women in Firefighting (Australia) n.d.) may even hold the record of the first all-female fire brigade in the world! In Victoria's Gippsland region, Aboriginal women in Lake Tyers hold the mantle of firefighting responsibilities in their community. The Lake Tyers Aboriginal Trust – Country Fire Authority (CFA) in Victoria has been active for over two decades (Smethurst 2020), and this team is thought to be the first all-Indigenous, all-female firefighting crew in Australia. Aboriginal women's

ranger teams are active in fire practice across Australia, including in the desert regions (Grant 2020). The Tjuwampa Women Rangers (2020) in Central Australia describe their two golden rules for burning: '*You can always add to a small fire, but you cannot take away from a big fire, and always burn into a creek, not out of the creek.*' The literature relating to Indigenous women's contribution to cultural burning in NSW is limited. This may be attributed to dominant patriarchal process more frequently involving men (Eriksen and Hankins 2015). In addition, it may be that the impacts of genocide have blurred the gendered knowledge custodianship boundaries, resulting in fire knowledge and practice being shared (Eriksen and Hankins 2015). The diaries of colonial explorers include observations of Aboriginal women and children burning. Thomas Mitchell's notes provide a clear indication that Indigenous people, including women and children, were discriminately applying fire in the landscape:

> *Fire, grass, kangaroos, and human inhabitants, seem all dependent on each other for existence … the native applies that fire to the grass at certain seasons, in order that a young green crop may subsequently spring up, and so attract and enable him to kill or take the kangaroo … [it is] females and children, who chiefly burn the grass.*
> *(Mitchell 1848)*

Similarly, an ethnohistorical review undertaken by Cahir *et al.* (2016) discusses Robinson's reference to Aboriginal women participating in burning in Victoria, during his time there as Chief Protector of Aborigines (1838–49). Eriksen and Hankins (2013, 2014, 2015) researched the gendered dimensions of fire in Australia and California (USA). Their work finds that modern-day land management burning is influenced by Aboriginal culture and sex, where men were responsible for landscape scale burning and women's burning was undertaken at a finer scale (Eriksen and Hankins 2015). Working with Martu Indigenous people in Western Australia, Bliege Bird *et al.*

(2008) found that Martu women were applying fire in a specific fashion that was distinct from that of Martu men. The findings include that women's burning was important for women's hunting needs and, as such, it was necessary that women's burning needs were incorporated into fire and conservation policy, in addition to the fire requirements of Martu men (Bird *et al.* 2004, 2005; Bliege Bird *et al.* 2008). These examples of the gendered and racialised dimensions of fire serve to demonstrate the place for Aboriginal women, as well as our roles and responsibilities in caring for Country and maintaining culture. Broadening from fire, Davies *et al.* (2018) found a distinction between Aboriginal Walpiri women's and men's engagement in natural resource management. Preliminary data from the author's own research reveal that Aboriginal women in NSW are participating, or desire to participate, in cultural burning where it is culturally appropriate to do so (Cavanagh *et al.* 2019; Cavanagh 2020b). Aboriginal women in NSW want to participate, but do so in ways that maintain local cultural protocols (Cavanagh and Standley 2020). Men are also keen to hold space for Aboriginal women's involvement in fire and natural resource management, as illustrated by Kowanyama man John Clark, who states, '[we] *need more girls too, more female rangers, not only men have knowledge of fire, so have the ladies*' (quoted in Robinson *et al.* 2016a). This gendered dimension of Indigenous fire knowledge is reflected internationally (Eriksen and Hankins 2015).

Aboriginal burning in the continental north and south

Many people think of Top End or remote area burning when discussing Aboriginal burning activities. In the northern regions of Australia, where savanna dominates the landscape, Indigenous people are engaging in fire in a very specific way through their participation in the carbon farming market (Langton 1998; Russell-Smith *et al.* 2013; Foley 2016; Robinson *et al.* 2016a, 2016b; Jackson *et al.* 2017; Ansell and Evans 2020;

McKemey *et al.* 2020b; Yibarbuk and Ansell 2020). The transferability of Indigenous fire as carbon farming to other areas of the continent is yet to be established. The carbon market is where carbon emissions are offset through the purchase of carbon units. For example, in August 2018 the Queensland Government announced it would offset the emissions from its fleet of vehicles with carbon credits generated from Aboriginal carbon farming (Queensland Government 2018). This is paying Aboriginal groups to care for Country. Here, carbon abatement is about savanna burning at a particular time of year. It works in this part of the continent because savannas are extremely fire-prone landscapes. Whether cultural burning in the south-east can create the same outcomes in terms of carbon farming remains to be seen. However, there are some readily comparable outcomes between Aboriginal burning in the north and south of Australia. Aboriginal participants in the north point out that carbon farming creates outcomes, such as getting more Indigenous people back out on Country, providing employment for Indigenous people where other secure employment is limited and having social cultural and environmental benefits (Langton 1998; Russell-Smith *et al.* 2013; Foley 2016; Robinson *et al.* 2016b; Jackson *et al.* 2017; Ansell and Evans 2020; McKemey *et al.* 2020b). Re-establishing deteriorated culturally important species such as emu is one Aboriginal community concern that has been targeted through carbon abatement programs in the north (Yibarbuk and Cooke 2001; Vigilante and Bowman 2004; Robinson *et al.* 2016b; Ansell and Evans 2020). Another concern was that bushfires were too big and destructive, leaving the landscape barren and unhealthy (Moorcroft *et al.* 2012; Robinson *et al.* 2016a). Carbon farming activity means returning people to Country to encourage re-establishing caring for Country, the return of animals into the landscape, reconnecting Aboriginal people with Aboriginal heritage sites, revitalising areas and stories due to increased activity on Country and reducing fuel loads around sensitive Aboriginal heritage (e.g. rock art) sites.

Concluding remarks

Indigenous knowledge and expertise must take precedence in the management of natural environments. Fundamentally, however, our knowledge should not be excerpted and cropped in models that do not suit or where Indigenous knowledge is impeded by restrictive power imbalances (Langton 1998; Muller *et al.* 2019). Fire will continue to be part of our relationship with Country, and we need to take notice of what is and is not working. This requires Aboriginal people and systems to lead the process, and more roles for Aboriginal people across environmental conservation practice, policy and research. There must be opportunities made for Aboriginal voices, including Aboriginal women's voices, to be heard and listened to. Given the need for this dialogue, it is important that the author's own research is attached to other bushfire research, such as the NSW Bushfire Risk Management Research Hub.

About the author

Vanessa Cavanagh is a Bundjalung and Wonnarua Aboriginal woman. Vanessa is an Associate Lecturer and PhD candidate in the University of Wollongong School of Geography and Sustainable Communities. Vanessa's research focuses on Aboriginal women's engagement in cultural burning in New South Wales (NSW). This mixed-method research is participatory, advocacy and auto-ethnographic, as Vanessa explores and promotes the multiple layers of Aboriginal women's roles. Vanessa has over two decades' experience in the environmental conservation sector in NSW, where she started her career in the National Parks and Wildlife Service and participated in remote area firefighting. In the Black Summer bushfires, Vanessa's childhood home was affected by the Gospers Mountain Fire, and she writes personally about returning to view the damage in Cavanagh (2020a). Vanessa appeared as a witness in the Royal Commission into National Natural Disaster Arrangements. Vanessa is affiliated with the New South Wales Bushfire Risk Management Research

Hub, Australia, and the Australian Centre for Culture, Environment, Society and Space.

Acknowledgements

The author acknowledges the participants in her research and their valuable contributions. The author also acknowledges the work of many Indigenous people who have and continue to care for Country. The author acknowledges the New South Wales Bushfire Risk Management Research Hub, Australia, and the Australian Centre for Culture, Environment, Society and Space for their financial contributions.

Endnotes

[1] This quote is from the author's current PhD qualitative research that explores Aboriginal women and cultural burning in NSW. The interaction is between two Aboriginal mothers and exemplifies the layers of importance for Aboriginal women's engagement.

[2] In this article the use of the words and phrases 'Aboriginal', 'Aboriginal peoples' and 'Aboriginal Australians' is in reference to the First Nations Peoples of the Australian mainland. The use of the words and phrases 'Indigenous', 'Indigenous peoples' and 'Indigenous Australians' is used where reference is being made to both Aboriginal and Torres Strait Islander peoples of Australia.

[3] The plural 'peoples' is used to reflect that these groupings represent multiple and diverse communities.

References

Ansell J, Evans J (2020) Contemporary Aboriginal savanna burning projects in Arnhem Land: a regional description and analysis of the fire management aspirations of Traditional Owners. *International Journal of Wildland Fire* **29**(5), 371–385. doi:10.1071/WF18152

Arabena K (2020) *'Country can't hear English': A guide supporting the implementation of cultural determinants of health and wellbeing with Aboriginal and Torres Strait Islander peoples.* Karabena Consulting, Riddell's Creek, <https://www.thecentrehki.com.au/wp-content/uploads/2020/07/Country_Cant_Hear_English_Cultural_DeterminantsGuide.pdf>.

Bird DW, Bliege Bird R, Parker CH (2004) Women who hunt with fire: Aboriginal resource use and fire regimes in Australia's Western Desert. *Australian Aboriginal Studies* **1**, 90–96.

Bird DW, Bliege Bird R, Parker CH (2005) Aboriginal burning regimes and hunting strategies in Australia's Western Desert. *Human Ecology* **33**(4), 443–464. doi:10.1007/s10745-005-5155-0

Bliege Bird R, Bird DW, Codding BF, Parker CH, Jones JH (2008) The 'firestick farming' hypothesis: Australian Aboriginal foraging strategies, biodiversity, and anthropogenic fire mosaics. *Proceedings of the National Academy of Sciences of the United States of America* **105**(39), 14796–14801. doi:10.1073/pnas.0804757105

Bowman DM, Williamson GJ, Prior LD, Murphy BP (2016) The relative importance of intrinsic and extrinsic factors in the decline of obligate seeder forests. *Global Ecology and Biogeography* **25**(10), 1166–1172. doi:10.1111/geb.12484

Burgess CP, Johnston FH, Berry HL, McDonnell J, Yibarbuk D, Gunabarra C, Mileran A, Bailie RS (2009) Healthy Country, healthy people: the relationship between Indigenous health status and 'caring for Country'. *The Medical Journal of Australia* **190**(10), 567–572. doi:10.5694/j.1326-5377.2009.tb02566.x

Cahir F, McMaster S, Clark I, Kerin R, Wright W (2016) Winda lingo parugoneit or Why set the bush [on] fire? Fire and Victorian Aboriginal people on the colonial frontier. *Australian Historical Studies* **47**(2), 225–240. doi:10.1080/1031461X.2016.1156137

Carpentaria Land Council Aboriginal Corporation (2020) Jigija Indigenous Fire Training Program. In *Prescribed Burning in Australasia: The Science, Politics and Practice of Burning the Bush.* (Eds A Leavesley, M Wouters and R Thornton) pp. 57–59. Australiasian Fire and Emergency Service Authorities Council, Melbourne.

Cary G, McKemey M (2020) Across the Country. In *Prescribed Burning in Australasia: The Science, Politics and Practice of Burning the Bush.* (Eds A Leavesley, M Wouters and R Thornton) pp. 54–55. Australiasian Fire and Emergency Service Authorities Council, Melbourne.

Cavanagh VI (2020a) Friday essay: this grandmother tree connects me to Country. I cried when I saw her burned. *The Conversation,* <https://theconversation.com/friday-essay-this-grandmother-tree-connects-me-to-country-i-cried-when-i-saw-her-burned-129782>.

Cavanagh VI (2020b) Entanglements – Vanessa Cavanagh. *There's no place like...* Australian Centre for Culture, Environment, Society & Space, University of Wollongong, <https://shows.acast.com/theres-no-place-like/episodes/entanglements-vanessa-cavanagh>.

Cavanagh V, Standley PM (2020) Walking in the landscapes of our ancestors – Indigenous perspectives critical in the teaching of Geography. *Interaction* **48**(1), 14–16.

Cavanagh V, Christianson A, Kristoff M (2019) Aboriginal women and caring for country in NSW, Australia with Vanessa Cavanagh. *Your Forest Podcast,* <https://your forestpodcast.com/good-fire-podcast/2019/10/16/39x2 1icgmd101pd7tj2qqzsajy0jh6>.

Clarke H, Penman T, Boer M, Cary GJ, Fontaine JB, Price O, Bradstock R (2020) The proximal drivers of large fires: a pyrogeographic study. *Frontiers of Earth Science* **8**, 90. doi:10.3389/feart.2020.00090

Clarkson C, Jacobs Z, Marwick B, Fullagar R, Wallis L, Smith M, Roberts RG, Hayes E, Lowe K, Carah X, *et al.* (2017) Human occupation of northern Australia by 65,000 years ago. *Nature* **547**, 306–310. doi:10.1038/nature22968

Costello O (2020) Fire has spirit. In *Prescribed Burning in Australasia: The Science, Politics and Practice of Burning the Bush.* (Eds A Leavesley, M Wouters and R Thornton) pp. 66–67. Australiasian Fire and Emergency Service Authorities Council, Melbourne.

Cunsolo Willox A, Harper SL, Edge VL, Landman K, Houle K, Ford JD (2013) The land enriches the soul: on climatic and environmental change, affect, and emotional health and well-being in Rigolet, Nunatsiavut, Canada. *Emotion, Space and Society* **6**, 14–24. doi:10.1016/j.emospa.2011.08.005

Davies J, Walker J, Maru YT (2018) Warlpiri experiences highlight challenges and opportunities for gender equity in Indigenous conservation management in arid Australia. *Journal of Arid Environments* **149**, 40–52. doi:10.1016/j.jaridenv.2017.10.002

NSW Department of Planning, Industry and Environment (DPIE) (2019) *Female firefighters blaze a trail.* [Media release] DPIE, <https://www.environment.nsw.gov.au/news/female-firefighters-blaze-a-trail?utm_source= miragenews&utm_medium=miragenews&utm_campaign= news>.

Eriksen C, Hankins DL (2013) Gendered dimensions of Aboriginal Australian and California Indian fire knowledge retention and revival. *Current Conservation* **7**, 22–26.

Eriksen C, Hankins DL (2014) The retention, revival, and subjugation of Indigenous fire knowledge through agency fire fighting in eastern Australia and California. *Society & Natural Resources* **27**(12), 1288–1303. doi:10.1080/08941920.2014.918226

Eriksen C, Hankins DL (2015) Colonisation and fire: gendered dimensions of indigenous fire knowledge retention and revival. In *The Routledge Handbook of Gender and Development.* (Eds A Coles, L Gray and J Momsen) pp. 129–137. Routledge, New York.

Feary S (2020) Indigenous Australians and fire in southeastern Australia. In *Prescribed Burning in Australasia: The Science, Politics and Practice of Burning the Bush.* (Eds A Leavesley, M Wouters and R Thornton) pp. 69–75. Australiasian Fire and Emergency Service Authorities Council, Melbourne.

Fletcher MS, Hall T, Alexandra AN (2021) The loss of an Indigenous constructed landscape following British invasion of Australia: an insight into the deep human imprint on the Australian landscape. *Ambio* **50**, 138–149. doi:10.1007/s13280-020-01339-3

Foley R (2016) It's time to invest in Indigenous carbon farming on Aboriginal lands' *The Guardian*, <https://www.theguardian.com/sustainable-business/2016/nov/16/its-time-to-invest-in-indigenous-carbon-farming-on-aboriginal-lands>.

Freeman D (2020) Aboriginal burning in southern Australia. In *Prescribed Burning in Australasia: The Science, Politics and Practice of Burning the Bush.* (Eds A Leavesley, M Wouters and R Thornton) pp. 239–241. Australiasian Fire and Emergency Service Authorities Council, Melbourne.

Gammage B (2011) *The Biggest Estate on Earth: How Aborigines Made Australia.* Allen & Unwin, Sydney.

Goddard C (2020) 'Country', 'land', 'nation': key Anglo English words for talking and thinking about people in places. *Journal of Postcolonial Linguistics* **2**, 8–27.

Grant J (2020) Women rangers' fire management in the Tanimi. In *Prescribed Burning in Australasia: The Science, Politics and Practice of Burning the Bush.* (Eds A Leavesley, M Wouters and R Thornton) p. 65. Australiasian Fire and Emergency Service Authorities Council, Melbourne.

Jackson S, Palmer L, McDonald F, Bumpus A (2017) Cultures of carbon and the logic of Care: the possibilities for carbon enrichment and its cultural signature. *Annals of the Association of American Geographers* **107**(4), 867–882. doi:10.1080/24694452.2016.1270187

Jones R, Thurber KA, Wright A, Chapman J, Donohoe P, Davis V, Lovett R (2018) Associations between participation in a ranger program and health and wellbeing outcomes among Aboriginal and Torres Strait Islander people in Central Australia: a proof of concept study. *International Journal of Environmental Research and Public Health* **15**(7), 1478. doi:10.3390/ijerph15071478

Langton M (1998) *Burning Questions: Emerging Environmental Issues for Indigenous Peoples in Northern Australia.* Centre for Indigenous Natural and Cultural Resource Management, Northern Territory University, Darwin.

Maclean K, Robinson CJ, Costello O (2018) *A National Framework to Report on the Benefits of Indigenous Cultural Fire Management. Final Report.* CSIRO, Canberra, <https://publications.csiro.au/rpr/download?pid=csiro:EP188803&dsid=DS1>.

McKemey MB, Patterson ML, Rangers B, Ens EJ, Reid NC, Hunter JT, Costello O, Ridges M, Miller C (2019) Cross-cultural monitoring of a cultural keystone species informs revival of Indigenous burning of Country in south-eastern Australia. *Human Ecology* **47**(6), 893–904. doi:10.1007/s10745-019-00120-9

McKemey M, Costello O, Ridges M, Ens EJ, Hunter JT, Reid NC (2020a) A review of contemporary Indigenous cultural fire management literature in southeast Australia. *EcoEvoRxiv.* doi:10.32942/osf.io/fvswy

McKemey M, Ens E, Rangers YM, Costello O, Reid N (2020b) Indigenous knowledge and seasonal calendar inform adaptive savanna burning in northern Australia. *Sustainability* **12**(3), 995. doi:10.3390/su12030995

McNiven IJ, Crouch J, Bowler JM, Sherwood JE, Dolby N, Dunn JE, Stanisic J (2018) The Moyjil site, south-west Victoria, Australia: excavation of a Last Interglacial charcoal and burnt stone feature: is it a hearth? *Proceedings of the Royal Society of Victoria* **130**, 94–116. doi:10.1071/RS18008

Mitchell TL (1848) *Journal of an Expedition Into the Interior of Tropical Australia: In Search of a Route From Sydney to the Gulf of Carpentaria.* Longman, Brown, Green and Longmans, London.

Moorcroft H, Ignjic E, Cowell S, Goonack J, Mangolomara S, Oobagooma J, Karadada R, Williams D, Waina N (2012) Conservation planning in a cross-cultural context: the Wunambal Gaambera Healthy Country Project in the Kimberley, Western Australia. *Ecological Management and Restoration* **13**, 16–25.

Muller S, Hemming S, Rigney D (2019) Indigenous sovereignties: relational ontologies and environmental management. *Geographical Research* **57**(4), 399–410. doi:10.1111/1745-5871.12362

Neale T, Carter R, Nelson T, Bourke M (2019) Walking together: a decolonising experiment in bushfire management on Dja Dja Wurrung country. *Cultural Geographies* **26**(3), 341–359. doi:10.1177/1474474018821419

New South Wales Rural Fire Service (NSW RFS) (2011) *Making a Difference: Women in the NSW Rural Fire Service.* NSW RFS, Sydney, <https://www.rfs.nsw.gov.au/__data/assets/pdf_file/0019/4267/Making-a-Difference-Women-in-the-NSW-Rural-Fire-Service.pdf>.

New South Wales Rural Fire Service (NSW RFS) (2019) Annual Report 2018/19. NSW RFS, Sydney, <https://www.rfs.nsw.gov.au/__data/assets/pdf_file/0004/129892/NSW-RFS-Annual-Report-2018-19-web.pdf>.

Pleshet N (2018) Caring for Country: history and alchemy in the making and management of Indigenous Australian land. *Oceania* **88**(2), 183–201. doi:10.1002/ocea.5188

Queensland Government (2018) *Palaszczuk Government to Offset Vehicle Pollution With Carbon Projects.* [Media statement] Queensland Government, Brisbane, <https://statements.qld.gov.au/statements/85206>.

Robinson CJ, Barber M, Hill R, Gerrard E, James G (2016a) *Protocols for Indigenous Fire Management Partnerships. Final Report.* CSIRO, Brisbane, <https://www.aidr.org.au/media/4916/protocols_for-indigenous_fire_management_partn.pdf>.

Robinson CJ, Renwick AR, May T, Gerrard E, Foley R, Battaglia M, Possingham H, Griggs D, Walker D (2016b) Indigenous benefits and carbon offset schemes: an Australian case study. *Environmental Science & Policy* **56**, 129–134. doi:10.1016/j.envsci.2015.11.007

Russell-Smith J, Cook GD, Cooke PM, Edwards AC, Lendrum M, Meyer CP, Whitehead PJ (2013) Managing fire regimes in north Australian savannas: applying Aboriginal approaches to contemporary global problems. *Frontiers in Ecology and the Environment* **11**(s1), e55–e63. doi:10.1890/120251

Smethurst S (2020) Meet the all-female Indigenous fire crew protecting community, family and sacred land. *The Australian Women's Weekly*, <https://www.nowtolove.com.au/news/local-news/indigenous-all-female-fire-crew-australia-62022>.

Smith W, Weir J, Neale T (2019) 'Hazards, culture and Indigenous communities, project annual report 2017–2018'. Bushfire and Natural Hazards CRC, Melbourne.

Steffensen V (2020) *Fire Country: How Indigenous Fire Management Could Help Save Australia*. Hardie Grant Publishing, Melbourne, Australia.

Tjuwampa Women Rangers (2020) You can always add to a small fire. In *Prescribed Burning in Australasia: The Science, Politics and Practice of Burning the Bush*. (Eds A Leavesley, M Wouters and R Thornton) p. 63. Australasian Fire and Emergency Service Authorities Council, Melbourne.

Vigilante T, Bowman DMJS (2004) Effects of individual fire events on the flower production of fruit-bearing woody tree species at Kalumburu, North Kimberley. *Australian Journal of Botany* **52**, 405–416.

Ward-Fear G, Balanggarra Rangers, Pearson D, Bruton M, Shine R (2019) Sharper eyes see shyer lizards: collaboration with indigenous peoples can alter the outcomes of conservation research. *Conservation Letters* **12**(4), e12643. doi:10.1111/conl.12643

Weir J, Freeman D (2019) 'Fire in the south: a cross-continental exchange'. Bushfire and Natural Hazards CRC, Melbourne, <https://www.bnhcrc.com.au/publications/biblio/bnh-5488>.

Weir J, Stacey C, Youngetob K (2011) *The Benefits Associated With Caring for Country*. Aboriginal Studies Press, Canberra.

Women in Firefighting (Australia) (n.d,) The Amazons c1901–1903. *Women in Fire Fighting (Australia) – An Archive*, <http://womeninfirefighting.blogspot.com/p/the-amazons-c1901-1903.html>.

Williamson B, Weir J, Cavanagh V (2020) Strength from perpetual grief: how Aboriginal people experience the bushfire crisis. *The Conversation*, <https://theconversation.com/strength-from-perpetual-grief-how-aboriginalpeople-experience-the-bushfire-crisis-129448>.

Yibarbuk D, Ansell J (2020) Fire management in Arnhem Land. In *Prescribed Burning in Australasia: The Science, Politics and Practice of Burning the Bush*. (Eds A Leavesley, M Wouters and R Thornton) pp. 49–53. Australasian Fire and Emergency Service Authorities Council, Melbourne.

Yibarbuk D, Cooke P (2001) Fire, fruit and emus. In *Savanna Burning: Understanding and Using Fire in Northern Australia*. (Eds R Dyer, P Jacklyn, I Partridge, J Russell-Smith and D Williams) p. 40. Tropical Savannas Cooperative Research Centre, Darwin.

7

Fire in pines of the Southeastern US

Steven R. Miller and Matthew K. Corby

Introduction to fire in the region

As the clouds of an early season thunderstorm drift across the sky, lightning strikes a pine tree, causing the cambium to pop and blow burning pieces of bark and wood onto the grasses and pine litter scattered across the surface. The importance of this being an early season storm is significant because, later in the season, thunderstorms are statistically less likely to start fires because the preceding storms have provided rain to the parched earth of spring. Lightning strikes early in the growing season are significantly more likely to start fires, and those fires are statistically more likely to burn more acres. The fire started by this lightning bolt will burn freely for days or weeks until the fire collides with a non-flammable barrier like a river or lake, or even the footprint of a previous fire; or it may burn until the next thunderstorm provides sufficient rain to overcome the heat generated by the fire.

Elsewhere, Native Americans carrying burning sticks stoop low to the ground to ignite their own fires among the grasses and pine litter (Figure 7.1). These Native Americans may have a myriad of purposes for lighting their fire: they may want to freshen forage to attract game; they may be improving their line of sight so they can see enemies and game at a longer distance; they may be clearing ground to plant crops around their village; perhaps they are encouraging native plants to flower more prolifically so that they will bear more fruit; or they may be burning the woods because the shrubs they burn will resprout with straighter and more flexible stems that can be more easily made into baskets. Although the reasons why Native Americans light fires may vary, one thing is certain: they knew how to light fires that would burn the landscape in a specific way and at specific times (seasons) to achieve their objectives.

For eons, lightning and Native Americans lit fires in the pines of the Southeastern US. In some places lightning dominated as the source of fire; in other places, the Native American influence was greater. Regardless of the source, those fires shaped and sustained the pine ecosystems. Although there are 10 species of pine that inhabit the Southeastern US, namely the eastern white (*Pinus strobus*), loblolly (*Pinus taeda*), longleaf (*Pinus palustris*), pitch (*Pinus rigida*), pond (*Pinus serotine*), sand (*Pinus clausa*),

Figure 7.1: Native Americans lighting fires in southern pines. Artwork by Patrick Elliott used with permission from Longleaf Alliance.

shortleaf (*Pinus echinata*), slash (*Pinus elliotti*), table mountain (*Pinus pungens*) and Virginia (*Pinus virginiana*) pines, this chapter focuses on the five that are more common and cover the larger extent, the loblolly, longleaf, shortleaf, pond and slash pines.

Fire history

It is estimated that Southern pines once covered more than 37 million hectares (Frost 2006). Those pine forests were maintained by frequent surface fires that occurred, depending on plant communities, as frequently as every year to as long as 12 years apart (Frost 2006). Those fires were essential for exposing the soil for the next generation of pine seedlings to germinate, controlling hardwood and brush species, encouraging the growth and reproduction of understorey herbs, grasses and sedges and maintaining the ideal habitat for a myriad of animal species (Van Lear and Harlow 2002; Oswalt *et al.* 2012). In the absence of fire, pine seedlings cannot successfully become established (Oswalt *et al.* 2012). Hardwoods and shrubs will increase in

both dominance and stature until they either serve as fuels for a much more intense fire that can threaten the pines themselves or they completely alter the ecosystem, impeding the herbaceous plants and the animals dependent upon them (Van Lear and Harlow 2002).

Common objectives for fire use

Historically, Native Americans used fire to provide food, tools and medicine. Fire supported native food production by encouraging forage production in groundcover species that would then attract grazing animals, preparing the ground for the cultivation of plants or encouraging the growth of berry-, nut- or tuber-producing species (Van Lear and Harlow 2002). Native Americans would use fire to trigger the sprouting of tree and brush species in such a way as to provide handles, arrows or fibres for weaving. Fire was also critically important for providing medicines for native cultures. For example, the Creek Tribe could identify and use over 400 species of plants that had medicinal properties, with most of those species being fire dependent (S. Thrower, pers. comm., 23 November 2019).

Early European settlers mimicked the native use of fire for similar purposes, although early settlers were more focused on grazing and crop production (Johnson and Hale 2002). From 1890 to 1930, this use of fire across the landscape began to be discouraged by the conservation and forestry organisations of the time (Wade *et al.* 2006). These organisations viewed fire on the landscape as a threat to the forest: many of the original forests had been cutover and frequent fires were viewed as a threat to efforts establishing pine seedlings and saplings (Oswalt *et al.* 2012). Some landowners were reluctant to stop burning and continued their tradition of burning, but in a diminished capacity.

In 1924, Herbert Stoddard began to investigate the decline of the bobwhite quail in south Georgia and north Florida (Stoddard 1931). Stoddard determined that the lack of burning and subsequent loss of fire frequency was contributing to the decline of the bobwhite quail and encouraged landowners to burn their pine lands and, in 1931, published a book entitled The Bobwhite Quail: Its Habits, Preservation, and Increase (Stoddard 1931). The book was originally met with resistance because it encouraged prescribed burning (Johnson and Hale 2002). Following the book's publication, prescribed fire began to grow in acceptance and use up to the present day, when it is commonly accepted and understood across the Southeastern US. Prescribed fire is recognised as an ecosystem process that is used to prepare sites for planting, encourage natural regeneration, reduce the hazard from wildfire, maintain or restore wildlife habitat, control invasive species and improve grazing (Wade *et al.* 2006).

Fuels

Many of the pine forests in the Southeastern US were originally grass dominated, and routine fire maintained those grasses (Oswalt *et al.* 2012). In pine forests maintained with fire, flames spread primarily through the grasses and pine litter. Those fires typically remain at the surface and have flame lengths ranging from 0.3 to 1.8 m (Anderson 1982).

The thick bark of Southern pines protects established trees from damage under most conditions (Oswalt *et al.* 2012). In the absence of fire, flammable shrubs, such as palmetto *Serenoa repens*, gallberry *Ilex glabra*, yaupon holly *Ilex vomitoria* and titi *Cyrilla racemiflora*, often invade pine forests, changing the habitat quality or characteristics for animals and markedly changing the fuel loading and fire behaviour (Wade *et al.* 2006). Fires in shrub-dominated areas have flame lengths of 1.5–5.8 m (Anderson 1982). These increased flame lengths enable fires to climb into the canopy of pine forests and the increased intensity may overcome the insulating properties of the bark, thus raising the mortality of overstorey pines (Wade *et al.* 2006).

Requirements and barriers for fire use

Prescribed fire is accepted in pines of the Southeastern US, but in some cases that acceptance has been hard fought and well earned (Wade *et al.* 2006).

Cultural and social issues with fire

There were efforts on the part of state and federal forestry agencies to eliminate the use of fire in the early 1900s. Forestry officials created a group referred to as the 'Dixie Crusaders', who travelled the South *educating* the residents about the evils of fire on the landscape and trying to abolish the use of fire (Johnson and Hale 2002; Wade *et al.* 2006). In the rural South, fire use continued, especially as associated with agriculture. The *art* of burning was handed down from generation to generation (Pyne 1982). Then, with the publication of Stoddard's book in 1931, prescribed fire began to take on the aspect of *science* (Johnson and Hale 2002). The science of prescribed fire gained momentum in 1958, with the establishment of the Tall Timbers Research Station, where Stoddard conducted his original work (Johnson and Hale 2002). From there, the science of prescribed fire in the Southeastern US grew in impact and magnitude. In the 1990s, a concerted effort began to educate the general public about the importance of prescribed fire, including the ecological improvement and wildfire risk reduction benefits (Wade *et al.* 2006). Although prescribed fire in the Southeastern US generally shares public support, individuals and groups concerned about smoke production and impacts still work to restrict or eliminate the use of prescribed fire (Wade *et al.* 2006). In an effort to communicate the effective use of fire and to address concerns regarding smoke, Florida established three regional prescribed fire councils (Miller 1998). Prescribed fire councils then began to spread across the US. By 2007, the various prescribed fire councils banded together to create the Coalition of Prescribed Fire Councils (Coalition of Prescribed Fire Councils 2019). As of April 2019, 39 states have prescribed fire councils that are members of the coalition. All 13 Southeastern US states have councils that are members of the Coalition (Coalition of Prescribed Fire Councils 2019).

Laws and policies governing the use of fire

As the Southeast becomes more urbanised, prescribed fire comes under increasing scrutiny from the public and from the legal system (Wade *et al.* 2006). In order to protect the rights of landowners and fire managers to use prescribed fire, 11 of the 13 Southeastern states have passed prescribed fire acts (Coalition of Prescribed Fire Councils 2018); Kentucky and Arkansas are the exceptions. Eleven of the 13 states have also developed certified burner programs to increase both the credibility and the skill levels of prescribed burners (Coalition of Prescribed Fire Councils 2018). Kentucky and Oklahoma have not yet developed certified burner programs.

Prescribed burner practitioners regularly report that concerns over legal liability is a significant barrier to the completion of planned operations (Wade *et al.* 2006; Coalition of Prescribed Fire Councils 2019). Every state in the Southeast has taken some steps towards limiting the liability a burner faces. Ten Southeastern states have taken actions to provide a limited level of liability protection for burners by providing a standard of simple negligence for prescribed burners, which

is better than the strict liability that exists in several states elsewhere in the nation. Three states, namely Florida, Georgia and South Carolina, have increased the standard to gross negligence for prescribed burners who are operating under the states' certified burner programs (Coalition of Prescribed Fire Councils 2018).

Regulatory requirements

Air quality restrictions and laws often make prescribed burning more challenging. Some states have combined their air quality permitting with the burn authorisation system (Coalition of Prescribed Fire Councils 2018). In some non-attainment areas, for example the six counties surrounding Atlanta, air quality concerns actually prohibit prescribed burning during certain times of the year (Wade *et al.* 2006). Most of the prescribed burning acts that states have passed attempt to address prescribe burners by limiting the ability for *nuisance smoke complaints* to get traction (Wade *et al.* 2006). In order to encourage burning and the ecological benefits from burning, some states actually go so far as to declare that the ability to prescribe burn is a *right* belonging to landowners (Wade *et al.* 2006).

As the world in which prescribe burning occurs becomes more complex, burners have found that banding together to form prescribed fire councils can be helpful (Miller 1998). These councils share training, communicate new ideas and challenges and can provide a common voice of reason when issues arise (Miller 1998).

Getting fire on the ground

Getting more fire on the ground in Southern pines is an *ecological imperative* (Wade *et al.* 2006). It is estimated that the combined efforts of federal, state and local governments and private landowners are only completing between 1% and 5% of the amount of fire needed to sustain the ecosystems of the Southeast on private lands and 35% on public lands (Wade *et al.* 2006; Hardin 2010). In order to increase this trend and to expand the acres burned, we discuss the ideal conditions of how to burn in Southern pines.

Prescriptions: weather, season and other conditions

The most critical prescription parameter to address may be the fire return interval. The Fire Effects Information System reports fire return intervals as short as 2 years for longleaf pine and 7 or 8 years for loblolly and pond pine (Abrahamson 2020). A first-entry burn is typically more difficult because timber litter has accumulated, grass species that normally serve as fuel may be suppressed and, depending on species, shrub and tree encroachment can either limit the ability of the fire to burn or contribute to increased fire behaviour (Varner *et al.* 2016).

The desired weather parameters will vary based on fuel loading and the season of the year; however, the general weather windows in which prescribed burns may be accomplished in Southern pines are as described in the following. The air temperature can vary significantly by season, but initial burns to reduce accumulated fuels should begin during the dormant season with air temperatures below 16°C (Waldrop and Goodrick 2012). Once accumulated fuels have been managed, and if there is a desire to move burning into the growing season, then maximum air temperatures can increase (Waldrop and Goodrick 2012). The range of fuel moisture is also subject to seasons and fuel loading. If a significant layer of duff or litter has accumulated, higher levels of fuel moisture are desired so that only the top layer of litter or duff is removed. Removing too much litter or duff during the first burn cycle can significantly damage fine feeder roots and contribute to increased pine mortality (Varner *et al.* 2016). Relative humidity affects fuel moisture and can significantly affect the amount of crown scorch produced during a prescribed fire. Relative humidity on the lower end of the range will also significantly increase the risk of spotting and crown scorch (Waldrop and Goodrick 2012). The ideal range of relative humidity is 30–50% (Waldrop and Goodrick 2012). Wind is important to encourage fire spread and disperse heat from the canopy (Waldrop and Goodrick 2012). The ideal range of wind speeds will vary based on the degree of canopy closure. The denser the stand, the more the canopy will restrict the wind and increase the desired wind speed (Waldrop and Goodrick 2012). The range of general wind speeds is 10–22 km h^{-1}, or in-stand wind speeds of 2–5 km h^{-1} (Waldrop and Goodrick 2012). Atmospheric stability, sometimes referred to as the *vertical wind*, is also important because it will affect the rate at which the smoke rises and disperses. A dispersion index of 35–70 can be acceptable, with the ideal range being 40–60 (Waldrop and Goodrick 2012). Ideal soil moisture is critical in the initial duff reduction burns. Different people identify the ideal soil moisture by measuring the days since rain or by following the Keetch–Byram Drought Index (KBDI), which is a numerical scale from 1 to 800, with 800 being extremely dry (Waldrop and Goodrick 2012). Initial burns should be conducted within 3 days of a wetting rain or with a KBDI in the range of 100–200. As duff is reduced, the acceptable maximum KBDI can increase to 350. The maximum KBDI in sandhills with little to no duff can be up to 500. As the KBDI increases, the risk of smouldering and root damage also increases (Waldrop and Goodrick 2012).

Typical burn unit, how it is determined, size and topography

When determining the layout of the burn unit, it is important to remember that fire is an ecosystem process that historically moved across entire landscapes until such time as the fire met a natural barrier or until the weather changed, stopping the fire spread. Originally, natural barriers included rivers, lakes, streams, exposed areas of rock or soil, previous fires, topography or areas of less-flammable vegetation. In the past 200 years, human-made barriers such as roads, trails, utility corridors, maintained turf or agricultural fields have also served to limit the spread of fire. To the extent possible, existing barriers should be used when laying out prescribed fires. Constructed fire lines may be necessary in places where natural or human-made barriers are not available.

Constructed fire lines can be expensive to create. In addition, depending on how they are constructed, fire lines may increase the risk of erosion, alter hydrology or provide a pathway for invasive plant establishment (Folkerts 1982). Human-made lines also contribute to the build-up of fuels near the fire line, because fire intensity is often lowest in these locations, and they can have significant ecological impacts (Ripley and Printiss 2005). For example, in Florida and Georgia in the 1980s and early 1990s, it was common to exclude isolated wetlands from prescribed burns with *hard fire lines* constructed by bulldozers. Those hard fire lines altered hydrology in various ways by interrupting the sheet flow of water and allowing shrubs to grow unchecked inside those fire lines (Folkerts 1982; Ripley and Printiss 2005). Soon isolated herbaceous wetlands became choked with titi and gallberry. The shrubs themselves also impacted hydrology by increasing evapotranspiration, thereby reducing the duration and frequency of the established hydroperiod (Ripley and Printiss 2005).

As the wetland ecosystem changed, several species of plants and animals were impacted by the change. Pitcher plants (*Sarracenia* spp.) require fire to control competing woody vegetation. In the absence of fire, pitcher plants could not compete and declined (Folkerts 1982). Flatwood salamanders *Ambystoma cingulatum* migrate between isolated wetlands and the surrounding pine forests. To complete their lifecycle, flatwood salamanders need to migrate through the ecotone separating the pine forest and the isolated wetlands. If that ecotone is interrupted by mechanical fire lines and shrub encroachment inside the fire line, the salamander cannot complete its migration (Ripley and Printiss 2005). Whenever possible, when laying out the burn unit, it should be done in such a way that the fire will be able to move through the edges of isolated wetlands within the unit. During the first few burns on a new site, this may mean burning under conditions when surface water is present in the wetlands. As surrounding fuels are reduced, it is possible to burn under slightly drier conditions, enabling the fire to creep

further towards the centre of the isolated wetlands. Smoke production and the risk of igniting organic soils within the wetlands may restrict the potential for incorporating isolated wetlands into a prescribed burn. As the fire becomes established, future burns should try to mix different wind directions. By altering how fire is applied, downwind fire shadows can be eliminated from the burn area.

Burn units can range from less than an acre to thousands of acres. The size of the burn unit is dictated by several factors, the first of which is the location of existing natural or human-made barriers. Another prominent factor dictating the size of the burn unit is likely to be ownership boundaries. However, if neighbouring landowners are also interested in prescribed burning, it may be possible to ignore common boundary lines and for neighbours to burn cooperatively across their common property lines.

An important factor in determining the size of the burn is the preferred fire behaviour and the rate at which the fire will spread across the desired area. Many states restrict the hours of the day when broadcast burning can occur, typically from some time after sunrise to some time near sunset. It is important to identify boundaries to prescribed burns that enable burns to be completed within the legal time frames. Staffing and equipment also contribute to determine burn unit boundaries, because the staffing and equipment available will dictate how many people can be dedicated to ignition and how many are available to hold the fire within the lines. With more resources available, more acres can be burned and the converse is also true. Finally, fuel loading within the burn unit becomes important because overwhelming the available smoke shed for an area can have large negative consequences, both on the day of the burn and far into the future for the burn program in general.

The role topography plays on burn zones is directly proportional to the amount of topography in the area. The greater the variability in vegetation patterns, slope, aspect etc., the more complex it becomes to lay out the burn zone and create the burn plan. Care should be exercised as slope increases, because fire spreads faster uphill. When elevation varies within the burn unit, ignition must be planned in such a way as to start uphill and to proceed downhill. Ideally, burn zones should be laid out in such a fashion that most of the edges occur on ridges or in valleys rather than midslope. When constructing fire lines, it is important to construct them with the potential for erosion in mind. When fire lines must go up- or downslope, they should include measures to minimise erosion, such as waterbars and wing ditches.

Common firebreaks

As mentioned previously, pre-existing natural and human-made firebreaks should be considered first. Sometimes the mere change in vegetation can serve as a firebreak if the adjoining vegetation is less flammable than the pine woods (e.g. some types of hardwood litter, green pasture grasses, maintained turf etc.). When attempting to use vegetation breaks as control lines, it is essential to know the conditions under which the less-flammable vegetation will and will not burn. Sometimes vegetation will only serve as an effective control line during specific seasons or at specific moisture levels. Other good examples of pre-existing breaks are wetlands (when they are wet), open water, roads, trails and tilled fields. If natural breaks are not sufficient to stop fire spread on their own, they may still be usable by augmenting them by raking, blowing leaves or mowing.

When pre-existing firebreaks are not adequate to limit the fire to the desired area, fire lines need to be created. When placing new fire lines, it can be helpful to locate them along vegetation changes, fence lines or trails. If possible, it is a good idea to try to leave the root systems of existing vegetation in place to limit the potential for erosion. This can be done by mowing the fire line as short as possible or by using a wet line. A wet line may either be sprayed in a pump-and-roll fashion (where the all-terrain vehicle [ATV] or truck supplying the water remains mobile) or it can be created using a stationary hose lay. Stationary hose lays may use nozzles and personnel, or they can utilise sprinkler heads. When using wet lines, it is critical to remember that the control effectiveness of the wet line lasts only as long as the water applied. If ignited fuels continue to burn after the applied water dries out, the fire can cross the previous firebreak. Wet lines should be patrolled until the threat of ignition across the line has passed. Adding foam or wetting agents can extend the effectiveness of plain water and make wet lines more effective by making them last longer.

Mechanically built fire lines typically rely on removing all flammable material down to mineral soil. These can be made by hand with shovels and other hand tools or by some sort of implement (harrow, disc, plough, rototiller, drag) pulled behind an ATV, tractor or bulldozer. Mechanical fire lines should be built at least one and a half times wider than the expected flame lengths, or one and a half times wider than the height of the surrounding flammable shrubs. The width required for an adequate fire line may be reduced by mowing the shrubs adjacent to the fire line. Mowing may also help establish a blackline during ignition.

Equipment used to ignite and extinguish fires

The most common tool used to ignite prescribed burns in Southern pines is the drip torch. A drip torch is a metal canister with a tube and wick. The drip torch works by having fuel drip across the wick, the wick igniting the fuel and the burning fuel then dripping onto the ground, igniting flammable vegetation. The fuel inside the drip torch is typically three parts diesel fuel to one part petrol. The benefit of the drip torch is that the fuel, once dripped onto the vegetation, will burn for few seconds to light the vegetation, allowing the person using the drip torch to continue. One challenge of this process is the need for a person carrying the drip torch to walk to the vegetation they want to ignite. Ignition within the block itself can be difficult if the vegetation or the terrain make it difficult to traverse.

A second common ignition tool is the fusee. Fusees are essentially road flares that have been modified so they can be linked together. Fusees are used by touching the burning end to the vegetation intended to burn. One disadvantage of the fusee is that the person using it must stop and hold it near the vegetation until it ignites.

An adaptation of the fusee is the flare gun. Flare guns propel small pieces of fusees between 30 and 100 m. The flare gun uses 22-calibre blank industrial actuators to ignite and propel the flare. The distance travelled depends on the type of actuator used. Although significantly more expensive than a drip torch, flare guns can ignite areas where terrain or fuels restrict access by personnel.

Plastic ignition spheres are another type of ignition tool that is effective when terrain limits access. These spheres contain potassium permanganate and are injected with ethylene glycol. The potassium permanganate and the ethylene glycol mix to become exothermic (giving off heat). The amount of glycol added determines both the delay of ignition and the overall temperature achieved by the reaction. Typically, 20–30 s after injection, the reaction will become hot enough to ignite the plastic spheres and, if in contact with vegetation, the plastic ignites the vegetation. These plastic spheres can be launched from hand-held launchers, vehicle-mounted launchers or dropped from aircraft. Recently, some manufacturers have developed systems for dropping these spheres from drones. Aerial ignition can be especially important when burning large areas or when burning areas where terrain limits personnel from safely walking inside the unit.

Similar to the tools used to ignite the fire, tools used to control the fire range in complexity. Simple tools include cutting hand tools: Pulaski, fire rake and shovel. The Pulaski was designed by a wildland firefighter and consists of a two-bladed axe, with one blade in the normal direction and one blade turned off 90° to resemble a hoe. The Pulaski is good for cutting roots and shrubs and creating a fire line. The fire rake is essentially sickle teeth riveted or welded side by side to a piece of angle iron

and attached to a hoe handle. Fire rakes are especially useful in pine litter and grasses for making handlines. Fire shovels are similar to regular shovels, except that their edges are sharpened for cutting small shrubs.

In pine litter and grasses, the fire flap can be used as a smothering tool. The flap is essentially a rubber mud flap from a truck attached to a long rake handle. When used to suppress fire, the flap can be dragged or patted on top of the fire to smother the flames. It is only effective when flame lengths are short and the fuel is horizontal. Another important hand tool is the backpack pump. The backpack pump can be either collapsible or a hard-sided tank. Typically, the backpack pump is a 19-L tank attached to a trombone-style hand pump. The operator aims the pump at the fire and then pumps the water by hand to suppress the fire. Backpack pumps are especially useful when a small amount of water is needed and the terrain limits access by vehicle. Petrol-powered leaf blowers can be helpful in constructing or maintaining fire lines when leaf litter is the primary source of fuel.

ATVs can be used for both fire ignition and fire suppression. Typically, ATVs will carry a water tank and an electric pump to deliver water through the hose. In the past decade, utility all-terrain vehicles (UTVs), sometimes called a side-by-side ATV, have become popular. UTVs have a greater load-carrying capacity, so they can carry more water, and they are typically equipped with petrol-powered pumps. The amount of water either an ATV or a UTV can carry is dictated by the weight capacity of the vehicle. The range is likely to be 55 L for a small ATV to around 400 L for larger UTVs.

Prescribed burners and firefighters are an ingenious bunch. They have figured out myriad ways to deliver water to fires in the woods. Some have turned their farm tractors into fire engines by adding tanks onto the three-point hitch or onto trailers pulled by the farm tractor. Others have focused on converting four-wheel drive trucks into fire engines by adding tanks and pumps. There are as many designs as there are fire managers. The important things to consider when devising a water delivery system are: the weight capacity of the vehicle, which determines the volume of the water tank; the amount and pressure of the desired water stream, which determines the size of the pump needed; the terrain that will need to be traversed, which dictates the ground pressure and the different types of wheels or tracks; and the type of expected fire behaviour, which determines the amount of water needed at the nozzle to be effective.

Many fire managers rely on heavy equipment and mineral soil fire lines as their primary tools for suppressing fire in the Southern pines. The size and configuration of the piece of equipment will be dictated largely by the shrub layer through which the vehicle will have to travel. In open forests of grass and timber litter, a small farm tractor may be able to pull a fire plough or heavy harrow to build a fire line. In areas where shrubs are present but do not present a significant barrier, a small dozer or skidder equipped with a fire plough can be effective. In areas where shrubs dominate and grow large, larger dozers with a plough attached will likely be necessary.

People-training needs and opportunities, cultural knowledge

Prescribed burners in many of the US states have joined together forming prescribed fire councils (Plate 6). These councils promote prescribed fire, address issues that restrict its use and enable members to share lessons learned. In 2009, the individual prescribed fire councils banded together to form the Coalition of Prescribed Fire Councils (Coalition of Prescribed Fire Councils 2018). The Coalition periodically surveys prescribed burners. One of the survey questions asked is, 'What prevents you from getting more burning done?'. Consistently, one of the top three answers is sufficient personnel and equipment (Coalition of Prescribed Fire Councils 2018). This perennial need for personnel and equipment has created an environment of sharing within the region (Pyne 2016). Agencies regularly establish cooperative agreements or memoranda of understanding that enable them to

share personnel and equipment. Recently, private landowners have formally followed suit by establishing prescribed burn associations.

Prescribed burn associations are essentially cooperatives in which private landowners agree to help one another apply fire across the entirety of their lands (NC State 2020). Landowners in five states in the Southeast (Oklahoma, Texas, Mississippi, North Carolina and Florida) have banded together to create prescribed burn associations. The United States Fish and Wildlife Service (USFWS) recognises both how vital prescribed burning is to maintaining wildlife habitat and how the lack of personnel has limited the amount of burning on the landscape. The USFWS has sought to overcome the barrier by providing grant funding through the states to hire crews to assist with prescribed burning (USFWS 2020).

Silviculture is defined as 'the art and science of controlling the establishment, growth, composition, health, and quality of forests and woodlands' (Smith *et al.* 1997). Similarly, prescribed burning is both art and science. The science aspect comes from classroom-style training; the art portion of the equation is typically learned through doing. Mentorship, either formal or informal, is critical to learning the art of prescribed burning. The balance between art and training needed to be a good prescribed burner depends on the availability of good mentors and the amount of time available to burn with those same mentors. As access to good mentors or the time spent burning with those mentors decreases, the importance of good classroom training increases. Classroom training on prescribed fire and fire management is available through state and federal forestry agencies and through land grant universities.

One of the benefits of joining a prescribed fire council or a prescribed burn association is the increased access to training (Miller 1998). The amount of training required to legally and successfully apply prescribed fire will vary by state and by the decision of the burner to seek the protection of their state's certified burner program. Plate 6c shows the states having certified burner programs.

In many states, being a certified burner provides the burner with a different level of liability protection than a non-certified burner, with Plate 6d showing the degree of liability protection provided (Coalition of Prescribed Fire Councils 2018). Each of the states hosting a certified burner program dictates the training needed to be certified. Typically, the training includes sections on fuels, fire behaviour, smoke management, ignition techniques and fire control or suppression.

Because the art of burning is learned through hands-on experience, the culture of fire is critically important. In his seminal work Fire in America, Steve Pyne (1982) referenced a section he titled Our Pappies Burned the Woods: A Fire History of the South. Pyne (1982) emphasised that it was the culture of prescribed burning that kept fire in play in the Southeast. There may have been some low ebbs in the fire culture of the Southeast when state and federal agencies tried to supress it, but it was never completely extinguished. That culture resurging as science once again supports the continued use of fire.

Fire behaviour

The ideal fire for Southern pines is a low-intensity, rapidly moving surface fire. Historically, surface fires were easy to maintain because the fires were so frequent that there was only a shallow layer of litter and duff, and smouldering ground fires were unlikely. Frequent fires also kept shrubs and hardwood trees from developing into an established mid-storey, and these fires pruned the lower branches of overstorey pines. The absence of mid-storey fuels and lower branches meant that fires were seldom able to climb into the canopy of existing mature pines. As inter-fire intervals increase, the depth of the litter or duff layer becomes greater and ladder fuels become more abundant (Wade et al. 2006). This increases the probability of both ground fires that threaten the roots of overstorey trees and crown fires that risk mortality of overstorey trees through heightened severity (Varner et al. 2016).

Will fire continue?

With or without prescribed fire, pyric ignition will continue in the Southeastern US (Wade et al. 2006). All fuel models existing beneath the Southern pines both require and promote burning (Oswalt et al. 2012). As the common saying goes in the South, 'it's not if it burns, it's when'. Aside from natural ignitions, the future of prescribed fire in the Southeast, at least in the near term, looks good. Legal protections implemented by the states limiting liability have increased the safety of individuals willing to place prescribed burns in their name and have allowed these same people to run more robust successful programs (Wade et al. 2006).

In addition to the legal protection, specifically in the Southeast, prescribed burning has never seen a greater awareness and acceptance from the general public (Coalition of Prescribed Fire Councils 2018). Fire councils are becoming more pervasive throughout the region and their messaging is becoming increasingly savvy. High-profile wildfires are routinely front page news items helping reinforce and showcase the danger of avoiding prescribed fire. Public awareness in the region is beginning to link the pretreatment of fuels using prescribed fire with reductions in the risk and severity of the inevitable natural ignitions.

What are future issues?

If the near-term future for prescribed fire in the Southeast is looking better, the long-term view is much more difficult to predict. The uncertain effects of climate change are playing havoc on fire planning and the implementation of those plans from year to year. Because a successful prescribed burning program is in equal parts planning and implementation, the difficulty of predicting those effects through time is beginning to have negative effects on burn programs throughout the Southeast.

The first and most immediate effect of climate change on prescribed fire in the Southeast is the loss of 'normal'. This loss of an expected normal condition can have large negative effects on the planning of a burn program. For example, in the

Southeast, rain and drought have historically been forecastable conditions, with the moisture from tropical rains transitioning into winter cold fronts that keep the ground moist and allow for cooler, less-impactful winter fires. This plannable window of lower-severity fires normally allows for entry-level burning in areas that have not seen recent fire.

These first fires coupled with high soil and fuel moisture allow lower-intensity burns to occur, removing understorey fuels while limiting overstorey mortality. Historically, these wet winter months would transition into a dry, droughty spring that would introduce the lightning season and the primary wildfire risk of the year. By late spring or early summer, the frequent thunderstorms would begin producing rainfall, and the moisture of the fire environment would begin to increase, limiting the wildfires and opening the window to more frequent prescribed fire.

As normal becomes less and less predictable, the tried and true methods of applying fire in the Southeast become harder to predict and manage. This difficulty in planning can lead to lost opportunities for applying fire to the landscape and areas with longer rotations between fire applications. Once routine frequency becomes lost in Southern fuels, burns become more difficult and the severity risk higher. This can often cause a downward spiral of fire in the area, making burning more difficult and the chance to miss future fire opportunities greater.

The second impact of climate change is the long-term shift in burning windows and required weather–fuel conditions that largely affect the implementation aspect of a burn program. This change is more subtle in Southern fuels because the frequency of fire is the most important aspect of a successful burn program. Each management unit within a burn program has a desirable range of weather and moisture parameters that will allow for the best possible burn from an ecological perspective, a resource damage perspective and a safety perspective. Long-unburned fuels need high moisture and cooler weather to limit ecosystem damage. Well-burned fuels may need higher winds or lower humidities to carry the fire across the extent of the area.

In all cases, a general trend of weather getting hotter and drier limits the total amount of productive burning days in the Southeast. The current understanding of putting off a day of burning to wait for a future day with better conditions may no longer be a long-term winning strategy. As those put-off days stack up, blocks that miss their burning rotation become more and more common. With fire frequency beginning to slip, implementing the burn program becomes incrementally more difficult through time. The idea of chasing the perfect ideal may jeopardise achieving 'good enough'.

Adjusting to a shorter burn season, or a season with fewer total burnable days, will demand either a reduction in acres burned or an increase in average acres burned per fire. In a region where the total of yearly burned acres comes nowhere near the acres needed for ecological maintenance, the only option for success in the future will be larger fires. If crews and equipment are not increased in lockstep with this option, individual fires will need to have a greater acceptance of severity and potential mortality of overstorey, as more will need to be done with less.

What will stop the use of fire?

The largest immediate risk to the use of fire in the Southeast is tied to the increasing urbanisation of rural areas. Most states in the South are seeing massive increases in immigration year to year. These people all require new housing, work locations and travel routes. New subdivisions, road networks, schools, retirement homes and hospitals are being built at a breakneck pace. All of this infrastructure poses smoke management hazards in a fire environment with an already limited smoke shed and introduces difficulty into the smoke management aspect of a prescribed burn operation.

Smoke management is the most difficult aspect of most burn programs, and the issue most likely to incur liability and cause complaints. There are defined health issues linked to smoke inhalation, and the public awareness has a limited tolerance for prolonged impacts. Unfortunately, for some burn managers, smoke management is learned through experience of what does not work. Figure 7.2 shows what is possible with good smoke management. Computer simulations and smoke mapping applications are becoming increasingly more reliable and predictive. However, the fire environment is a difficult thing to model and most burn managers will err on the side of caution where smoke impacts are concerned. This can lead to a loss of frequency of fire and the issues mentioned previously.

A prescribed fire program is only as successful as its last burn and, with poor planning, a well-run program can be undone by routinely mismanaged smoke. The increasing smoke hazards and limited smoke sheds are creating a fire environment where both the opportunity for and severity of accidents are becoming greater. In addition to individual

programs, from a public perspective, all prescribed fire is linked regardless of agency or private individual. When one entity mismanages its smoke and causes an issue, all fire programs regionally will suffer a loss of public support and a set back in their ability to apply fire to the landscape. Again, this will lead to loss of fire frequency and an increasing difficulty applying fire and managing the smoke it creates. This recursive circle could, by feeding upon itself, limit or even stop fire in the long term.

Will fire continue to be used?

Fire will continue to be used in the Southeast going forward because the wildfire risk under the Southern pines will not reduce by itself and prescribed fire, at least for now, is seen publicly as the best way to limit the impacts. That is not to say there will not be difficulty.

Fire managers must mitigate new and complex smoke environments while continuing to educate the public on the need to produce that smoke. The

Figure 7.2: Prescribed burn in the urban interface showing good smoke management. The community is a retirement community, with residents viewing the burn from their golf carts. Photograph courtesy of Steven R. Miller.

idea that a burn program as a whole is more important than any single burn operation may cause fire to be applied in a different manner or alter day-to-day decision making. Finally, burn managers need to realise that fire application across the entire region is represented by their individual burn efforts and when one entity makes a poor decision, all programs suffer from the collective loss of public support (Pyne 2016).

Fire managers will need to prepare for a loss of normal and the effects that will have on long-term planning. Realising that old routines for fire application throughout the year may not be viable any longer and adjusting desired outcomes may be necessary into the future. Because frequency is the most important aspect of fire application in the Southeast, these changing conditions will cause the seasonality of fire to matter less and less as the ability to keep fire on the landscape becomes more difficult to manage.

Fire managers will be obligated to remain flexible as general weather patterns become hotter and drier through time. Planning for limited burn windows and a reduced number of acceptable burn days per year will become an integral part of success. The future will not have as much opportunity to apply fire on the landscape from permanently altering weather conditions.

The burn programs under Southern pines of the future will need to be much more tolerant of increased severity and possible resource damage. Putting off a burn today to limit potential severity may just incur more severity down the road when the loss of frequency becomes unavoidable. Waiting for the perfect day may no longer be a viable option. Successful burn programs will need to accept greater risk and damage to resources now to ensure fire occurs into the future at the amount required by the ecosystem.

Given all this uncertainty, there are two things that are not uncertain: (1) in some manner, fire will continue to occur under the pines of the Southeast; and (2) the burn managers of the future will need to be flexible, creative and willing to manage risk in order to successfully meet these new challenges.

References

Abrahamson I (2020) *Fire Effects Information System (FEIS)*. US Department of Agriculture, Forest Service, Fort Collins, <https://www.feis-crs.org/feis/>.

Anderson HE (1982) 'Aids to determining fuel models for estimating fire behavior'. General Technical Report INT-GTR-122, US Department of Agriculture, Forest Service, Intermountain Forest and Range Experimental Station, Boise.

Coalition of Prescribed Fire Councils (2018) *2018 National Prescribed Fire Use Survey Report*. Coalition of Prescribed Fire Councils, Newton, <https://docs.google.com/a/prescribedfire.net/viewer?a=v&pid=sites&srcid=cHJl c2NyaWJlGZpcmUubmV0fGNvYWxpdGlvbi1vZi1wcm VzY3JpYmVkLWZpcmUtY291bmNpbHN8Z3g6NTEzZ DhlMGRhNDU1ZmY2>.

Coalition of Prescribed Fire Councils (2019) *2019 Membership Summary*. Coalition of Prescribed Fire Councils, Newton, <https://drive.google.com/file/d/12T-6lhwp2rmPDFMa UzZQRGEuZi5alTH5/view>.

Folkerts GW (1982) The Gulf Coast pitcher plant bogs. *American Scientist* **70**, 260–267.

Frost CC (2006) History and future of the longleaf pine ecosystem. In *Longleaf Pine Ecosystems: Ecology, Management, and Restoration*. (Eds J Shibu, E Jokela and D Miller) pp. 9–42. Springer-Verlag, New York.

Hardin ED (2010) Institutional history of prescribed fire in the Florida Division of Forestry: lessons from the past, directions for the future. In *Proceedings of the 24th Tall Timbers Fire Ecology Conference: The Future of Fire: Public Awareness, Health, and Safety*. (Eds KM Robertson, KEM Galley and RE Masters) pp. 35–42. Tall Timbers Research Station, Tallahassee.

Johnson AS, Hale PE (2002) The historical foundations of prescribed burning for wildlife: a southeastern perspective, General Technical Report NE-288. In *Proceedings of The Role of Fire for Nongame Wildlife Management and Community Restoration: Traditional Uses and New Directions*. (Eds WM Ford, KR Russell and CE Moorman) pp. 11–23. US Department of Agriculture, Forest Service, Northeastern Research Station, Newton Square.

Miller SR (1998) Florida's regional fire councils: tools for fire management. In *Proceedings of the 20th Tall Timbers Fire Ecology Conference*. 7–10 May 1996, Boise. (Eds TL Pruden and LA Brennan) pp. 41–43. Tall Timbers Research Station, Tallahassee.

NC State (2020) *Prescribed Burn Associations*. North Carolina State University, College of Natural Resources, Raleigh, <https://research.cnr.ncsu.edu/blogs/southeast-fire-update/prescribed-burn-associations/>.

Oswalt CM, Cooper JA, Brockway DG, Brooks HW, Walker JL, Connor KF, Oswalt SN, Conner RC (2012) 'History and current condition of longleaf pine in the Southern United States'. General Technical Report SRS–166, US Department of Agriculture, Forest Service, Southern Research Station, Asheville.

Pyne SJ (1982) Our pappies burned the woods: a fire history of the south. In *Fire in America: A Cultural History of Wildland and Rural Fire*. (Ed SJ Pyne) pp. 143–160. Princeton University Press, Princeton.

Pyne S (2016) *Florida: A Fire Survey*. University of Arizona Press, Tucson.

Ripley R, Printiss D (2005) 'Management plan for flatwoods salamander populations on national forests in Florida – final report to Florida Fish and Wildlife Conservation Commission'. The Nature Conservancy, Northwest Florida Program, Bristol.

Smith DM, Larson BC, Kelty MJ, Ashton PMS (1997) *The Practice of Silviculture: Applied Ecology*. 9th edn. Wiley and Sons, Hoboken.

Stoddard HL (1931) *The Bobwhite Quail: Its Habits, Preservation and Increase*. Scribner's, New York.

US Fish and Wildlife Service (2020) *Partners*. United States Fish and Wildlife Service, Washington, DC, <https://www.fws.gov/partners/>.

Van Lear DH, Harlow RF (2002) Fire in the eastern United States: influence on wildlife habitat, General Technical Report NE-288. In *Proceedings of The Role of Fire for Non-game Wildlife Management and Community Restoration: Traditional Uses and New Directions*. (Eds WM Ford, KR Russell and CE Moorman) pp. 2–10. US Department of Agriculture, Forest Service, Northeastern Research Station, Newton Square.

Varner JM, Kreye JK, Hiers JK, O'Brien JJ (2016) Recent advances in understanding duff consumption and post-fire longleaf pine mortality, General Technical Report SRS-GTR-212. In *Proceedings of the 18th Biennial Southern Silvicultural Research Conference*. 2–5 March 2015, Knoxville. (Eds CJ Schweitzer, WK Clatterbuck and CM Oswalt) pp. 335–338. US Department of Agriculture, Forest Service, Southern Research Station, Asheville.

Wade D, Miller S, Stowe J, Brenner J (2006) Rx fire laws: tools to protect fire: the 'ecological imperative'? General Technical Report NRS-P-1. In *Proceedings of the Fire in Eastern Oak Forests: Delivering Science to Land Managers Conference*. 15–17 November 2005, Columbus. (Ed. MB Dickinson) pp. 233–262. US Department of Agriculture, Forest Service, Northeastern Research Station, Newton Square.

Waldrop TA, Goodrick SL (2012) 'Introduction to prescribed fires in Southern ecosystems, Science Update SRS-054'. US Department of Agriculture, Forest Service, Southern Research Station, Asheville.

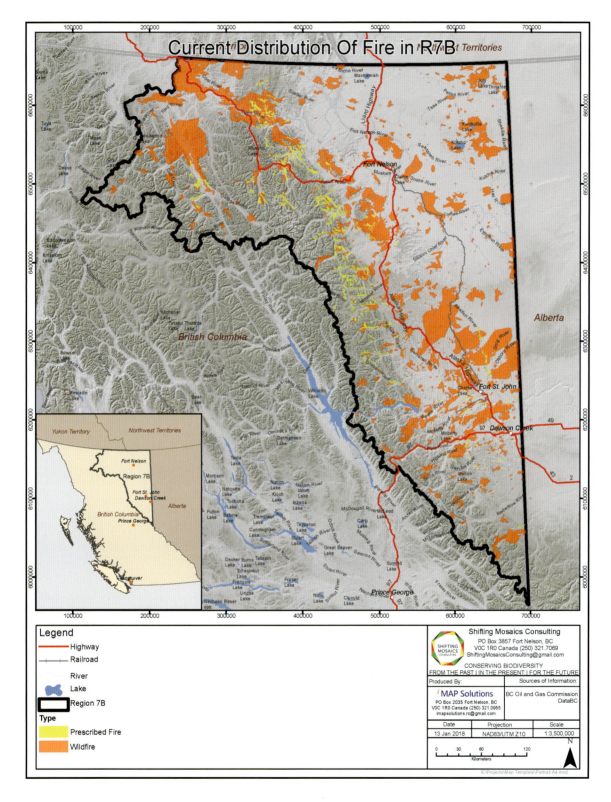

Plate 1: Current distribution of fire across the landscape of Region 7B as analysed by Shifting Mosaics Consulting in 2018 (Leverkus 2015; Leverkus *et al.* 2017, 2018a, 2018b, 2018c).

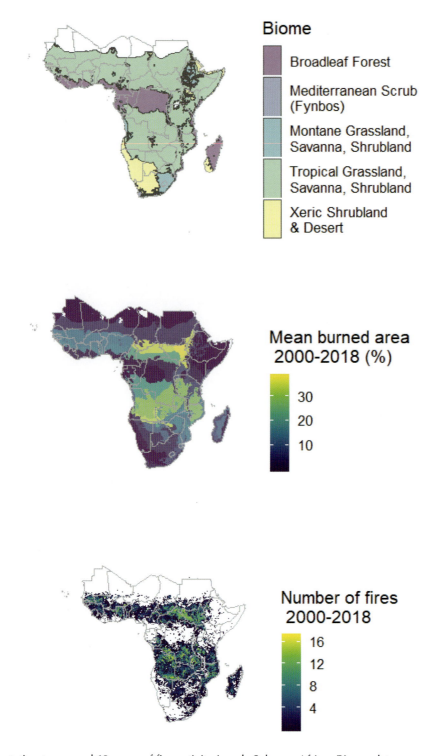

Plate 2: Broad vegetation types and 19 years of fire activity in sub-Saharan Africa. Biome data are modified World Wildlife Foundation Terrestrial Ecoregions from The Nature Conservancy's Geospatial Conservation Atlas (https://geospatial.tnc.org). Fire data are from the moderate-resolution imaging spectroradiometer (MODIS) burned area product MCD64A1.

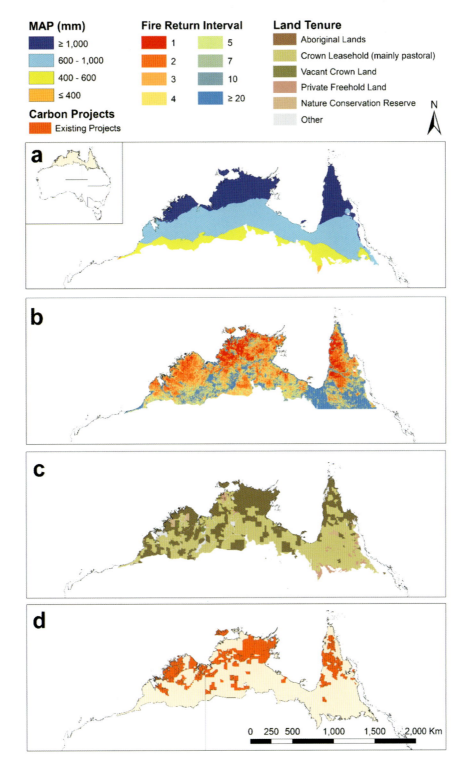

Plate 3: The (a) extent (inset) and mean annual precipitation (MAP) of tropical savannas in northern Australia, (b) fire return interval, in years, for 2000–19 for the area covered by North Australian Fire Information (NAFI) fire mapping, (c) current dominant land tenure (Aboriginal lands include Aboriginal freehold, leasehold, reserves and exclusive possession native title) and (d) existing carbon credit projects. Geospatial data sourced from (a) Fick and Hijmans (2017), (b) NAFI (https://firenorth.org.au/nafi3/), (c) Geoscience Australia (2004) and (d) the Clean Energy Regulator (2019).

Prehistoric

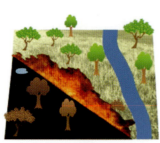

Pre-human
- Lightning ignition only
- Late dry season
- High intensity

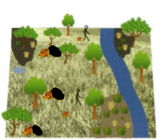

Traditional Aboriginal fire use
- High spatial and temporal heterogeneity
- Ignition by hand
- Low intensity

Post-European Settlement
- Some prescribed burning
- Unmanaged lands burned by large, high intensity wildfires

Right Way Fire/Cultural Burning
- Increasing spatial and temporal heterogeneity
- Ground and aerial ignition
- Increasing amount of low intensity, early dry season

Present

Plate 4: The evolution of fire regimes in the tropical savannas of Australia and their dominant characteristics.

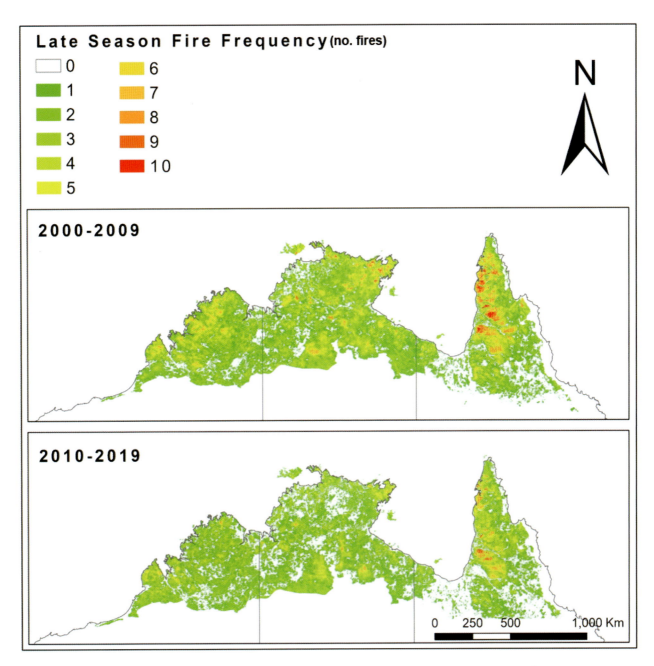

Plate 5: Frequency of late season fires across the northern tropical savanna from 2000 to 2009 and from 2010 to 2019, decades that roughly correspond to the transition of management from unmanaged to active fire management, including by Aboriginal Traditional Owners. Geospatial data sourced from North Australia and Rangelands Fire Information (https://firenorth.org.au/nafi3/).

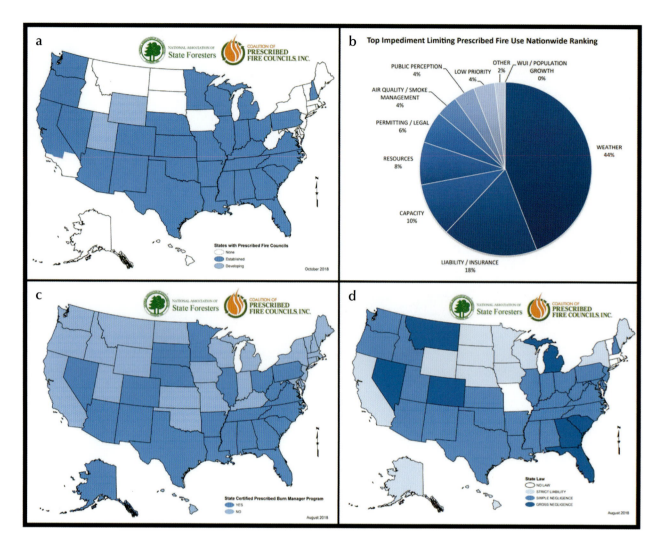

Plate 6: (a) Map showing states with prescribed fire councils. (b) Chart showing results from the Coalition of Prescribed Fire Councils survey regarding impediments to prescribed burning. (c) Map showing states with certified burner programs. (d) Map showing the level of liability protection provided for prescribed burners. Images courtesy of the Coalition of Prescribed Fire Councils, Inc.

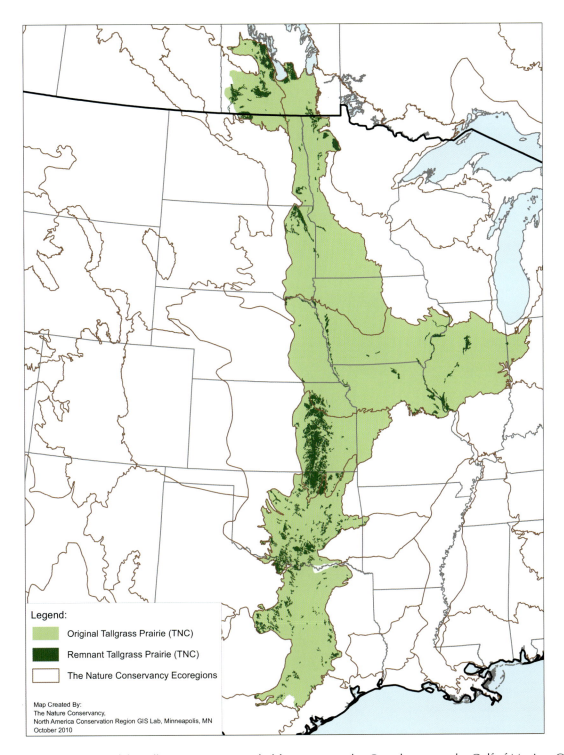

Plate 7: The historic extent of the tallgrass prairie extended from present day Canada to near the Gulf of Mexico. Only approximately 4% of the tallgrass remains as prairie due to land conversion, primarily to farming, woodland and development. The largest contiguous tallgrass expanse remaining in North America is the Flint Hills region of Kansas and Oklahoma, located in the central US. Map created by The Nature Conservancy (TNC), North America Conservation Region, GIS Laboratory, Minneapolis, MN, October 2010.

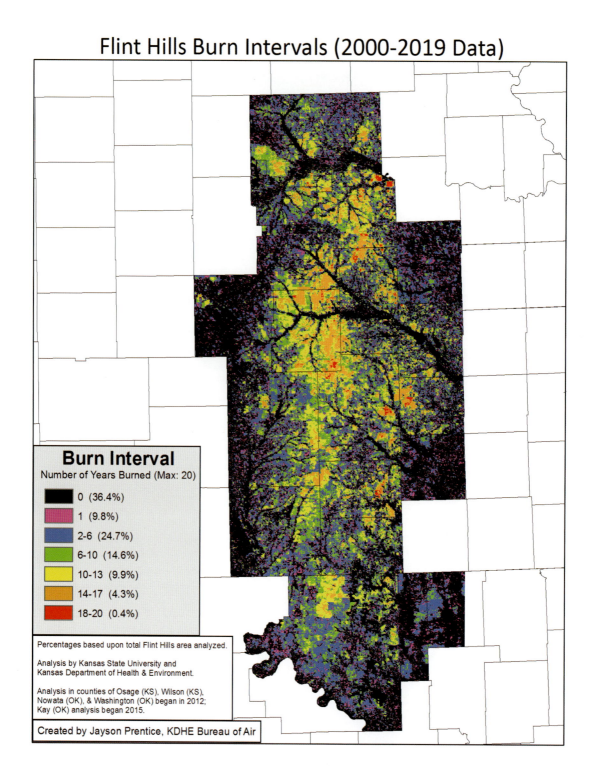

Flint Hills Burn Intervals (2000-2019 Data)

Burn Interval
Number of Years Burned (Max: 20)

- ■ 0 (36.4%)
- ■ 1 (9.8%)
- ■ 2-6 (24.7%)
- ■ 6-10 (14.6%)
- ■ 10-13 (9.9%)
- ■ 14-17 (4.3%)
- ■ 18-20 (0.4%)

Percentages based upon total Flint Hills area analyzed.

Analysis by Kansas State University and
Kansas Department of Health & Environment.

Analysis in counties of Osage (KS), Wilson (KS),
Nowata (OK), & Washington (OK) began in 2012;
Kay (OK) analysis began 2015.

Created by Jayson Prentice, KDHE Bureau of Air

Plate 8: High-fire frequency is a characteristic of the Flint Hills. Approximately 40% of rangelands burned at least once in 20 years, and approximately 4.5% burned 14–20 times in 20 years. The absence of fire results in conversion to woodlands in approximately 40 years. Image created by Jayson Prentice, Kansas Department of Health and Environment Bureau of Air.

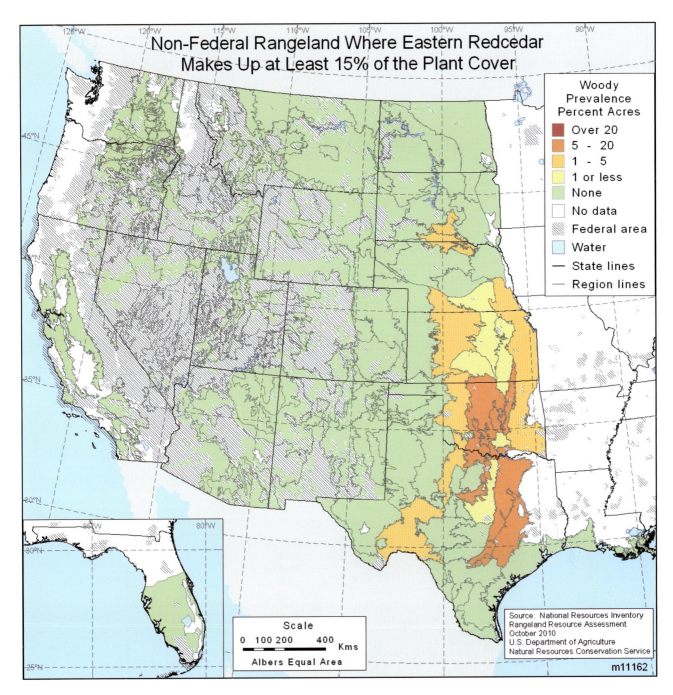

Plate 9: Eastern red cedar is rapidly converting rangeland to woodland in many parts of the remaining tallgrass prairie. Prescribed burning is the only feasible way to stop the conversion process and maintain open grasslands. Image courtesy of Patrick E. Flanagan, National Resources Inventory National Statistician.

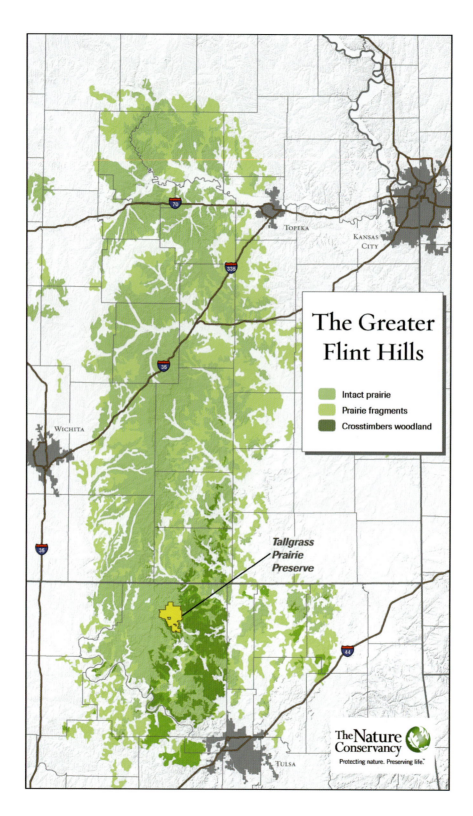

Plate 10: Map of the Greater Flint Hills region of eastern Kansas and north-eastern Oklahoma showing the dominant native vegetation associations. Note the location of the Tallgrass Prairie Preserve. Image courtesy of Tony Brown.

Aerial Photograph - 2015 NAIP Image
Tallgrass Prairie Preserve, Osage County, OK

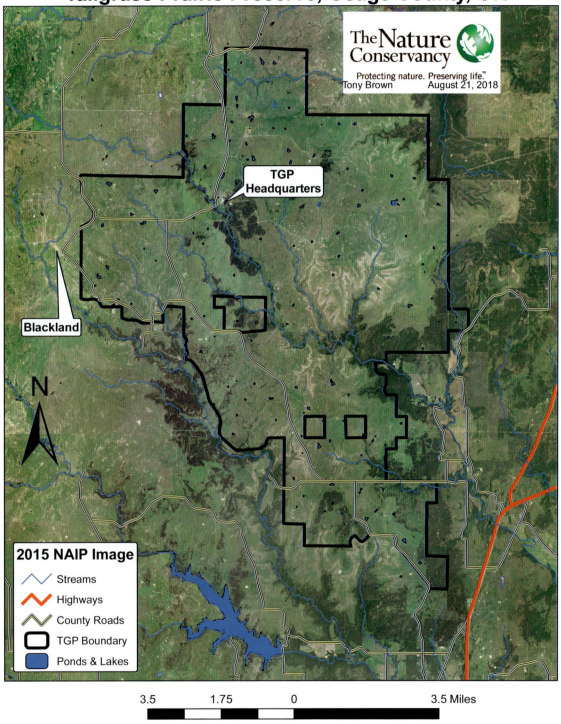

Plate 11: Aerial photograph of the Tallgrass Prairie Preserve (TGP). Lightly coloured areas are tallgrass prairie vegetation; darkly coloured areas are cross-timbers woodlands vegetation. Image courtesy of Tony Brown. NAIP, National Agriculture Imagery Program of the U.S. Department of Agriculture, Farm Service Agency.

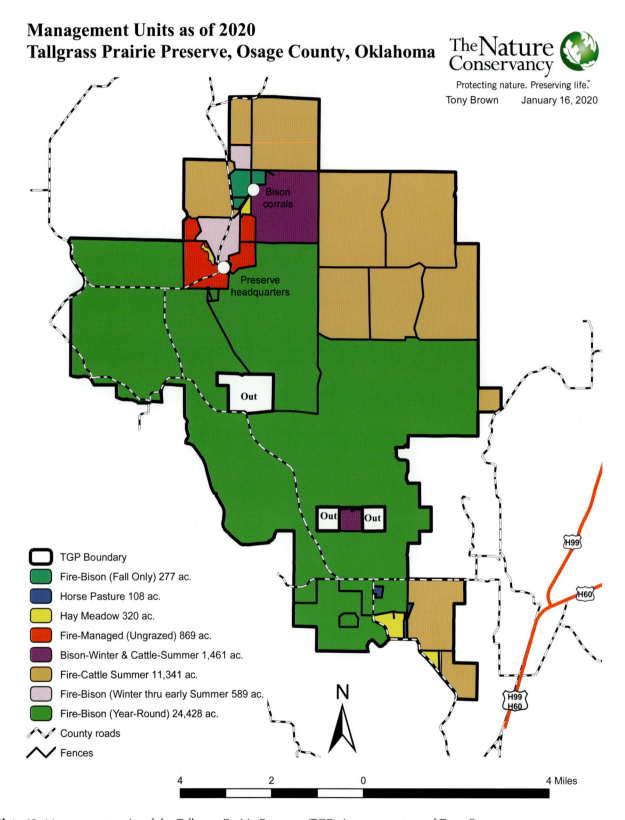

Management Units as of 2020
Tallgrass Prairie Preserve, Osage County, Oklahoma

The Nature Conservancy

Protecting nature. Preserving life.™

Tony Brown   January 16, 2020

Bison corrals

Preserve headquarters

Out

Out   Out

H99

H60

Legend:
- ☐ TGP Boundary
- ■ Fire-Bison (Fall Only) 277 ac.
- ■ Horse Pasture 108 ac.
- ■ Hay Meadow 320 ac.
- ■ Fire-Managed (Ungrazed) 869 ac.
- ■ Bison-Winter & Cattle-Summer 1,461 ac.
- ■ Fire-Cattle Summer 11,341 ac.
- ■ Fire-Bison (Winter thru early Summer 589 ac.
- ■ Fire-Bison (Year-Round) 24,428 ac.
- ⋀ County roads
- ⋀ Fences

N

4   2   0   4 Miles

H99
H60

Plate 12: Management units of the Tallgrass Prairie Preserve (TGP). Image courtesy of Tony Brown.

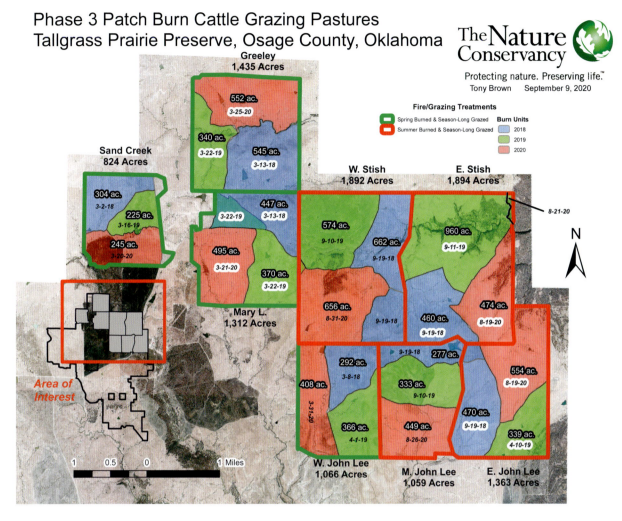

Plate 13: Patch burn cattle grazing research treatments at the Tallgrass Prairie Preserve. Image courtesy of Tony Brown.

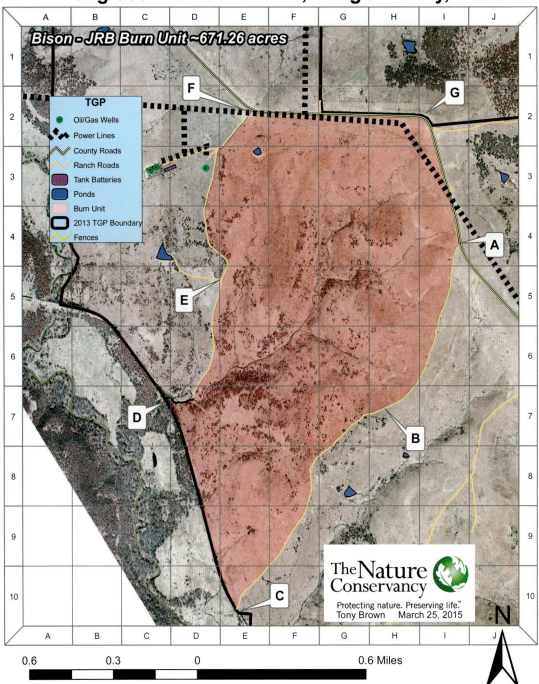

Plate 14: Representative burn unit map carried in the field for every prescribed burn at the Tallgrass Prairie Preserve (TGP). Points labelled A–G are intended to assist in reporting crew locations during radio communications. The burn crew is often separated into two squads to conduct prescribed burns. The red-shaded area is the planned burn unit area. Image courtesy of Tony Brown.

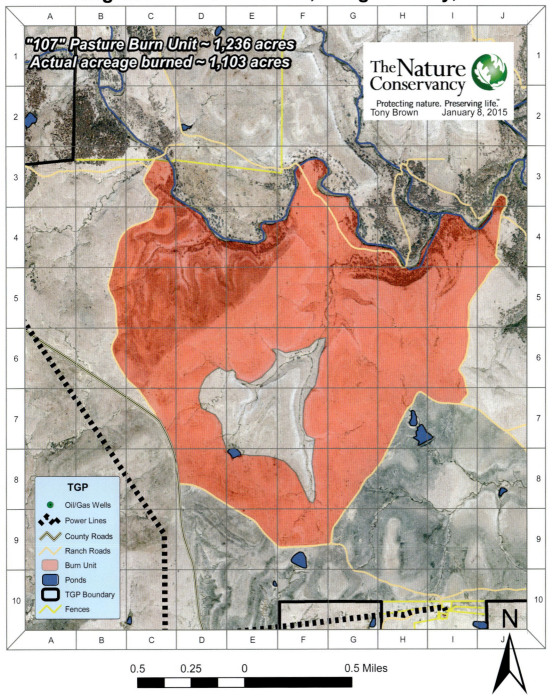

Plate 15: Prescribed burn unit map for 16 September 2014, Tallgrass Prairie Preserve (TGP). The unit burned overnight as relative humidity increased and winds died down. Note the unburned portion within the unit. Image courtesy of Tony Brown.

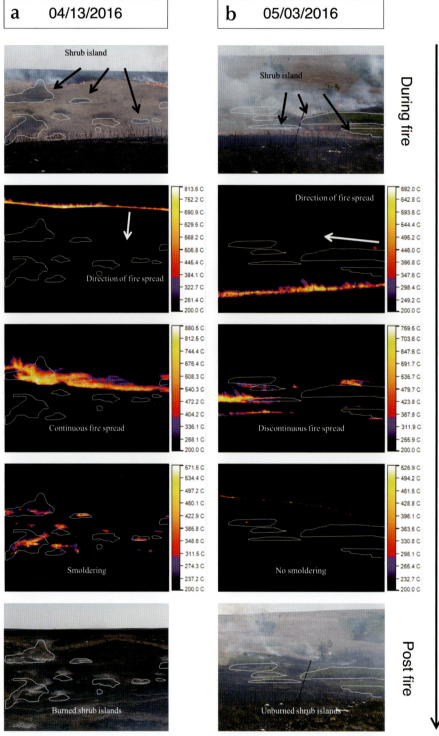

Plate 16: Thermal imaging captured fine-scale spatial fire behaviour across two landscapes burned under dry conditions (a) and moist (b) conditions in long-term watersheds on the Konza Prairie Long-term Ecological Research Station (Kansas, USA). When fuels were dry, fire burned continuously through shrub islands and smouldered for more than 30 min after the flaming front passed. When fuels were moist, fire burned discontinuously and did not burn through shrub islands, leaving shrub islands relatively untouched by fire. Photograph courtesy of Christine Bielski.

8

The West *wasn't* burning …

Douglas Cram

Fire that's closest kept, burns most of all –
William Shakespeare

When the idea for this western US chapter was first brainstormed, the placeholder title was *The West is Burning*. It was the quick and obvious choice considering the stream of headlines flowing from the West.[1] US headlines from fires like the 2018 Camp Fire (Paradise, CA), the 2017 Tubbs Fire (Santa Rosa, CA) or the 2018 Thomas Fire (just north of Los Angeles, CA) seemed to be ever-present (and now, more recently, the firestorm that has engulfed the West Coast during the summer of 2020). Gone are the days of wildfire news being restricted to some narrow 'fire season', be it the spring (e.g. southwest) or later summer (north-west). Moreover, gone are the days of being able to remember the year, and sometimes even the name, of all the other fires that used to be significant, but now seem minor in comparison, such as the 2003 Aspen Fire in Arizona, the 2006 Day Fire in California and the 2012 High Park Fire in Colorado. Today, the only way to keep track of the all the wildfires in the West is to search for a list on the Internet, and even that information becomes dated with each passing month without checking back in to learn of new record-setting fires.

Given this sometimes-unpleasant reality, that we live in a fire region, continent and world, it has essentially become cliché to say, 'The West is burning'. However, from the perspective of prescribed burners, this cliché is inaccurate and misplaced. For prescribed fire practitioners, the West is *not* 'burning'! It may be on fire, but it is not as a result of 'burning'. Moreover, if the West had been burning[2] for the past 120 years, it would not be in nearly the same predicament it finds itself today (i.e. in a fire deficit or hole that arguably can only be remedied by more fire, or other types of fuel reduction techniques). And the hole is deep, maybe even too deep to emerge from and expect landscapes to function or look like they did over 200 years ago. For example, research indicated California historically burned between 1.6 million and 4.5 million hectares each year before European settlement (*c.* 1800; Stephens *et al.* 2007). Clearly, this amount of fire is not realistic from a combined prescribed, managed and wildfire perspective;

there are simply too many people and competing values, even for a relatively sparsely populated West.

Ironically, the roots of not burning began in the West with the 1910 'Big Burn'. Unfortunately, this event (in northern Idaho, western Montana and eastern Washington) was not a 1.2-million hectare prescribed fire, but rather a wildfire that set the West not only on a strict course of fire suppression for the next 50 years, but also fire exclusion, a doctrine that was entirely wrongheaded, not just sometimes wrong. That is to say, sometimes wildfires, or parts of wildfires, need to be suppressed because of values at risk and pending weather conditions (e.g. sustained winds >32 kph). However, at other times, allowing wildfires to burn to achieve a host of management objectives is biologically defensible and even socially acceptable, within ordinary limits. But fire exclusion was never a good policy idea. And, in fact, it was only a matter of time before the 'truth' came billowing to the surface regarding the essential role fire played in the environment. Fire exclusion is characterised as the (unofficial) complementary policy to fire suppression that acted to exclude using fire as a tool for land management purposes (i.e. prescribed fire). Fortunately, the golden days of fire exclusion in the West, the general period between the Big Burn and the 1960s and 1970s, have passed.

In a thought exercise (c. 1910), we can see and argue that if A (fire suppression) is 'good', then B (fire exclusion) must also be 'good', or at least enforced. And therein lays the chink in the armour of fire suppression: burners and the idea of burning would not go away; the request to use fire was ecologically germane. Specifically, early fire ecologists recognised the role fire played in ecosystems, and eventually federal agency managers and practitioners in the 1960s and 1970s began pursuing burning options with more vigour; the drip torch could not be kept in the bag. In a bit of insight that speaks to the consternation of the times, Raymond Conarro (1942) wrote about the back-and-forth arguments between the fire exclusionist and the controlled burner in his *Journal of Forestry* article

where he introduced the term 'prescribed burning'. Of note, both factions were south-eastern foresters/ecologists concerned with the growth, reproduction and sustainability of the Southern pines but, again, the burners would not relinquish and put out their torches. Interestingly enough, this 'controversial' back and forth came on the heels of the 1935 US Forest Service 10 a.m. fire suppression policy (i.e. a so-called policy of the agency that decreed wildfires should be suppressed by 10 a.m. the day following their initial report). In other words, while one school of thought was pursuing full suppression, the antithesis was taking shape and slowly starting to build momentum.

But there was another force at work, at least in the south-west, at the turn of the 19th century that may have subconsciously supported the idea of fire suppression in the minds of a casual observer and that was a lack of surface fire. The primary driver behind this phenomenon was the introduction of large numbers of livestock from Mexico, tens of thousands of head of cows, as well as large numbers of horses and sheep (Love 1916). As physicists say, for every action there is an equal and opposite reaction; in this case, the opposite reaction was the reduction of fine fuels that significantly slowed or eliminated spreading surface fire. Of course, this makes perfect sense to any burner. When burners are looking at a site for burn potential, the first thing they look at is fine fuel, not necessarily canopy fuels from standing trees. Thanks to the excellent fire ecology work of dendrochronologists, tree rings and fire scars provide a picture of the fire regimes across the south-west to include this time period (Figure 8.1). In studying this figure, we see the cessation of frequent fire around 1900 that may have presented a picture that conflated an absence of fire with forest health. Regardless, this was the beginning of the fire suppression and exclusion period.

Excluding *'laissez-faire* folk burning', as Stephen Pyne coined it (Melvin 2018), or 'prescribed burning', as Raymond Conarro (1942) called it, had a stifling and long-lasting effect that we still see and feel today. For example, who has the keys to the drip torch shed: the state, the landowner or both? Turning around

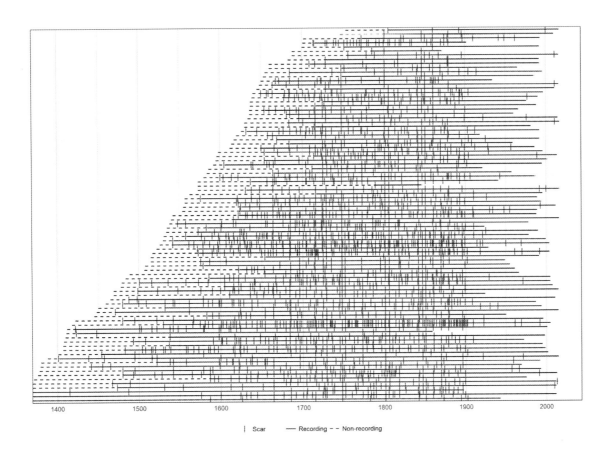

1400	1500	1600	1700	1800	1900	2000

| Scar   — Recording - - Non-recording

Figure 8.1: Fire history for major fires in the Jemez Mountains, New Mexico dating back to 1400. Horizontal lines are the sampled time spans for individual trees and vertical black tick marks are fire dates recorded on those trees. Notice the frequency of fires before 1900 and the abrupt cessation of fires after 1900. Also, consider and appreciate the fire behaviour that scarred individual trees multiple times but did not kill the tree (i.e. an indication of surface fire). Fire history provided by Ellis Margolis from the United States Geological Survey.

this doctrine of fire exclusion that started 110 years ago with the Big Burn continues to be a slow process. However, in the West, the drip torches have been lit and there is plenty of fuel to burn.

The West *is* burning ... a little

Indeed, western torches have been lit, and the question is no longer about whether prescribed fire is a viable tool, but rather how it can be expanded. What are the specific objectives? When is the best time of year? How can technology be used? And, in some states, who should be burning and what training, if any, is appropriate? For example, Lenya Quinn-Davidson, from the University of California Cooperative Extension, said in 2020, '*In trying to*

increase the pace and scale of prescribed fire, we're actually fighting some really deep cultural attitudes around who gets to use it and where it belongs in society' (Weil 2020). Regardless of the answer to these questions, as burn practitioners look across the western landscape, the magnitude of the challenge is immense. The sheer number of hectares that would benefit from the reintroduction of fire is beyond the current operational capacity. But there is no time like the present and, relatively speaking, the West is just getting started:

> *Despite recognition of the value of prescribed fire in scientific literature and policy, a number of factors impede its widespread implementation in the United States. Social acceptance of prescribed*

fire is a key factor, making consistent and effective outreach an important part of efforts to increase prescribed fire implementation. (Katie McGrath (2020), Colorado State University)

Why use prescribed fire in the West?

Goals for prescribed fire use in the West fall into four broad categories, ecological, natural resource security, public safety and cultural (see The Original Culture of Burning below), which is not to say a burn cannot be designed to meet all four simultaneously. Ecological goals include land management, conservation and restoration projects that are generally environmental in nature, such as reintroducing frequent fire back into a mixed conifer or ponderosa pine forest for purposes of reducing trees per hectare or reducing fire frequency in a Great Basin rangeland dominated by cheatgrass that is being managed for greater sage-grouse. These goals tend to be shaped and guided by knowledge of the historic fire regime of a particular area and how that

regime affected native vegetation. Knowledge of the historic mean fire return interval, as well as understanding fire severity, is helpful when developing fire prescriptions to meet ecological goals.

Natural resource security goals include using prescribed fire to increase the resilience of watersheds, timber stands or woodlands to natural disturbance events, principally wildfires, but also insect and disease outbreaks. A prime example in the south-west, which is emblematic of the entire West, is the Santa Fe Municipal Watershed in the Sangre de Cristo Mountains of New Mexico. This upper-elevation watershed provides surface water via run-off that is captured by a series of human-made reservoirs (Figure 8.2). The water is then piped into a water treatment facility located at the base of the watershed for filtration and subsequently consumed by residents of the city of Santa Fe, New Mexico. Concerted attention, especially in the use of autumn and spring prescribed burning (Figure 8.3), is given to securing this natural

Figure 8.2: Laura McCarthy, State Forestry for New Mexico, points to a hillside near a Santa Fe, New Mexico, reservoir where forest density has been reduced using mechanical techniques and surface fuel loads have been reduced using prescribed fire. Photograph by Alan W. Eckert; used with permission from The Nature Conservancy.

Figure 8.3: Pictures from a 2016 autumn prescribed burn on the Santa Fe Municipal Watershed. The objective of the second-entry prescribed fire was to reduce surface fuel loads, but not down to mineral soil. To achieve this objective, the burn was conducted with moderate litter and duff fuel moistures so as to not consume the entire substrate. The watershed, which is located on lands administered by the US Forest Service, is closed to public access primarily due to concerns about accidental wildfire ignitions. Continued prescribed fires in the future may help alleviate this concern. (a) Thinned ponderosa pine stand following a second prescribed burn. (b) Reduced litter layer following a prescribed burn. (c) Sign posted at a gate to the watershed.

resource for its ecological services that directly benefit the citizens of Santa Fe. Although the city recently added local well water as well as piped water from a Colorado watershed to diversify its portfolio of water sources, it still pulled 80–90% of its drinking water from surface waters via watersheds, watersheds that are at risk from high-severity wildfires. In fact, the majority of water that is consumed in the West is from high-profile river systems (i.e. Columbia, Missouri, Rio Grande, Colorado) that originate in upper-elevation watersheds. Recognising this expansive reach of watersheds and their importance to downstream users, the Nature Conservancy established the Rio Grande Water Fund in 2014 to support upstream forest restoration projects in order to ensure a continuous downstream supply of clean water. This model is based on a strategy of valuing forests by having users paying for environmental services (Tacconi 2012). In the West, this resource security model could be expanded to all watersheds in continuous need of fire management to include combinations of thinning and burning.

Reducing fuel loads and changing future fire behaviour and smoke emissions all collectively embody the goal of burning for public safety. Of all the reasons prescribed fire is used in the West (Table 8.1), fuel reduction is the overarching reason given by agency and private burners as their first priority (Ryan *et al.* 2013). Logically, this makes sense given the fire behaviour potential in western landscapes. In fact, western stakeholders have also come to painfully recognise that wildfire itself is just the tip of the iceberg in terms of hazards related to high-severity wildfire. Post-fire realities in the form of flooding and debris flows can persist for years following wildfire, presenting long-lasting public safety concerns. In a recent worst case scenario, the residents of Montecito, California, experienced a devastating flood and debris flow that killed 23 people following a high-intensity rainfall event (100 mm over 2 days) on the >121 000-ha high-severity fire scar from the 2017 Thomas Fire. If prescribed fire can reduce subsequent fire behaviour and severity, and in turn minimise post-fire hazards, this proactive management would be supported and welcomed by stakeholders. In fact, according to social science research (McCaffrey 2006), 80–90% of citizens surveyed across the West do approve of prescribed fire as a management tool. They also have a greater understanding of the reasons for prescribed fire than they are given credit for, and that understanding and approval increases even further when additional trust and dialogue are built with practitioners (McCaffrey 2006). For example, survey respondents understood fuel reduction objectives,

but were that much more excited and supportive when discussing the simultaneous benefits for wildlife (McCaffrey and Olsen 2012). Generally speaking, the public is on board with burning for public safety reasons.

How is prescribed fire expanding in the West?

Aside from federal agencies using prescribed fire to meet management targets, the private, non-profit and commercial sectors are aggressively pursuing novel ideas to increase the use of prescribed burning across the landscape. In addition, the states themselves are engaging in reforms and efforts to change statutes and policy to better facilitate the use of prescribed fire. Some states, like Colorado, are further ahead, but others, like California, Oregon, Washington and New Mexico, are making progress and applying lessons learned from peer states. Higher education institutions, including cooperative extension service units from across western states, are also contributing significant effort, resources and ideas to help catalyse a movement rooted in fire science research and knowledge. In a nod to the South, prescribed fire councils have been established in 8 of the 11 western states. These organised and intentional groups are proving to be valuable, reasoned voices for prescribed fire in their respective states and are occupying a space that, before their arrival, was completely void in terms of representation, perspective and knowledge.

At the forefront of this effort to expand burning is the Prescribed Fire Training Exchange program, better recognised by the acronym TREX. This cooperative training model, started in 2008, is led principally by staff at The Nature Conservancy's North America Fire Initiative, who, true to the

Table 8.1.   Common objectives for using prescribed fire in the West

1.   Reduce live and dead fuel loads, thereby changing subsequent fire behaviour (e.g. reduced high-severity hectares and associated effects, including those related to smoke)
2.   Manipulate vegetation for wildlife habitat objectives, aesthetics and native plant communities, suppress the influence of woody plants and improve forage quality and utilisation
3.   Prepare sites for seeding and planting
4.   Participate in traditional burning practices

mission, also work closely with numerous diverse partners. Cooperative learning and burning are the crux of the program, plain and simple. The West, with its checkerboard land ownership status, is best managed, at least at the landscape scale, in a cooperative melting pot of local stakeholders. As such, on the ground, drip torch in hand, TREX partnerships are multilayered between professional fire practitioners from federal and state agencies, tribes, employees from non-profit organisations, local governments, volunteer fire departments and, to some extent, private citizens willing to endure the mandatory educational and physical requirements required by federal agency burners. These diverse TREX partnerships allow skills, resources and staff to be leveraged in unique ways that maximise training, treatment and outreach opportunities, but at a uniquely local scale. Considering the vast reaches of the West differentiated by various fuel types and fire regimes, this local, and thereby cultural, approach is well suited to expand the knowledge of burning. For example, as the TREX program continues to grow, unique training sessions have been created for all-female and all-Spanish-speaking crews. Outcomes from this cooperative effort are the building and growing of prescribed burning capacity across the West. This includes expanding knowledge, skills and experience in burning that ultimately leads to a culture of proactive fire starters as a first line of defence rather than reactionary fire fighters vexed by unprecedented fire behaviour.

It should be noted that TREX events follow National Wildfire Coordinating Group (NWCG) training standards and criteria (https://www.nwcg.gov/). The adherence to this training standard marks an interesting dichotomy between western and more southern cultural burning approaches as it relates to training philosophies, specifically the steadfast choice to follow and adhere to NWCG standards when burning in the West. The NWCG was formed in the US following destructive fire seasons in the early 1970s, but notably the fire season of 1970, which saw hundreds of thousands of hectares burned, hundreds of homes destroyed

and lives lost. The intent of the NWCG was to establish a national set of fire training, procedural and equipment standards for federal fire firefighters such that safety, coordination and efficiency would be standardised when responding to wildfires across the US, particularly in the topography-accentuated mountains of the West where crown fires are king. As it relates to TREX events, this training standard does not significantly affect professional fire practitioners, but it does represent a potential burden for non-affiliated and private burners, although this can be overcome with on-the-spot training and testing before burning. Nonetheless, at the end of the training event, the experience gained is the same, and therefore ubiquitously valuable when applied on the next burn, with or without NWCG requirements.

The heretofore unprecedented drive by western states to expand prescribed fire has many roots. And although fuel reduction with intent to change fire behaviour is the principal and pressing motive, an undercurrent moves as well. That is to say, western forests are uniquely defined by an overarching land use: federal administration. And although these federal lands provide beloved multiple use, they come with a burdensome trade-off: sluggish progress towards proactively addressing increasing fuel loads. This reality, further stressed by a changing climate, ultimately threatens the uninterrupted use of multiple resources in the event of a large, high-severity wildfire. As such, diverse stakeholders from across western states are looking for direct and indirect opportunities to inject catalytic grassroots agents into the system to move the needle on expanding prescribed fire and ultimately improve forest health. Prescribed fire, although temperamental to use, is such an agent that is far-reaching and far less controversial and expensive than mechanical fuel reduction approaches. Moreover, in some ways, western states are essentially trying to (re)develop a culture of burning, a model successfully on display in the Midwest (e.g. Kansas and Oklahoma) and the South, but not seen west of the 100th meridian since before European exploration (i.e. tribal burning). When western burners look east, they see a federal agency surrounded by an influential culture of burning (and thinning), a small fish in a big pond; in the West, the inverse holds true and the sphere of influence is seemly limited to one, big, fish.

When is prescribed fire used in the West?

An oversimplification of the paradigm shift that started to occur in the West in the 1960s and 1970s with regard to prescribed fire may have sounded something like this: 'Okay. Maybe you are right, maybe we should be burning. So, when is the best time?' This illustrates one of the first questions practitioners would have asked after agreeing to use fire. When should we use fire and at what time of year?

The answer to these questions in the South is easy: 'Every day is a burn day.' This oft-heard and repeated axiom of Southern burners reflects their culture of burning, not to mention the ecology of Southern pines. Similarly, in the Midwest, there are similar sentiments as burners continue to experiment and explore with growing season burning. But again, what about the West? Historically, the answer to these question was, 'When fire is easiest to control.' However, this response did not necessarily consider the question, 'What are the (ecological) management objectives?'

In the 1960s, western ecologists such as Dr Harold Biswell and others were getting traction on the idea that fire was a necessary natural disturbance; that is, a time-immemorial process initiated by lightning and adopted by indigenous people as well as an ecological process that needed no surrogate such as the axe, plough and cow, as coined by Aldo Leopold (1933) in Game Management. However, as Stephen Pyne (2015) wrote in Between Two Fires, the firefighters were the institution providing fire-related answers in the West in the 1960s because they had the monopoly on fire, albeit through the lens of suppression. As such, the answer came from a place that first and foremost supported the suppression objective. After all, the early moniker was 'controlled burn'. Further, because it would be the firefighters who would be

lighting these burns, 'whenever it was easiest to control' was the logical answer.

To date, most of the prescribed fires in western forests are conducted on the margins of historical fire seasons. For example, in the south-west the peak of the historic fire season is May and June, a time when fuels are at their driest point and winds are at their greatest; this is also a time directly before the wettest part of the year, a period known locally as the monsoon season. As such, the two predominant (broadcast) burning seasons in the south-west are autumn (after fuels have dried out following the monsoon and, in some cases, following freezing to cure fine fuels, such as grasses) and late spring (a narrow but particular window when fuels are drying out after winter snow melt and temperatures are warming up, but wind events are often in the forecast). Table 8.2 lists when different western regions conduct their prescribed burns and why.

Incidentally, in the future, hopefully more practitioners in the West will start asking not just when should we burn, but when should we burn *again*? However, currently, the backlog of land that needs to be burned for the first time is in the millions of hectares on federal land (according to the Landscape Fire and Resource Management Planning Tools Project, also known as LANDFIRE; LANDFIRE 2020), so the prospect of a robust discussion on fire frequency may be for the next generation of managers and practitioners.

Research literature (Kerns *et al.* 2006; Fuhlendorf *et al.* 2011; Kerns and Westlind 2013; Zald *et al.* 2020) suggests that season of burning is not an overarching determining factor when it comes to ecological outcomes (within ordinary limits). Typically, the ecological outcomes of interest are related to understorey attributes, such as species composition and diversity. Where there are differences in fire effects that can be attributed to burn season, as reported in the literature (Zald *et al.* 2020), they tend to be relatively short lived and, more importantly, are attributed as much or more to burn severity than to season of burn. In other words, to achieve desired ecological outcomes, prescription inputs that affect

Table 8.2. Western US regional broadcast burn seasons and explanations for the rationale

Region	Burn seasons and explanation
North-west (Washington, Oregon)	Ponderosa pine and mixed conifer burn seasons include: (1) late spring, while fuels are drying out following winter precipitation; and (2) the early autumn, before rain and snow increase closer to winter months
	Despite the prominent role of fire (i.e. low, mixed and high severity) in moist mixed conifer forests (Stine *et al.* 2014), the use of prescribed fire is limited in these sites compared with adjacent dry mixed confer sites. The burn seasons for this cover type is essentially the same as dry mixed conifer sites because the two sites are often burned together because of their proximity and connectivity
Northern and Central Rockies (Idaho, Montana, Nevada, Utah, Wyoming, Colorado)	Interior mixed conifer forests are burned: (1) in the spring after winter snow has melted until the beginning of the summer growing season; and (2) in the autumn after the dry, windy and volatile summer fire season is over and before winter precipitation sets in
California (forest, woodland, grassland)	Grasslands: Late-phenology invasives like yellow star-thistle, medusahead and barbed goatgrass can be effectively treated with prescribed fire in the late spring/early summer, after other grasses and plants have gone to seed but before the target species have fully matured. Burning these species in other times of the year will not meet the desired objective
	Oak woodlands: California has more than 20 species of oaks, many of which have a history of frequent fire. For deciduous oaks like Oregon white oak and California black oak, prescribed fire can be used to reduce encroachment and competition from conifers and shrubs and reduce pest issues in acorns. Burning typically takes place in autumn and winter, taking advantage of cured grass (autumn) or oak litter (winter) to carry the fire
	Mixed conifer forests: California has a wide variety of conifer forest types with different fire regimes and management needs. In mixed conifer forest types, burning can take place throughout the year when appropriate conditions occur. However, the emphasis tends to be on autumn windows, when fuels are dry enough to carry the fire and be consumed, but impending winter precipitation can mitigate long-term holding concerns. Spring burning is also common in these forest types, but requires extra care and mop-up going into California's months-long dry season. Winter burning is less common, but winter windows do occur and can provide important opportunities for burning, especially in forests with a long-needle pine and/or deciduous oak component
South-west (Arizona, New Mexico)	Two predominate ponderosa pine and mixed conifer burn seasons include: (1) late spring, while fuels are drying out following winter snow melt and temperatures are increasing, but the challenge is to avoid erratic and gusty wind events, especially as the temperature increases and humidity decreases; and (2) late autumn while fuels are drying out following the monsoon season and, in some cases, after fine fuels have cured out following freeze events, but before snow flies in late November and December

burn severity are worth considering. Of note, in the arid south-west, post-fire precipitation events, or lack thereof, can make or break the ability to achieve ecological objectives even if the burn results at the time of the burn were exactly as intended.

Western forest ecologists point out that high-severity fires over tens of thousands of contiguous hectares following a wildfire are a far more significant factor in driving ecological outcomes than subtle differences in season of burn. And, as such, for many burns, changing fuel structures using prescribed fires regardless of the season of burn is

the overarching and important management objective in the short term. Generally speaking, this management objective can be achieved in any season with prescribed fire. Of course, the degree to which fuel reduction can be achieved depends on numerous factors, most notably fuel and weather conditions at the time of the burn, as well as decisions, such as ignition patterns.

This is not to suggest season of burn is without merit. As an example, practitioners in the Midwest and South have been, and continue, experimenting with growing season burns. To date, the West has not significantly experimented with growing season burns. However, federal agencies in the West have continued, and even increased, their use of allowing lightning-ignited wildfires to do their time-honoured work of rapid fuel decomposition. This can be considered a surrogate prescribed fire policy that is conducted during the peak of the historical fire season. Incidentally, this surrogate prescribed fire policy has endured a plethora of name changes over the past 60 years to include variations of the following: let burn, wildland fire use, prescribed natural wildfire, ecological use of fire for resource benefit and simply wildfire. The emphasis to use this natural tool has increased over the past 10 years. In fact, it has been anecdotally shared in personal conversations that administrators in the south-west regional office of the Forest Service have inverted their approach to these fires; that is, the first option and desire is to manage lightning fires for resource benefit and, barring that possibility, full suppression (or some combination of the two depending on circumstances). Not only is this a significant change on all levels from ecological to budgetary to liability, but it also represents a symbolic change from the now infamous 10 a.m. policy. That policy *always* prioritised full suppression by 10 a.m. the next day. Today, following fire use principles, fire management decisions can extend to the next day, and the next day, and the next day throughout the monsoon season or until the snow flies, thereby allowing fire to play a more natural role in the environment. This is the West's version of 'Every day is a burn day'. Let's call that a 'paradigm shift'.

Where is prescribed fire used in the West?

The National Interagency Coordination Center provides data on the number of prescribed fires and hectares burned each year on county, state and federal lands. These data are generated from information provided on the Incident Command System Incident Status Summary Form 209 (ICS-209). Although this form does not capture private landowner burning, it nonetheless adequately tells the story of prescribed fire at a landscape level as performed by governing bodies. Results from ICS-209 forms indicated Oregon, Arizona and California burned the greatest number of hectares between 2002 and 2017 (Table 8.3). Specifically, these three states burned over 0.4 million hectares during this time period (~26 700 ha per year on average). The remaining western states burned between ~81 000 and 364 000 ha over the 15-year time period (~5260–24 000 ha per year on average). As would be expected, the Forest Service was responsible for the majority of these hectares (1.8 million hectares), followed by the Bureau of Land Management (0.57 million hectares), Bureau of Indian Affairs (0.27 million hectares), US Fish and Wildlife Service (0.26 million hectares) and the National Park Service (0.08 million hectares; Table 8.3). Unfortunately, when we look at these numbers across time (i.e. 15 years), either by state or by governing body, we see a trend for maintaining the status quo in terms of the area burned. Or, as the placeholder title of this chapter suggested, the west is burning … a little, but not enough to report a growing trend in hectares burned across the region (Figures 8.4, 8.5).

The Coalition of Prescribed Fire Councils is another source of data to evaluate trends in prescribed fire hectares in western states. Although these data may not be as precise as those from the ICS-209 forms, they do have some ability to capture private landowner burning. In their first survey conducted in 2011, Florida, Georgia and Oklahoma reported the greatest 'forestry' areas burned (>0.4 million hectares by each state in 2011, with the term 'forestry' meaning forest and range burning in this case; Melvin 2012). As for the West, no one, two or three states stood out from the pack; rather, all 11 states fell within two categories, namely the '1001–50 000 acres' (~405–20 234 ha) and '50 001–250 000 acres' (~20 235–101 171 ha) categories (Melvin 2012). That trend did not change in the next survey, conducted in 2014 (Melvin 2015). In fact, the overall area of burning declined slightly in the West. Similarly, in the 2017 survey, the West had four states (down from seven and six states in 2011 and 2014 respectively) in the '50 001–250 000

Table 8.3. Prescribed fires and area burned in 12 western contiguous US states between 2002 and 2017 by responsible governing party

Data are from the National Interagency Coordination Center (2020). The governing burn parties or ignitors were the Bureau of Indian Affairs (BIA), Bureau of Land Management (BLM), County (CNTY), Department of Defence (DOD), US Fish and Wildlife Service (FWS), National Park Service (NPS), State (ST) and the US Forest Service (USFS). AZ, Arizona; CA, California; CO, Colorado; ID, Idaho; MT, Montana; NM, New Mexico; NV, Nevada; OR, Oregon; UT, Utah; WA, Washington; WY, Wyoming

State	BIA No. fires	BIA Area burned (ha)	BLM No. fires	BLM Area burned (ha)	CNTY No. fires	CNTY Area burned (ha)	DOD No. fires	DOD Area burned (ha)	FWS No. fires	FWS Area burned (ha)	NPS No. fires	NPS Area burned (ha)	ST No. fires	ST Area burned (ha)	USFS No. fires	USFS Area burned (ha)	Total No. fires	Total Area burned (ha)
AZ	2258	141 628	279	45 747	0	0	5	1458	57	19 131	100	20 102	13	331	6087	384 288	8799	612 684
CA	228	9239	364	13 501	59	325	19	1892	789	118 874	668	28 528	125	5862	8413	229 786	10 665	408 007
CO	82	4879	468	23 634	444	4613	33	3221	137	10 656	157	3442	101	2183	1570	115 456	2992	168 082
ID	108	5258	349	46 756	9	0	1	51	48	3715	1	40	1998	47 902	3394	179 751	5908	283 475
MT	369	21 491	357	30 453	75	751	0	0	196	25 924	69	717	954	19 552	4999	134 599	7019	233 488
NM	209	15 480	291	114 612	0	0	0	0	91	29 930	46	3151	15	5738	690	184 584	1342	353 496
NV	1	6	163	16 600	0	0	0	0	85	9535	68	9280	76	2906	89	6270	482	44 597
OR	237	30 391	3363	203 527	0	0	0	0	307	31 522	25	1045	51	2586	7962	353 002	11 945	622 072
UT	9	3354	245	26 986	0	0	0	0	35	6370	76	6892	393	11 117	751	99 495	1509	154 214
WA	345	36 836	85	4873	0	0	0	0	405	10 874	62	2342	15	613	2491	64 159	3403	119 697
WY	5	359	295	50 600	25	1526	0	0	19	335	106	2074	6	180	362	32 476	818	87 550
Total	3851	268 922	6259	577 289	612	7215	58	6622	2169	266 865	1378	77 613	3747	98 971	36 808	1 783 865	54 882	2 941 673

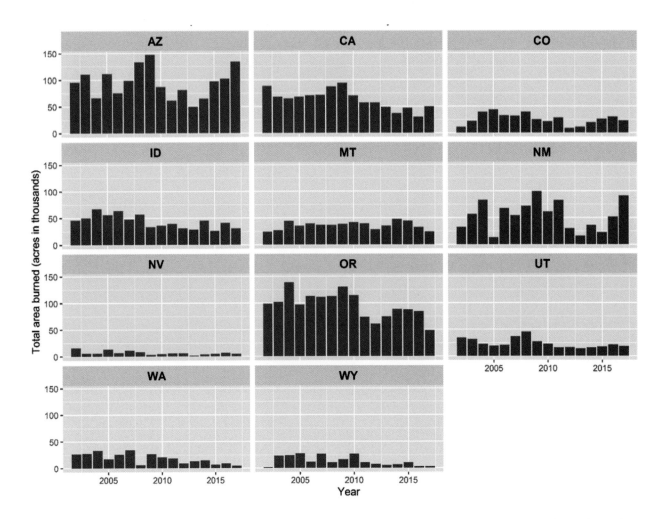

Figure 8.4: Time line of prescribed acres burned in 12 western contiguous US states between 2002 and 2017 by eight governing parties, including the Bureau of Indian Affairs, Bureau of Land Management, County, Department of Defence, US Fish and Wildlife Service, National Park Service, State and the US Forest Service. (Data from the National Interagency Coordination Center (2020).)

acres' category (Melvin 2018). Although fire managers and ecologists would like to see an increase in the western prescribed fire areas burned, the surveys indicate that even though the area burned in the West is not necessarily growing, there is a solid baseline over a 6-year period from which to continue to expand efforts.

Original culture of burning

Generally speaking, indigenous peoples across North America were using fire upon the arrival of

Europeans (Vale 2013). It is not definitively known with great specificity, but suffice to say indigenous people have been using fire for the last 14 000 years in North America (Stewart 2002; Vale 2013). Although the degree to which this anthropogenic use of fire affected ecological systems at the landscape scale is debated (see Minnich 1988; cf. Anderson 1997), the fact that there was a cultural relationship between people, fire and land has been quantified (Stambaugh *et al.* 2018).

Unfortunately, as the story goes, between fire suppression and exclusion mindsets and, in some

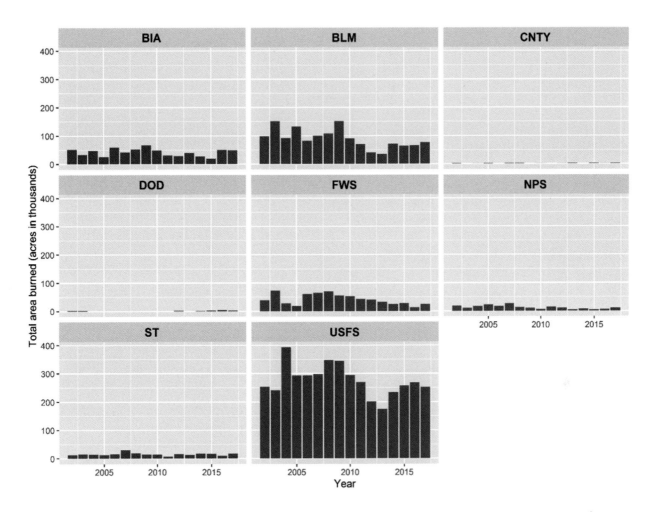

Figure 8.5: Time line of prescribed acres burned by eight governing parties in 12 western contiguous US states between 2002 and 2017. Governing parties include the Bureau of Indian Affairs (BIA), Bureau of Land Management (BLM), County (CNTY), Department of Defence (DOD), US Fish and Wildlife Service (FWS), National Park Service (NPS), State (ST) and the US Forest Service (USFS). (Data from the National Interagency Coordination Center (2020).)

cases, legislative policy negatively affecting indigenous people (e.g. the *Indian Removal Act* of 1830, the 1850 *Act for the Government and Protection of Indians* and the 1887 *Dawes General Allotment Act* 1887), the ability of Native Americans to continue traditional cultural burning was constricted. As such, the original culture of anthropogenic burning in North America was all but erased from the landscape, with the only lifeline to the past (save a few fire-scarred trees; Stambaugh *et al.* 2018) being the oral storytelling tradition. However, today, that time-honoured oral tradition proved to be enough heritage to reignite the torches across the West on Native American lands. In 2020, in the midst of a modern-day fire storm engulfing California, Oregon and Washington, there were any number of headline stories about Native Americans using prescribed fire to manage western landscapes, including the Karuk, Yurok, Hupa, Miwok, Chumash and Modoc in the north-west, the San Carlos Apache in Arizona and the Mescalero Apache in New Mexico, among others. The evolving narrative in the West following record-breaking fire season after record-breaking fire season is the West must learn to live with fire … and who better to learn from than the original western burners? Don't have a drip torch? Just use some dried and bound wormwood to light your backfire.

Unmanned aerial systems

In 2016, faculty from the University of Nebraska published an article about unmanned aerial systems, better known as drones, and how they may be used in fire management (Twidwell *et al.* 2016). Specifically, the article explored how a prototype drone system could do more than just monitor smoke and fire from above, and actually ignite fire. The combination of merging drone capabilities with aerial plastic ignition spheres was a stroke of genius. These plastic spheres are filled with potassium permanganate and mechanically injected with glycol (antifreeze). They are launched from a helicopter to land on the ground, igniting 30 s later following the chemical reaction inside the ball and thus creating an ignition point. In hindsight, it seemed an obvious pairing but, as is often the case, it took bold individuals to push through the unknowns and take a chance on an idea. In fact, Twidwell *et al.* (2016) had an entire section devoted to institutional and operational barriers to use. That was 4 short years ago. Today, the system is fully functional and has blossomed into a standalone company selling 'Ignis' units to federal, state, contract and private burners in the US, Canada and Australia. In particular, several Hot Shot crews (i.e. US federal firefighting units consisting of 20 specially trained individuals) stationed in the western US have purchased these systems and trained in-house pilots in order to expand their capabilities when called upon for wildland and prescribed fires assignments. Suffice to say, these 'ping-pong ball' systems mounted on helicopters are expensive and have an inherent risk factor. Drones igniting back and head fires on prescribed and wildland fires in the middle of the night with sustained winds are an undeniable game changer. What will inventors think of next?

Prescribed fire escapes in the West …

There are two types of burn bosses: the one that's had a spot fire, and the one that's getting ready to have a spot fire – John Weir

For better *and* worse, a chapter on prescribed fire in the West cannot ignore infamous escapes (Table 8.4). The memories and painful outcomes from these events are seared not only into the minds of the affected communities and victims, but also into the minds of the burn crew that

Table 8.4. Notable escaped prescribed burns and one related incident in the western US

AZ, Arizona; CA, California; CO, Colorado; NM, New Mexico

Date	Fire	Précis
July 1999	Lowden Ranch, CA	A 40.5-ha prescribed fire ignited by the Bureau of Land Management: the burn was ignited with an energy release component at historical maximum levels. A litany of policy and implantation errors (Shepard *et al.* 1999) occurred, culminating in four successive spot fires, the last of which could not be contained. The fire ultimately burned 809 ha and destroyed 23 homes
May 2000	Cerro Grande, NM	A 364-ha prescribed fire ignited by the National Park Service: the burn was ignited on a Thursday evening, with operations continuing through to 2:00 a.m. A fire line slop-over occurred by 10:00 a.m. on Friday and a wildfire was declared by 1:00 p.m. on Friday. The fire ultimately burned ~17 400 ha, destroyed 235 homes and caused an estimated US$1 billion in damages
March 2012	Lower North Fork, CO	A 20-ha prescribed fire ignited by the Colorado State Forest Service: 4 days after ignition and mop-up, a wind event carried embers from smouldering unburned interior fuels across the fire line; two spot fires were contained, but a third (just 3 m × 3 m when discovered) in masticated fuels quickly grew to wildfire status. The fire ultimately burned 1600 ha, destroyed 25 homes and tragically killed three people
October 2016	Green Base Prescribed Fire, AZ	A 405-ha prescribed fire ignited by the US Forest Service: there were numerous vehicle crashes on Interstate 40 after midnight, including one fatality, due to smoke on the highway (although an official investigation and report is not available or was never issued)

struck the match. On the beneficial side, calling attention to escaped burns presents yet another opportunity to report on the statistical track record of prescribed burns (<1% escape per year; Dether and Black 2006; Weir *et al.* 2019) while also providing an opening to remember that with great (fire) power comes great responsibility. The mistakes and oversights of the past that resulted in loss of life and property cannot be forgotten; they are a reminder that safety and prudence must continue to be co-equal with management goals when planning and conducting burns. On the negative side, dwelling on escapes clouds the sky. Escapes are to burning what shark attacks are to surfing: exceptionally rare, but bound to occur eventually. Unfortunately, intensive media coverage (which is to be expected) following escaped prescribed fires often results in seeding half-truths (e.g. that prescribed fire is dangerous), breeds scepticism and opposition and, in general, has the potential to sour the public on the idea of using prescribed fire as a useful tool.

Catch-22?

Better known in the US by its acronym, the NWCG is associated with terms and US firefighting jargon such as 10 & 18, red cards, pack tests, task books, incident response pocket guide, S-130, S-190, RT-130, 6 min for safety, watch out situations, standard firefighting orders, hierarchy and slightly fewer acronyms than the US military (i.e. CRWB, CTR, ENGB, FAL1, FELB, FEMO, FIRB, FFT1, FFT2, FOBS, GISS, HRSP, ICT1, ICT2, ICT3, LSC, OSC, PIO, PSC, SOF, STAM, STCR, UASP). The mission of this well-known (within the wildland fire world) institution is simple: establish national interagency wildland fire operating standards. Standards improve safety, the number one goal for all fire operations regardless of whether they are federal or private, state or local, structure or wildland, prescribed or wildfire. Towards this end, the NWCG is the gold standard in the US, epitomised by Hot Shot crews stationed across western national forests.

However, what if the objective is to train private practitioners in the use of prescribed fire? Is the NWCG a suitable option? Is it the only option? Arguably, the NWCG is not suited or designed to meet the needs of private burners. Given this conundrum (i.e. gold standard yet incompatible), the following question is raised: is there an appropriate rigorous and comprehensive training course for non-federal, non-professional, private practitioners in the use of prescribed fire that is not the NWCG?

In the West, the answer to that question is generally no (at the present time). However, because this is a recognised impediment to increased burning in the West, there are several efforts afoot to address and solve this problem. As described earlier, TREX is one approach, although participation in this program does require completion of the basic NWCG fire courses (i.e. S-130, S-190) and a pack test, but thereafter an individual can take the knowledge learned and potentially conduct burns on private property or elsewhere.

An alternative approach to NWCG training for private practitioners are the state-funded training curricula that lead to certification, also known as certified prescribed burn manager (CPBM) programs. Currently, the only operational models of this approach are found outside the West (i.e. Texas, Florida, Alabama, Georgia and other states). Although Colorado passed legislation that created a CPBM program in 2013, it is steeped in NWCG requirements: it includes 32 h of coursework and, upon completion, it does not extend the limited civil liability protections beyond pile burning (i.e. no liability standards for broadcast burning) for private individuals. California and Washington are currently (*c.* 2020) working on CPBM programs, so it is too soon to tell what route these states will take. However, in New Mexico, a final report to the state legislature (i.e. House Memorial 42 – Expanding Prescribed Fire Use in New Mexico; July 2020) by a working group of local stakeholders recommended an appropriately rigorous and comprehensive training program for private practitioners that will not require NWCG certification.

Black Range Ranger District, Gila National Forest

Over 4000 ha in one prescribed burn? Where, Florida? No, the Black Range Ranger District in the Gila National Forest, New Mexico (Figure 8.6). Was this conducted in the autumn to include pile burning hectares? No, this landscape burn was conducted in the spring of 2018 in the middle of burn bans implemented by neighbouring counties and just 3 weeks after an adjacent neighbouring forest lost a 728-ha prescribed burn and had to declare it a wildfire that ended up burning 3600 ha. This Black Range modus operandi that has emerged and evolved over the past three decades constitutes a culture of burning that now annually completes around 20 000 ha each year, and around another 9000 ha with managed wildfire (depending on the fire season).

This culture of burning (Figure 8.7) started in earnest 30 years ago on the Black Range with the development of the Indian Peaks project, a 36 000-ha burn plan footprint, broken up into 20 burn units. Some units have now seen as many as four re-entrees over the years. The first entrees

Figure 8.6: Pictures of the Black Range Ranger District of the Gila National Forest, New Mexico, where prescribed fire is a tool widely used across the landscape to achieve management goals. (a) Welcome sign at the entrance to the fire base. (b) Members of the Black Range Ranger District fire crew igniting a prescribed fire. (c) Post-fire forest stand conditions adjacent to the Continental Divide Trail on the Gila National Forest.

Figure 8.7: The unofficial logo of the Black Range Fire Fighters. Logo provided by Dennis Fahl, Fire Management Officer, Black Range Ranger District, Gila National Forest.

were cool burns to remove built up pine needles but, over time, they have increased the fire intensity to achieve different prescribed outcomes, such as increased canopy base height or, as it is affectionately referred to in the Black Range, 'live low limb', a factor that increases the resilience of the stand to withstand future wildfires. This burn plan epitomises all the 'rights': right location (remote), right fuel type (ponderosa pine), right objectives (maintaining frequent fire) and right social licence (general acceptance from local stakeholders). Given all the stars aligning in the Black Range, it could be argued that all these 'rights' make achieving success easier. However, that would only account for half the equation: prescribed fires, especially on federal land, need committed people to plan and implement them year after year. To paraphrase Martha Graham, who said, *'Fire is the test of gold; adversity, of strong men'*, fire is the test of watersheds; burning, of commitment. This is where the culture of burning comes into play. The district ranger, line officers, biologists, managers and on-the-ground practitioners all work collaboratively before, during and after the burn to ensure successful outcomes. Positive intent is assumed by all. This unique environment has resulted in a respected culture that is

known within the federal fire circles as a desirable place to work if you want to learn and burn. The Black Range is leading the way for the agency in the south-west and beyond as an example to be replicated across the landscape in the bid to increase hectares burned.

Apples and oranges

Within this chapter characterising prescribed burning in the West, there have been many references to burning in the Midwest (e.g. Oklahoma and Texas) and South (e.g. Florida and Georgia), geographic locations that house traditional cultures of burning. Although these hot beds for burning are admired for their pioneering exploits and leadership attributes, as well as accomplishments achieved with the drip torch, they are not like the West.

The principal difference is, of course, topography. The West has vast regions of rugged and remote mountains characterised quintessentially by the Rocky Mountains, stretching from Canada to Mexico. These rugged mountainous regions are unique for their peaks and saddles, deep canyons and ridges, wide ranging aspects and elevation changes, lack of access and plenty of 26-m-tall trees ready to fuel a crown fire stoked by sustained winds. The impact of this third leg of the fire behaviour triangle cannot be overstated when *considering* the *complexity*, *cost* and *consequences* of an escaped (*crown*) fire (the five Cs). Fortunately, there are but only a few examples of this disparity between the West and the rest of the country (Table 8.4), but the examples we have are not lost in the minds of burn bosses operating in mountainous terrain and, moreover, they are certainly not lost on the insurance industry. Although wildfires in the West may seem to fall into another category (i.e. not prescribed burns), the five Cs of recent megafires further reinforce the potential liability concerns regarding an escaped prescribed fire in mountainous terrain. These concerns include tens of thousands of contiguous hectares burned at high severity, six- and seven-figure suppression costs, billions of dollars in damages, years of post-fire flooding and debris flows and the loss of life and limb. The point is, the West may never be able to keep pace with the South or Midwest in terms of annual hectares burned or cultivating a culture of burning: it's apples and oranges.

Acknowledgements

Thanks go out to Sabrina Lucero and Dr Pradip Saud for help in preparing raw data for tables and figures. In addition, many thanks to Lenya Quinn-Davidson from the University of California Cooperative Extension Service for contributing expertise and ideas to improve and complete Table 8.2. Thanks to Ellis Margolis and Craig Allen from the US Geological Survey for providing the comprehensive composite fire history for the Jemez Mountains, New Mexico (Figure 8.1). Thanks also to The Nature Conservancy, Laura McCarthy, Anne Bradley and Alan Eckert for extending permission to use their photograph. Finally, thanks to Dennis Fahl, Toby Richards and all the Black Range Rx Burners for allowing me to observe and learn from your craft.

Endnotes

1   For the purposes of this chapter, the West is considered to be the 11 western contiguous states (i.e. Arizona, California, Colorado, Idaho, Montana, Nevada, New Mexico, Oregon, Utah, Wyoming, and Washington).

2   For the purposes of this chapter, burning is considered to be for the intent of forest and rangeland management, not agricultural objectives (e.g. burning row crop residues left in the field following harvest).

References

Allen C, Touchan R, Swetnam T (1995) Landscape-scale fire history studies support fire management action at Bandelier. *Park Science* 15, 18–19.

Anderson M (1997) California's endangered peoples and endangered ecosystems. *American Indian Culture and Research Journal* 21, 7–31. doi:10.17953/aicr.21.3.06q15 85l4j05113n

Conarro R (1942) The place of fire in southern forestry. *Journal of Forestry* 40, 129–131. doi:10.1093/jof/40.2.129

Dether D, Black A (2006) Learning from escaped prescribed fires – lessons for high reliability. *Fire Management Today* 66, 50–56.

Fuhlendorf S, Limb R, Engle D, Miller R (2011) Assessment of prescribed fire as a conservation practice. In *Conservation Benefits of Rangeland Practices: Assessment, Recommendations, and Knowledge Gaps.* (Ed. D Briske) pp. 75–104. U.S. Department of Agriculture, Natural Resources Conservation Service, Washington, DC.

Kerns B, Westlind D (2013) Effect of season and interval of prescribed burn on ponderosa pine butterfly defoliation patterns. *Canadian Journal of Forest Research* 43, 979–983. doi:10.1139/cjfr-2013-0153

Kerns B, Thies W, Niwa C (2006) Season of prescribed burn in ponderosa pine forests: implications for native and exotic plant species. *Ecoscience* 13, 44–55. doi:10.2980/1195-6860(2006)13[44:SASOPB]2.0.CO;2

LANDFIRE (2020) *LANDFIRE Vegetation Condition Class layer, LF 2.0.0.* U.S. Department of the Interior, Geological Survey, <http://www.landfire.gov/>.

Leopold A (1933) *Game Management.* Scribner's Sons, New York.

Love C (1916) History of the cattle industry in the Southwest, II. *The Southwestern Historical Quarterly* 20, 1–18.

McCaffrey S (2006) Prescribed fire: what influences public approval. In *Fire in Eastern Oak Forests: Delivering Science to Land Managers, Proceedings of a Conference.* 15–17 November 2005, Columbus. General Technical Report NRS-P-1. (Ed. M Dickinson) pp. 192–196. U.S. Department of Agriculture, Forest Service, Northern Research Station, Newton Square.

McCaffrey S, Olsen C (2012) 'Research perspectives on the public and fire management: a synthesis of current social science on eight essential questions'. General Technical Report NRS-104, U.S. Department of Agriculture, Forest Service, Northern Research Station, Newton Square.

McGrath K (2020) *Building a Prescribed Fire Program on the Colorado Front Range: The Role of Landowner Engagement.* Southwest Fire Science Consortium, Flagstaff, <https://www.swfireconsortium.org/2020/01/30/building-a-prescribed-fire-program-on-the-colorado-front-range-the-role-of-landowner-engagement/>.

Melvin M (2012) 'National prescribed fire use survey report'. Coalition of Prescribed Fire Councils, Newton.

Melvin M (2015) 'National prescribed fire use survey report'. Coalition of Prescribed Fire Councils, Newton.

Melvin M (2018) 'National prescribed fire use survey report'. Coalition of Prescribed Fire Councils, Newton.

Minnich R (1988) *The Biogeography of Fire in the San Bernardino Mountains of California: A Historical Study.* University of California Press, Berkeley.

National Interagency Coordination Center (2020) *Historical Year-end Fire Statistics by State and Year*. National Interagency Coordination Center, Boise, <https://www.nifc.gov/fire-information/statistics>.

Pyne S (2015) *Between Two Fires: A History of Contemporary America*. University of Arizona Press, Tucson.

Ryan K, Knapp E, Varner J (2013) Prescribed fire in North American forests and woodlands: history, current practice, and challenges. *Frontiers in Ecology and the Environment* **11**, e15–e24. doi:10.1890/120329

Shepard E, Johnson R, Palmer S, Kraushaar J, Burnham R, Pincha-Tulley J, Hood L, Lentz D, Buckley D, Hoffmeister R, Glenn G, Cole D, Fontana C (1999) 'Lowden Ranch prescribed fire review – final report 1999'. U.S. Department of Interior, Bureau of Land Management, Boise.

Stambaugh M, Marschall J, Abadir E, Jones B, Brose P, Dey D, Guyette R (2018) Wave of fire: an anthropogenic signal in historical fire regimes across central Pennsylvania, USA. *Ecosphere* **9**, e02222. doi:10.1002/ecs2.2222

Stephens S, Martin R, Clinton N (2007) Prehistoric fire area and emissions from California's forests, woodlands, shrublands, and grasslands. *Forest Ecology and Management* **251**, 205–216. doi:10.1016/j.foreco.2007.06.005

Stewart O (2002) *Forgotten Fires: Native Americans and the Transient Wilderness*. University of Oklahoma Press, Norman.

Stine P, Hessburg P, Spies T, Kramer M, Fettig C, Hansen A, Lehmkuhl J, O'Hara K, Polivka K, Singleton P, *et al.* (2014) 'The ecology and management of moist mixed-conifer forests in eastern Oregon and Washington: a synthesis of the relevant biophysical science and implications for future land management'. General Technical Repot PNW-GTR-897, U.S. Department of Agriculture, Forest Service, Pacific Northwest Research Station, Portland.

Tacconi L (2012) Redefining payments for environmental services. *Ecological Economics* **73**, 29–36. doi:10.1016/j.ecolecon.2011.09.028

Twidwell D, Allen C, Detweiler C, Higgins J, Laney C, Elbaum S (2016) Smokey comes of age: unmanned aerial systems for fire management. *Frontiers in Ecology and the Environment* **14**, 333–339. doi:10.1002/fee.1299

Vale T (2013) *Fire, Native Peoples, and the Natural Landscape*. Island Press, Washington, DC.

Weil E (2020) They know how to prevent megafires. Why won't anybody listen? *ProPublica*, <https://www.propublica.org/article/they-know-how-to-prevent-megafires-why-wont-anybody-listen>.

Weir J, Kreuter U, Wonkka C, Twidwell D, Stroman D, Russell M, Taylor C (2019) Liability and prescribed fire: perception and reality. *Rangeland Ecology and Management* **72**, 533–538. doi:10.1016/j.rama.2018.11.010

Zald H, Kerns B, Day M (2020) Limited effects of long-term repeated season and interval of prescribed burning on understory vegetation compositional trajectories and indicator species in ponderosa pine forests of northeastern Oregon, USA. *Forests* **11**, 834. doi:10.3390/f11080834

9

Pyric legacy: prescribed burning in the Flint Hills region, USA

Carolyn Baldwin, Jeff Davidson and Lars Coleman

Introduction

A strong fire culture has existed in the Great Plains for centuries (Pyne 1982; Anderson 1990; Stewart 2002). Indigenous burning created the conditions for the diverse and unique assemblages of flora and fauna that were present when Europeans first arrived on the immense prairies that spanned the North American continent (Plate 7; Wells 1819; Mitchell 1978; Anderson 1990; Williams 2002).

Much of the tallgrass prairie has been cultivated and much of the prairie remains as small remnants of the once-vast rangelands (Samson and Knopf 1994). Today, approximately two-thirds of the remaining tallgrass prairie lies within the undulating rock-ledge region of Kansas and Oklahoma called the Flint Hills (Figure 9.1; Samson *et al.* 2004; Middendorf *et al.* 2009; Obermeyer 2012). This largest remaining tract of tallgrass prairie is highly valued for its concatenation of native plants and animals in a landscape intact enough to function as an ecosystem.

The Flint Hills region was recognised early during the European settlement process as highly suitable for livestock production, especially cattle

grazing (Malin 1942; Kollmorgen and Simonett 1965). The use of prescribed fire in managing this land was initially discouraged by the science community. However, ranchers soon recognised the benefits of fire and began burning within a decade of settlement (Hoy 1989). Today, Flint Hills land managers, primarily ranchers, continue to use prescribed burning to maintain healthy prairies that are home to native plants and wildlife, livestock and rural communities (Figure 9.2).

Fire return intervals are short, in the range of 1–3 years, because longer intervals result in brush management problems that may require more intensive and expensive management (Ratajczak *et al.* 2016; Briggs *et al.* 2002b). In these mesic prairies, conversion from open rangeland to closed canopy woodland can take as little as 40 years (Steinauer and Collins 1996; Briggs *et al.* 2002a; Blair *et al.* 2014).

An average of approximately 0.9 million hectares of Flint Hills rangeland are intentionally burned each year (Plate 8; Kansas Department of Health and Environment 2020). Burning is not evenly distributed because certain regions of the

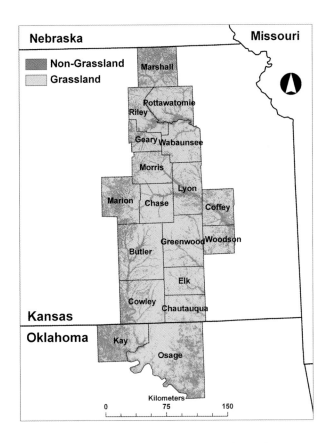

Figure 9.1: The Flint Hills region is not definitively defined, but includes counties in both Kansas and Oklahoma. Grassland in this region rapidly converts to woodland without fire. River and streams are delineated in this image by the unburned woodlands growing along their banks. Image by Douglas G. Goodin and Rhett Mohler. Reproduced with permission from Mohler and Goodin (2012).

Figure 9.2: The Flint Hills landscape where fire is most prevalent consists of open grasslands with trees and shrubs confined to valleys. Vegetation consists of warm-season tallgrasses and forbs, with rapid growth in the spring after burning. Rock outcrops are common. Photograph courtesy of Carolyn Baldwin.

Flint Hills are burned at more frequent intervals than others (Ratajczak *et al.* 2016).

Vegetative characteristics

Flint Hills rangelands are often characterised by the abundance of four native grass species, namely big bluestem *Andropogon gerardii* Vitman, little bluestem *Schizachyrium scoparium* (Michx.) Nash, switchgrass *Panicum virgatum* L. and Indiangrass *Sorghastrum nutans* (L.) Nash. These four species can make up 60% or more of the biomass produced each year in the Flint Hills rangelands (Abrams and Hulbert 1987). At the end of the winter

dormant season, when only a very few cool-season native species such as sedges remain green, a blanket of dead vegetative material composed of grass and forb leaves, stems and litter covers the rangelands (Knapp and Seastedt 1986).

Prescribed burns in April favour native warm-season grasses in the highly diverse plant community of the Flint Hills (Launchbaugh and Owensby 1978). Central US native plants are well adapted to fire, with extensive root systems (Weaver 1958) and symbiotic underground microbial associations (Wilson and Hartnett 1998) that support rapid aboveground growth after fire (Svejcar 1990). Grasses have meristematic tissue located near the soil surface that is not damaged by prescribed fire (Benson *et al.* 2004). Older parts of bunch grasses, in the centre of the clone, can be burned out, leaving a ring of vigorous new growth that, when combined with grazing, results in new plants or clones (Figure 9.3). Specifically, the time of burning is tied to the growth of big bluestem in the spring (Launchbaugh and Owensby 1978).

Because growth begins earlier in the more southern regions of the Flint Hills, prescribed burning also begins earlier in these locations.

Figure 9.3: Bunchgrasses often have the centre of the clump charred during a prescribed burn. Prescribed burning stimulates new grass growth from meristematic tissue near or below ground level. Photograph courtesy of Carolyn Baldwin.

Prescribed burning ends as stocker cattle arriving by truck in the latter part of April and early May are turned out to graze. In many years ranchers fail to burn as many hectares as they would like, generally due to adverse weather conditions.

In addition to enhanced livestock production, the most common reasons for prescribed burning in the Flint Hills are the removal and management of undesirable woody species and plants, to promote healthier and more vigorous plant communities, enhancing prairie wildlife habitat, and for wildfire mitigation.

Livestock grazing and fire

Frequency of burning is an individual rancher or landowner decision and can depend on weather conditions, brush encroachment, grazing contract requirements, type of grazing system, livestock type and labour availability, among other factors. The percentage of a county that burns in any one year can range from 11% to 56% (Mohler and Goodin 2012).

Flint Hills rangelands are working lands, supporting ranching families and rural communities. Approximately two-thirds of the livestock grazed on these lands are stocker cattle, young animals that are weaned but not yet ready for finishing in a feedlot (Beam 2010). These animals have high potential for weight gain during this growth phase. The Intensive Early Stocking (IES) grazing system is closely attuned to regional grassland ecology and enjoys widespread adoption (Smith and Owensby 1978). In this system, the rangeland is burned when warm-season grass species, such as big bluestem, just begin growth in the spring following the winter dormant season, generally in April (Engle and Bidwell 2001).

Burning stimulates grass growth in several ways, including solar warming of the blackened soil surface and the removal of accumulated litter that would shade growing plants (Hulbert 1969). Under these conditions, native grasses and forbs endemic to the Flint Hills begin rapid growth immediately after the burn. Because not every blade of vegetation is burned, livestock can begin grazing as early as several days afterwards.

With rapidly growing, highly nutritious forage available to rapidly growing 'teenage' cattle, gains can be impressive, in the range of 0.9–1.4 kg per day (Hoy 2009) or even 1.8 kg per day for thin, aged (3 years old) steers (B. Obermeyer, pers. comm., 2020). Stockers managed with this grazing system can be expected to gain approximately 14 kg more in the approximately 2.5-month grazing period than if the rangeland were not burned before grazing (Launchbaugh and Owensby 1978). With IES, the stocking rate is twice what would be used for season-long stocking (15 April–15 October), but because animals graze only half the growing season, plants have a long recovery period to replenish root reserves before dormancy. This is relevant to prescribed burning because the large accumulation of ungrazed grass during the second half of the growing season results in a greater fuel load with more continuity than with season-long stocking, where grazing patches result in more variable consumption of material.

The interval needed to burn the rangeland for brush control can be as long as 3–5 years (Fuhlendorf *et al.* 2008), but the need to burn for maximum stocker gains is annual because the benefit is of short duration. By mid-summer, when vegetation begins to mature, stocker gains are similar to those on rangeland that has not been burned (Launch-baugh and Owensby 1978). All the increase in weight gains occurs in the first 70 days or so after the burn, and the effect does not carry over into the next year (Owensby 2019).

There are numerous modifications of IES and the use of other burn–grazing strategies, including patch burn grazing, where only a portion of a paddock is burned at any one time (Fuhlendorf and Engle 2001); partial removal of stockers at 70 days, with the remainder removed at the end of the grazing season (October; Owensby and Auen 2013); late summer burning for specific weed control purposes; and other permutations depending on financial, labour, wildlife and range management goals. Livestock may be rancher owned or custom grazed. Similarly, land may be rancher owned or leased from non-resident owners (Kollmorgen and Simonett 1965; Smith and Owensby 1973). There are both formal lease clauses and informal understandings between landowners and ranchers that the land will be burned as part of routine management activities (Anderson 1967; Kansas State University Agricultural Economics and Kansas Department of Agriculture 2019).

The remaining one-third of livestock in the Flint Hills is composed of cow-calf operations, where animal performance is not directly tied to prescribed burning. However, burning at 2- to 3-year intervals is still needed to maintain brush-free pastures. In all instances, if there is a woody plant problem, more intensive burning, and possibly shorter burn intervals, will be required to manage and decrease undesirable plants (Ratajczak *et al.* 2016). Burning and grazing under light to moderate conditions are highly interactive and both are necessary for the highest biological diversity and most productive Flint Hills rangelands (Hickman *et al.* 2004).

Requirements for and barriers to fire use

There is no overall control of prescribed burning in the Flint Hills region. Although there are state and county regulations regarding burning, by far the most important regulation is self-regulation. With no direct supervision, it is up to individual ranchers to correctly assess the risks and take appropriate precautions to safely conduct fires. This requires an understanding of how fire behaviour is affected by uneven terrain, fuel characteristics, humidity, wind speed and ignition rate, plus consideration of the type and amount of crew and equipment available and an estimation of how likely and where the fire may escape, among other factors (Hoy 1989). Safety concerns over smoke duration, direction and density must also be factored in. And finally, honest self-evaluation of overall preparedness must occur when deciding whether or not to light the fire.

Kansas legal requirements

In Kansas, prescribed burning falls under regulation Kansas Administrative Regulation (K.A.R) 28-19-648 Agricultural Open Burning and K.A.R. 128-19-646 Responsibility for Open Burning, which can be summarised as follows:

1. The local fire control authority (generally the county dispatcher) will be notified immediately before burning begins.
2. Smoke will not be allowed to become a safety hazard on roads or at airports.
3. The person conducting the burn is generally responsible for the fire and will supervise the fire until it is extinguished.
4. The property owner or manager of the property being burned will be assumed to have permitted the fire.

An additional regulation, K.A.R. 28-19-645a, is only applicable during April and applies only to Flint Hills counties and three urban counties in an attempt to address air quality issues by restricting open burning while extensive rangeland burning is occurring. The key provision of this regulation is that only rangeland burning can occur during this time period, and other open burning is prohibited.

Although not required in Kansas, it is considered courteous to let neighbours know about prescribed burning plans before ignition (Launch-baugh and Owensby 1978).

Oklahoma legal requirements

In Oklahoma, prescribed burning falls under Statutes §2-16-24.1, §2-16-25 and §2-16-26. The key provisions are:

1. You must be legally entitled to burn the property as an owner, authorised tenant or agent of the owner/authorised tenant (Statutory Reference: O.S. Title 2 S 16-25).
2. You must provide adequate fire lines, sufficient manpower and firefighting equipment to contain your fires to the property you are authorised to burn and stay with the fire until it is extinguished.
3. In the protection areas of eastern Oklahoma (generally east of Highway 69), you must obtain approval from the Forestry Division at least 4 h before burning (Statutory Reference: O.S. Title 2 S 16-28; Oklahoma Forestry Services 2019).
4. Burning someone else's land without permission is unlawful.
5. A written permission process must be used if a state of extreme fire danger has been declared.
6. Neighbours and local fire authorities must be notified before conducting a prescribed burn.

Because so much of the prescribed burning in the Flint Hills occurs during late March and April, and only on days when weather conditions are suitable for burning, more than 40 000 ha can be burned in a single day. This concentration of burning becomes more prevalent later in the burn season if there have been few suitable days to burn. Concentrated burning can result in smoke being transported hundreds of kilometres away, but smoke problems are generally more local. Prevailing winds during this time of year are generally from the south or south-west, so smoke tends to move north. Although there are some complaints in Kansas during the burn season, by far the largest number of complaints received from the Kansas Flint Hills Smoke Management website (www.ksfire.org) are when smoke contributes to poor air

quality in Nebraska, a state adjacent to Kansas to the north.

The smoke problem has been persistent enough to merit US Environmental Protection Agency notice, and a Flint Hills Smoke Management Plan (SMP; Kansas Department of Health and Environment 2010) has been implemented to encourage the voluntary selection of dates for burning when impairment of air quality (ozone and particulate matter 2.5) is least likely to occur. To provide rancher guidance, an online smoke model is provided by the Kansas Department of Health and Environment that shows the likelihood of smoke impacting air quality monitor readings (www.ksfire.org; Craig *et al.* 2012). The model incorporates meteorological forecasts, including wind speed and direction, transport wind height and direction and inversions, as well as hectares of rangeland still likely to burn during the current burn season and estimated fuel load. Although smoke contributions to impaired air quality have not been eliminated, the SMP and attendant outreach to the ranching community and urban areas have resulted in more understanding by both sides on the reasons for burning and the impact smoke can have.

Local smoke impacts are expected by Flint Hills residents during the prescribed burning season. It is not uncommon to have small drifts of ash on the streets, reduced visibility and a very strong smell of smoke. Although unpleasant, annoying and potentially affecting the health of sensitive populations, most residents accept this as part of living within a fire-dependent ecosystem.

Smoke issues are exacerbated by nightly inversions, when the boundary layer of air is lower than during the daytime. Wind speeds often decrease at night, adding to the potential for smoke to settle near the ground and flow down topographical drainages. After sunrise, the boundary layer tends to rise and smoke disperses. Transported smoke issues tend to be greatest at sunrise when people begin their daily activities and before the boundary layer rises. By midday, transported smoke issues rarely remain. This presents a challenge to those responsible for afternoon outdoor school sports and recreation activities, because decisions need to be made in the early morning so parents can make alternative arrangements for their children's after-school care. Better forecasting and communication of likely weather and smoke conditions later in the day are needed.

Counties can and generally do have regulations in addition to state regulations, and requirements can vary substantially (Kansas Flint Hills Smoke Management 2019). Some counties require burn permits, some do not. Those counties requiring notification collect, at a minimum, the burner's name, the location of the burn and an estimate of how many hectares will be burned. Reporting the start and end time of a burn is generally required so that emergency vehicles are not dispatched unnecessarily. Generally notifications are made to the county sheriff's office dispatcher.

When weather conditions are adverse for prescribed burning, as determined by county commissioners in conjunction with local volunteer fire departments (VFDs), burn bans can be declared to prevent prescribed burning. These bans are typically temporary in nature and only a day or two in duration. Sometimes individual ranchers are allowed to burn during a ban based on the fire department's personal knowledge of the individual's experience and skill with prescribed fire and burn unit characteristics.

Virtually all of the Flint Hills region is served by local VFDs, which are staffed by trained community members who volunteer for both wildland and structural fire responses. Fire equipment is purchased through taxes and grants, and is sometimes facilitated by state forest service access to US military surplus equipment that is modified for wildland firefighting. Vehicles specifically designed and designated to respond to wildland fires are often referred to as 'brush trucks', as distinct from structural firefighting vehicles. Brush trucks are often custom fitted by the local VFD with equipment best suited to local conditions. Because of the rugged terrain and long distances from water refill points, brush trucks are heavy duty and have water supplies on board appropriate for manoeuvrability, as well as equipment for drawing water from both pressurised water systems and open water sources, such as ponds and streams. Rugged tanker trucks are also common for carrying water to remote locations. VFD crews may include ranchers familiar with wildland fire because of their experience with prescribed rangeland burning.

Locally, most residents in the Flint Hills, especially those who have lived there for any length of time, are comfortable with the extent of prescribed burning that occurs. They understand that the air may be smoky, with ash dropping on the streets, for a day or two each year, and residents with health issues affected by smoke understand they will need to take precautions when this happens.

Complaints about air quality are more common among new residents, who may not understand the necessity of prescribed burning to maintain these landscapes. Those unfamiliar with prescribed fire may also fail to recognise the danger of building on the edge of the prairie. Little or no regulation exists for landowners building in these highly flammable, fire-maintained landscapes, with the result that inappropriate building and landscaping methods are often used, such as wood decks and coniferous landscape plantings near structures. The result can be a nearly indefensible landscape of large homes constructed and surrounded by highly flammable biomass, often eastern red cedar (*Juniperus virginiana*) mixed with tall grass, with less than ideal access for firefighting.

This mix of non-urban, non-rural native vegetation is called the wildlife–urban interface (WUI) and occurs most commonly near rapidly growing communities in the Flint Hills (Middendorf *et al.* 2009). The problem can be exacerbated by landowners fearing or choosing not to conduct prescribed burns on their land, which rapidly becomes covered with highly flammable eastern red cedar. As this land conversion occurs, prescribed burning becomes less of a land management option because it is riskier and less likely to achieve the needed level of woody plant control without high fire intensities only achievable outside the usual burn parameters.

Most ranchers do not limit their prescribed burning activity due to legal concerns because of their experience with fire, how Kansas and Oklahoma state liability law is interpreted in court, the rarity of prescribed burning-related lawsuits and because many farm and ranch insurance policies include prescribed burning as a covered normal management activity. A major exception is concern about smoke on roadways and resulting fatalities. Ranchers burning close to major roads and interstate highways take extra precautions and wait for off-road wind directions before burning. However, there have been fatalities directly linked to prescribed burn smoke impairing driver visibility.

Most instruction in prescribed burning is traditional ecological knowledge, as skills, methods and understanding of how fire affects native rangeland and livestock is passed to younger generations. More formal training is available through burn workshops and on-the-ground training, which are often the primary method of learning for non-ranching landowners. Other sources of expertise available include land management agency programs and consultations, primarily the Natural Resources Conservation Service, state, federal and non-governmental organisation wildlife managers and K-State Research and Extension.

Getting fire on the ground

Planning which hectares to burn often begins a year in advance. Because it is rare to be able to burn as many hectares as desired each year, ranchers use an informal prioritisation process. Parcels of land that were not burned the previous year, areas that received more rain or less grazing and therefore have a greater accumulation of biomass and parcels of land with woody encroachment are typically a higher priority for burning. Changes in the ranching operation, such as the amount of land managed, can also affect priorities. Burn objectives generally include control of woody species and increased forage quality and quantity. Additional objectives can be incorporated into a single burn. Although written burn plans are not required,

some ranchers do write a burn plan as part of the preparation process. The components of a burn plan are part of a rancher's planning process even if not formalised or written down. Ranchers doing their own burning often have years of experience, beginning in their youth.

Prescribed burning often occurs within a community context. Neighbours are frequently contacted well in advance of a prescribed burn, often resulting in a group effort where multiple burn units are more efficiently burned with a single ignition. Larger burns are often safer because there is an increased supply of equipment and number of crew available and less perimeter, where fire can escape, per hectares burned. Combining burn units increases the chances that natural landscape features can be used as fireguards, reducing the length and complexity of manual firebreak construction. Unlike other areas of the Great Plains, formal burn associations are not found in the Flint Hills at the current time. However, the burn association concept of neighbours helping neighbours is very much in evidence.

Burn unit size can range from less than four to tens of thousands of hectares (B. Obermeyer, pers. comm., 2020). Land ownership in the Flint Hills is laid out on the standard US Public Land Survey System grid system, with the section (~260 ha) and quarter section (~65 ha) the most typical units. Ranches can often be several square kilometres in extent, but smaller land ownership patterns are also common. Many of the larger ranches are owned by non-resident landowners, who lease the land to local ranchers to manage.

Burn units are determined primarily by land ownership, management unit boundaries and the ability to create or use existing fireguards. Topography can be quite rugged, with exposed rocks and steep terrain, and burn units often are sized to allow access around the perimeter with vehicles (Figure 9.4).

Although a burn unit is often delineated in advance, if conditions are favourable or neighbours decide to burn too, the final burn unit size may be substantially larger than originally planned. Although seemingly casual and spontaneous, such

Figure 9.4: After a burn, the rocky surface of the soil is most apparent. Topography and rocks discouraged the wholesale conversion to croplands common at other tallgrass prairie sites in North America. Photograph courtesy of Carolyn Baldwin.

decisions are actually based on years of prescribed burning experience, familiarity with crew and equipment capabilities and knowledge of the local rangeland and its management. The ability to make independent decisions without regulatory interference is highly prized.

Fireguards are often existing landscape features such as roads, cattle trails along fence lines and creeks. Mowing can be used for firebreaks, but the length of the burn unit perimeter, the need to move mowed material away from the break and inaccessible terrain often make this a less-suitable option, especially on large burn units. Crop fields of generally <40.5 ha are found throughout the Flint Hills along creek bottoms (Middendorf *et al.* 2009), and these can also be used as fireguards. Tilled fireguards are almost non-existent, except perhaps around a highly valued structure or on military lands. It is recommended that the width of a constructed fireguard is at least 10 times the height of the vegetation or a minimum of approximately 9 m (Kansas Natural Resources Conservation Service 2011), but, in practice, the width of the fireguard varies widely. Heavy or volatile fuels such as red

cedar near the edge of the burn unit necessitate wider fireguards. Where available, roads and pasture trails are the preferred fireguards because they offer vehicle access around the perimeter of the burn unit, as well as an already prepared area of little or no vegetation. Additional crew and equipment can be deployed where fireguards are considered less than optimal. The ideal serendipitous fireguard is an already burned area adjacent to the burn unit, which is often an option as the burn season progresses. Fireguards are generally selected and/or prepared in advance of the burn season.

Weather is the greatest constraint to achieving prescribed burning goals. April is a period of often sudden temperature and wind shifts, with fronts passing through and precipitation likely. In general, burn prescriptions call for wind speeds between 8 and 32 kph, and relative humidity in the range of 30–60% (Kansas Natural Resources Conservation Service 2019). Other weather factors, such as forecast cold fronts and precipitation following the burn, are considered. The soil surface is often damp this time of year, which makes the fire less likely to escape. Prescribed burning in drought conditions, with a very dry soil surface, greatly increases the chance a fire will escape.

A second major constraint for prescribed burning is labour. Crews are generally made up of family members, employees and neighbours, and coordinating schedules can be a challenge so that everyone can be on the burn at the same time. Generally, contacting potential crew members begins informally before the burn season as the intent to burn is discussed. Starting several weeks ahead of the burn season, as burn planning becomes more complete, crew members are contacted and burn dates are proposed as schedules are consulted and weather forecasts become nearer term. Eventually a specific date and time are selected, and the crew assembles at the site. Given that most crew members will have had experience burning the unit and have worked together in the past, crew briefings are typically minimal, although any new or temporary hazards, such as

standing water or construction work, are usually pointed out. A general plan of how the unit is to be burned is understood and crew members perform their designated tasks without much discussion.

Unless otherwise delegated, the person who owns or manages the land is the burn boss and carries the responsibility for the burn. Contingency planning generally consists of calling the local fire department if the fire escapes.

Mobile telephones are ubiquitous and used for communicating with crew members and county staff as needed. Small hand-held radios are also commonly used.

Formal protective gear is virtually unknown when burning on private lands, but is generally required for agency staff burning on state lands or assisting landowners on a private land burn. Typical clothing on a prescribed burn would include jeans, boots, chaps, cap or hat, gloves, other normal clothing and a jacket if the weather requires it (Figure 9.5).

Figure 9.5: Ranchers rarely use specialised protective clothing while conducting prescribed burns. Most ranchers conduct burns while wearing the jeans, jackets, hats and boots typical of everyday wear. Photograph courtesy of Kansas State University Department of Agronomy.

Equipment

Individual ranchers generally own some or all of the equipment needed to conduct prescribed burning on their own land. Minimally, this tends to consist of a sprayer unit mounted on a four-wheel drive pickup or other off-road vehicle, all-terrain vehicles (ATVs) or utility task vehicles (UTVs) with ignition devices and sprayers attached, and a back-up water supply on a separate vehicle. Equipment can be basic or elaborate depending on the needs and desires of the rancher.

Fire suppression is achieved with both sprayers and hand tools. Sprayers in their most simple form consist of a tank, pump, hose, wand with nozzle and power source. ATV and UTVs commonly use the vehicle battery as a pump power source. Small petrol (gasoline) engines are typically used as a power source for sprayers mounted in pickup trucks. Vehicles specifically designed for fire suppression may have large swivelling nozzles directly mounted on the vehicle, but a hand-held nozzle is more common. Small hand-pump sprayers worn as a backpack are available, but are less commonly used. Sprayers are considered essential equipment for burning in the Flint Hills.

Sprayers are most commonly deployed along the edges of a fire. A wet line can be laid down along a fireguard to prevent fire spread outside the burn unit. If sprayer output is substantial, the wet line it creates can be used as a fireguard immediately ahead of ignition. Sprayer units follow along behind the ignition line and suppress fire that is moving outside the burn unit. Sprayers are also used to put out escapes, spot fires and smouldering fuels, such as cow faecal pats, where they pose an escape problem. In addition to sprayers, manual suppression tools for less-intense fire situations include flappers, backpack blowers, fire brooms and rakes.

The need to ignite large acreages rapidly has led to the design of novel ignition equipment. Historically, stringing fire was done by dropping wooden matches or by dragging a rake, burning hay bale or tyre. More modern ignition sources include the commercial drip torch, which is filled with a mixture of ~30% petrol and 70% diesel. Drip torches are generally hand-held and are used while either walking or riding an ATV or UTV. After replacing the fill cap on the drip torch, a small amount of fuel is allowed to flow out the pad at the tip by inverting the torch. The pad is then lit using a lighter or matches. Lighted fuel drips from the pad as the torch is carried along in an inverted position, creating an ignition line. The drip torch is generally not in direct contact with the grass. The torch is extinguished by blowing it out. A drip torch offers flexibility in its use because a fire line can be strengthened by repeated passes or odd corners and fuel types can be addressed individually.

Although commercial drip torches are used, other home-built ignition devices are actually more common. Perhaps the most prevalent of the innovative ignition devices is the shop-built fire stick, which often consists of a 3.8- or 5-cm diameter steel pipe with a threaded cap on the upper end and an angled reduction elbow fitted with a slotted plug threaded on the ground end (Figure 9.6a; Hoy 1989).

The plug of the shop-built fire stick has a narrow slot cut across the threads or a hole drilled in it to allow the flow of fuel from inside the pipe. The width of the slot determines how much fuel is dispensed. The cap on the upper end often has a welded steel loop to allow the fire stick to be dragged with a vehicle. There are also other arrangements for mounting fire sticks on ATVs. The fire stick is filled with 100% petrol, the cap is replaced and the fire stick is then attached to a vehicle, generally an ATV or UTV. The fire stick is ignited by allowing the fuel to drip out for a short amount of time and then dropping a match into the fuel-saturated grass. The fire stick will continue to burn until it is placed in a fully upright position, whereupon it will go out by itself. If the fire stick is held in a horizontal position, it will continue to burn, but it can be elevated above the ground surface to stop ignition. As the fire stick is dragged along behind the vehicle through the grass, it ignites a continuous line of fire (Figure 9.6b). The use of a single fuel reduces the need to carry additional fuel types or mixes.

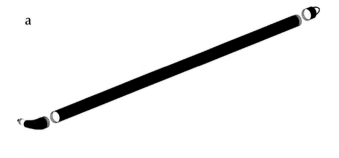

Figure 9.6: (a) A fire stick is a shop-built piece of ignition equipment used in the Flint Hills. It rapidly lights a continuous line of fire in the grass when pulled by an all-terrain or utility vehicle. Photograph courtesy of Carolyn Baldwin. (b) A fire stick in action. Photograph courtesy of Kansas State University Department of Agronomy.

Timing

Weather forecasts are checked several times a day during the burn season, as selecting an appropriate day to burn is critical to achieving management objectives. Assembling crew and transporting equipment to the site are time consuming and calling off a burn at the last minute because of weather can be frustrating. Every effort is made to select a day when weather conditions remain within the desired parameters for the entire period of the burn and possibly longer. Strong fronts with strong winds and weather anomalies such as dust devils and fire whirls during or closely following a burn can reignite or transport smouldering fuels such as cow pats and start a wildfire. A handheld wind meter is sometimes used to measure wind speed on-site. Generally, wind speed and direction are the most critical criteria when deciding to start ignition.

Many burns in the Flint Hills are started between midmorning and midafternoon, after the dew has evaporated and fuels have been warmed by the sun (Figure 9.7). However, ignition can occur during virtually all daylight hours. Small burns of a couple of hundred hectares or less are often planned to be extinguished by dark. Large burns greater than 4050 ha often burn through the night after the perimeter has been well secured. Humidity rises typically with nightfall, while temperatures and wind speed decrease, reducing fire intensity and smoke dispersion. Because of the reduced fire intensity, some burns are intentionally set to burn at night, but this practice is increasingly frowned upon because of concerns regarding smoke dispersion.

Ignition

The most typical ignition pattern is a ring burn (Figure 9.8). Starting on the downwind side of the burn unit at a given point, two ignitors begin stringing fire in opposite directions. This fire is the backfire, burning slowly into the wind along the fireguard. The fire is carefully monitored and any movement of the fire into or across the fireguard is immediately extinguished. This creates a widened, blackened fireguard that will later be used to stop the headfire. The backfiring process is often time consuming and requires skill. As the fire continues burning into the wind, ignitors begin to string fire from the ends of the backfire up the sides of the burn unit. Again, the fireguards are carefully monitored. The movement of ignitors is coordinated so that one ignitor does not get too far ahead of the ignitor on the opposite side of the fire. These

Figure 9.7: Although prescribed burns are initiated during daylight hours, the size of some burns will cause them to continue burning through the night after the perimeters are secured. Photograph courtesy of Tom Gross.

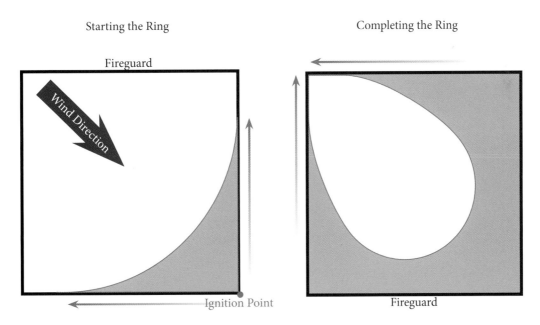

Figure 9.8: A ring fire is the most common type of ignition strategy. Starting at a downwind side or corner, a backfire is lit and closely monitored to create a fuel break. Gradually both sides of the burn unit are lit simultaneously. After an adequate fuel break has been created on the downwind and flank sides of the fire, the upwind side is lit, creating a headfire that burns into the fuel breaks. Photograph courtesy of Carolyn Baldwin.

secondary ignitions, called flank fires, are parallel to the wind. As the backfire and flank fires continue to burn, a horseshoe-shaped blackened fireguard is created, with the active fire line on the interior side. A period of fireguard growth, with no additional ignition, often follows until the fireguard is considered adequate to contain the headfire.

Finally, the ignitors string fire from the sides of the burn unit towards the middle of the windward side. This creates the headfire, which is the most intense and fast moving part of the burn. Backfire and flank fire flame lengths are generally small (9–1.8 m tall), but can rapidly increase in size (6–9 m tall) as the headfire is lit. The headfire is the fastest moving fire and rapidly consumes the fuel remaining in the burn unit. It burns into the blackened area created by the backfires and flank fires and goes out. Mop-up consists of monitoring the burn unit perimeter to make sure no fire escapes across the fireguards. Smouldering fuels, most often cow pats, are watered down around the perimeter to reduce the chance of fire reigniting after the crew has left.

After burn completion, the crew gathers up the equipment and makes a final check to see that the fire is extinguished. Heavy patches of fuel, especially woody material, may continue to smoulder for hours or even days afterwards, and require periodic checks to make sure embers have not been transported by the wind across the fireguard. Ember transport and resulting fire escape are key concerns when frontal weather systems are predicted within 24 h after a fire.

After a spring fire, grasses start to grow rapidly, which is enhanced by solar warming of the blackened soil surface. A flush of new green growth is soon visible. Moist soils increase the speed with which grass regrows. Livestock grazing can begin within days of a fire, and pastures are generally stocked by the beginning of May.

Fire and the future

Present-day ranchers consider prescribed burning in the Flint Hills as a continuation of land management practices started by Native Americans long before Euro-American settlement. There is a definite feeling of connection to prior generations of land managers. Ranchers and agency staff agree that without prescribed burning, this largest remaining contiguous North American tallgrass prairie ecosystem will be lost. Both endemic flora and fauna are adapted to prescribed burning at frequent intervals, and human communities in the Flint Hills are also adapted. The tacit agreement between landowners, communities, scientists, agencies and government units that high rates of prescribed burning are desirable creates a culture of fire that has endured several challenges.

At present, offsite smoke is a major concern with the current prescribed burning regime, and continues to be addressed through voluntary actions. There is an inherent conflict between the smoke produced by prescribed burning and the desired air quality. A broader view of ecosystem processes would include the improvement in air quality during the year as growing grasses remove carbon from the atmosphere during the growing season (Suyker et al. 2003). Some of this captured carbon is stored underground (Derner et al. 2006). Other carbon is incorporated into leaves and stems and will be released by fire once again, either the slow fire of decomposition or the rapid fire of a prescribed burn. Increased smoke regulation is the single biggest threat to reducing or eliminating needed fire.

An additional threat is the increase of eastern red cedar encroachment (Plate 9) due to infrequent or discontinued burning, especially in the WUI (Hoch and Briggs 1999), which makes prescribed burning of adjacent lands more difficult and risky (Figures 9.9, 9.10). All increased regulation of prescribed fire will decrease the amount of prescribed burning that occurs. Changes to the legal and insurance environment could also decrease or eliminate prescribed burning in the Flint Hills. In contradiction to these potential threats, Flint Hills ranchers' strong belief, supported by science, in the absolute necessity of burning provides a context in which increased regulation is politically unpopular and avoided.

Figure 9.9: At small sizes, red cedar is readily controlled with prescribed burning. Fire intensity increases as red cedars burn. Photograph courtesy of Eva Horne.

Figure 9.10: Red cedar is an invasive native conifer that rapidly colonises Flint Hills prairies in the absence of fire. Photograph courtesy of Carolyn Baldwin.

Healthy prairies provide numerous ecosystem services, including water storage and filtration, wildlife habitat and aesthetic enjoyment. Ecotourism is increasing as non-Flint Hills residents enjoy the magnificent wide-sky vistas, prairie wildlife in abundance, room to surrender to quiet and solitude outdoors and the mystic experience of being surrounded by fires and smoke during the burn season, especially the dramatic lines of fire that crawl across the hills at night.

Fire behaviour in well-managed prairies without woody species is relatively predictable because fuels are mostly continuous grass and surface fires are normal. Local pockets of heavier vegetation or more flammable plants can produce brief increases in fire intensity, whereas wet spots, heavily grazed areas and rocky outcrops reduce localised fire intensity.

The spread of woody species is increasing in the Flint Hills as elsewhere in the tallgrass ecosystem (Briggs *et al.* 2002b). Eastern red cedar is a highly volatile fuel that can send up showers of embers, increasing the need for larger fireguards and more frequent fire, as well as increasing the risk of conducting prescribed burns (Kansas Natural Resources Conservation Service 2019). Small red cedars (<1 m tall) are easily and safely burned within the context of a typical grassland burn. However, as size increases, so do the risks and the need for more intense fire to achieve control under conditions where there is less continuous grassland fuel to ignite the trees as the canopy closes. Larger red cedars can be ignited in a grass–red cedar matrix when fine fuel loads, red cedar moisture levels and weather conditions are favourable. However, when larger red cedars ignite during a burn, risk is increased as crowns torch and the resulting embers are carried by the wind far in excess of grassland-only burns (Weir 2009). If conditions are suitable, crown-to-crown torching can occur. Although not characterised chemically, the smoke from red cedars is darker and heavier than that from grass.

Although eastern red cedar does not resprout after fire, the tree carcasses can remain upright for a decade or more when larger trees are burned (Harr *et al.* 2014). If carcasses are allowed to stand in place, they become roosting sites for birds, which deposit seeds and restart the infestation. In addition, working livestock can be made more difficult where there are numerous tree carcasses. The removal of tree carcasses includes cutting, piling and then burning them, which is comparatively expensive (Coffey 2011).

Other shrubby woody encroachment is similarly resistant to prescribed burning, where an increase in motte size results in decreased control with typical prescribed burns (Ratajczak *et al.* 2011). A combination of fire, chemical and mechanical control and targeted grazing over a period of decades may be needed to reverse woody encroachment and restore native endemic species (Ditomaso *et al.* 2006). As an endangered North American ecosystem, the need for prescribed burning at frequent intervals is both necessary and desirable to preserve the tallgrass prairie (Ratajczak *et al.* 2016).

A common question is that if the prairie has to be burned, does it all have to be burned at the same time and cause smoke issues? To capture maximum gain from stocker cattle, burns need to be conducted within a specific time period in the spring to align with grass growth and the grazing season. For other objectives, the need to burn in April is less absolute, and other pyric herbivory (fire and grazing) systems may afford similar benefits (Engle and Bidwell 2001). Patch burn grazing is a system where generally approximately one-third of a pasture is rotationally burned each year. The burned area provides the highest-quality nutrition for livestock and wildlife; the unburned portion of the pasture provides rest for the vegetation from the heavy grazing that occurs the year of the burn, as well as litter and standing dead material for the wildlife that need this type of habitat. The advantages of patch burn grazing include a reserve of lower-quality but still grazable forage during drought years and possible wildlife benefits. The disadvantages include all the same preparation effort while only burning a part of the pasture, and the preference for larger burns with neighbours without the need to protect parts of a pasture from fire. In general, patch burn grazing is seen as requiring more work than burning an entire pasture.

Summer burning occurs when the paddock is burned during the growing season, generally in July through early September (Figure 9.11). Advantages of summer burning include a less-intense, more easily managed fire than during the dormant season, the ability to control troublesome weeds such as sericea lespedeza (*Lespedeza cuneata*;

Figure 9.11: Growing season burns are less common but occasionally occur in the Flint Hills. Photograph courtesy of Melissa Harvey, Kansas State University.

Olson and Baldwin 2018) and increasing the chances that all the acreage that needs to be burned is treated. Disadvantages include the loss of forage as green grass is consumed and the potential loss of stocker cattle gains the following year. Research is continuing to more fully understand the impact of summer burns on stocker gains and native rangeland vegetation. Anecdotal evidence is that summer fire is increasing in the Flint Hills. Smoke plumes are often visible, and there is much experimentation with fire as ranchers strive to care for their land in the best and most feasible manner.

Currently, Flint Hills private landowners and ranchers, scientists, state and county agencies, conservation organisations and the wildlife community are all in agreement that prescribed burning at frequent intervals is required to maintain the Flint Hills ecosystem. Although there is disagreement on the most appropriate fire return interval, there is no disagreement about the need for fire. In the Flint Hills, fire is not only accepted, but is also promoted; policies and regulations allow and expect extensive prescribed burning with minimal interference; and prairie plants and animals thrive with frequent fire on the landscape. The pyric legacy of Native Americans lives on in the fire culture of the Flint Hills (Hoy 1989).

Acknowledgements

The authors are grateful to the numerous ranchers and agency staff who provided interviews critical to the preparation of this manuscript. Kyle Griffith was instrumental in recording the interviews, and his work is greatly appreciated. Partial funding was provided by the Joint Fire Science Program through the Great Plains Fire Science Exchange. The authors also acknowledge the many people living and working in the Flint Hills who have contributed to our understanding of this special place.

References

Abrams M, Hulbert L (1987) Effect of topographic position and fire on species composition in tallgrass prairie in northeast Kansas. *American Midland Naturalist* **117**, 442–445. doi:10.2307/2425988

Anderson K (1967) Grazing management and fire in the Flint Hills. *Transactions of the Kansas Academy of Science* **70**, 171–176. doi:10.2307/3627115

Anderson R (1990) The historic role of fire in the North American grassland. In *Fire in the North American Tallgrass Prairies*. (Eds S Collins and L Wallace) pp. 8–18. University of Oklahoma Press, Norman.

Beam M (2010) Beef production in the Flint Hills. In *Ranching on the Tallgrass Prairie*. (Ed. M White) pp. 102–104. New Prairie Press, Manhattan.

Benson E, Hartnett D, Mann D (2004) Belowground bud banks and meristem limitation in tallgrass prairie plant population. *American Journal of Botany* **91**, 416–421. doi:10.3732/ajb.91.3.416

Blair J, Nippert J, Briggs J (2014) Grassland Ecology. In *The Plant Sciences, Volume 8: Ecology and the Environment*. (Ed. RK Monson) pp. 389–423. Springer, New York.

Briggs J, Hoch G, Johnson L (2002a) Assessing the rate, mechanisms, and consequences of the conversion of tallgrass prairie to *Juniperus virginiana* forest. *Ecosystems* **5**, 578–586. doi:10.1007/s10021-002-0187-4

Briggs J, Knapp A, Brock B (2002b) Expansion of woody plants in tallgrass prairie: a fifteen-year study of fire and fire–grazing interactions. *American Midland Naturalist* **147**, 287–294.

Coffey A (2011) Private benefits of eastern redcedar management and the impact of changing stocker value of gain. MSc thesis. Oklahoma State University, United States.

Craig K, MacDonald C, Wheeler N, Healy A, Zahn P, Gross T, Watson D (2012) A prescribed burn decision support system for the Kansas Flint Hills region. In *Proceedings of the 11th Annual Community Modeling and Analysis System Conference*. 15–17 October, Chapel Hill. <https://pdfs.semanticscholar.org/0641/01bd713946e7031a231da5ab005600093220.pdf>.

Derner J, Boutton T, Briske D (2006) Grazing ecosystem carbon storage in the North American Great Plains. *Plant and Soil* **280**, 77–90. doi:10.1007/s11104-005-2554-3

Ditomaso J, Brooks M, Allen E, Minnich R, Rice P, Kyser G (2006) Control of invasive weeds with prescribed burning. *Weed Technology* **20**, 535–548. doi:10.1614/WT-05-086R1.1

Engle D, Bidwell T (2001) Viewpoint: the response of central North American prairies to seasonal fire. *Journal of Range Management* **54**, 2–10. doi:10.2307/4003519

Fuhlendorf S, Engle D (2001) Restoring Heterogeneity on rangelands: ecosystem management based on evolutionary grazing patterns. *Bioscience* **51**, 625–632. doi:10.1641/0006-3568(2001)051[0625:RHOREM]2.0.CO;2

Fuhlendorf S, Archer S, Smeins F, Engle D, Taylor C (2008) The combined influence of grazing, fire, and herbaceous productivity on tree–grass interactions. In *Western North American Juniperus Communities: A Dynamic Vegetation Type* (Ed. O Van Auken) pp. 219–238. Springer, New York.

Harr R, Morton L, Rusk S, Engle D, Miller J, Debinski D (2014) Landowners' perceptions of risk in grassland management: woody plant encroachment and prescribed fire. *Ecology and Society* **19**, 41. doi:10.5751/ES-06404-190241

Hickman K, Hartnett D, Cochran R, Owensby C (2004) Grazing management effects on plant species diversity in tallgrass prairie. *Journal of Range Management* **57**, 58–65. doi:10.2307/4003955

Hoch G, Briggs J (1999) Expansion of eastern red cedar in the northern Flint Hills, Kansas. In *Proceedings of the Sixteenth North American Prairie Conference, No. 16*. (Ed. J Springer) pp. 9–15. University of Nebraska, Lincoln, <https://images.library.wisc.edu/EcoNatRes/EFacs/NAPC/NAPC16/reference/econatres.napc16.ghoch.pdf>.

Hoy J (1989) Controlled pasture burning in the folklife of the Kansas Flint Hills. *Great Plains Quarterly* **9**, 231–238.

Hoy J (2009) Cattle in the Flint Hills. In *Discovering This Place*. (Ed. Marty White) pp. 41–48. New Prairie Press, Manhattan.

Hulbert L (1969) Fire and litter effects in undisturbed bluestem prairie in Kansas. *Ecology* **50**, 874–877. doi:10.2307/1933702

Knapp A, Seastedt T (1986) Detritus accumulation limits productivity of tallgrass prairie. *Bioscience* **36**, 662–668. doi:10.2307/1310387

Kansas Department of Health and Environment (2010) 'State of Kansas Flint Hills smoke management plan'. Kansas Department of Health and Environment Division of Environment Bureau of Air, Topeka.

Kansas Department of Health and Environment (2020) *Flint Hills Prescribed Fire Update 2020 Summary May 15, 2020.* Kansas Department of Health and Environment, Topeka, <https://www.ksfire.org/new-media-archives/weekly updates/2020/2020_Flint_Hills_Summary_May_15.pdf>.

Kansas Flint Hills Smoke Management (2019) County burning information. Kansas Flint Hills Smoke Management, Topeka, <https://www.ksfire.org/burn-info/>.

Kansas Natural Resources Conservation Service (2011) 'Firebreak construction specifications S-394-1'. United States Department of Agriculture Kansas Natural Resources Conservation Service, Salina.

Kansas Natural Resources Conservation Service (2019) 'Prescribed burning construction specifications 338'. United States Department of Agriculture Kansas Natural Resources Conservation Service, Salina.

Kansas State University Agricultural Economics and Kansas Department of Agriculture (2019) Bluestem pasture release 2019. Kansas State University, Manhattan, <https://www.agmanager.info/land-leasing/land-buying-valuing/land-use-value-research/bluestem-pasture-release-2019>.

Kollmorgen W, Simonett D (1965) Grazing operations in the Flint Hills-bluestem pastures of Chase County, Kansas. *Annals of the Association of American Geographers* **55**, 260–290.

Launchbaugh J, Owensby C (1978) 'Kansas rangelands: their management based on half a century of research'. Bulletin 622, Kansas Agriculture Experiment Station, Manhattan.

Malin J (1942) An introduction to the history of the bluestem pasture region of Kansas: a study in adaptation to geographical environment. *The Kansas Historical Quarterly* **2**, 3–28.

Middendorf G, Becerra TA, Cline D (2009) Transition and resilience in the Kansas Flint Hills. *Online Journal of Rural Research and Policy* **4**, doi:10.4148/ojrrp.v4i3.109>.

Mitchell J (1978) The American Indian: a fire ecologist. *American Indian Culture and Research Journal* **2**, 26–31. doi:10.17953/aicr.02.2.v736211336358254

Mohler R, Goodin D (2012) Mapping burned areas in the Flint Hills of Kansas and Oklahoma, 2000–2010. *Great Plains Research* **22**, 15–25.

Obermeyer B (2012) Defining the Flint Hills. In *The Prairie: Its Seasons and Rhythms.* (Ed. L Hamilton) pp. 117–123. New Prairie Press, Manhattan.

Oklahoma Forestry Services (2019) *Burn Within the Law.* Oklahoma Department of Agriculture, Food, and Forestry, Oklahoma City, <http://www.forestry.ok.gov/rxburn-law>.

Olson K, Baldwin C (2018) 'Maximizing effectiveness of growing season burns for sericea lespedeza control'. Joint Fire Science Program Great Plains Fire Science Exchange Publication 2018-1, Manhattan.

Owensby C (2019) Reasons for burning. In *Prescribed Burning Notebook.* (Ed. C Baldwin) p. 3–13. Kansas State University Research and Extension, Manhattan.

Owensby C, Auen L (2013) Comparison of season-long grazing applied annually and a 2-year rotation of intensive early stocking plus late-season grazing and season-long grazing. *Rangeland Ecology and Management* **66**, 700–705. doi:10.2111/REM-D-13-00014.1

Pyne S (1982) Our Grandfather Fire: fire and the American Indian. In *Fire in America: A Cultural History of Wildland and Rural Fire.* pp. 71–83. University of Washington Press, Seattle.

Ratajczak Z, Nippert J, Hartman J, Ocheltree T (2011) Positive feedbacks amplify rates of woody encroachment in mesic tallgrass prairie. *Ecosphere* **2**, 121. doi:10.1890/ES11-00212.1

Ratajczak Z, Briggs J, Goodin D, Luo L, Mohler R, Nippert J, Obermeyer B (2016) Assessing the potential for transitions from tallgrass prairie to woodlands: are we operating beyond critical fire thresholds? *Rangeland Ecology and Management* **69**, 280–287. doi:10.1016/j.rama.2016.03.004

Samson F, Knopf F (1994) Prairie conservation in North America. *Bioscience* **44**, 418–421. doi:10.2307/1312365

Samson F, Knopf F, Ostlie W (2004) Great Plains ecosystems: past, present, future. *Wildlife Society Bulletin* **32**, 6–15. doi:10.2193/0091-7648(2004)32[6:GPEPPA]2.0.CO;2

Smith E, Owensby C (1973) Effects of fire on true prairie grasslands. *Fire Ecology Conference Proceedings* **12**, 9–22. <https://talltimbers.org/wp-content/uploads/2018/09/9-SmithandOwensby1972_op.pdf>

Smith E, Owensby C (1978) Intensive-early stocking and season-long stocking of Kansas Flint Hills Range. *Journal of Range Management* **31**, 14–17. doi:10.2307/3897624

Steinauer E, Collins S (1996) Prairie ecology – the tallgrass prairie. In *Prairie Conservation: Preserving North America's Most Endangered Ecosystem.* (Eds F Sampson and F Knopf) pp. 38–52. Island Press, Washington, DC.

Stewart O (2002) The effects of burning of grasslands and forests by aborigines the world over. In *Forgotten Fires: Native Americans and the Transient Wilderness.* (Eds H Lewis and K Anderson) pp. 113–216. University of Oklahoma Press, Norman.

Suyker A, Verma S, Burba G (2003) Interannual variability in net CO_2 exchange of a native tallgrass prairie. *Global Change Biology* **9**, 255–265. doi:10.1046/j.1365-2486.2003.00567.x

Svejcar T (1990) Response of *Andropogon gerardii* to fire in the tallgrass prairie. In *Fire in the North American Tallgrass*

Prairies. (Eds S Collins and L Wallace) pp. 19–27. University of Oklahoma Press, Norman.

Weaver J (1958) Classification of root systems of forbs of grassland and a consideration of their significance. *Ecology* **39**, 393–401. doi:10.2307/1931749

Weir J (2009) Why conduct prescribed burns. In *Conducting Prescribed Burns: A Comprehensive Manual*. Texas A&M University Press, College Station.

Wells R (1819) On the origin of prairies. *American Journal of Science* **1**, 331–338.

Williams G (2002) Aboriginal use of fire: are there any 'natural' plant communities? In *Wilderness and Political Ecology*. (Eds C Kay and R Simmons) pp. 179–214. University of Utah Press, Salt Lake City.

Wilson G, Hartnett D (1998) Interspecific variation in plant responses to mychorrhizal colonization in tallgrass prairie. *American Journal of Botany* **85**, 1732–1738. doi:10.2307/2446507

10

An NGO and prescribed fire: The Nature Conservancy's Joseph H. Williams Tallgrass Prairie Preserve (USA)

Robert G. Hamilton

Introduction to fire in the region

The Joseph H. Williams Tallgrass Prairie Preserve (hereafter the Preserve) is a 16 050-ha natural area located in Osage County, in north-eastern Oklahoma. Established in 1989, the Preserve is owned and managed by The Nature Conservancy, an international non-profit conservation organisation whose mission is to protect the lands and waters on which all life depends. The Conservancy is active in 72 countries and in every US state, and works to maintain fire's role where it benefits people and nature.

The Preserve is embedded within the southern end of the 2-million hectare Greater Flint Hills of Kansas and Oklahoma, which comprises the largest extant native tallgrass prairie landscape in North America. The Oklahoma portion of the Greater Flint Hills landscape is locally known as 'the Osage' and 'Osage Hills' (Figure 10.1). Two distinct native vegetation associations are found in the Greater Flint Hills landform (Plate 10). The tallgrass prairie landscape in the north-western portion is underlain by limestone and shale and is dominated by big bluestem *Andropogon gerardii*, Indiangrass

Sorghastrum nutans, composite dropseed *Sporobolus compositus*, switchgrass *Panicum virgatum* and little bluestem *Schizachyrium scoparium*. The south-eastern portion of the Greater Flint Hills landform is underlain by sandstone and shale and supports cross-timbers vegetation (tallgrass prairie and upland oak woodlands of post oak *Quercus stellata* and blackjack oak *Quercus marilandica*). The Preserve is located where these two vegetation associations meet, consisting of ~90% tallgrass prairie grassland and 10% upland cross-timbers woodlands and riparian forests (Plate 11). Fuels for fire management primarily consist of a matrix of tallgrass prairie dominated by tall grass and forbs (Figure 10.2), and cross-timbers woodlands with oak leaf litter and tallgrass prairie (Figure 10.3). The mean herbage production of the tallgrass prairie is ~4000 kg per hectare per year, but levels can be significantly higher in areas that have not received recent fire or grazing. Small-patch plant communities are also embedded in the tallgrass prairie and cross-timbers matrix, and include wet prairies, seeps, springs, streams and riparian woodlands.

Figure 10.1: Tallgrass prairie landscape of the Osage Hills in the southern portion of the Greater Flint Hills, Osage County, Oklahoma. The native wildflower in the foreground is the compass plant *Silphium laciniatum*. Photograph taken by Robert G. Hamilton within the bison fire unit of the Tallgrass Prairie Preserve.

Figure 10.2: Tallgrass prairie vegetation that provides abundant fine fuels for fire management.

Figure 10.3: Cross-timbers vegetation that provides oak leaf litter and tallgrass prairie vegetation for fire management.

The Flint Hills pre-settlement fire regime was likely similar to that of other Great Plains grasslands. For the Northern Plains region, Higgins (1986) reports seasonal fire peaks in March through May and September through October, with a smaller peak in July through August. Historic sources of ignition were lightning strikes and burning by Native Americans. The scale of pre-settlement fires likely ranged from small-scale lightning strike burn patches during the growing season (high fuel moisture and low-intensity fires) to large-scale human-set burns in the non-growing or dormant season (low fuel moisture and high-intensity fires). Estimates of pre-settlement tallgrass prairie fire frequencies range from every 5–10 years (Wright and Bailey 1982) to two to five times every 10 years (Hulbert 1973).

Ranching is the primary land use in the Flint Hills, with annual spring burning coupled with intensive early stocking of yearling cattle (double stocked for the first half of the growing season) being the most widely applied range management practice over the past four decades (Launchbaugh and Owensby 1978; Smith and Owensby 1978; Vermeire and Bidwell 1998). Thus, fire is regularly applied on an annual basis by ranch managers across a sizeable portion of the privately owned Flint Hills landscape. Unfortunately, from a conservation perspective, this fire–grazing regimen typically results in habitat uniformity and a largely homogeneous landscape with lowered biodiversity. Homogenising range practices are considered to be one of the leading sources of ecological stress in the Flint Hills (The Nature Conservancy 2000).

Ecosystem variability, or heterogeneity, has been described by numerous authors as the root of biological diversity at all levels of ecological organisation, and should therefore serve as the foundation for ecosystem and conservation management (Christensen 1997; Ostfeld et al. 1997; Wiens 1997; Fuhlendorf et al. 2006). The Great Plains of North America evolved with fire and ungulate grazing, and these two agents of natural disturbance are considered to be keystone processes of the prairie ecosystem (Axelrod 1985; Milchunas et al. 1988; Knapp et al. 1999). The close interaction between grazers and fire is believed to be the primary means of achieving heterogeneity and the full range of natural variation in Great Plains

grasslands (Biondini et al. 1989; Vinton et al. 1993; Steuter et al. 1995; Hartnett et al. 1996; Fuhlendorf and Engle 2001; Fuhlendorf et al. 2009, 2010; Leis et al. 2013; Monroe and O'Connell 2014). Therefore, utilisation of the fire–grazing interaction to promote landscape heterogeneity, and thus support native biodiversity, has been the primary land management goal at the Preserve (Hamilton 1996, 2007).

The Preserve uses two separate fire–grazing management regimes to enhance landscape heterogeneity and biodiversity (Plate 12). First, a bison herd was introduced in 1993 and now consists of 1400 animal units (~2200 head with spring calves) grazing on 9900 ha. The herd has year-round access to its entire management unit and is free to interact with randomly selected burn patches that reflect the original seasonality and frequency of fire. There is a significant bison–fire interaction, with strong bison grazing selection for recently burned patches that offer increased forage quality in the prairie's regrowth following a burn (Figure 10.4). The fire–bison interaction produces a vegetative

Figure 10.4: Bison grazing on lush spring regrowth of a winter burn patch. Note the unburned patch in the background, dominated by accumulated low-quality thatch from previous growing seasons that is not attractive forage for bison.

structural and compositional heterogeneity in an ever-shifting landscape patch mosaic that is supporting the complete array of native tallgrass prairie biodiversity.

Although the fire–bison regime has proven to be very effective for biodiversity conservation, it is not likely to be exportable to the private ranching industry that dominates the Flint Hills. The conservation challenge is to develop and implement cattle management regimes that incorporate some of the same 'biodiversity-friendly' elements as fire–bison. To that end, the Conservancy has been working with Oklahoma State University since 2001 to research and develop cattle-grazing regimes that promote heterogeneity. Over 4400 ha at the Preserve are dedicated to cattle 'patch burn grazing' research and demonstration (Plate 13). The research results have been encouraging thus far: heterogeneity and biodiversity can be enhanced with little or no decrease in livestock production (Allred *et al.* 2014). An additional outreach strategy engages area ranchers to restore greater prairie chickens through range management practices that produce grassland habitat diversity.

In summary, developing and maintaining an effective prescribed fire program is critical to the success of the Tallgrass Prairie Preserve. This chapter details how the Conservancy developed the Preserve fire program and how it has evolved over the past 30 years, provides an accounting of the program's results and discusses future challenges.

Requirements and barriers for fire use

The native tallgrass prairie landscape of the Flint Hills still exists because it was too rocky for European settlers to plough. Instead, it was settled by ranchers, and the prairie has been maintained as a native rangeland resource. Continued use of fire since settlement has also played a critical role in limiting the invasion of woody species into the native prairie ecosystem. The Flint Hills is unique in the Great Plains in that fire never left the landscape after European settlement. This privately owned native grassland has had a continuous fire culture, with ranchers and land managers being comfortable using fire as a land management tool. In addition, there is a strong tradition of neighbours helping neighbours conduct prescribed burns, and the local towns and citizens are generally tolerant of smoke during the burn season.

Conservancy policy restricts its ability to burn with other parties due to liability concerns. However, the Conservancy has signed fire management agreements with several large private ranch neighbours and a Fire Management Memorandum of Understanding with the Oklahoma Department of Wildlife Conservation. These agreements allow the involved parties to assist each other with prescribed fire, with each party serving as the burn boss on their own burns.

In this region of Oklahoma, there are no permits required before conducting a prescribed burn on private property. Title 2, Sections 16-28 and 16-28.2 of the Oklahoma Forestry Code provide some liability protection for landowners conducting prescribed burns under certain conditions. However, to obtain this protection, the owner or manager is responsible for: planning the burn; providing proper notification to neighbours and local authorities; conducting the burn according to the plan; providing adequate equipment and manpower to control the fire and confine it to their property; and preventing impacts downwind from smoke.

Regarding the Preserve fire management program, the highest risk is probably putting smoke across the public county gravel roads within the property. In addition to local traffic, the Preserve's public roads receive approximately 20 000 visitors per year, many of whom are from out of state. Most of these visitors have likely never encountered dense smoke obscuring their view of the roadway, and their reactions can be quite unpredictable. To ensure public safety if significant smoke is affecting the road, the Preserve burn crew will park a fire truck with flashing emergency lights at either end of the smoky stretch of road (in the clean air) and restrict traffic flow. Preserve fire truck operators communicate with each other by 40-W cab-mounted radios, and only one passing vehicle at a time is allowed through and no other vehicles are allowed in until the first vehicle emerges. It is unpredictable how drivers will respond to driving through smoke; some drivers stop or turn around in the smoke and head back out the way they came in.

Getting fire on the ground

The Preserve Prescribed Burn Plan is developed and reviewed by Conservancy fire management staff with extensive fire management experience; it is a 20-page document that must be renewed every 5 years. This single written plan serves as an efficient 'umbrella' document for all individual prescribed burns to be conducted during that 5-year term. Addenda to the Prescribed Burn Plan are the Fire Management Plan (science supporting the use of fire) and the Wildfire Response Plan. For each individual burn unit, a one-page incident action plan is carried in the field (Figure 10.5), with an aerial photograph-based burn unit map printed on the other side (Plate 14). These documents are filed after the burn, in addition to the go/no-go checklist, pre-burn fire weather, smoke dispersion and fuel moisture forecasts and post-burn reports of the same data. All of this pre-burn forecast and post-burn fire weather data are acquired from OK-FIRE (http://www.mesonet.org/index.php/okfire/home), a weather-based decision support system that has been developed for wildland fire managers throughout Oklahoma. OK-FIRE products use the Oklahoma Mesonet, the state's automated weather station network, and the National Weather Service's 84-h North American Mesoscale (NAM) model. The Preserve is extremely fortunate to host the Foraker weather station of the Oklahoma Mesonet network.

The Preserve Prescribed Burn Plan provides fairly wide-ranging parameters for fuel and weather conditions in order to give the burn boss some reasonable flexibility in making the go/no-go decision and execution of prescribed burns. The prescription for dormant-season burns (October–May) is a maximum temperature of 30°C, minimum relative humidity of 20% and a maximum wind speed of 32 kph. The prescription for growing-season burns (June–September) is a maximum temperature of 38°C, minimum relative humidity of 20% and a maximum wind speed of 32 kmh. However, relative humidity levels usually range from 25% to 50% for dormant-season burns and from 40% to 60% for growing-season burns.

Observed fire behaviour for dormant-season burns on the Preserve is typical for that commonly used season of prescribed fire in the Great Plains. Those burns usually involve fine fuels that are predominately dead and have very little to no green component, and the fire usually moves quickly and thoroughly across the entire unit. However, conducting growing-season burns has some significant differences and challenges. Often containing a high percentage of green fine fuels and burning under relatively high relative humidity, growing-season burns often move slowly and do not totally combust all fuels, or leave unburned patches within the burn unit (Plate 15). Summer burns also release spectacular smoke plumes; most of which is water vapour released from burning high-moisture fuels (Figure 10.6). An additional challenge with summer burns can arise from burning through cross-timbers fuels. If sufficient heat is generated in shrubby cross-timbers, the fire will crown into the overlying oak tree canopy, even during growing-season conditions when the oak leaves are lush and green. As with many upland oak-dominated savannas and woodlands, the cross-timbers are a fire-adapted native plant community (Figure 10.7).

The smallest burn units (1–100 ha) on the Preserve are hazard reduction 'firebreaks' around structures or ecological burns in ungrazed areas, whereas the largest (several hundred to several thousand hectares) are ecological burns in the fire–bison and fire–cattle managed areas. Within the 9900-ha fire–bison area, potential burn units are randomly selected from areas on the landscape that contain the minimum fine fuel needed to carry a fire (~900 kg ha^{-1}). Prescribed burns in the fire–bison unit reflect the ecosystem's original seasonality (spring, summer and winter) and frequency of fire (overall 3-year fire return;

Incident Action Plan, TNC-Tallgrass Prairie Preserve, Osage County, Oklahoma

Incident Name:		Date Prepared:	Prepared By:
	Operational Period:	From:	To:

General Management Goals:

- Ensure the safety of fire personnel and the public.
- Maintain an ecologically appropriate fire regime for the Tallgrass Prairie Preserve

Specific Burn Objectives:

- Burn at least 75% of the area within the burn subunit.
- Reduce herbaceous litter by at least 90% and rejuvenate native prairie plants.
- Top-kill at least 70% of invasive woody seedlings and saplings.

Control Operations:

- Ignition will begin with a test fire in representative fuels on the down-wind side of the unit, and will proceed by building black line on the down- wind side(s) of unit. .
- Strips will be used along holding lines to create black line. Backing fire from point source ignition will be the primary interior ignition technique in order to reduce fire behavior and minimize spotting. Flanking fire and strip head firing will also be used to assist in burning out the unit in a timely manner.
- **Water Sources (see map):** several man-made cattle ponds are within or adjacent to the burn unit. Several prairie streams are within or adjacent to the burn unit.
- **Secondary Control Lines:** The nearest county road, oil production road, or ranch road (all of which are graveled). Depending on the order of treatment, units burned earlier in the season (or in previous years) will themselves be firebreaks for later units.

Special Instructions:

- **Spots outside the unit**; watch carefully and be prepared.
- **Holding Plan:** Each holding crew will be equipped with at least one fire truck or ATV sprayer. Appropriate crew members will immediately suppress any escapes or spot fires. Crews will call for assistance with large escapes.
- **Mop-up:** All flaming materials within 10 yards of the line will be extinguished, with particular attention to burning heavy fuels within 50 yards of the line and cow pies within 6 feet of the fireline edge.

Medical Plan:

During the operational briefing EMTs (if any are present) will be identified to all personnel. First aid kits will be available on the burn in each fire truck. In the event of an injury, provide first aid promptly and notify the fire line supervisor and the Burn Boss as soon as possible. Injuries will be evaluated and treated by on-site resources to the extent possible. If injuries exceed the qualifications, abilities or materials of on- site resources then the Burn Boss will call 911; evacuate the patient to nearest county road for pick-up by the ambulance.

Safety Message:

- **LCES!** (Lookouts, Communications, Escape routes, Safety zones)
- **Watch out** for rocks, gullies, snakes, ground nesting wasps and bees, and check for ticks.
- **Mitigate for smoke** concerns: use respirators, step into fresh air for breathers, rotate crew members as needed.
- **Monitor for heat stress;** especially on summer burns. Monitor crew health and keep hydrated.
- **Maintain good situational awareness**, especially working around equipment.

Communications - one of the following tactical (line-of-sight) channels will be identified at briefing:

Frequency	Channel Name	Channel # (TNC)	Frequency	Channel Name	Channel # (TNC)
XXXX	TNC FIRE	1	XXXX	Neighbor Ranch	
XXXX	TNC FIRE (no PLT)	2	XXXX	BIA Fire	

Figure 10.5: Incident action plan carried in the field for every prescribed burn at the Tallgrass Prairie Preserve. ATV, all-terrain vehicle; BIA, Bureau of Indian Affairs; EMT, emergency medical technician; PLT, private line transmission (subfrequency); TNC, The Nature Conservancy.

Figure 10.6: Impressive vertical smoke plume generated by a prescribed burn on 17 September 2018 at the Tallgrass Prairie Preserve.

Figure 10.7: Post-burn canopy scorch following a summer prescribed burn in cross-timbers savanna at the Tallgrass Prairie Preserve. The burn was conducted on 28 July 2008 and the photograph was taken on 1 September 2008. The large tree in the foreground is a post oak (*Quercus stellata*).

approximately one-third of the unit burned annually). The interaction between fire and bison results in a process-driven mosaic of patches, moving across the landscape through the seasons and years (Figure 10.8). Within the 4400-ha cattle patch burn grazing area, the boundaries of the burn units are fixed and the units are burned in a set 3-year rotation (Plate 13).

A flexible process is used to select and design burn units on the Preserve. Once a general area is selected, consideration is then given to existing potential firebreaks on the landscape to determine the final burn unit boundaries (county and internal ranch roads, major stream courses, adjacent recently burned and grazed patches with low fuels). No pre-burn development of firebreaks is done (no mowing, disking or blacklining). However, the

Preserve commonly uses its fire trucks to create temporary wet line firebreaks where none exist, or to reinforce an inadequate existing firebreak (Figure 10.9). Heading out across the prairie in tall (unmowed) grass or along an existing inadequate firebreak, the first truck will shoot a cone of water down through the fine fuel, positioning the edge of the spray zone where the front tyre will track. A second fire truck will then immediately follow, soaking an additional adjacent swath of vegetation. The result is an approximate 10-m strip of saturated fine fuel with a defined sharp edge created by the first truck's tyre track. Immediately following is the ignitor (usually on an all-terrain vehicle [ATV]), using a drip torch to set the fire on the dry side of the tyre track. After the fire has burned back a few metres from the wet line edge, an additional third (and sometimes fourth) truck will follow, soaking the firebreak edge to ensure it holds. Depending on the amount of fine fuels and fire weather conditions, such a crew can create approximately 1–2 km of wet line before having to pause to refill the fire trucks with water. The resulting wet line firebreak will typically show compressed vegetation from the vehicle tyres tracks, but this impact will quickly

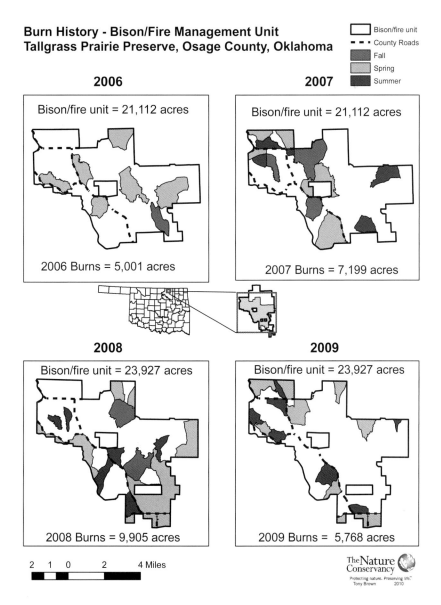

Figure 10.8: Fire history within the fire–bison management unit at the Tallgrass Prairie Preserve (2006–09). Image courtesy of Tony Brown.

fade (Figure 10.10). The typical surround-type ignition process is used to complete the prescribed burn process. Ignitors (with drip torches) typically drive ATVs, and holding and mop-up of the burn unit boundary is usually conducted by a crew member driving an ATV or utility task vehicle (UTV) with a slip-on spray unit (Figure 10.11). Kicking burning faecal pats into the burn unit is a major mop-up task on burn units that have cattle or bison grazing.

The Preserve fire management philosophy is that the whole process of planning and executing burns must be efficient and comfortably repeatable in order to keep pace with the approximately three dozen prescribed burns that must be conducted each year. On an annual basis, approximately 5000–6000 ha is burned on the Preserve, and the Conservancy assists rancher neighbours in burning twice that much. As a result of the Preserve's consistently productive fire program,

Figure 10.9: Five-ton fire trucks creating a temporary wet line firebreak during a growing season prescribed burn at the Tallgrass Prairie Preserve (17 September 2014). The first two trucks are creating a swath of soaked vegetation, followed by the ignitor on an all-terrain vehicle and finally a third fire truck to secure the firebreak edge. Photograph courtesy of Harvey Payne.

the Oklahoma program usually places as one of the Conservancy's most productive in the US on an annual basis. Over the past 30 years (1990–2019), the Preserve burn crew has conducted 865 prescribed burns on 159 100 ha. In addition, the Conservancy has assisted rancher neighbours in burning 244 700 ha of their properties. During that time, the Conservancy has also controlled 145 wildfires on the Preserve (25 lightning set)

and helped control 95 wildfires on adjacent ranches.

The Preserve's highly mechanised approach to fire management is a primary reason for its high productivity, and this equipment has undergone significant evolution through the years to improve capability and reliability. The original water sprayer units developed at the Preserve were 1500-L slip-on sprayers mounted on a trailer and pulled by a farm tractor (Figure 10.12) and a 3785-L slip-on sprayer mounted on the bed of a 2-ton four-wheel drive farm truck (Figure 10.13a). Both these spray units had diaphragm water pumps that were low volume and high pressure. Unfortunately, these vehicles had a tendency to get stuck in the mud and the sprayers lacked knockdown power under conditions of high fuel loads or high winds.

The next fire equipment innovation at the Preserve was 'Daisy' (big and yellow), a 3785-L, four-wheel drive articulating diesel vehicle (Figure 10.13b). This vehicle had the advantage of wide flotation tyres that greatly reduced problems with mobility on wet soils. However, it was very slow (maximum speed ~20 km h^{-1}) and had a low volume diaphragm sprayer, both of which hindered its ability to effectively respond to wildfires during extreme conditions.

Figure 10.10: (a) Completed growing-season prescribed burn wet line firebreak at the Tallgrass Prairie Preserve (4 August 2020). (b) Completed dormant-season prescribed burn wet line firebreak at the Tallgrass Prairie Preserve (6 January 2009).

Figure 10.11: Prescribed burn ignition from an all-terrain vehicle with a drip torch at the Tallgrass Prairie Preserve. Photograph courtesy of Harvey Payne.

Figure 10.12: Farm tractor pulling a trailer-mounted sprayer at the Tallgrass Prairie Preserve (1994). Photograph courtesy of Harvey Payne.

The breakthrough regarding fire control equipment in Osage County came from the Oklahoma Department of Agriculture Forestry Services. Beginning in the early 1990s, the Department initiated a new 'ranch-based rural fire department' program in the Osage Hills region of Oklahoma. Large ranches were encouraged to sign a Cooperative Fire Equipment Agreement with the Department, which established the cooperator as a ranch-based fire department and put the ranch on a waiting list for surplus military equipment.

Once the vehicle arrived, the cooperator had 4 months to outfit the vehicle as a fire truck. Within a few years, several hundred fire trucks were placed across the region. This program dramatically and successfully shifted the ranching community to large surplus military vehicles to control wildfire and manage prescribed fire. The highly mechanised approach works well in this region, where the terrain and soils can usually be navigated with large vehicles. Large military vehicles also have the payload capacity to carry large amounts of water to supply the high-volume spray pumps needed to effectively control fire in the abundant fine fuels produced by the tallgrass prairie. The tallgrass prairie landscape also supports abundant surface water supplies (streams and human-made ponds for watering livestock), which allows for easy refilling. And, most importantly, there is a talented group of mechanically inclined ranchers that builds and maintains this equipment. Now, when the call goes out for help on a large wildfire, often a dozen or more surplus military fire trucks will quickly respond from the ranch-based rural fire departments. It is very impressive how this modest investment by the State of Oklahoma has further strengthened the fire culture of the Osage Hills, both in the effectiveness of wildfire control and improved application of prescribed fire.

The quality of the surplus military equipment and the sophistication of fire truck outfitting have also evolved through the years. Initially, Gama Goats were the most available surplus military vehicles. The Gama Goat was a 1.25-ton six-wheel drive semi-amphibious vehicle developed for use by the US military in the Vietnam War (Figure 10.13c). The cab of the vehicle carried the driver and one passenger, whereas the rear trailer carried troops or cargo. Conversion of Gama Goats to be used as fire trucks commonly involved mounting a slip-on sprayer unit in the rear trailer and replacing the canvas cab roof with a steel roof. The Gama Goats were very manoeuvrable, but they were under-powered if more than a 750-L sprayer was mounted on the rear trailer. There also were no after-market parts available for these vehicles, so they became difficult to maintain.

The next generation of vehicles available through the Oklahoma Department of Agriculture Forestry Services were six-wheel drive military trucks. The first of these were 2.5-ton trucks. Cooperators often installed 3785- to 4500-L water tanks on the beds of these trucks (Figure 10.13d). At the Preserve, air-assisted power steering was also added, as were dual front tyres to correct the shortcoming of the vehicle's front-end to sink in the mud. More recently, 5-ton trucks became available and are still very popular. These trucks have power steering as a standard feature, and have more power and a greater payload capacity. Cooperators often install 4500- to 6800-L water tanks on the beds of these trucks (Figure 10.13e). At the Preserve, the standard military tyres and dual wheels on the rear axles are replaced with single floatation-type tyres to improve performance on soft soils. Water sprayer units are typically 20-hp Honda fire pumps that are relatively high volume and low pressure, providing good fire knockdown capability in high winds and dense grass fuels. In the past few years, a significant innovation in the region has been to install a high-tech spray nozzle on a swivel arm on the front of the truck, with the nozzle's direction, spray pattern and volume all operated by the truck's driver via electronic controls in the cab. This one-person, one-truck arrangement is labour efficient and much safer than the old standard design requiring a 'gunner' person to stand on a platform on the front of the truck to operate the sprayer nozzle. To refill the truck's water tank, two high-volume 'trash pumps' are mounted on the bed of the truck, which require only approximately 10 min to refill the tank from a pond or stream. In this landscape, there is typically such a source of water within several kilometres to refill the fire trucks.

Most recently, some private landowners (including the Conservancy) have been purchasing even bigger vehicles available in the surplus military market. The HEMMT is a military 10-ton eight-wheel drive vehicle that often comes already outfitted with a 9500-L tank (Figure 10.13f). The Preserve has also recently purchased a similar eight-wheel drive vehicle manufactured by Oshkosh Corporation, which articulates in the middle for greater manoeuvrability (Figure 10.13g). Both vehicles have been outfitted with the same front-mounted sprayer nozzle, high-volume water sprayer pump and refill pump arrangement as mentioned above. They have also been outfitted with an emergency horizontal spray nozzle on the front that produces a 500-L min^{-1} spray of water, allowing for aggressive tactics on wildfire suppression. Both these fire trucks carry a large supply of water, have high-volume sprayer pumps that are effective in dense grass fuels and high wind, operate well in wet and muddy soils due to their wide flotation-type tyres and can operate at highway speeds (100 km h^{-1}).

Consistent programmatic support (funding and administration), retention of the talented Preserve fire management staff and flexibility for program evolution through time are the primary reasons the Conservancy has had a successful fire management program at the Tallgrass Prairie Preserve. The Preserve burn crew comprises Conservancy staff who are full-time, permanent employees at the Preserve. These staff know the Preserve and its landscape features, as well as their fire equipment (they built it and maintain it), intimately. Having a talented and seasoned burn crew and all the necessary equipment on-site allows for a very flexible and short lead time for go/no-go decisions and what burn unit to target. It is worth noting that none of the Preserve fire staff works full-time on fire management; they all have other significant science or stewardship job duties. However, fire becomes the top priority during burn seasons.

Historically, the Conservancy has been burning its own lands and assisting its partners on theirs for almost 60 years. Its first prescribed burn was conducted in April 1962 on the Helen Allison Savanna Preserve in Minnesota. The Conservancy held its first in-house fire school for prescribed fire practitioners in the autumn of 1985 at the Niobrara Valley Preserve, Nebraska. For the next 20 years,

Figure 10.13: (a) A 2-ton four-wheel drive fire truck at the Tallgrass Prairie Preserve (1993). (b) 'Daisy', a four-wheel drive articulating diesel fire truck, at the Tallgrass Prairie Preserve (1994). (c) A Gama Goat six-wheel drive fire truck at the Tallgrass Prairie Preserve (1998). Photographs (a–c) courtesy of Harvey Payne. (d) A 2.5-ton six-wheel drive military truck converted to a fire truck at the Tallgrass Prairie Preserve (2008). Note the man ('gunner') standing on the front platform of the truck, directing the output of the water sprayer. (e) A 5-ton six-wheel drive military truck converted to a fire truck at the Tallgrass Prairie Preserve (2020). Note the high-tech spray nozzle mounted on the front of the truck, which is operated from within the cab by the driver (no second 'gunner' person is needed on the front of the truck to direct the water spray). (f) HEMMT surplus military 10-ton eight-wheel drive fire truck at the Tallgrass Prairie Preserve (2020). (g) Oshkosh 10-ton eight-wheel drive fire truck at Tallgrass Prairie Preserve (2020).

the Conservancy maintained a two-track fire-training system. Those staff pursuing qualification as a Fire Leader within The Nature Conservancy pursued in-house fire training, and a mentoring and experience pathway. In contrast, those staff needing qualifications to burn with federal agency partners pursued fire certification through the National Interagency Incident Management System (NIIMS). In 2005, the Conservancy discontinued the in-house fire-training path, requiring all fire management staff to follow the NIIMS training, experience and task book process. At the Preserve, the policy has been to maintain two staff certified as a Prescribed Fire Burn Boss Type 2 (RXB2) to make sure there is redundancy in that key position in order to maintain an active fire program. Training for that position is a huge personal and institutional investment: it took 9 years for the Preserve's newest burn boss to achieve certification. Other staff on the Preserve burn crew are certified at the NIIMS Fire Fighter Type 2 level.

Future of fire in the region

Considering the strong fire culture in the Flint Hills, prescribed fire should continue to be a viable land management tool for the foreseeable future. The economic incentive to enhance cattle weight gains by burning is not likely to decrease, and the utility of fire to control encroaching woody plants is appreciated by ranchers and land managers. Recently, the use of summer burns appears to be gaining some interest as a possible strategy to help control *Lespedeza cuneata*, the region's primary non-woody invasive plant problem, and to spread out the prescribed fire workload (and smoke impacts) from the current focus on spring burns. Finally, appreciation for the essential role of pyric herbivory in maintaining native grassland heterogeneity (and thus, biodiversity) is gaining ever-more respect within grassland conservation circles. Prescribed fire, if responsibly managed, should continue to flourish in the Flint Hills.

Issues that could negatively affect that future include growing citizen and regulatory discomfort with smoke and its negative safety and human health impacts. A tragic incident involving loss of life or property could severely tarnish the reputation of fire in the eyes of the public and politicians, leading to a backlash of regulations and rules that reduces the viability of fire as a management tool. Prescribed fire practitioners should always remember their responsibility to look out for the greater good of the industry.

Acknowledgements

The Tallgrass Prairie Preserve burn crew is an amazing group of smoke-eaters who know how to get the job done. Tremendous respect and appreciation go to Gene Big Soldier, Joe Bob Briggs, Tony Brown, Kevin Chouteau and Perry Collins. Likewise, huge thanks to the generous and capable ranchers of the Osage that we have had the pleasure of burning with through the years.

References

Allred BW, Scasta JD, Hovick TJ, Fuhlendorf SD, Hamilton RG (2014) Spatial heterogeneity stabilizes livestock productivity in a changing climate. *Agriculture, Ecosystems & Environment* **193**, 37–41. doi:10.1016/j.agee.2014.04.020

Axelrod DI (1985) Rise of the grassland biome, central North America. *Botanical Review* **51**, 163–201. doi:10.1007/BF02861083

Biondini ME, Steuter AA, Grygiel CE (1989) Seasonal fire effects on the diversity patterns, spatial distribution, and community structure of forbs in the northern mixed prairie, USA. *Vegetatio* **85**, 21–31. doi:10.1007/BF00042252

Christensen NL (1997) Managing for heterogeneity and complexity on dynamic landscapes. In *The Ecological Basis for Conservation: Heterogeneity, Ecosystems, and Biodiversity*. (Eds STA Pickett, RS Ostfeld, M Shachak and GE Likens) pp. 167–186. Chapman and Hall, New York.

Fuhlendorf SD, Engle DM (2001) Restoring heterogeneity on rangelands: ecosystem management based on evolutionary grazing patterns. *Bioscience* **51**, 625–632. doi:10.1641/0006-3568(2001)051[0625:RHOREM]2.0.CO;2

Fuhlendorf SD, Harrel WC, Engle DM, Hamilton RG, Davis CA, Leslie DM (2006) Should heterogeneity be the basis for conservation? Grassland bird response to fire and grazing. *Ecological Applications* **16**, 1706–1716. doi:10.1890/1051-0761(2006)016[1706:SHBTBF]2.0.CO;2

Fuhlendorf SD, Engle DM, Kerby J, Hamilton R (2009) Pyric herbivory: rewilding landscapes through the recoupling of fire and grazing. *Conservation Biology* **23**, 588–598. doi:10.1111/j.1523-1739.2008.01139.x

Fuhlendorf SD, Townsend DE, Elmore DE, Engle DM (2010) Pyric-herbivory to promote rangeland heterogeneity: evidence from small mammal communities. *Rangeland Ecology and Management* **63**(6), 670–678. doi:10.2111/REM-D-10-00044.1

Hamilton RG (1996) Using fire and bison to restore a functional tallgrass prairie landscape. *Transactions of the North American Wildlife and Natural Resources Conference* **61**, 208–214.

Hamilton RG (2007) Restoring heterogeneity on the Tallgrass Prairie Preserve: applying the fire-grazing interaction model. In *Proceedings of the 23rd Tall Timbers Fire Ecology Conference: Fire in Grassland and Shrubland Ecosystems.* (Eds RE Masters and KEM Galley) pp. 163–169. Tall Timbers Research Station, Tallahassee.

Hartnett DC, Hickman KR, Fischer-Walter LE (1996) Effects of bison grazing, fire, and topography on floristic diversity in tallgrass prairie. *Journal of Range Management* **49**, 413–420. doi:10.2307/4002922

Higgins KF (1986) 'Interpretation and compendium of historical fire accounts in the northern great plains'. Research Publication 161, US Fish and Wildlife Service, Washington, DC.

Hulbert LC (1973) Management of Konza prairie to approximate pre-white-man fire influences. In *3rd Midwest Prairie Conference Proceedings*, Kansas State University, Manhattan. (Ed. LC Hulbert) pp. 14–16. Division of Biology, Kansas State University, Manhattan.

Knapp AK, Briggs JM, Collins SL, Hartnett DC, Johnson LC, Towne EG (1999) The keystone role of bison in North American tallgrass prairie. *Bioscience* **49**, 39–50. doi:10.2307/1313492

Launchbaugh JL, Owensby CE (1978) 'Kansas rangelands: their management based on a half century of research'. Bulletin 662, Kansas Agricultural Experiment Station, Manhattan.

Leis SA, Morrison LW, Debacker MD (2013) Spatiotemporal variation in vegetation structure resulting from pyric-herbivory. *Prairie Naturalist* **45**, 13–20.

Milchunas DG, Sala OE, Lauenroth WK (1988) A generalized model of the effects of grazing by large herbivores on grassland community structure. *American Naturalist* **132**, 87–106. doi:10.1086/284839

Monroe AP, O'Connell TJ (2014) Winter bird habitat use in a heterogeneous tallgrass prairie. *American Midland Naturalist* **171**, 97–115. doi:10.1674/0003-0031-171.1.97

Ostfeld RS, Pickett STA, Shackak M, Likens GE (1997) Defining scientific issues. In *The Ecological Basis for Conservation: Heterogeneity, Ecosystems, and Biodiversity.* (Eds STA Pickett, RS Ostfeld, M Shachak and GE Likens) pp. 3–10. Chapman and Hall, New York.

Smith EF, Owensby CE (1978) Intensive early stocking and season-long stocking of Kansas Flint Hills range. *Journal of Range Management* **31**, 14–17. doi:10.2307/3897624

Steuter AA, Steinauer EM, Hill GL, Bowers PA, Tieszen LL (1995) Distribution and diet of bison and pocket gophers in a sandhill prairie. *Ecological Applications* **5**, 756–766. doi:10.2307/1941983

The Nature Conservancy (2000) 'Ecoregional conservation in the Osage Plains/Flint Hills Prairie'. The Nature Conservancy, Midwestern Resource Office, Minneapolis.

Vermeire LT, Bidwell TG (1998) 'Intensive early stocking'. Oklahoma State University Extension Facts F-2875, Oklahoma Cooperative Extension Service, Stillwater.

Vinton MA, Hartnett DC, Finck EJ, Briggs JM (1993) Interactive effects of fire, bison (*Bison bison*) grazing, and plant community composition in tallgrass prairie. *American Midland Naturalist* **129**, 10–18. doi:10.2307/2426430

Wiens JA (1997) The emerging role of patchiness in conservation biology. In *The Ecological Basis for Conservation: Heterogeneity, Ecosystems, and Biodiversity.* (Eds STA Pickett, RS Ostfeld, M Shachak and GE Likens) pp. 93–107. Chapman and Hall, New York.

Wright HA, Bailey AW (1982) *Fire Ecology.* John Wiley and Sons, New York.

11

Prescribed burn associations: US landowners getting fire on the ground

Russell Stevens and Morgan Treadwell

Introduction to prescribed burn associations

Aldo Leopold, the father of modern wildlife management, in 1933 wrote *'... wildlife can be restored by the creative use of the same tools which have heretofore destroyed it – axe, cow, plow, fire, and gun'* (Leopold 1933). Most people think about 'tools' as ways mechanics or carpenters correct problems or create and build speciality items. Range management is really no different; the manager in this case applies Leopold's management tools to address ecological problems. For example, the manager may use grazing to manage plant communities or brush management to sculpt wildlife habitat. For the most part we generally associate the use of these tools with positive outcomes. Conversely, we often do not consider the effects of overusing or neglecting to use these tools. This neglect or overuse can have negative, often cascading, effects, especially when addressing issues ecologically. The neglect or exploitation of the five tools outlined by Leopold have had marked effects across the agricultural landscape. We have been witness to the overuse of these tools in the Southern Great Plains; the Dust Bowl of the 1930s may be the most historically recognisable example. The current onslaught of wildfires across the US, Australia and other regions of the world is a result of neglecting the use of prescribed fire.

The application of prescribed fire is more of a process than a tool. Fire is probably the least understood, and certainly the least used, of the tools Leopold defines. Fire and grazing were the two major disturbances that shaped the plant communities not only in the Great Plains, but also across North America as a whole. Mother Nature and Native Americans caused fires all across North America. The right combination of rainfall, drought and lightning is how Mother Nature started fire. Native Americans saw how bison and other animals were attracted to burned areas and began using fire to their advantage. They also used it for warfare (Anderson 1990).

With no knowledge of fire science and no method or understanding of how to fight fire, early European settlers were terrified of fire. Their lack of knowledge and fear of fire also applied to cities and towns. Over time, prevention rose to the top of the list as the best method of fighting fire.

Therefore, fire was bad. This thinking was likely exacerbated by huge, destructive city fires, as well as wildfires in national forests. This lack of knowledge and fear, and the US Forest Service's Smokey the Bear campaign, all but eliminated the use of fire across North America. The suppression of fire for over 150 years has created ecological problems and a reduction in productivity on our grazing lands. When combined with years of overgrazing, the problems are exacerbated (Pyne 2015). Woody plant encroachment has caused untold hectares of once usable habitat to become useless for animals that depend on open grasslands. Some of these species, such as the lesser prairie chicken and monarch butterfly, are or have been proposed to be listed as endangered. In addition, as brush encroaches on open grasslands, forage production is greatly diminished, reducing the number of many species of wild and domestic herbivores.

To combat the woody plant invasion on the Great Plains, a grassroots movement to restore fire began in the mid-1990s. This involved the formation of localised cooperative associations, or prescribed burn associations (PBAs). The first such associations were formed in Nebraska (*c.* 1995), Texas (*c.* 1997) and Oklahoma (*c.* 2001; Weir *et al.* 2016). The concept of PBAs has proven a tremendous success and has spread to numerous other states. Illinois, Missouri, Louisiana and Mississippi now have PBAs, and several other states are in the planning phase (Weir *et al.* 2016). In 2019, the Humboldt County PBA was formed in California. This PBA currently has 85 members and wants to reverse the 100-year history of aggressive fire suppression in California, believing it can be done in a safe, effective, affordable and fun way (University of California, Division of Agriculture and Natural Resources 2019).

Thanks to demonstration and research, the use of prescribed fire has increased over the past few decades. The benefits of prescribed fire and the science and methodology of implementing prescribed fire safely and to accomplish specific goals are becoming more widely understood and accepted, and incorporated by PBAs (Twidwell *et al.* 2013). Today, prescribed fire is used not only during the

dormant months, but also during the growing season to reduce brush encroachment, improve forage quality and quantity for livestock and to manage wildlife habitat (Figure 11.1). Fire, when used alone, can accomplish many goals a manager may have. Prescribed fire in conjunction with good grazing management forms the best extensive management tool (process) available to manage native plant communities for food, fibre, habitat and other ecological services. Fire and grazing are cost-effective for landowners and beneficial for plants and animals that evolved under fire and herbivory.

The visibly and obvious mounting problems caused by the elimination of fire on the landscape and the new information that fire science is generating have created a lot of interest from landowners as to how to apply fire to their property. Unlike the cow, axe, plough and gun, it is very difficult for one person to apply fire correctly and safely. To address this issue, some landowners have worked with neighbours to share labour, equipment and knowledge to apply fire. This grassroots idea led to larger groups of neighbours helping each other within larger geographical areas through the formation of PBAs. These associations are simply comprised of groups of people with a common interest and a desire to

Figure 11.1: Conducting prescribed burns during the growing season can retard woody plant encroachment and enhance wildlife habitat and forage quality for livestock.

work together in order to apply more fire in their region. The objective of forming PBAs is to provide education, training, equipment and manpower to landowners so they can achieve their resource management goals. These associations are also extremely beneficial to communities through reductions in allergenic eastern red cedar populations and dangerous fuel load accumulations responsible for increasing the incidence of wildfire (Twidwell *et al.* 2013).

Canada, Australia, Portugal, Spain, France and South Africa are incorporating prescribed fire in their management plans, and other countries are in developmental stages. The management plans of these countries are to accomplish goals similar to those of many PBAs in the US: improve forage and habitat and reduce the impact of wildfires (International Association of Wildland Fire 2017). Although the acceptance of the importance of prescribed burning is increasing around the world, it is not widely accepted. Misunderstanding and social pressure to avoid short-term negative impacts and the fear of escaped fires prevent or reduce the implementation of prescribed fire (International Association of Wildland Fire 2017). The concept of PBAs can be very useful in these situations. Sharing knowledge and equipment in order to accomplish common goals for managing plants and animals can build confidence, knowledge, safety and therefore acceptance.

Most people involved with PBAs want to use fire to help them accomplish specific goals, such as controlling or reducing woody plants in order to increase grazeable hectares for cattle, improving forage quality or improving habitat for wildlife (Weir *et al.* 2016). Local, state, federal and private organisations should work collaboratively and diligently together to empower landowners to join their lands, resources and talents together to help them achieve these goals and to improve our natural resources. Empowering landowners to burn is the only way to significantly increase the amount of fire applied.

Why PBAs work

Regardless of the subject or discipline, there is no better way to learn about a specific issue than from those with experience. Many landowners attend educational events because they have met other like-minded producers and have realised the worth of networking with them. Producers enjoy learning from other producers who have similar operations, challenges and questions. Gaining first-hand knowledge from other landowners regarding tips on everything from deals on feed and seed, to working livestock, fencing and watering techniques, management of white-tailed deer and grazing, dealing with timely weather and market events and tools of the trade is priceless.

Working groups or associations comprised of like-minded producers can be beneficial to the overall success of a producer's operation. Landowners with the mindset to share information regarding their management techniques and operational successes and failures, who are willing to listen to the same experiences from other producers, can derive huge benefits from being a part of a working group or association.

PBAs are the heart and soul of a fire culture in a community. There are no requirements to what a PBA should look like or how the PBA even functions. The only crucial and uniting element of all PBAs throughout the US is landowners helping landowners get more fire safely and effectively on the ground (Figure 11.2). This common goal unites and defines all PBAs. Although each PBA will be unique in terms of its own challenges, experience, strengths and weaknesses, the excitement, desire and fortitude to apply fire is always consistent.

Every landowner will have different objectives for implementing a prescribed burn, including, for example, wildlife habitat, wildfire mitigation, the quality and quantity of herbaceous forage, brush suppression or even reclamation of overgrown rangeland pastures. The unique thing about the PBA perspective is that these goals and justifications are secondary to the landowner's right to burn. A landowner's right to manage their private property for whatever reason is a blessing throughout the southern Great Plains of the US, whereas other states, particularly western states, are dominated by current policy dictated by state

Figure 11.2: A prescribed burn association preparing to conduct a dormant-season prescribed fire.

and federal land agencies. PBAs facilitate that decision-making process by promoting inclusivity of like-minded individuals who understand the role and process fire plays on our landscapes.

PBAs work and have unharnessed potential to apply more fire because of the community that a PBA embodies. Community adds meaning and purpose to overcoming rangeland challenges and creates stronger connections among landowners facing similar challenges. Like any community, PBAs serve as a strong catalyst for a meaningful life. Sharing the highs and lows of working and making a living off rangelands with peers gives a stronger sense of purpose and acceptance. Landowners belonging to a PBA can serve as mentors, cheerleaders and supporters when community and culture are at the forefront of the group. Building a community of like-minded individuals is a vulnerable thing to do because each landowner reveals parts of the operation that may not be perfect, or even the possibility of an escape prescribed burn. But, that is what makes PBAs so successful! Total transparency from a grassroots program that offers help, knowledge, resources and labour, and local leadership are advantages to serving and contributing to a PBA. Some of the most successful PBAs

have members from all walks of life, backgrounds, ranching experience and talents. For example, a PBA in West Texas consists of several retired schoolteachers, a pastor, banker, mechanic, veterans, absentee landowners and fifth- and sixth-generation ranchers; their PBA is their community. The result? More fire on the ground because of a strong fire culture in a community with like-minded individuals who look out for one another before, during and after a prescribed fire.

This community (the PBA) will be your biggest advocate and best teacher. By participating in a PBA, you are more likely to get more hands-on burn experience, experience different jobs and assignments on a prescribed burn and learn from each burn boss as each landowner executes his or her respective fire. On a PBA prescribed fire, it is very likely that a retired schoolteacher will approach and implement a prescribed burn much differently than a fifth-generation landowner. And that's ok! There are plenty of scenarios that may align for a successful and safe prescribed burn, but there are also an equal number of strategies to accomplish that prescribed fire. Learning from the best, communicating and soaking in the big picture of a PBA fire will grow members' confidence and foster the PBA community. This community will also support you through rough times. When you are struggling, the PBA community will help you to help yourself up. When you are celebrating, it will celebrate with you. These kinds of connections add a stronger sense of purpose and meaning in ranch life. If you are hoping to implement some changes in your ranch management, you can call on people in your PBA to hold you accountable. If you are stuck in a range management rut and are not sure what to do next, you can consult your PBA and rely on its members for support, encouragement and guidance.

Knocking on your neighbour's door, asking for help and seeking knowledge allows for resources, equipment and labour to be shared for a safe and successful prescribed burn. Gaining experience and confidence from your PBA community is why PBAs work! Neighbour helping neighbour reduces risks, enhances knowledge transfer and understanding and fosters a fire culture community. There is strength in numbers and even more strength when it is local neighbours helping, teaching and learning from other local neighbours. Just as folks gather around the coffee shop to talk about news, or families and neighbours come together for branding, a PBA collectively bands together with the same goal: more fire on the ground and a community that supports, embraces and encourages a fire culture.

Building PBAs

Many landowners interested in forming an association don't quite know where or how to begin. There are many ways to form an association but, however formed, there are some important steps to consider.

To be successful, an association should be a locally led, grassroots effort. Government and non-government agencies can assist by serving as advisors, providing technical assistance and removing bureaucratic roadblocks, but without local leaders and local involvement, an association will fail, period. Creating and maintaining a locally led association is absolutely the single most important aspect to consider. State and government agency employees can have a critical role in assisting a PBA, but they should not serve as leaders. Employees should focus on filling gaps that landowners do not have the time or skill to do, such as coordinating membership meetings with the officers and maintaining contact among all PBA members. Lack of activity will end the life of a PBA. Another role that state and government employees can provide is assistance with developing burn plans, one of the biggest perceived obstacles for a landowner. This can be accomplished at membership meetings with employees experienced with prescribed fire. Once landowners understand what a burn plan consists of, it is no longer an obstacle. Some local or rural volunteer fire departments (VFDs) collaborate with PBAs in order to provide assistance in case of an escaped fire, and to provide their firefighters knowledge of the difference between a prescribed fire and a wildfire.

There are two basic options to organise an association and both will work. The first option is to organise loosely with or without officers, and the second is to formally elect officers and develop bylaws, articles of incorporation and other pertinent information required by the state. If the association wants to become a non-profit corporation, such as a 501(c)(3), formal organisation is required. In the US, a 501(c)(3) status makes an association or any other qualifying organisation a 'non-profit' and eligible to apply for a broader range of grants and receive charitable donations that are tax deductible by the donor. This can be beneficial to the PBA as well as to the donor. Often donors don't even own land, but want to be a part of helping a neighbour or friend improve it. It also encourages absentee landowners who are unable to assist with burning to participate by providing financial support.

Getting started seems to be a common concern, but there are many ways to begin forming an association. The following considerations are beneficial:

- visit neighbours and/or other landowners in the local area to determine the level of interest
- contact people involved with other similar associations
- organise an informal meeting and meal to discuss interest and potential; if possible, include key landowners or individuals in the community and people with experience in other associations
- generate rough ideas for goals and objectives. There are many possible goals and objectives; seek everyone's input and realise goals and objectives can be adjusted or changed as the association matures
- ask for commitment from key landowners or influential members of the community
- organise a more formal meeting and meal to discuss geographical boundaries and the preference for an informal or formal structure (note, a formal structure can be developed later if needed)
- identify several key people to share responsibilities; successful associations have several people involved with coordinating and scheduling.

Be sure to plan meetings and fun events at least once every year and consider incorporating education into these events. Resources such as university, government and private agencies are available to help with educational events, and this is an excellent way for these organisations to stay involved and support local, landowner-led associations. A critical role for local leaders is to be sure these events happen and all members of the association are kept informed.

Not all landowners are of the mindset or have the personality type to fit into local PBAs. It's natural for some landowners to be introverted and feel very uncomfortable speaking up in a group. It's also natural for some landowners to be on the opposite extreme: very vocal and tending to talk a lot more than others in the group.

There are many benefits of forming an association. Major benefits include sharing of equipment and labour, the management of natural resources, such as wildlife habitat and populations over a larger area, and accomplishing or influencing other activities as a result of a group of people working together. It's not easy and requires time, but these benefits are worth it.

PBAs for hunters, cattlemen and recreation

Dr Dale Rollins (Rolling Plains Quail Research Ranch, Roby, TX, USA) always asks the question to his extension audience, 'Which hat are you wearing? A cowboy hat, a camo ballcap, or a fishing hat?', meaning, are you a rancher, hunter or a recreationalist? The cool thing about PBAs is that it doesn't matter which hat you have on!

If you are a hunter, then most likely you have a commitment to optimise plant diversity, offering an array of wildlife habitats. Prescribed fire serves as an important process to reduce woody plant canopy cover and to manipulate plant species composition to meet the dietary needs of wildlife species, including white-tailed deer. Development of more complex management strategies using prescribed fire almost naturally requires the assistance of a PBA. PBAs can assist in the decision-making process regarding practicality, understanding of vegetative responses and post-fire management.

As a wildlife manager, landowners should be active within a PBA because fire is the only tool to produce a response from every single plant species. Top-killing brush, or suppressing brush, still promotes a unique response that is desirable from a woody browse perspective. Browsing following fire typically increases the mortality of resprouting species. In contrast, browsing after fire may temporarily reduce the height of the sprouting species without causing plant mortality. Profuse browsing following fire is typical due to the increased palatability and forage quality of the tender new growth.

Forb production following fire is another good example why the hunter should be involved with a PBA. Fire typically improves forb composition and species richness by activating germination and growth patterns (Weir and Scasta 2017). Pronounced seasonal effects of fire on forbs have been thoroughly documented, showcasing the potential for PBAs to manipulate forb composition and production with fire (Weir and Scasta 2017).

Nearly all native wildlife species are attracted to a recently burned area and may temporarily concentrate in the burned unit due to new species growth. In addition to preference to recently burned areas, fawn production, fawn biomass and antler size of 2-year-old male deer were greater during the first year after burning in South Texas (Fulbright and Ortega-Santos 2006).

On rangelands, 'multiple use' is a popular term to describe the numerous benefits or services from rangelands, and this typically involves both hunting and livestock production uses. A local PBA can serve as an efficient community to help with brush management and forage improvement for both livestock and wildlife habitat. As some effects of prescribed fire are temporary, landowners need to nurture their PBA community because of the importance of fire frequency to accomplish or maintain their land use goals.

The difference between fire frequency and fire return interval is often misunderstood. Fire frequency refers to the recurrence of fire in a given area over time and is often stated as the number of fires per unit time in a designated area. The fire return interval is the time between fires in a designated area. Where present, tree scars are the most common indicator of fire frequency and fire return interval in a particular area, assuming the sampled trees were scarred during each fire event. For example, if tree scars indicate a particular location burned in 10 out of 30 years, then the fire frequency would be once every 3 years. Counting growth rings between tree scars provides estimates of fire return intervals. If, in our example, the 10 fire events occurred in years 2, 8, 9, 15, 16, 17, 21, 24, 28 and 29, the fire return intervals would be 6, 1, 6, 1, 1, 4, 3, 4 and 1 year respectively.

Based on prescribed fire research in the southern Great Plains, Oklahoma State University (OSU) developed a rule of thumb that says the application of prescribed fire once every 3 years maintains brush abundance. To reduce brush, burn more often than once every 3 years, whereas brush encroachment usually occurs when properties are burned less often than once every 3 years. More specifically, depending on precipitation and site productivity, OSU recommends a 2- to 5-year return interval to manage resprouting shrubs and trees and a 5- to 15-year return interval to reduce fire-sensitive species such as eastern red cedar, whereas for grasslands, time since fire is the most important variable to monitor (Guyette et al. 2012). These are all good guidelines to follow, but closer evaluation of the results of applying prescribed fire at specific locations is always more helpful.

For our recreationalist, encroaching juniper species and other invasive woody brush provides another example of using plant growth to establish fire return intervals. Depending on the amount of annual rainfall over time and soil productivity, in most situations juniper species will not become too large in 3 years or less to control with fire. Maintaining a plant community balance of native grasses, forbs and browse species is key for any rangeland owner. Even if the pastures are being managed for aesthetic purposes, a landowner must consider the maturing structure of woody plants, the reduced amount of herbaceous plants, continued juniper growth and an overall desire to provide a functioning plant community with adequate wildlife habitat and diversity. This is where your local PBA steps in and facilitates the reset button for plant diversity and brush suppression with prescribed fire.

Comparing current plant structure and diversity to what is desired for the property should always be the guiding factor in determining when to apply fire. Rainfall is the driver. More rainfall provides the opportunity to burn more frequently, whereas less rainfall means longer fire return intervals. Decisions based on these factors will always be more effective than planning by the calendar.

With the potential that PBAs bring, there is no excuse for landowners with prescribed burning goals to be short on labour, equipment or even knowledge. Associations for prescribed burning may be the answer many landowners are looking for. However, the focus does not always need to be tailored for livestock or wildlife or aesthetics. The need or opportunity to collectively manage for plant diversity is key. Using a PBA to manipulate nutrient dynamics, soils, vegetation, grazing patterns and the grazing behaviour of animals can be beneficial regardless of a camo ballcap, cowboy hat or fishing hat. All perspectives play important roles in land stewardship, and a PBA can further facilitate, enhance and nurture that stewardship role.

Overcoming PBA challenges

By far, the biggest challenge to PBAs is collaborating and working with people. This is manifested in many ways, such as different levels of knowledge among association members, association members with dominating personalities, determining the annual burn schedule and equipment sharing, among others. The obstacles that people place in front themselves are the most difficult aspects to overcome. The actual application of prescribed fire or other management practice of interest to the association is rarely difficult because there are proven guidelines to follow.

Maintaining local leadership over time is also a big challenge. In most cases, it is difficult to get a landowner from the local group to step up to the task of leadership. Usually, the local landowners look to state or federal agency personnel to fill the leadership role, which is rarely successful because state and federal employees have other tasks to perform and are not as committed as a local landowner who is a member of the association. The tasks associated with leading a local PBA are not numerous or difficult; any that present difficulty can be addressed with the help of state or federal agency personnel. This support role is the best role for state and federal agency personnel. Landowners are busy tending to their own operations and a

landowner who steps up to lead the association can quickly tire of the efforts to keep everyone informed and schedule and preside over meetings. This becomes increasingly frustrating when members fail to attend meetings, often due to the lack of applying fire because of drought or other weather conditions that prevent safe burning. Members need to understand that the application of prescribed fire will vary annually and the reasons for this. The most successful leaders of local PBAs challenge the association to constantly brainstorm ways and ideas to continue to provide informative and educational activities and events pertaining to prescribed fire regardless of actual burning activity.

With newly formed PBAs, equipment is often limiting. In addition, every member is new and they all want help burning their property in the same year that the association was formed. These factors often limit the number of properties that can be burned safely, thus discouraging some of the members, sometimes to the point that they drop their memberships. These factors may also create the temptation for some members to borrow equipment when others are busy in order to conduct the burn on their own, usually with a limited crew and under unsafe conditions, risking injury and damage to neighbouring property due to escaped fire (not to mention creating a dark cloud over the local PBA concept among local authorities and the general public). This is not always limited to individual members of the association. Lack of equipment, combined with the urge to address all members' requests to burn with members of a newly formed association that really do not yet understand the science of safely applying prescribed fire, can also lead to disastrous outcomes. State and federal agency personnel can play a key role in this regard by providing educational events focusing on the importance of creating a prescribed burn plan for each burn and advising the association on how and when to conduct prescribed fires safely (Figure 11.3). Prescribed fire councils, state PBAs and other entities can also play key roles in helping equip local PBAs.

Figure 11.3: The Tall Timbers Prescribed Burn Association routinely conducts prescribed fires with state and federal agency personnel to enhance learning and knowledge transfer.

Many factors influence whether prescribed fire achieves particular land management goals. Weather conditions, such as relative humidity and temperature, and the amount of fuel during the burn are probably the biggest factors. Rainfall and the presence or absence of grazing affect the amount of fuel, fuel moisture and fire return interval. Season of burn also influences the outcome of the prescribed fire. All these factors affect prescribed fire intensity, which, in turn, affects decisions regarding the proper fire return interval necessary to achieve the desired goal(s). Therefore, it is vital that PBA members monitor annual rainfall on their property to predict forage growth and manage their grazing to ensure adequate fuel loading in order to optimise the outcome of their prescribed burn when the association gets around to burning their

property. Rainfall and other weather variables are the drivers of plant growth. It is not necessary to be preoccupied planning prescribed burning events based on the calendar. Rather than planning to burn in year 1 and again 3 years later, use an adaptive grazing management plan and/or monitor plant growth to burn when plant growth, not a calendar date, indicates that it is time based on the goals for the property. Knowing this in advance can help an individual member of an association communicate and coordinate their prescribed burning needs more efficiently. However, extended periods of excessive rainfall or drought can reduce burning activity within an association, creating a need for several properties to be burned during the same year when prescribed burning conditions return.

State and local laws and regulations are arguably the biggest challenge for local PBAs. In fact, there are many states that have such imposing laws and regulations pertaining to outdoor burning that it is extremely difficult for local PBAs to navigate them in order to conduct a lawful burn. These laws and regulations, combined with the liability consequences of breaking them or simply having an escaped fire due to an act of nature, are often a huge deterrent to forming an association in many states. Many states require insurance in order to have coverage in the event of damage caused by an escaped prescribed fire. There are extremely limited options available to obtaining liability insurance for prescribed burning. However, coverage is often provided in the ranch insurance policy that most landowners have in the US.

These laws and regulations are written and put into effect by people with good intentions but ignorant of the importance and use of prescribed fire. They are often quick to impose lengthy statewide or regional burn bans in complete ignorance of the speed at which conditions can change to make the application of prescribed fire safe. Often these burn bans can eliminate the opportunity to burn for an entire season. There are some states that have worked hard to create and maintain a fire culture among landowners and a public awareness of prescribed fire. Oklahoma, Kansas and Florida are examples. Even in these states, there is constant pressure from local authorities, numerous city and rural fire departments and state politicians to further regulate the use of prescribed fire through the modification of outdoor burning laws. In addition, some federal agency personnel advocate the need for 'red card' training, which consists of training on how to combat wildfires and passing the physical requirement of carrying 45 lb for 3 miles (~20 kg for 4.8 km) in under 45 min, for landowners who want to conduct prescribed fire. At best, red card training is remotely applicable to a landowner wanting to apply prescribed fire.

To help ensure the ability of landowners to apply prescribed fire, it is crucial to guard against unnecessary laws and regulations pertaining to prescribed fire. Thorough knowledge of the science of prescribed fire, fire behaviour and how to complete a burn plan is all that a landowner needs in order to conduct a burn. Too much regulation simply discourages landowners, resulting in very little or no application of fire at the local level. State and federal agencies and other organisations have a system in place to conduct prescribed fire for the landowner. This is well intended, but there simply are not enough state and federal agencies and personnel, or other organisations, to get fire on the ground. Landowners must be empowered to apply prescribed fire on their property or we will see very little fire applied. State and federal agency personnel and numerous other organisations can provide the necessary education to landowners. It is also crucial to work towards creating numerous local PBAs. Changes in laws and regulations begin at the local level. Local landowners who are members of PBAs can have a very influential voice. State associations and prescribed fire councils can also assist local PBAs by helping members educate their local and state politicians as to the importance of prescribed fire and how it can be applied safely.

Funding is a challenge to all PBAs at the local or state level. Association members sometimes purchase and donate equipment to their association, but this is not common. Some associations have completed all steps necessary to be formally recognised as a non-profit by their state. This provides an opportunity for them to apply for grants that provide funding for equipment and to accept tax-deductible donations from individuals or organisations. Some prescribed burning equipment will last for years with proper care. However, mechanical equipment must be replaced after a few years. Associations must plan accordingly. State associations, prescribed fire councils and local politicians can play a valuable role by helping local PBAs obtain grants or contact individuals for donations of new and used equipment. The Oklahoma Prescribed Burn Association (OPBA; https://www.ok-pba.org) is an excellent example of a state association helping local PBAs. The OPBA serves as an umbrella association for all the local PBAs in Oklahoma. It is a non-profit organisation that secures funding to supply equipment and education to the local PBAs. Drip torches, slide-in sprayers, equipment trailers, all-terrain vehicles, fire rakes and road signs are examples of the equipment the OPBA has supplied to local PBAs. The OPBA also coordinates with OSU, Noble Research Institute (NRI), Natural Resources Conservation Service and the Oklahoma Conservation Commission to conduct several prescribed burn training sessions each year. Each training session involves the discussion of burn plan contents and, weather permitting, an actual demonstration burn for participants to see and gain a little experience.

In the US, there are cost-share programs available for individual landowners. Available funding depends on the state, because not all states dedicate the same amount of funds for prescribed burning. In addition, these cost-share programs are not applicable to PBAs. However, for members of an association, these funds are good opportunities to enable them to apply fire. There is a sign-up period and subsequent approval process that must be navigated by the applying landowner. This can sometimes require up to a couple of years to complete, which is discouraging to the landowner, especially if they have plans for their association to burn their property in a more immediate time frame.

PBAs feeding into fire culture

PBAs should be grassroots programs with local people in charge. However, technical assistance opportunities and guidance from personnel of state or federal agencies (e.g. Natural Resource Conservation Service, US Fish and Wildlife Service, state parks and wildlife, state forestry service or extension) and non-profit organisations (e.g. Pheasant Forever and many others) can be beneficial. Many of these groups can provide financial or technical assistance, training, workshops or equipment to PBAs. However, PBAs are a direct reflection of the community and, therefore, will only prosper when someone from that community steps forward to lead, encourage and nurture the PBA.

Numerous states have successfully formed fire councils as a collective prescribed fire voice. It is imperative that fire councils recognise and include PBAs. Just as the community of a PBA comes together, so must all state fire practitioners. As all prescribed fire managers face new and increasingly complex challenges, fire councils can serve as strong voice for the future of a fire culture. Fire councils and PBAs should effectively work together to facilitate communication among their members, provide a focal point for sharing ideas and information and create opportunities for prescribed fire collaboration. The NRI, universities, state and national government entities, non-governmental organisations (NGOs) and other natural resource-based organisations largely focus on providing assistance to individual producers or large groups of producers, which is very much needed and should continue (Figure 11.4). These organisations realise the value of working with producer groups and do some work with them even though it is not their main focus. The feedback from the producers involved has been overwhelmingly positive, and networking is what they value the most. Involving PBAs in working groups to brainstorm ways and ideas to continue to provide informative activities and events for each group helps keep these organisations in touch with the needs of PBAs, and keeps the groups from becoming stagnant.

Umbrella PBAs have also been formed in states or regions that serve as a source for education, training and equipment for local PBAs. State or regional associations also represent local PBAs on a political level to provide input on laws and regulations pertaining to prescribed fire. In addition, most state or regional PBAs are 501(c)(3) organisations in order to obtain grants to support local PBAs in the form of educational events, trainings and equipment. Members of state and regional PBAs are usually comprised of landowners and resource professionals, as well as officers or employees of state or federal organisations, and possess an excellent ability to create collaborations among all interested parties to support local PBAs and their efforts to apply fire to the landscape.

PBAs are a necessary and required component of a fire culture. Without landowner support, prescribed fire will be muted as a range management option. Just as a torch needs an ignition to be effective, so our fire culture needs the local ignition that PBAs provide. The common goal for agencies, landowners and NGOs of putting more fire on the ground is only achieved when neighbours are helping and learning from their neighbours, and stewardship is prioritised through community. On rangelands, PBAs are that community.

Figure 11.4: Federal, state, and non-governmental organisations can conduct educational events to assist prescribed burn association members and help keep the association active.

Unique examples of PBAs

PBAs take on many different shapes and forms, and there is no perfect strategy or recipe for success. The OPBA has been a very effective example for other PBAs and states to follow (Figure 11.5). Their vision revolves around a very simple premise to serve as the premier organisation that significantly increases the application of prescribed fire on the Oklahoma landscape. Members of the OPBA accomplish a significant amount of prescribed burning each year by facilitating the training, equipping, education and organisation of member PBAs and individual landowners. Members of the OPBA also routinely make legislative visits in order to promote and protect the right of Oklahoma landowners to use prescribed burning as a safe, economical and effective land management practice. Without a doubt, the OPBA has been very successful and maintained a long-term prescribed burn presence by promoting prescribed fire as a natural process necessary to maintain the health of Oklahoma lands, uniting existing and creating new PBAs in the state, and coordinating dynamic local, area, state, regional and national partnerships focused on prescribed fire, such as the Great Plains Fire Summit held every other year throughout the Great Plains. Leaders of the OPBA prioritise and facilitate communication among PBAs and other member

Figure 11.6: A prescribed burn demonstration led by a prescribed burn association is an effective recruiting tool for new ranch managers and interested helpers.

associations while also providing outreach and education activities to increase the knowledge of PBA members and all Oklahomans through educational events and activities pertaining to the benefits of prescribed fire (Figure 11.6). Essentially, the OPBA is successful because it provides a voice on important issues for PBA members throughout the state, assists with locating funding sources for PBAs and facilitates member access to prescribed burning equipment.

Perhaps the greatest accomplishment of the OPBA with regard to the practice of prescribed fire is the creation of the Burn Entry Form Report, which has expanded to include additional states like Texas. This form is crucial to keeping track of hectares burned, as well as summarising the large impact that prescribed fire has at state and regional levels. For example, the OPBA reported through the Burn Entry Form system that from 2015 to 2020, 591 individual prescribed fires were reported (470 burns had volatile juniper species present within their burn unit), totalling 54 065 ha in total, with an average burn unit size of 91 ha. A total of 22 PBAs representing 40 Oklahoma counties reported their prescribed fire results. The total number of prescribed fires conducted (Figure 11.7) and the total number of hectares burned each year (Figure 11.8)

Figure 11.5: The Oklahoma Prescribed Burn Association (OPBA) strives to coordinate dynamic local, area, state, regional and national partnerships focused on prescribed fire, while also facilitating communication and collaboration among prescribed burn associations and other member associations.

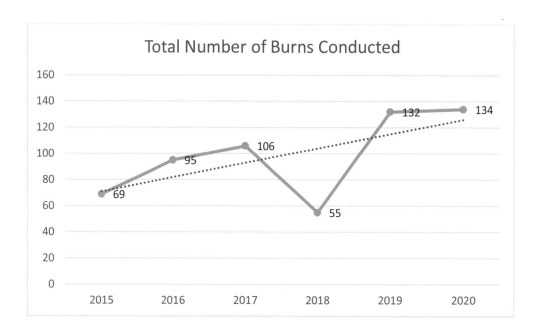

Figure 11.7: Total number of prescribed fires reported by prescribed burn associations in Oklahoma.

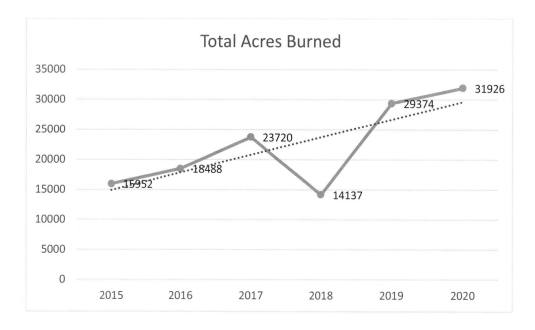

Figure 11.8: Total number of acres burned by prescribed burn associations in Oklahoma.

has increased between 2015 and 2020, but the average burn unit size has remained relatively stable (Figure 11.9).

Interestingly, spot fires (Figure 11.10) occurred during 89 of the 591 prescribed fires reported, with most being less than 0.04 ha in size. Of those 89

prescribed fires that reported spot fires, only 15 fires reported spot fires greater than 0.4 ha, two fires reported spot fires greater than 4 ha and three fires reported spot fires less than 40 ha. The presence of volatile juniper species was noted in 90% of the spot fires reported. In addition to the reported

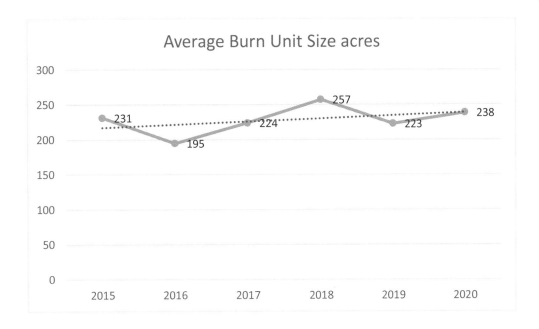

Figure 11.9: Average burn unit size as reported by prescribed burn associations in Oklahoma.

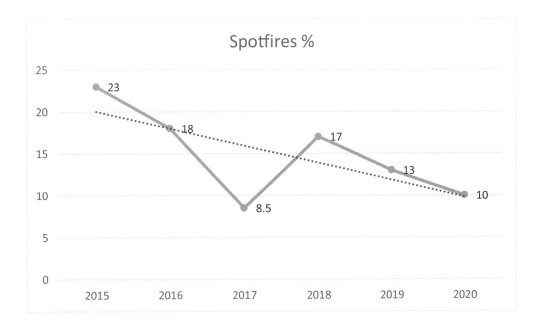

Figure 11.10: Total number of spot fires per year as reported by prescribed burn associations in Oklahoma.

spot fires, escape fires (Figure 11.11) only occurred during 23 of the prescribed fires reported from 2015 to 2020, with most being less than 4 ha in size.

Smoke issues or complaints were reported for 0.1% of the total prescribed fires, whereas six prescribed fires (0.01%) reportedly involved insurance claims and none of the reported fires was involved with any liable or negligent lawsuits.

More PBAs are conducting prescribed fires during the growing season (Figure 11.12). This is likely due to landowner goals of increased brush suppression and/or increased forb diversity for

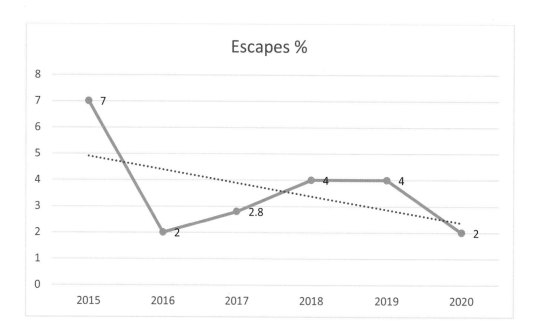

Figure 11.11: Total number of escaped fires per year as reported by prescribed burn associations in Oklahoma.

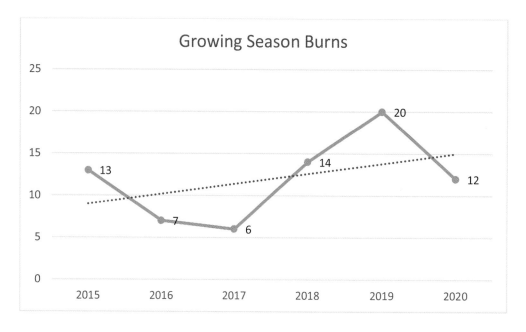

Figure 11.12: Number of growing-season prescribed fires conducted by prescribed burn associations in Oklahoma by year from 2015 to 2020.

wildlife habitat, which are often the result of growing-season prescribed fires. However, March and April remain two of the most popular months in which conduct prescribed fire by PBAs in Oklahoma (Figure 11.13).

Upper Llanos PBA, Texas

Another great example of a PBA is the Upper Llanos PBA (ULPBA) in west-central Texas. The ULPBA has a diverse set of members and routinely burns as much as weather conditions will

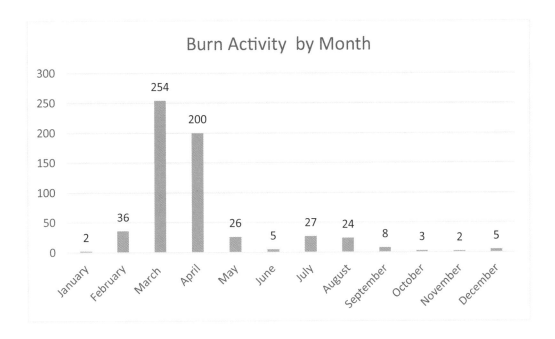

Figure 11.13: Total number of prescribed fires conducted in each month by prescribed burn associations in Oklahoma from 2015 to 2020.

allow. The ULPBA considers itself a proactive conservation organisation based in Kimble County, Texas. The ULPBA currently has approximately 54 members and associate members, most of whom are actively involved with the organisation. The ULPBA is governed by a 10-member board of directors, which is elected by the membership at an annual meeting and does not receive any compensation for its service. The goal of the ULPBA is to enhance the productivity of the land and provide more water to the aquifer by reducing run-off, erosion and competition from juniper, while simultaneously reducing wildfire fuels. A primary objective of the ULPBA has also been to educate members and the public about the methods and benefits of prescribed burning when strictly adhering to safe and proven guidelines. Through the years, numerous articles and essays have been published, meetings to which the public is invited held and information disseminated electronically. The group was originally formed on 16 June 2004 as the Kimble County PBA, with 26 members, as one of 11 chapters of the larger Sonora-based Edwards Plateau PBA

(EPPBA). After becoming independent of the EPPBA on 17 February 2012, the State Certificate of Incorporation name was amended to ULPBA, and the IRS 501(c)(3) designation as a public charity was granted on 24 August 2012. In 2008, approximately 4000 hectares of Kimble County rangeland was burned successfully under prescriptions approved in comprehensive burn plans. Due to this extreme success and the reputation of the organisation, the president and vice president were invited to speak at the National Conference on Grazing Lands Conservation Initiative in Reno, Nevada.

In April 2011, a lightning strike resulted in a massive wildfire in Kimble County. Responding quickly to the call for help, ULPBA members were some of the first on the scene at the Oasis Pipeline Wildfire, which caused the evacuation of a large area in south-western Kimble County and threatened the town of Junction. ULPBA members' training and knowledge of rangeland fire made them an invaluable asset in the very early stages until the Forestry Service and other authorities assumed command. The ULPBA continues to spearhead training and education, partnering with other prescribed burning organisations and agencies in Texas and the central US. For many years, detailed information on each completed burn has been submitted to the OPBA's Burn Entry Form Report.

There are a number of necessary qualifications required for any organization to be successful. There has to be an identifiable need and people willing to give freely of their time and talents to serve that need. There must be folks with organizational skills and there must be skilled communicators. In Kimble County we have just enough folks left in the ranching community to recognize the need to work the land to prevent the complete encroachment of woody species. These old ranchers have spent a lifetime fighting droughts, markets, predators, and the takeover of a juniper dominated canopy which all attempt to take much needed money from their bank accounts. Naturally, they have always looked for better, more economical ways to assist them. When Texas A&M AgriLife Extension and [Natural Resource Conservation Service] introduced these folks to prescribed fire as a macro-management tool these ranchers organized what would eventually become ULPBA in 2004. ULPBA has benefitted from several different leaders. The only common denominator I can discern is that these were all 'people persons' with the ability to unite the very different members and seem to get others to willingly donate their time and talents to the overall cause. From an organizational standpoint ULPBA had Wanda Blackburn to completely care for all clerical duties of the organization. Though Wanda rarely attends a burn, she files burn plans, administrates the group email, takes care of all mailouts, files the minutes of all meetings, secures grants, and reports burn acreage to the OSU database. Several other folks have stepped up to organize and maintain equipment as well as schedule burns. Probably the most important component of a Rx [prescribed] burn is communication between team members. The
same is true for keeping any organization informed and engaged. After struggling with many different ways to communicate to members, regulatory agencies, and others with information and scheduling, ULPBA found group electronic communication to be the most beneficial. Group emails seem to be preferred over group texts (for some unknown reason). This form of communication is utilized to communicate upcoming burns, notify county officials and area fire departments, inform regulatory agencies, as well as networking information from Rx burners throughout the state. I would be remiss to not recognize the support this organization receives from our county government which allows us to perform burns during burn bans. The county judge and commissioners have the foresight to realize the benefit Rx burning has to the safety of its residents. I have been told that this type of organization is solely dependent on a strong leader and that when that leadership is gone, for whatever reason, the organization will soon be gone as well. The longevity of ULPBA has proven that when the cause is broadly supported by the community it serves the organization will survive the test of time. (Sam Jetton, ULPBA Vice President, pers. comm.)

Dedication

It is with a heavy heart we dedicate this chapter to our colleague and good friend Russell L. Stevens who passed away on 23 June 2021 after a long and courageous battle with cancer. For over 30 years Russell was a very active promotor of prescribed fire, burn associations, range and wildlife management throughout the southern Great Plains, USA. His knowledge, passion and most of all his friendship will be greatly missed by all.

– John Weir and Morgan Treadwell

References

Anderson RC (1990) The historic role of fire in the North American Grassland. In *Fire in North American Tallgrass*

Prairies. (Eds SL Collins and LL Wallace) pp. 8–18. University of Oklahoma Press, Norman.

Fulbright TE, Ortega-Santos JA (2006) *White-Tailed Deer Habitat: Ecology and Management on Rangelands.* Texas A&M University Press, College Station.

Guyette RP, Stambaugh MC, Dey DC, Muzika RM (2012) Predicting fire frequency with chemistry and climate. *Ecosystems* **15**, 322–335. doi:10.1007/s10021-011-9512-0

International Association of Wildland Fire (2017) *Prescribed Fire: A Tool For Our Time.* International Association of Wildland Fire, Missoula, <https://www.iawfonline.org/article/prescribed-fire-a-tool-for-our-time/>.

Leopold A (1933) *Game Management.* University of Wisconsin Press, Madison.

Pyne S (2015) *Between Two Fires: A Fire History of Contemporary America.* University of Arizona Press, Tucson.

Twidwell D, Rogers WE, Fuhlendorf SD, Wonkka CL, Engle DM, Weir JR, Kreuter UP, Taylor CA, Jr (2013) The rising Great Plains fire campaign: citizens' response to woody plant encroachment. *Frontiers in Ecology and the Environment* **11**, 64–71. doi:10.1890/130015

University of California, Division of Agriculture and Natural Resources (UCANR) (2019) *California's First Prescribed Burn Association Shows Why We Need More in the State.* UCANR, Davis, <https://ucanr.edu/blogs/blogcore/postdetail.cfm?postnum=31049>.

Weir JR, Scasta JD (2017) Vegetation responses to season of fire in tallgrass prairie: a 13-year case study. *Fire Ecology* **13**, 137–142. doi:10.4996/fireecology.130290241

Weir JR, Twidwell D, Wonkka CL (2016) From grassroots to national alliance: the emerging trajectory for landowner prescribed burn associations. *Rangelands* **38**, 113–119. doi:10.1016/j.rala.2016.02.005

Fire management in heather-dominated heaths and moorlands of north-west Europe

G. Matt Davies, Vigdis Vandvik, Rob Marrs and Liv Guri Velle

A (very) brief history of fire in oceanic heath and moorland ecosystems

The heathland ecosystems of north-west Europe have been shaped by fire for millennia (Gimingham 1972; Simmons 2003). Although this may seem surprising for a region not exactly noted for a fire-conducive climate, a unique combination of ecological, environmental and cultural factors means fire continues to play a dominant role in many habitats. Managed fire is widespread in some regions; for example, Yallop *et al.* (2006) estimated that an average of 114 km² of moorland in England was burned by managed fires each year between 1996 and 2000. Changes in climate, land use, political priorities and social perceptions of fire mean that the future character of fire use is increasingly uncertain. Some of the contrasts, and similarities, in trends and histories of fire use across this ecologically and culturally diverse region are well illustrated by the current status of prescribed burning in the UK and Norway. In both these countries, fire is particularly associated with heathland and moorland ecosystems. Gimingham (1972) used Warming's (1909) definition of northern European

heathlands as *'a treeless tract that is mainly occupied by evergreen, slow-growing, small-leaved dwarf shrubs which are largely Ericaceae'*, although there are often graminoids, forbs and bryophytes in the understorey. Heathlands are thus open habitats and are derived via a long history of human management. The ericaceous species *Calluna vulgaris* (L.) Hull (hereafter *Calluna*) is particularly important to, and to some extent emblematic of, European Atlantic heathlands and moorlands as a whole. The relationship between fire, *Calluna* and other heathland species is long-enough established that there is evidence of evolutionary responses through enhanced seed germination in response to smoke in historically managed regions (Bargmann *et al.* 2014; Vandvik *et al.* 2014). *Calluna*-dominated heaths and moorlands exist throughout Europe, although they differ somewhat in their ecological composition and occur across varying soil types and climatic conditions. These ecosystems have significant cultural and conservation importance (Thompson *et al.* 1995a, 1995b; Kvamme *et al.* 2004; Dodgshon and Olsson 2006; Kaland and Kvamme 2013), but have seen substantial declines in their area. Key threats include land use conversion, climate change, deposition of atmospheric pollution, increasing wildfire activity and declines in traditional agricultural land uses (Webb 1998; Fagúndez 2013; Hovstad *et al.* 2018). Fagúndez (2013) summarised research showing declines in heathland of 99% in Belgium, 60–70% in Sweden and Denmark and 95% in the Netherlands. In Norway, 30–50% of the heathland area has been lost over the past 50 years, and 50–80% is in poor ecological condition, largely due to abandonment of traditional management (Hovstad *et al.* 2018). Losses and degradation in the UK have been significant but more modest (Thompson *et al.* 1995b), due, at least in part, to the unique economic and cultural status of these ecosystems in that country.

There is some debate about the character of prehistoric heathland fire regimes and the role of humans within them. Most recently, Halsall (2019) suggested that climate is the main driver of heathland vegetation dynamics but that fire accounts for up to 30% of the variance in vegetation in England, Sweden, Denmark and Germany during the last 13 500 years. Landscapes of the early Holocene were predominantly forested. There is substantive evidence that Mesolithic societies used fire to manipulate their environment (e.g. Moore 2000; Innes and Blackford 2003; Innes *et al.* 2010; Ryan and Blackford 2010). Some studies have suggested that increased fire activity during the mid-Holocene period may have occurred naturally in association with changes in climatic conditions (Brown 1997; Grant *et al.* 2014). Increasing fire activity has been previously associated with decline in pine (*Pinus sylvestris* L.) woodlands in the Scottish Highlands around the same time, but more recent studies have emphasised the resilience of these systems to fire (Froyd 2006) and evidence for pine growth release following burning (Lageard *et al.* 2000). Forest cover declined, and heathlands expanded, through the Neolithic, Bronze Age and Iron Age periods, and abundant charcoal evidence suggests fire was likely to have been an important part of this process (e.g. Karg 2008). The managed use of fire undoubtedly played a central role in the expansion of lowland dry heaths in southern Britain (Groves

et al. 2012). In coastal Norway, ample palaeoecological research links heathland initiation with human clearance of forests from 4000 BC onwards. By the end of the Bronze Age, *Calluna* heathland dominated the coastal landscapes all the way up to the Vesterålen archipelago (Prøsch-Danielsen and Simonsen 2000; Tveraabak 2004; Hjelle *et al.* 2010). These findings, demonstrating the pivotal role of humans in driving the deforestation and development of the heathland landscape, were originally controversial because they contrasted the traditional view that heathland development was driven by climatic changes (e.g. Sernander 1912, 1929). The shift in our understanding of the origin of coastal heathlands was driven by the pioneering work of Kaland (1979, 1986), who found substantial local variation in the timing of the onset of heathland formation and demonstrated the use of fire to clear forest and maintain open heathland habitats. Charcoal records generally document recurrent fire activity in heathlands from first clearance and continuously through records, supporting the use of fire as an integrated part of prehistoric heathland management regimes (Prøsch-Danielsen and Simonsen 2000; Tveraabak 2004; Hjelle *et al.* 2010; for a review, see Vandvik *et al.* 2014).

Many heathland vegetation communities in the British uplands are associated with areas of blanket peat, and here there remains uncertainty about the relative importance of climatic versus human influence in initiating peat formation (e.g. Tipping 2008). Blanket peatland began to dominate the British uplands from the mid-Holocene onwards. Human land use, particularly forest clearance and fire use, has previously been argued to be a significant driver of peat initiation in these areas, but more recent work (Tipping 2008; Gallego-Sala *et al.* 2016) suggests that climate changes alone explain the observed patterns and trends of peat accumulation. Estimating the frequency of fire during these prehistoric periods is fraught with difficulty due to the paucity of appropriate evidence. A single study used crossmatched pine chronologies to determine that there was 90 years between two fires that burned a bog in northern England (Chambers *et al.* 1997).

By the early medieval period, substantial areas of the British Isles had been cleared of forest and heathland and moorland landscapes were well established. Fire appears to have been a regular feature of pastoral management systems in the uplands. Dodgshon and Olsson (2006) describe that, in Scotland, references to 'muirburn' (a regional colloquialism for heather burning) date back to 1400 AD, when the Scottish parliament ruled it could only be done in March. Legislation from the same era prohibits using fire in a manner that damages woodland. A by-product of this form of management was an increase in the number of red grouse (*Lagopus lagopus scotica*) on the moors, and the hunting of this bird gradually moved from being a landowner's hobby to the primary economic activity of a large number of estates. The importance of grouse shooting, to both the upland economy and as a pursuit of the aristocracy, became such that a crash in grouse populations around the turn of the 19th century led to a full-scale inquiry by the House of Lords (Lovat 1911). Today, in the Scottish Highlands and the north of England, the importance of large rural estates, grouse shooting and deer stalking remain relatively undiminished despite increases in labour, less favourable attitudes towards such pursuits among the wider public (Grandy *et al.* 2003) and pressures for land reform (e.g. Wightman 1996). Palaeoecological studies (e.g. Yeloff *et al.* 2006; Chambers *et al.* 2013) suggest that changes in management coincident with the start of the Industrial Revolution may have initiated peatland degradation in some settings. More recent significant anthropogenic impacts include the effects of deposition of atmospheric pollution (Caporn and Emmett 2008), changes in grazing regimes (Anderson and Yalden 1981) and peatland drainage (Stewart and Lance 1983, 1991; Holden *et al.* 2007), all of which make understanding the impacts of fire in and of itself somewhat difficult.

Burning remains an integral component of the management of British upland heaths, but elsewhere the traditional use of fire has declined substantially (e.g. Ascoli *et al.* 2009; Kvamme and Kaland 2009; Mause *et al.* 2010; Fernandes *et al.* 2013). Even in the UK there has long been concern about the ecological consequences of declines in traditional agricultural burning practices in lowland heaths, because here grouse moor management has not provided a continued incentive for management. More recently, there has been growing interest in restoring European heathland habitats and work to understand how the targeted use of fire and grazing may play a role in that (Sedláková and Chytrý 1999; Niemeyer *et al.* 2005; Ascoli *et al.* 2009). Fire management is an integral part of the Norwegian Action Plan to restore heathlands, and is included in the descriptions of the habitat type and its ecology in Norwegian nature type classification and red-list assessments (Kaland and Kvamme 2013; Hovstad *et al.* 2018). Nevertheless, prescribed burning has become a deeply polarising subject, especially in the UK, due to the need to understand trade-offs between ecosystem services (Harper *et al.* 2018), interactions between fire and more recent land management and anthropogenic impacts (Davies *et al.* 2016a) and the scale dependence of conclusions about the outcomes from burning (Davies *et al.* 2016b).

Conditions and prescriptions for fire use in *Calluna*-dominated heathlands

Variation in fuel structure

The driving force behind the ecology heaths and moorland is heather, *Calluna*. Left to its own devices, this dwarf shrub will live for at least 40–50 years and has traditionally been seen to regenerate in a cyclical fashion, passing through four stages: pioneer, building, mature and degenerate (Figure 12.1; Watt 1955; Gimingham 1988). Such ideas were formed on the basis of observations of *Calluna* on dry heathland sites in the south of England. In the uplands, building phase *Calluna* often forms dense monocultures that shade out other species. Deep layers of pleurocarpous mosses often form beneath its canopy, and these are a poor seedbed for seedling establishment (de Hullu and Gimingham 1984;

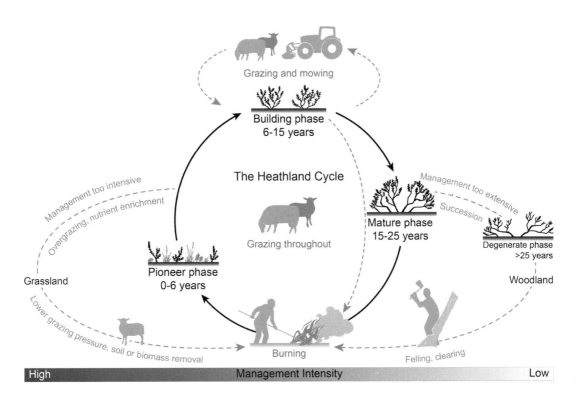

Figure 12.1: The traditional heathland management cycle and change in *Calluna* structure with age. Based on the stages of the *Calluna* cycle from Watt (1955). In the pioneer phase, young seedlings develop or shoots regrow from stem bases until canopy closure occurs in the building phase. Building phase structures can be maintained by grazing and mowing, but overgrazing can lead to conversion to grassland. Plants begin to lose vigour in the mature phase and gaps begin to open up. In the degenerate phase, significant gaps form and older stems become more prostrate; *Calluna* seedlings colonise the gaps and a mixed-age stand results, with individual bushes showing different life phases. Continued lack of management leads to woodland encroachment. Reproduced from Velle *et al.* (2021).

Davies *et al.* 2010a) in the gaps that begin to form as stands age. It is therefore now generally accepted that the cycle as envisaged by Watt (1955) is not applicable to large *Calluna* stands on upland moors (Gimingham 1988; Legg 1995). Furthermore, *Calluna* may maintain its dominance through the process of layering, where prostrate stems produce adventitious roots into moss mats, allowing the plants to maintain their vigour and cover (MacDonald *et al.* 1995). Although there are regional variations in post-fire vegetation development, and thus the length of the different heathland phases, the heather cycle, and related knowledge linked to the vegetation dynamics and composition of the different phases, is actively used in Norwegian heathland management. Managers are encouraged to burn the heather stands as they become mature.

Palaeoecological studies suggest that *Calluna* abundance increased in response to changing management, including burning, in the late-Holocene (Prøsch-Danielsen and Simonsen 2000; Tveraabak 2004; Hjelle *et al.* 2010; Vandvik *et al.* 2014; Davies 2016). More recently severe burns combined with overgrazing and atmospheric nitrogen deposition have led to substantial areas of such habitats becoming dominated by graminoids, notably *Eriophorum* spp., *Molinia caerulea* L. and *Nardus stricta* L. (Stevenson and Thompson 1993). In British raised and blanket bogs, *Calluna* dominance has often been taken to be a sign of degradation resulting from altered hydrology due to drainage and burning, although direct evidence for such an effect is surprisingly weak (e.g. Stewart and Lance 1991). *Calluna* can, in fact, be dominant in areas where there has been no artificial drainage, for example in the Moor House catchment in northern England (Milligan *et al.* 2018), and in Norway it is considered a dominant species in multiple mire-type communities.

Although heathlands are thus characterised by the dominance of *Calluna* and other dwarf shrubs, there has been comparatively little work to describe variation in their fuel structure and composition. The general structure of heather-dominated fuels has been described as being analogous to a miniature forest with a crown layer composed of live and dead shrub fuels and surface fuels dominated by bryophytes, lichens and litter (Figure 12.2). Although fuels *per se* are not well described, there has been a substantive effort to classify European habitats and plant communities. Classification systems have evolved substantially in the past two decades and a somewhat bewildering array now exists (Table 12.1; Figure 12.2), with several relevant to consideration of the composition of heathland fuels. Specific quantitative descriptions of fuel characteristics exist for few of these habitats, but the dominance of *Calluna* forms a common denominator across many of them.

Due to their agronomic and ecological importance, there has been considerable research on biomass and productivity in heather-dominated moorlands (e.g. Milne *et al.* 2002; Diemont *et al.* 2013; Alday *et al.* 2015). Age-related changes in vegetation biomass are moderated by the effects of variation in climatic conditions and interactions with other disturbances, notably grazing. Unfortunately, these data mostly lack adequate specificity and detail with regard to all but the broadest inferences regarding fire behaviour. What data do exist on fuel structure mostly come from studies of heathlands in the Scottish Highlands and northern England (Table 12.2), and a more limited number of sites in Norway.

Fuel load and structure vary considerably across the *Calluna* cycle, but not all stages have been adequately characterised. In many dry and wet heath communities, *Calluna* forms most of the fuel load, although layers of moss and litter may also hold appreciable biomass and, if dry enough to burn, can contribute significantly to fire behaviour. In the

data for wet and dry Calluna-dominated heathland communities analysed by Davies *et al.* (2008, 2009a), *Calluna* accounted for, on average, 96% of the fuel load above the moss and litter layer (range 62–100%). Changes in the structure of vegetation through the *Calluna* cycle (Figure 12.1) lead to progressively greater heterogeneity in fuel load and canopy density, including the formation of canopy gaps (Davies *et al.* 2008). This heterogeneity and 'gappiness' can have significant implications for fire behaviour (Davies *et al.* 2009a), with gaps slowing fire spread under lighter wind speeds. Dead fuels become a progressively more important component of the fuel load as stands age. Watson *et al.* (1966) estimated that the proportion of dead shoots in *Calluna* was substantially greater in the degenerate phase (37%) than in the pioneer (27%), building (22%) and mature (21%) phases. Over-winter frost damage has been observed to cause large-scale dieback events (Hancock 2008), as can outbreaks of the heather beetle *Lochmaea suturalis* (Thomson, 1866).

In wet heaths and bogs, herbaceous fuels dominated by, for example, *Molinia caerulea*, *Eriophorum* spp. and *Scirpus* spp. can become more important, while layers of pleurocarpous moss may be replaced by *Sphagnum* spp. Other ericaceous shrubs such as *Erica* spp. and *Vaccinium* spp. vary in importance depending on soil moisture and other environmental conditions. In dry heaths, fuels may contain appreciable amounts of gorse (*Ulex* spp.), which can be associated with particularly intense fire behaviour (Figure 12.3). *Juniperus communis* can also be present in many heathlands, and is particularly common in less intensively managed sites in Norway. It can also lead to high fireline intensities due to its highly flammable, resinous foliage. Heather-dominated fuel beds also occur beneath the canopies of many woodland and forest communities, including remnant native Caledonian pine forests in the Scottish Highlands and pine and birch woodlands naturally regenerating on former heathland areas. In some such settings, the limited available data suggest very high fuel loads (total up to 3.4 kg m^{-2}) and bulk densities (up to 5.5 kg m^{-3})

Figure 12.2: Heathland vegetation and fuels showing remarkable consistency in composition and structure in *Calluna*-dominated habitats, including (a, b) upland dry heath, (c) lowland dry heath and (d) a transitional upland wet heath, namely blanket bog. (a, b) In the upland dry heath, evidence of prescribed fire in the form of burned strips and differences in vegetation structure can be seen. (d) Note the stand of fire beaters left out on the lowland heath. (e) A vertical cross-section through a mature-stage *Calluna* canopy showing the predominately live (green) canopy, abundant dead aerial fuels (grey) in the lower canopy and the pleurocarpous moss ground fuels; the bands on the measuring stick are 10 cm. (f) A close-up of a building-phase *Calluna* in a Norwegian heath. (g) Patch-scale variation in *Calluna* canopy status affects the balance between dead and live fuel abundance. Such 'browning' of *Calluna* is a common phenomenon in colder climates and may be caused by overwinter frost damage and moisture stress, as well as outbreaks of the heather beetle (Watson *et al.* 1966; Hancock 2008; Davies *et al.* 2010b). Image credits: (b) 'East side of Clashanruich from Lary Hill' by Nigel Corby (licenced under CC BY-SA 2.0); (c) 'Fire-beaters by the track, Town Common' by Jim Champion (licenced under CC BY-SA 2.0); (d) 'Bog-bashing territory' by Eric Jones (licenced under CC BY-SA 2.0); all other images taken by the authors.

can accumulate in the longer-term absence of fire (MB Bruce and G Servant, unpubl. data). Information to inform the prediction of fire behaviour is limited, but fuel bed descriptions (Table 12.2), suitable for use with the Rothermel fire behaviour model and associated software (e.g. BehavePlus, FlamMap), have been produced for *Calluna–Molinia* heathland fuels in Italy (Vacchiano and Ascoli

2015) and for some stages of dry and wet heath fuels in Scotland (Davies 2006).

Aside from vegetation, ground fuels (duff and peat) are of great significance in many heathland and moorland systems managed through burning. Burning on 'deep peat' (i.e. >40 cm deep) has raised concerns that fire may alter hydrological and chemical processes, with implications for aquatic

Table 12.1. Cross-walk of key European habitat classifications relevant to describing variation in *Calluna*-dominated heathland fuel structure

We include associations that can include substantial *Calluna* cover even where this may exist due to historic management or degradation. The table shows the formalised habitat name and code; numbers in square brackets indicate the number of subordinate associations. Annex I habitat codes are given in parentheses. For the European Nature Information System (EUNIS), where available we provide the revised and historic codes. Based on Strachan (2017). BAP, Biodiversity Action Plan; NiN, Natur i Norge; NVC, National Vegetation Classification

EUNIS[A]	Annex I[B]	NVC (UK)[C]	UK BAP[D]	Phase I Habitat (UK)[E]	NiN (Norway)[F]
Wet heath (S4–1/F4.1) [3]	Northern Atlantic wet heaths with *Erica tetralix* (4010) Temperate Atlantic wet heaths with *Erica ciliaris* and *Erica tetralix* (4020)	H3: *Ulex minor–Agrostis curtisii* heath H4: *Ulex gallii–Agrostis curtisii* heath H5: H5 *Erica vagans–Schoenus nigricans* heath M14: *Schoenus nigricans–Narthecium ossifragum* mire M15: *Scirpus cespitosus–Erica tetralix* wet heath M16: *Erica tetralix–Sphagnum compactum* wet heath	Upland heathland Lowland heathland	D2: Wet dwarf shrub heath E1.7: Wet modified bog	T34-1: Acid north-facing heath T34-4: Intermediate rich north-facing heath T34-11: Acid moist heath T34-12: Intermediate rich moist heath
Dry heath (S4–2/F4.2) [6] • F4.21: Submontane *Vaccinium–Calluna* heaths [6] • F4.22: Sub-Atlantic *Calluna–Genista* heaths [12] • F4.23: Atlantic *Erica–Ulex* heaths [9] • F4.24: Ibero-Atlantic *Erica–Ulex–Cistus* heaths [9] • F4.25: Boreo-Atlantic *Erica cinerea* heaths [0] • F4.26: Inland dune heaths [2]	Dry sand heaths with *Calluna* and *Genista* (2310) Dry sand heaths with *Calluna* and *Empetrum nigrum* (2320) European dry heaths (4030) Dry Atlantic coastal heaths with *Erica vagans* (4040)	H1: *Calluna vulgaris–Festuca ovina* heath H2: *Calluna vulgaris–Ulex minor* heath H3 H4 H7: *Calluna vulgaris–Scilla verna* heath H8: *Calluna vulgaris–Ulex gallii* heath H9: *Calluna vulgaris–Deschampsia flexuosa* heath H10: *Calluna vulgaris–Erica cinerea* heath H12: *Calluna vulgaris–Vaccinium myrtillus* heath H16: *Calluna vulgaris–Arctostaphylos uva-ursi* heath H18: *Vaccinium myrtillus–Deschampsia flexuosa* heath H21: *Calluna vulgaris–Vaccinium myrtillus–Sphagnum capillifolium* heath	Upland heathland Lowland heathland	D1: Dry dwarf shrub heath D5: Dry heath/ acid grassland mosaic E1.8: Dry modified bog	T34-2: Acid coastal heath T34-3: Acid dry coastal heath T34-5: Intermediate rich coastal heath T34-6: Intermediate rich dry coastal heath T34-7: Weakly calcareous coastal heath T34-8: Weakly calcareous dry coastal heath T34-9: Calcareous coastal heath T34-10: Calcareous dry coastal heath

EUNIS[A]	Annex I[B]	NVC (UK)[C]	UK BAP[D]	Phase I Habitat (UK)[E]	NiN (Norway)[F]
Raised bogs (D1.1) • D1.11131: Ling dwarf shrub hummocks • D1.122: Drained raised bogs • D1.123: Ditched raised bogs	Active raised bogs (7110) Degraded raised bogs still capable of natural regeneration (7120)	M1: *Sphagnum auriculatum* bog pool community M2: *Sphagnum cuspidatum/recurvum* bog pool community M3: *Eriophorum angustifolium* bog pool community M15 M16 M17: *Scirpus cespitosus–Eriophorum vaginatum* blanket mire M18: *Erica tetralix–Sphagnum papillosum* raised and blanket mire M19: *Calluna vulgaris–Eriophorum vaginatum* blanket mire M20: *Eriophorum vaginatum* raised and blanket mire M25: *Molinia caerulea–Potentilla erecta* mire	Lowland raised bog	E1.6.2: Raised bog	Several landforms within BS-3TO peatlands, including 3TO-HA Atlantic raised bogs
Blanket bogs (D1.2) • D1.22: Montane blanket bogs, *Calluna* and *Eriophorum vaginatum* often dominant [7] • D1.23: Boreo-Atlantic blanket bogs [5]	Blanket bogs (if active bog; 7130)	M1 M2 M3 M15 M19 M20	Blanket bog	E1.6.1: Blanket bog	3TO-TE blanket bogs

[A] European Environment Agency (2020); [B] European Commission DG Environment (2013); [C] Elkington *et al.* (2001); [D] Joint Nature Conservation Committee (JNCC 2019); [E] JNCC (2010); [F] Halvorsen *et al.* (2016).

Table 12.2. Variation in average fuel bed characteristics across European Nature Information System (EUNIS) habitat classifications and stages of the *Calluna* cycle

Asterisks indicate fuel classes based on limited (less than five) observations, and these data should be treated with caution. Data are aggregated from previous studies, including Davies *et al.* (2008, 2009a, 2016c). Norwegian data are previously unpublished

Country	Class	EUNIS	*Calluna* stage	Canopy depth (cm)	Moss/litter depth (cm)	Moss/litter (kg m^{-2})	Dead fine (1-h) fuels (kg m^{-2})[A]	Herbaceous fuels (live and dead; kg m^{-2})	Live woody (kg m^{-2})
UK	Lowland	Dry heath*	Mature	–	–	0.51	0.15	0.03	1.08
		Wet heath	Degenerate	–	–	1.05	0.15	<0.01	0.29
	Upland	Blanket bog	–	–	–	0.85	0.04	0.27	0.30
		Dry heath[B]	Pioneer*	11.18	0.95	0.50	0.15	0.01	0.40
			Building	21.54	2.62	0.55	0.13	<0.01	0.74
			Mature	35.78	7.16	1.29	0.21	<0.01	1.05
			Degenerate*	40.75	9.10	1.67	0.20	0.01	0.88
		Wet heath	Undefined	–	–	0.47	0.23	0.15	0.56
Norway	Lowland	Wet heath	Pioneer	8.88	1.83	0.44	0.02	0.06	0.31
			Building	9.97	2.01	0.28	0.03	0.14	0.46
			Late building	24.03	3.90	0.57	0.03	0.07	0.48
			Mature	27.19	3.89	0.54	0.03	0.09	0.94

[A] Norwegian sampling was not focused on fuel structure *per se*. The 1-h fuels only include entirely dead plants and not dead material within living shrubs as with UK data.

[B] Equivalent to National Vegetation Classification Community H12.

Figure 12.3: Heathland fire behaviour in Britain showing burns in the (a) late pioneer, (b) building and (c) mature stages of *Calluna* and (d) fire in a mixture of *Calluna* and gorse *Ulex europaeus*, where flames >4 m length are apparent from the gorse and dwarf those in adjacent *Calluna* fuels. In (a), note the spread of the fire through the lower canopy where dead fuels dominate. The posts in (b) enabled recording of the spread rates and flame lengths (cross-bars are at 1 and 2 m). (e, f) Back-burns in mature Norwegian heaths. Image credits: (a, d–f) the authors; (b) Colin Legg (licenced under CC BY-NC-SA 4.0); and (c) Elaine Boyd (licenced under CC BY-NC-SA 4.0).

ecosystems, vegetation communities and carbon storage (e.g. Brown *et al.* 2015; Grau-Andrés *et al.* 2019a). The vulnerability of peat and organic soil carbon stocks is a significant concern due to potential feedbacks to climate change and implications for peatland ecosystem services more widely (e.g. Worrall *et al.* 2010). Peat and organic fuel loads within European heaths and moors are highly variable. The depth of organic material may be as little as a couple of centimetres in dry heathlands and up to several metres in raised and blanket bogs.

Fuel moisture dynamics

Variations in both live and dead fuel moisture in heathland fuels remain poorly understood. Given that in *Calluna*-dominated fuel beds the majority of the fuel is live, there has been greatest interest in understanding controls on this component. *Calluna* live fuel moisture content has been observed to follow a seasonal cycle typical of many other live fuel types. Its moisture content has been observed to range from an average of approximately 115% in summer to 67% in early spring. Values during spring prescribed burning operations monitored by Legg *et al.* (2007) were in the range 55–95%. However, in spring, when the majority of burning is completed and wildfire activity is generally greatest, live *Calluna* can exhibit rapid fuel moisture fluctuations, crashing to values as low as 45% in periods combining clear sunny skies and cold or frozen ground (Davies *et al.* 2010b). Over-winter damage to leaf cuticles by abrasion and the reduced efficiency of water status regulation have been posited as explanations.

Calluna dead fuel moisture dynamics were recently investigated by Log (2020), who demonstrated large variation in moisture diffusion coefficients and successfully validated a numerical drying model under laboratory conditions. Moreover, in a drying experiment, Log *et al.* (2017) demonstrated that dead old *Calluna* showed significantly faster drying rates than live, young *Calluna* and plants in the building phase, as well as drought-damaged old but still live plants (typically having some dead small branches). Using dead gorse fuels, Anderson and Anderson (2009) also demonstrated

very rapid response times within well-aerated shrub canopies. This aligns with casual observations that heather stands can be ignited a matter of hours after rain where this is followed by suitable drying conditions (e.g. clear skies, strong winds, reduced humidity). Dead fuel moisture content during the prescribed burns monitored by Legg *et al.* (2007) ranged between 15% and 29%. A more limited number of studies investigated the moisture dynamics of surface (moss and litter) fuels. During typical periods for prescribed burning, the moisture content of pleurocarpous mosses has been observed to vary between 72% and 552% (Legg *et al.* 2007). Moisture contents may be even higher in the *Sphagnum* mosses, which become more common in wet heath and bog communities. Grau-Andrés *et al.* (2018), for instance, observed average moss layer fuel moisture contents of 271% and 365% during experimental prescribed fires at an upland dry heath and lowland raised bog respectively. The moisture content of pleurocarpous moss carpets may decline substantially during periods of drought and extended dry weather. At such times, these ground fuels may contribute a substantial proportion of the available fuel load (Table 12.2), with significant effects on fire behaviour, burn severity (Grau-Andrés *et al.* 2018) and the relative effectiveness of suppression and control strategies and tools. The moisture content of moss and litter fuel layers demonstrates tolerable relationships between fuel moisture and predictions from the Fine Fuel Moisture Code (FFMC; Grau-Andrés *et al.* 2015) of the Canadian Fire Weather Index System (Van Wagner 1987). This has been posited as an explanation for the comparatively strong performance of the FFMC in predicting periods of increased wildfire activity in Scotland (Davies and Legg 2016).

Flammability and fire behaviour in heathland fuels

There is a surprisingly long history of investigation into heathland fire behaviour. Indeed, some of the earliest attempts to develop physically based fire behaviour models used such fuels (e.g. Thomas 1963, 1971) and demonstrated that reduced bulk density and increased wind speed result in faster spreading fires. Fires in *Calluna*-dominated heathland fuels can display high rates of spread and fireline intensities, but these vary significantly across varying age and community-related differences in fuel structure, as well as with differences in fire weather (Table 12.3; Figures 12.3, 12.4). Prescribed burns in heavy heathland–pinewood edge fuels completed by Bruce and Servant (2003) exhibited exceptionally intense behaviour, with headfire flame length of 3–4 m and estimated fireline intensities between 6800 and 15 400 kW m^{-1}. For the same burns, flank and backing fire flame lengths were recorded at between 0.5 and 1.5 m.

The process of heathland fire spread is interesting to observe; due to the fuel structure of dense *Calluna* stands, the fire initially advances through the lower canopy, which contains abundant dead fine twigs and foliage. The upper, predominantly live, canopy is preheated and dried by the advancing lower-canopy fire and ignites shortly after (Figure 12.3). Similar to other shrub fuel types, studies have demonstrated key controls on heathland fire rate of spread and intensity include fuel bed depth, wind speed and live fuel moisture content (Davies *et al.* 2009a). Empirical models have been produced for fire rates of spread (Davies *et al.* 2009a), fireline intensity, flame lengths (Davies *et al.* 2019) and canopy temperatures (Hobbs and Gimingham 1984) in *Calluna*-dominated heathland fuels. Fire behaviour nomograms have also been produced for flame length and fireline intensity (Figure 12.4). Legg *et al.* (2007) estimated combustion completeness during prescribed burns to range

between 37% and 91% for shrub and herbaceous fuels (mean 79%; 0.93 kg m^{-2}), but only between 0% and 17% (mean 5%; 0.03 kg m^{-2}) for moss and litter layers. In contrast, Allen *et al.* (2013) observed an average of 71% shrub fuel consumption and 56% for litter based on comparisons of burned and unburned areas. Using a similar approach, Davies *et al.* (2016c) observed average moss and litter combustion completeness of 70% following wildfires.

Understanding ignition potential is critical to modelling wildfire risk and forecasting suitable conditions for prescribed burning. Davies and Legg (2011) demonstrated that ignition of the *Calluna* canopy from a flaming source (drip torch) is predominantly controlled by the moisture content of the lower canopy (containing a mixture of suspended dead fuels and fine live branches <2 mm in diameter; Figure 12.2). Above a threshold moisture content of approximately 70%, fires failed to establish and spread. Elsewhere, critical moisture thresholds have been identified for pleurocarpous mosses (15% based on a simulated smouldering ignition; Davies *et al.* 2009b) and gorse (dead fuel moisture content <36% for ignition and <19% for spread; Anderson and Anderson 2009). Santana and Marrs (2014) assessed flammability thresholds for a range of fuels in a laboratory setting using a simulated smouldering source and identified critical thresholds of 19–27% for the litter of various ericaceous heathland shrubs and approximately 35% for gorse litter. For ignition of the *Calluna* canopy, Santana and Marrs (2014) found dead fuel moisture and the proportion of dead fuels to be significant drivers of ignition success from smouldering sources. Critical moisture

Table 12.3.   Variation in mean (±s.d.) fire behaviour across four different *Calluna*-dominated stand structures recorded by Davies *et al.* (2009a, 2019)

Individual burns within each *Calluna* stage were completed on different days, and the substantial within-stage variability in behaviour illustrates the importance of fire weather conditions

Calluna stage	Rate of spread (m min^{-1})	Fireline intensity (kW m^{-1})	Flame length (m)
Building ($n = 8$)	2.33 ± 1.96	531.52 ± 456.81	0.75 ± 0.29
Late building ($n = 9$)	3.41 ± 2.61	1054.89 ± 988.56	1.10 ± 0.28
Mature ($n = 7$)	6.96 ± 2.08	2186.47 ± 516.62	1.46 ± 0.72
Degenerate ($n = 2$)	4.68 ± 1.77	1025.24 ± 597.32	1.82 ± 0.80

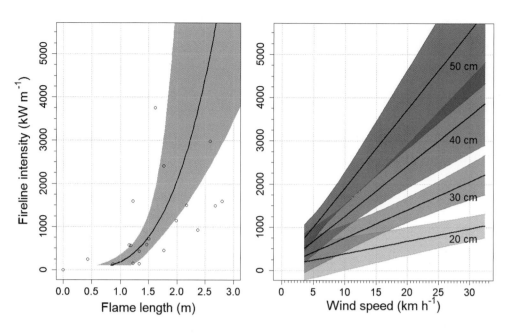

Figure 12.4: A fire behaviour nomogram based on predictions from Davies *et al.* (2019). The right predicts fireline intensity as a function of wind speed for four different fuel heights; the left predicts flame length from the estimated fireline intensity. The figure is organised so that the predicted intensity can be read across to predict flame length. Black lines show the predicted values and the shaded areas around the lines demarcate the 95% confidence intervals of the modelled fireline intensity or flame length. Observed flame lengths and intensities, from experimental managed burns on *Calluna*-dominated moorland in Scotland between spring of 2006 and autumn of 2009, are shown as circles. Reproduced from Davies *et al.* (2019; licenced under CC BY 4.0).

contents ranged from 19% to 35% depending on the proportion of dead fuel in the canopy. In another study, Santana and Marrs (2016) found that for the common heathland graminoids *Molinia caerulea*, *Eriophorum angustifolium* and *Eriophorum vaginatum*, fuel moisture content values corresponding to a 50% ignition probability from a flaming source were approximately 48% for the former two species and approximately 36% for the latter.

Ignition thresholds for peat are comparatively well characterised, with research on the topic from both European and North American peatlands (e.g. Frandsen 1997; Grishin *et al.* 2006). Using peat from the UK, Rein *et al.* (2008) defined a critical moisture of 125% for ignition. More recent research has demonstrated that established smouldering fires can spread an appreciable distance into moister peat (Prat-Guitart *et al.* 2016), with moistures of extinction being as high as approximately 250% (Huang and Rein 2015). Spread rates are a function of both bulk density and moisture content,

with propagation observed to range between 1 and 5 cm h⁻¹ (Prat-Guitart *et al.* 2016). The consumption of deep organic soils in peatlands is generally limited by a high water table. During the spring managed burning season, it is not unusual for the water table to be at, or very close to, the ground, moss or *Sphagnum* surface. This, combined with cold soil temperatures and saturation of the moss or litter layer itself, limits consumption or substantive downward heat transfer (Grau-Andrés *et al.* 2017a). However, drought, or degradation of peat due to drainage, can lead to significant changes in patterns of fuel moisture (Prat-Guitart *et al.* 2017), soil heating (Grau-Andrés *et al.* 2017a, 2018) and burn severity (Granath *et al.* 2016; Grau-Andrés *et al.* 2018). Davies *et al.* (2013) highlighted this in the case of smouldering fire in a conifer plantation; here, a fire originating on adjacent heathland ignited dry, degraded peat deposits within the forest, causing release of 9.6 ± 1.5 kg C m⁻². Despite the concern about the effects of burning on peatlands, evidence suggests that, depending on the hydrological setting, intact systems can be relatively resilient to occasional fires when surface and ground fuel layers are below the ignition threshold (Ingram *et al.* 2019). Ironically, considering the attention paid to fire effects on blanket bogs in the UK, recent research suggests that it is deposits of thin organic soils in dry heathlands that may be at more risk of loss during or following fire (Grau-Andrés *et al.* 2018; Wilkinson *et al.* 2020).

Heathland prescribed burning practice in the modern era

Objectives for fire use

Traditional heathland land use regimes were fine-tuned to exploit outfield resources in the cool, moist regions of north-west Europe, where year-round free-range grazing depended on the availability and nutritional quality of heather for winter fodder. Burning promotes the regrowth of young heather shoots from the protected stem bases, and the fertilising effect of ash increases forage value for several years following a fire (Gimingham 1972; Skre *et al.* 1998). This made fire an important tool for enhancing the productivity of heathlands throughout northern Europe. Indeed, there are interesting etymological connections between practices across the region. In Dartmoor National Park (south-west England) the use of fire for agricultural practices is known to date back to the Mesolithic (Caseldine and Hatton 1993) and is today known as 'swaling', linking it to the Low German *swelan* (to singe grass) and Old Norse *svæla* (to smoke out). In Norway, this ancient land use practice persisted into the 20th century, allowing cross-disciplinary investigations combining palaeoecology, archaeology, history and ecology to disentangle the functioning and dynamics of the heathland farming system (Kaland and Kvamme 2013; Kaland *et al.* 2014). The land use practice was based on small-scale burns with a fire rotation of 15–25 years (longer rotations in more exposed or northern regions), resulting in a patchy landscape with

a mosaic of areas in different successional stages. Fires were always set during winter, after cold and/or wet spells to ensure the soil was frozen or waterlogged to avoid damage to both it and the seed bank (Kaland and Kvamme 2013). In Norway, heathland burning and grazing practices are seen as integral to the heathland agroecosystem, and as crucial to its conservation (Kvamme *et al.* 2004; Halvorsen *et al.* 2016), restoration (Velle *et al.* 2012) and economic sustainability (Velle *et al.* 2008).

In the UK, current management practice is strongly associated with habitat requirements of red grouse *L. lagopus scotica* and the objective of producing large population surpluses for game shooting. Management generally aims to produce a patchwork of all *Calluna* stand stages by burning a series of small fires or long thin strips no more than 30 m across (Figure 12.5). The reasons behind this lie in the territorial behaviour of grouse as traditional burning produces a mixture of heather ages within each approximate 1-ha territory (Palmer and Bacon 2001). Grouse graze on young nutritious shoots of the pioneer and early building stages, but also require taller heather in which to nest and hide from predators. Burning is also widely used to improve grazing for sheep and deer and, in areas where these are the dominant economic resource, fires tend to be larger. Although UK heathland burning thus has a strong association with game and livestock production, the actual uses and outcomes of fire in heathland habitats are, in reality, much more diverse. As Davies *et al.* (2016b) and Velle *et al.* (2014) point out, disturbances, including fire and grazing, are critical in maintaining open heathland habitats that can have high conservation value. Fire use is thus not limited to agricultural and sporting settings. Lowland heaths are resilient to fire (Bullock and Webb 1995), and Lovegrove (2016) demonstrated the importance of burning for maintaining lowland heath habitats. Within the New Forest National Park of southern England Lovegrove (2016) showed differential plant community outcomes between cutting and burning management. Burning can be used to improve the conservation value of habitats for wildlife

Figure 12.5: (a–g) Examples of heathland burning practice in the UK. (a) The heathland landscape mosaic created by rotational heather burning in the Scottish Highlands; (b) multiple managed fires spreading across moorland in northern England; (c, d) old Norse sheep (c) and red grouse (d), the primary agroeconomic focus of traditional managed burning in Norway and the UK respectively; (e) recently burned patches from traditional management on a Scottish hillside; (f) burned patches (lighter colours) on a Norwegian heathland; and (g) patch burning that used mowed firebreaks. (h–j) Examples of poor practice include visually intrusive intensive management with individual burn units divided by regular, straight cut breaks (h), burning into or adjacent to watercourses and steep gullies (i) and burning upslope leading to loss of control (j; note the V-shaped fire scar resulting from a burn rapidly accelerating upslope and escaping control). Image credits: (a) Copernicus European, Very High Resolution Image Mosaic (VHRIM); (b) 'Controlled burning on Great Hograh Moor 2' by Colin Grice (licenced under CC BY-SA 2.0); (d) 'Red grouse on Burley Moor' by John Winder (licenced under CC BY-SA 2.0); (e) 'Muirburn on slopes of Gurlet' by Russel Wills (licenced under CC BY-SA 2.0); (g) 'Patterns from heather burning' by Jim Barton (licenced under CC BY-SA 2.0); (h) 'Muirburn patterns, Feuar's Moor' by Richard Webb (licenced under CC BY-SA 2.0); (i) 'Long Grain' by Chris Eilbeck (licenced under CC BY-SA 2.0); (c, f, j) images taken by the authors.

(Gimingham 1992) and species-rich lichen communities (Davies and Legg 2008). The latter case nicely illustrates the controversies in the UK because the site involved in the study, which demonstrated biodiversity benefits from managed fire, is owned by a nature conservation charity that has since banned burning on its property. Prescribed burning has been investigated as a tool for habitat improvement for threatened capercaillie populations in Scotland (Hancock *et al.* 2011), to improve conditions for pine establishment during reforestation and woodland expansion efforts (Hancock *et al.* 2005) and as a means to increase the fruiting of mycorrhizal fungi (Amphlett *et al.* 2006). Historically, prescribed fire was also used as a tool to clear heathland vegetation before afforestation (e.g. McNab 1931; Evans 1948).

In the UK, pressure from environmental groups for a ban on burning on deep peat has grown in recent years and today most agencies discourage managed burning in areas with deep (<50 cm) peat deposits. This is primarily due to concerns about the effects of fire on peatland hydrology and ecosystem carbon dynamics (e.g. Clay *et al.* 2009; Brown *et al.* 2015; Grau-Andrés *et al.* 2019a). The carbon issue has become contested, with several studies suggesting that black carbon production, and fire effects on peat bulk density, allow carbon sequestration even in peatlands managed by fire (e.g. Heinemeyer *et al.* 2018; Marrs *et al.* 2019). Nevertheless, significant areas of British blanket peatland (approximately one-third of Sites of Special Scientific Interest, and more than half Natura 2000 sites) are classified as being in 'unsatisfactory' condition, with evidence of fire cited as a key reason for this (Williams 2006). There is, however, an obvious illogicality here because if there is permission for managed burning, then this should not be used as evidence of poor condition regardless of its ecological results. Although it is reasonable to suggest that significant uncertainty about the effects of fire should lead to a precautionary approach to its use on peatlands (Douglas *et al.* 2016), it is not immediately clear what 'precautionary' should entail within systems that have been associated with fire for millennia. There is evidence to suggest that *intact* peatlands are

resilient to low-severity fires (e.g. Grau-Andrés *et al.* 2019b). However, it is also undoubtedly true that severe burns, or severe burning in association with other disturbances such as heavy grazing, can lead to state changes in peatland systems (Maltby *et al.* 1990; Legg *et al.* 1992; Blundell and Holden 2015). The significant issue for many peatlands in the UK is that they have been degraded by an array of interacting disturbances, including drainage, nutrient deposition from atmospheric pollution and overgrazing (Holden *et al.* 2007). The inappropriate use of fire can exacerbate the degradation associated with such disturbances, and drainage in particular is known to cause step changes in burn severity (e.g. Davies *et al.* 2013; Granath *et al.* 2016). Whether fire on peatlands is in fact damaging in all situations remains an open question and a subject of much recent controversy (e.g. Davies *et al.* 2016a; Baird *et al.* 2019; Marrs *et al.* 2019).

Moving forward, peatland fire management must place emphasis on developing an ecological approach to the use of fire where specific prescriptions for its use are defined and trade-offs clearly quantified. Learning from traditional practices (e.g. long-standing expertise on fire control in the UK and Norwegian practices to minimise soil impacts) certainly has a role to play, but objectives will need to be targeted to 21st century priorities. Burning is important in managing fuels and in maintaining heterogeneity in habitat and community structure that benefits biodiversity (Velle *et al.* 2014). Fire has also been proposed as a tool to reinvigorate *Sphagnum* in wet heathlands where *Molinia* and *Calluna* may shade it out, leading to its replacement with feather (pleurocarpous) mosses. *Sphagnum* spp. are obviously initially impacted by burning (Noble *et al.* 2019a), but many species appear to be resilient, showing rapid recovery afterwards (Grau-Andrés *et al.* 2017b; Taylor *et al.* 2017). In the UK's single long-term peatland burning regime experiment at the Moor House National Nature Reserve (Ecological Continuity Trust 2020), the most frequent (10-year rotation) burn treatments had higher *Sphagnum* abundance than adjacent control areas (Lee *et al.* 2013; Milligan *et al.*

2018; Noble *et al.* 2018a). Interestingly, larger-scale correlative studies have shown *Sphagnum* to be negatively associated with burned and grazed locations and sites subjected to greater deposition of atmospheric nitrogen pollution (Noble *et al.* 2018b). Furthermore, some *Sphagnum* species have shown declines synchronous with evidence for anthropogenic fire use (McCarroll *et al.* 2016). In all cases, untangling the effects of fire and other disturbances remains challenging. Rewetting drained peatlands is *the* critical restoration need across many peatland habitats in the UK (Parry *et al.* 2014; Granath *et al.* 2016) and arguments over the use of fire should not detract from this. It is generally not recommended to burn drained or degraded peatlands because this may inhibit recolonisation by *Sphagnum* and/or promote a greater dominance of *Calluna* and *Molinia* than is desirable. Recently, some in the management community have proposed that burning may be a useful pretreatment before attempting re-establishment of *Sphagnum*, but the single study to date did not demonstrate any short-term benefits (Noble *et al.* 2019b).

There has been growing interest in the use of managed burning as a tool for wildfire fighting and risk management (Figure 12.6). The latter is a particular concern in the context of fuel accumulation and flammability changes due climate change, reductions or cessations of traditional management in some areas and increasing emphasis on reforestation (Sutherland *et al.* 2008). High fire risk in some peatlands undergoing restoration (Wiltshire *et al.* 2019) suggests prescribed burning, or other fuel management strategies, should be an important consideration in this process. To add to these challenges, some areas of the country, notably the post-industrial, economically deprived South Wales valleys, experience an endemic culture of what one might politely term 'recreational fire setting' (Jollands *et al.* 2011). The Fire Service in one such region, namely South Wales, has been at the forefront of using prescribed fire for fuel reduction and has contributed to the use of suppression fire in some of the UK's recent large wildfires. In Norway, the combination of biomass build-up in former agricultural landscapes and climate change has increased the number of wildfires and put wildland–urban interface management on the agenda. Unlike prescribed burning, which happens during winter, wildfires can occur during summer and may do considerable damage to soils and seed banks, as well as potentially to settlements and human lives and livelihoods. Log *et al.* (2020) point out that wildfire risk is now a concern across the boreal coastal heathland region. This increased risk poses specific human health impacts, including stress related to the loss of jobs, psychological effects due to the loss of possessions, the effects of exposure to smoke and heat and the immediate, or delayed, loss of lives, with rural and vulnerable populations being disproportionally affected (Metallinou and Log 2017). In western Norway, professional training in safe and ecologically sound burning practices has spurred the rise of local 'Heath Burning Societies', consisting of small-holder farmers who collaborate to assist each other in planning and conducting safe management burns (Log *et al.* 2020). Collaboration with local firefighters has been growing, with these societies now building competence in fire and fire risk management and helping local firefighters with preventive burning to reduce landscape fire risk, as well as being an extra force in putting out wildfires (Metallinou 2020). Collaborative fire management groups involving private and public landowners and the emergency services are also common in the UK, particularly in Scotland and northern England. Local knowledge and collaboration within civic groups, the exchange of experience with other groups and recognition from and collaboration with the local fire brigade may significantly increase group identity and perceived as well as actual competence (Metallinou 2020).

Many of these fire initiatives and uses are in the early stages of implementation and development. Interestingly, fire management in the UK seems to be in the process of 'relearning' some of these skills, because there is documented use of

Figure 12.6: Variations in heathland prescribed burning tools and techniques in the UK and Norway. (a) Traditional burning of a coastal heathland in Norway using back-burning and beaters. (b) A heathland burning cooperative in Norway using leaf blowers to control a prescribed burn. (c) Employees of the Forestry Commission and a local estate control a fire using a rubber 'flapper' and a backpack water sprayer during a collaborative prescribed fire exercise. (d) Igniting mature heather from a recently burned patch using a drip torch. (e, f) Members of the South Wales Fire and Rescue Services using strip and spot ignition strategies during fuel reduction burns. (g) A gamekeeper igniting a fire from a recently cut firebreak using a butane burner. (h) Burning in a Scottish blizzard using long-handled metal beaters; the fire is being ignited using a modified backpack sprayer. (i) Igniting a patch of gorse *Ulex europaeus* from a grassy ride. (j) The late Professor Charles Gimingham demonstrating a high-pressure fire fogging unit mounted on a pick-up truck. (k) An all-terrain vehicle with a mounted fire fogging unit and various fire beaters used on a Scottish grouse moor. (l) A member of the UK fire and rescue services demonstrating the outcome of using a rubber 'flapper' on a high-intensity fire. Image credits: (a, c, j, k) the authors; (b) Annlaug Fludal (Norsk Landbruksrådgiving); (d) Elaine Boyd (licenced under CC BY-NC-SA 4.0); (e, f) Craig Hope (licenced under CC BY-NC-SA 4.0); (g) Guillermo Rein (licenced under CC BY-NC-SA 4.0); (h) Michael Bruce (licenced under CC BY-NC-SA 4.0); (i) Colin Legg (licenced under CC BY-NC-SA 4.0); and (l) Adam Smith (Game and Wildlife Conservation Trust).

prescribed burning by public agencies for wild-fire suppression (e.g. Sangar 1928; Graham 1939) and fuel management (e.g. Murray 1931; Williams 1936) as far back as the early to mid 20th century. This was a period when wildfire risk was a constant concern due to the risk of fires ignited by steam trains and the flammability of abundant young conifer plantations that had been established following the First World War (e.g. Charters 1939). Further research is needed on controls on

the effectiveness of prescribed fire in mitigating wildfire effects during high-risk periods to minimise ecosystem carbon losses (e.g. Allen *et al.* 2013), protect ecosystem function (e.g. Legg *et al.* 1992; Gray *et al.* 2020) and safeguard property and human health (e.g. Log *et al.* 2017; Metallinou and Log 2017). The use of remote sensing and burning maps may both assist with the policing of the use of prescribed burning and provide information to help with firefighting (Allen *et al.* 2016).

Legal requirements for fire use

> ### Box 12.1: Regulations on heather burning introduced by Robert III of Scotland in 'Burning of Muris' (from Findlay 1964)
>
> *It is a statute to be keiped and observed throu' the haille realme, and there sail be na muirburne or burning of heder bot in the month of March, and not thereafter induring the time of somer, or of harvest under the pane of fourtie shillings.*
>
> Translation: It is a statute to be kept and observed through the whole realm that there shall be no muirburn or burning of heather except in the month of March and not in summer or at harvest time. Penalty for non-compliance is forty [Scots] shillings (ca. £550 in 2019).

In the UK, managed burning has been regulated in some form for several centuries. For example, Findlay (1964) recounts the rules introduced by Robert III of Scotland at the turn of the 15th Century (Box 12.1). In the modern era prescribed burning and wildfire fighting fall under the purview of the devolved administrations in Wales, Scotland and Northern Ireland. This has resulted in slightly different regulations across each of the UK's constituent nations (Table 12.4). Legal dates of burning vary between the nations, although all provide a process for acquiring licences to burn outwith the defined season. Applications for such licences are restricted to where fire is to be used for ecosystem management and restoration, research and public safety purposes.

The legal context for burning in the UK is also rapidly changing. As noted previously, there is controversy regarding the use of fire and its effects on 'deep' (i.e. deeper than 40 cm) peat. In Scotland, a recent public review (Werritty 2019) recommended the development of a more robust licensing and training framework for heathland management including prescribed burning. In November 2020, the Scottish Government announced its intention to bring forward such legislation. In England, a voluntary moratorium on burning peatland vegetation was introduced by the country's environment and conservation agency Natural England (2020), but the level of compliance with this policy was unclear (e.g. Wildlife and Countryside Link 2020).

Matters came to a head in early 2021 when the Westminster government (responsible for environmental legislation pertaining to England) announced that a bill would be introduced to significantly restrict the use of management burning on peatlands where they fall within a protected site (Department for Environment, Food & Rural Affairs (DEFRA) 2021). Although touted in some quarters as a 'ban' on burning, the actual proposal is for a system of licensing, but with an apparent general presumption against allowing fire use. Bizarrely, the announcement of the 'ban' will not apply to areas where there are significant opportunities for intense fire behaviour (e.g. 'steep slopes') or where fire has the greatest opportunity to damage sensitive plant communities and soils (e.g. 'where scree makes up half the land area'). Although plans remain vague, the bill will apparently still permit licenced burning for the purposes of wildfire risk management and for 'a conservation purpose'. Nevertheless, conversations with fire research colleagues in the UK have revealed that difficulties obtaining permits for research burns on peatlands have already emerged. Combined, these plans mean there is the potential for a coming sea change in the regulatory environment for prescribed burning in the UK.

In Norway, coastal heathlands are a selected habitat type (*Utvalgt naturtype*) under the Biodiversity act (*Naturmangfoldloven*) since 2015. This gives the coastal heathlands, including their management

Table 12.4. Legal basis and requirements for undertaking managed burning in the British Isles and Norway

Managers failing to comply with legal obligations can face fines under several laws and may see reductions in agricultural subsidies that, in the UK, are now tied to 'cross-compliance' with standards for the Good Agricultural and Environmental Conditions of Land (Rural Payments Agency 2021). All jurisdictions now provide a process for seeking a licence to complete prescribed burning operations out of season where these can be justified as necessary for ecological or safety/risk management reasons. A detailed summary of all UK legislation relevant to completing prescribed burning is provided in Murgatroyd (2002a). DAFM, Department for Agriculture Food and the Marine; DEFA, Department of Environment, Food and Agriculture; DEFRA, Department for Environment, Food & Rural Affairs

Country	Burning season	Principle legislation	Guidance/code
Wales	1 October–15 March[A]	*The Heather and Grass Burning Code Regulations (Wales) 2008*	The Heather and Grass Burning Code for Wales (Welsh Assembly Government 2008)
Scotland	1 October–15th April[B]	*Hill Farming Act 1946*	The Muirburn Code (Scottish Natural Heritage 2017)[E]
Northern Ireland	1 September–14 April	*Game Preservation Act 1928*	The Heather and Grass Burning Code (DEFRA 2007)
England	1 October–31 March[C]	*The Heather and Grass Burning Code Regulations (England) 2007*	The Heather and Grass Burning Code (DEFRA 2007)
Eire	1 September–31 April	*Wildlife Act 1976* (as amended)	Prescribed Burning Code of Practice – Ireland (DAFM 2018)
Isle of Man	1 September–15 March[D]	*Heath Burning Act* (2003)	Heath Burning Code (DEFA 2010)
Norway	15 September–15 April	*Forskrift om brannforebygging* (2016), *Naturmangfoldloven* (2009)	Unpublished national management plan template required[F]

Managers must:
  Develop a Burn Management Plan that can be inspected by relevant authorities on request (Wales) or that uses a national template (Norway)
  Notify neighbours and the fire service in advance of burning
  Obtain consent from the relevant government agency if burning is to take place within a protected area (e.g. Site of Special Scientific Interest, Special Areas of Conservation, Special Protection Areas)
  Ensure sufficient and appropriate equipment and personnel are available to control the fire
  Ensure equipment is fit for purpose
  Forthcoming legislation in Scotland and England will ban burning on deep peat (>40 cm deep) within protected areas without a licence. It is unclear what the licencing requirements will be, but stated possible reasons include for demonstrated restoration, conservation or wildfire management purposes

Managers *must not*:
  Ignite any fires between sunset and sunrise
  Burn 'sensitive areas' or damage sensitive flora, fauna and ancient buildings, structures or sites
  Intentionally or recklessly kill, injure or damage the 'places of shelter or nesting' of wildlife species
  Create smoke that is a 'nuisance' (Scotland) and/or that may have health impacts
  Damage woodland or protected ancient monuments
  Burn within 30 m of a public highway (Scotland) or in a way that will endanger highway users (England)
  Leave a fire unattended or leave a burned site where there is still smoke production
  Endanger anyone's health and safety
  Burn individual areas >10 ha, expose bare soil over a single area >0.5 ha, burn a single area >0.5 ha on slopes >45° or where more than half the area is rock or scree, leave more than 25 m of exposed soil along the bank of a watercourse, leave soils smouldering[G] for >48 h (England and Wales)

[A] The burning season is extended to 31 March in Severely Disadvantaged Area of Less Favoured Areas (SDA LFA). These areas correspond to regions of the country with 'natural handicaps' in terms of agricultural productivity and have benefited from targeted subsidies under the European Union Common Agricultural Policy (OECD 2002).
[B] Extended to 30 April with landowner permission.
[C] Extended to 15 April in SDA LFA.
[D] Licence required; extendable to 31 March with a Special Extension Licence.
[E] A supplemental best-practice handbook is also available (Scottish Government 2011).
[F] For an example of a completed plan using the template, see Thorvaldsen and Velle (2020).
[G] It is not clear why anyone would want any soil smouldering!

and protection, special status and protection. Generally, the use of open fire in outfields is prohibited between 15 April and 15 October. This is usually unproblematic for fire management of heathlands, because the burns traditionally happen in winter. However, the fire service can also prohibit the use of fire in periods of high fire risk, and prolonged winter droughts can postpone the burning season until rains occur, potentially late into the spring. A promising path towards solving such issues is direct contact and collaboration between heathland farmers' societies and the fire service (Log *et al.* 2020; Metallinou 2020).

Training requirements

In the UK there is currently no mandated training or certification required in order to participate in or lead managed burning. However, formalised training on fire control and prevention has been available since at least the 1960s (Hendry 1964). Today, the practical use of fire on heathlands remains dominated by land managers on private estates and somewhat in the realms of 'traditional' knowledge. Traditional burning practice has become increasingly codified in the last 10–20 years, in addition to adopting several technological innovations; for example, National Occupational Standards for wildfire fighting are maintained by LANTRA (n.d.). Although professional training is available from private and charitable organisations, most knowledge is gained by managers on the job through apprenticeships or work placements. Qualifications that can require understanding and use of prescribed burning include the work-based (c.f. apprenticeship) National or Scottish Vocational Qualifications in Game/Gamekeeping and Wildlife Management (City & Guilds 2011; Scottish Qualifications Authority 2020) and Countryside Management (City & Guilds 2012). Modules related to heather or habitat management require participants to demonstrate a basic understanding of controls on fire behaviour and issues associated with burn management planning, as well as ignition and suppression tools and techniques. The former UK Forestry Commission (whose responsibilities have since been devolved and reorganised in Wales and Scotland) had also developed a detailed set of guidance documents on planning and controlling prescribed burns and wildfires (Murgatroyd 2002a, 2002b).

As in the UK, there is no mandatory training or certification to perform prescribed burning in Norway. There are many examples of farmers along the coast who have revived the traditions of burning to enhance the qualities of the coastal heathlands, not only good pastures, but also as habitats for several vulnerable species relying on seminatural habitats. In Norway, heather burning courses are organised by several interest groups, such as The Norwegian Environmental Agency's national coordinator for coastal heathlands the Norwegian Old Norse Sheep Association (Norsk Villsaulag) in collaboration with the civic heather burning group, and the agricultural advisory service. These courses are often financially supported by regional and national schemes. Over the past 10 years there has been a growing interest in traditional heathland management, which includes both burning and grazing strategies.

Current prescribed burning practices

Codification of generally recognised 'best practices' was completed in the seminal Lowland Heathland Management Handbook by Gimingham (1992). The guidelines Gimingham (1992) described were primarily written with respect to lowland heathland management, but are equally applicable to upland settings (Box 12.2). More recently, a best practice handbook was released by the Scottish Government (2017b) as a supplement to the Muirburn Code. In general, heathland management has been organised around the assumption that vegetation should burned when *Calluna* reaches the end of the building phase (i.e. on an average 15-year rotation) or when approximately 30 cm tall, although this should vary according to productivity, habitat type and grazing level. Research suggests that on some moors the rotation may be significantly longer (Hester and Sydes 1992; Allen *et al.* 2016; Davies *et al.* 2016a), but there is also evidence of increasingly intensive managed burning activity in some regions (Yallop *et al.* 2006). Recent research by Douglas *et al.* (2015) using aerial photographs found evidence of burning in 19% of the approximately 45 000 1-km^2 grid squares they sampled, with the percentage area burned varying from 1% to 95%. Douglas *et al.* (2015) found substantive differences between the composite nations of Great Britain, with the proportion of the moorland area burned being approximately 19% in England, 16% in Scotland and 6% in Wales; one-third of the burned area (466 km^2) was found to overlie areas of 'deep peat'. Yallop *et al.* (2006) surveyed a sample in the Peak District within the English uplands using similar methods and found that 17% of moorland habitat had been burned within the previous 4 years, with a median return interval on 'consistently managed' sites of approximately 20 years (ranging from <15 to >60 years). Yallop *et al.* (2006) also identified evidence for an approximate doubling in the area of new burns between 1980 and 2000. More recently, Thacker *et al.* (2015) quantified an increase in burn area on deep peat from 5.3 km^2 year^{-1} in 1945–59 to 38.9 km^2 year^{-1} in 2010. Some of this increase may be associated with the requirements of agri-environment schemes that required moorland managers to burn 10% of their moor each year to enhance *Calluna* growth. Many of the moorland managers could not meet this requirement (Allen *et al.* 2016). This apparent intensification of management practice on some grouse moors, perhaps associated with the introduction of tools that allow more burning to be completed more rapidly, may lie behind the concerns expressed by conservation groups. Nevertheless, research by both Yallop *et al.* (2006) and Allen *et al.* (2016) showed that managed burning practice within the Peak District (northern England) generally adhered to good practice guidelines. Evaluation of aerial photographs showed burned patches met recommended size guidelines and that the occurrence of large burned areas, indicative of escaped fires, was low. Current recommendations are somewhat simplistic though, and it is not appropriate to think that all heathlands should be managed uniformly and intensively. Thompson *et al.* (1995b), for example, emphasised the importance of achieving a diversity of fire return intervals, including leaving some areas unburned, to produce mosaic landscapes comprising *Calluna* of different stages, scrub woodland and riparian areas that are protected from fire. In Norway, Velle and Vandvik (2014) emphasised the importance of considering differential rates of post-fire succession across environmental gradients.

Prescribed burns are completed using a mixture of traditional and modern hand and power tools. Fire beaters (Figure 12.6) are perhaps the best recognised, most widely adopted and most important tool used by managers. Responsible managers will have at least one all-terrain vehicle (ATV) with a high-pressure fire fogging unit on standby during burning operations, although the terrain makes this challenging in Norway (Figure 12.2). Traditional beaters were often fashioned from birch branches and twigs, but Allan (1935) writes that by the early 20th century those using them were seen as *'old-fashioned, behind the times, bound by prejudice'*, despite their cost-effectiveness and efficacy in some situations. We also know from Allan (1935) that by the 1930s beaters were increasingly fashioned from wire, wire netting and sheet metal. Modern designs use similar materials and vary somewhat, but the basic premise is that a long-handled (2–3 m), flat-headed implement is used to beat, or in shorter fuels scrub, out the fire by smothering it and compacting the flaming heather canopy into the ground. In suitable conditions, particularly where ground fuels remain saturated, the tool can be used to rapidly extinguish the fire line. Shorter-handled 'flapper'-type beaters, fashioned from a rubber conveyer belt, are also common, particularly with fire brigades. Although fire beaters can be highly effective, they rapidly lose their efficacy at higher fire intensities because radiant heat prevents a close approach to the fire and stimulates the reignition of beaten areas, and the lack of a moist moss or litter layer reduces the cooling and smothering effect. In fact, at times fire beaters may accentuate fire spread as the beating action spreads embers and encourages spotting. There has been comparatively little research on the relative effectiveness of different fire-suppression tools in heathland fuels. However, Graham (1939) noted that that traditional birch wood beaters were of limited use in herbaceous fuels and where uneven or rocky ground prevented effective smothering of the fire. Graham (1939) also recommended the use of 'Canadian water packs' as an effective supplemental tool. To the best of our knowledge, backpack water sprayers have not been widely adopted to date. Murgatroyd and Bruce (2009) examined the suppression efficiency of different tools and found that long-handled, wire-mesh headed beaters substantially out-performed shorter-handled rubber 'flappers', albeit in rather different fuel types: head and flank suppression rates were 100 m per person per h for flappers in *Molinia*-dominated fuels (estimated rate of spread 37 m min^{-1}) and 250–300 m per person per h for mesh beaters in *Calluna* fuels (estimated rate of spread 7 m min^{-1}). Murgatroyd and Bruce (2009) also compared suppression using combined fogging systems and beater teams versus fogging alone and found that adding beater teams increased water use efficiency and team suppression rates. However, per-person suppression rates were reduced due to the larger team required. The water use efficiency of high-pressure fogging units was four- to fivefold greater for fogging units than for conventional Hathaway pumps and sprayers, although the latter had the highest suppression rates (Murgatroyd and Bruce 2009). More recently adopted tools include leaf blowers (Metallinou 2020; Figure 12.6), which have been shown to be effective for controlling lower-intensity flank and back fires, as well as fires in rugged terrain.

Managers regularly make used of natural and constructed firebreaks. Natural or existing firebreaks may include tracks and roads (although it is illegal to burn within 30 m of a public highway in Scotland), ridgetops, lakes, streams, wetlands and cliffs. In winter and early spring at higher elevations and more northerly latitudes, snow patches may also be used. There is a lack of clarity about the use of ditches, streams and other waterbodies as firebreaks, with some best-practice guidelines appearing to advocate their use in some situations and others strongly advising against it (e.g. Welsh Assembly Government 2008). The Scottish Muirburn Code (Scottish Natural Heritage 2017), for instance, states '*Watercourses should not be used as primary firebreaks. In an emergency they can be considered as a back-up to cover the failure of a primary firebreak.*' Brown and Holden (2020) have shown that the practice of burning adjacent to watercourses (Figure 12.5) unfortunately remains relatively common. Burning has been demonstrated to have significant effects on aquatic ecosystems (Ramchunder *et al.* 2013) and on flood peaks in streams draining peatlands, although there is also evidence that the latter can be mitigated to an extent by avoiding burning and restoring vegetation adjacent to watercourses (Gao *et al.* 2016). On regularly managed heathlands under low-risk conditions, it is often possible to use more recent burns as firebreaks (i.e. those completed within the past 1–3 years), but care must be taken because, in dry weather, unconsumed layers of moss and litter may dry out rapidly and readily carry a fire even in the absence of significant shrub or herbaceous fuel. In flat terrain, managers may use ATV- or tractor-mounted flails and mowing decks to cut firebreaks before burning (Figure 12.6). This can be an effective approach under the right conditions, but cut breaks can dry out readily and loose effectiveness. In such situations, cut breaks can be supplemented with wet lines. On more intensively managed heathlands, the unsympathetic use of cutting to produce a network of cut breaks can have detrimental aesthetic impacts (Figure 12.5). Foam wet lines are occasionally used, but these, and wetting agents, have not seen particularly widespread adoption outwith wildfire suppression operations.

Traditional management displays somewhat limited variability in the tactics for setting fires. They are generally burned under light to moderate winds as headfires and ignited as narrow strips 15–30 m wide. In the Peak District, mean (±s.e.m.) fire patch sizes were measured at 2370 ± 70 m^2, which equates to dimensions of approximately 71 m × 71 m or 50 m × 100 m (Allen *et al.* 2016). Fires are allowed to advance with the wind, with the margins controlled by beaters to limit lateral growth (Figure 12.6). Fires are ignited using a wide variety of tools, including drip torches, propane blowtorches and backpack sprayers adapted with brass nozzles, where the fuel mix is sprayed onto the vegetation in a line and then ignited (Figure 12.6). Burning with the wind can result in high fire intensities and rates of spread but, when the ground fuel moisture content is above ignition thresholds, burning with the wind generally results in limited heating and consumption of ground fuels. Such fires are colloquially referred to in the UK as 'cool burns' as opposed to 'hot burns', which result in the consumption of moss and litter layers and larger woody heather stems. Headfire intensities, flame lengths and fire front depths generally prevent a direct attack to extinguish the fire. Instead, the flanks are controlled to gradually reduce the fire front width and intensity before the head is knocked down.

Published management recommendations (e.g. DEFRA 2007; Welsh Assembly Government 2008; Scottish Government 2017b) suggest that back fires should generally be avoided because of the risk of extensive soil heating. To our knowledge there has been no robust analysis of the association between fire rate of spread, fuel consumption and soil heating in heathlands, and current guidance appears to presuppose that moss and litter layers have a fuel moisture content capable of supporting combustion. Classic research on duff consumption (e.g. Van Wagner 1972) reveals moisture content to be a critical control on the depth of combustion. Furthermore, Grau-Andrés *et al.* (2017a) showed that, during prescribed burns where there was an intact moss or litter layer (moss fuel moisture content ranging from 103% to 398%), soil temperatures never exceeded 21°C at the soil surface and 7°C 2 cm below this. Although Grau-Andrés *et al.* (2017a) did not measure fire intensity or spread, reanalysis of fires described in Davies (2006) reveals a weak association between the rate of spread and the depth of moss consumption (consumption never exceeded 1 cm), but none between the rate of spread and the duration of temperatures above 50°C at the moss surface. Back-burning

under conditions where moss or soil moisture is high (>100%) appears unlikely to lead to extensive consumption, and slower rates of spread produced in high-wind conditions will extend the prescription window for safe burning. Back fires are sometimes used for preparing firebreaks, and a wider array of ignition strategies is used during fuel reduction burns by the fire and rescue services. However, slower rates of spread when burning against the wind do create a logistical constraint on using this approach as a general practice. Recommendations regarding the interaction of fire and slope tend to also be somewhat simplistic, with it having been suggested the managers burn across slopes to minimise the risk of fire escapes and soil erosion. This ignores the potential for considering the interaction of slope and wind and, again, potentially limits potential burn windows and flexibility in planning ignition and control strategies.

The adoption and use of personal protective equipment during prescribed burning operations varies significantly. It is not unusual to see land managers wearing the standard-issue tweed of many traditional sporting estates (Figure 12.6). It is also not unusual to see managers wearing rubber boots (wellingtons), as there can often be standing water when burning wet heaths and bogs. Fire-retardant clothing has become more common in recent decades, particularly among public agencies and organised civic groups, but otherwise participants generally wear less-flammable natural fibres, such as cotton, denim and wool (the latter is often a good idea because it can actually be very cold at times when fire is applied). Leather gloves and plastic face shields will also generally be worn, along with bandanas or handkerchiefs over the face to reduce the impacts of smoke and high radiant heat in close proximity to a fire. Some management guidance (DEFRA 2007) suggests that practitioners should '*always keep a heat-sensitive part of the body exposed as a vital indicator of danger*'. We would note to those referring to this advice that some body parts are more sensitive and vital than others, and they may instead wish to ensure they are well protected from the risk of burns.

Box 12.2: Summary of best practice recommendations for traditional managed heathland burning based on Gimingham (1992), Scottish Government (2017b) and traditional Norwegian practices

Fire frequency

Fire frequency should be a function of site productivity, with the mean fire return interval generally not less than ~8 years. Minimum desirable return intervals may be as much as 25 years in the least-productive areas. All heathlands should demonstrate heterogeneity in fire frequency, with some areas designated as 'fire free' to ensure plant and wildlife diversity is maximised.

Firebreaks

Managers should plan in advance where a fire will be extinguished. Suitable firebreaks may include tracks, snow patches, 'greens' dominated by live herbaceous vegetation or recent burns where any remaining ground fuels (moss or litter) are moist enough not to ignite. Wet lines and cut firebreaks may be used where these are created immediately before the fire; the rapid drying of fine heathland fuels means that such breaks can rapidly lose their effectiveness.

Ignition pattern[1]

Fires should generally be burned with the wind and ignited in narrow strips no more than ~50 m wide (ideally ≤30 m wide). Back-burning should be avoided to reduce the potential for the consumption of moss and litter layers and prolonged heating or charring of peat deposits. Fires should not be ignited to burn uphill, but burned across the slope to minimise the risk of escape and the potential for soil erosion.

Burning conditions

Burn under light to moderate winds sufficient to direct the fire without resulting in uncontrollable behaviour. Wind speed should not exceed 3 on the Beaufort scale. The moisture content of ground fuel layers should be high enough to prevent their extensive consumption. English guidance suggests burning should not take place above 4 on the Beaufort scale or in conditions with no wind (the latter is presumed to lead to slow-moving fires with more extensive ground fuel heating and consumption; there is presently no evidence to support or refute this).

Fire size, shape and area

Total fire area is of less relevance than the width of the fire. Although fires may be of any length, they should not be wider than 50 m. Limiting the width of the fire front ensures fires remain under control (due to the relationship between fire front width and the intensity and rate of spread), and ensures a patchwork of heathland vegetation structures is maintained. Ideally, burned patches should remain relatively small (between 0.5 and 2 ha). Ensure burned areas remain well distributed and preference winding sinuous shapes over straight edges to reduce negative consequences for visual aesthetics and to maximise the ecological benefits of burn edge habitat.

Fire effects and protecting the soil

Managers should generally seek to achieve low severities (aka 'cool' burns) that avoid prolonged heating of the soil, minimise the consumption of moss and litter layers and leave behind abundance *Calluna* 'stick'. Where there are organic soils, this can be achieved by burning when soil is saturated or frozen. However, older *Calluna* stands regenerate primarily from seed, and germination and establishment are maximised where bare peat or soil is exposed. Such severe burns may affect soil erosion and carbon dynamics, and it is thus generally preferable to concentrate burning on areas where vigorous vegetative regeneration is likely. This may not be possible in the case of the restoration of under-managed old heaths requiring trade-offs between soil protection and *Calluna* regeneration.

Fire-free and fire-sensitive areas

All areas of moorland should have areas planned to be protected from burning. This includes both leaving some heather-dominated vegetation to develop into older stages and structures, as well as the protection of fire-sensitive areas. The following areas should generally not be burned: nesting sites for birds of prey; woodlands and scrub; areas with eroding or shallow (<5 cm deep) soil; peat 'haggs' and areas with exposed peat; exposed summits and ridges with wind-clipped vegetation; montane and alpine heaths; maritime heaths where salt spray limits growth; steep hillsides and gullies; areas where bracken is present; 'tall vegetation' adjacent to watercourses; and, in Wales, areas of degenerate stage or 'rank' heather. The Scottish Muirburn Code (Scottish Natural Heritage 2017) advises that fire-free buffer zones 2 m wide should be established around watercourses less than 2 m wide and that buffers should be extended to a width of 5 m for wider watercourses and lochs or lakes. Welsh guidance suggests there should be no burning within 10 m of watercourses (Welsh Assembly Government 2008), whereas English guidance suggests a 5-m buffer (DEFRA 2007). Recommendations on burning peatland also vary. The Scottish Muirburn Code (Scottish Natural Heritage 2017) states fire should not be used on blanket and raised bogs with peat >50 cm and where *Calluna* cover is <75%, whereas the Welsh and English codes communicate a broader presumption against burning peat bogs and wet heath communities.

[1] See main text for a discussion of current recommendations regarding firing patterns

Overall, there would appear to be some scope for broadening the range of tactics used within traditional practice, improving technical understanding of fire behaviour and increasing formalised training for practitioners. Balancing this against protecting and respecting significant traditional knowledge is a challenge (Fernandes *et al.* 2013). Some non-traditional groups (e.g. regional fire and rescue services, and the South Wales Brigade in particular) using prescribed burning for fire suppression or fuel reduction have developed a more technical approach to burning and greater variation in tactical approaches. Collaborative training exercises, and regional fire management groups, involving public agencies, emergency services and private land managers have also been important in advancing practice (Figure 12.6).

Conclusions: a challenging future for managed burning

The use of prescribed fire in northern heathlands finds itself at a critical juncture. Many ecologists and land managers advocate for its importance in maintaining ecologically important cultural landscapes and the sustainability of agroecosystems. The fire services also increasingly recognise its importance in the management of hazardous fuels, wildfire risk management and wildfire fighting. However, attitudes in other sectors have hardened against burning. In the UK, several significant

land-owning organisations (e.g. National Trust for Scotland, John Muir Trust, United Utilities, Yorkshire Water) and several large private land owners have ceased burning by their managers and/or tenants. Some of this change has come in the context of growing emphasis on 're-wilding' managed landscapes (with several of its influential proponents authoring fairly vitriolic polemics against any use of fire; e.g. Monbiot 2016). Division has grown within the scientific community too. More recently, the debate has become particularly 'hot' regarding issues of carbon sequestration, for example Heinemeyer *et al.* (2018) versus Evans *et al.* (2019) and Marrs *et al.* (2019) versus Baird *et al.* (2019). Furthermore, a critique of the experimental design of a large-scale study of managed burning that had suggested predominantly negative effects on aquatic ecosystems and peatland hydrology (Ashby and Heinemeyer 2020) has also raised controversy and a response that included somewhat distasteful accusations of funding bias (Brown and Holden 2020). Contrasting the situation in the UK and Norway is thus fascinating as the two countries appear to be moving in opposite directions, albeit from very different current contexts. To some extent this lays bare how debates over fire in the UK have become beholden to ancillary arguments about other aspects of moorland management (e.g. land ownership, hunting, wildlife crime). This lack of trust between various stakeholders is already impacting perceptions of new tools and approaches (Edgeley and Paveglio 2016), and may thus limit adaptive capacity of managers in the face of political and environmental change. We completed drafting this chapter during a week in which the UK Parliament debated banning heather burning, and a bill that severely restricts managers' ability to use fire is now proposed. The fact this seems like a reasonable policy to many conservation-minded people in the UK, whereas in Norway similar groups are actively working to reintroduce fire, cannot be explained on the basis of fire ecology. The reality is that simplistic debates about fire are a distraction from, and create impediments to, holistic management and restoration of heathland landscapes. It is equally simplistic to suggest that 'traditional management' is the right answer everywhere. In reality, somewhere between the situation in Norway and the UK there is a happy medium where fire is used sustainably to protect carbon stocks, enhance valuable heathland habitats, maintain rural livelihoods and traditions, create room for more complex mosaic landscapes and reduce impacts on sensitive areas such as streams and other waterbodies. As the threats to heathlands and associated biodiversity increase, red-listing of these habitats and heathland species may mandate conservation involving traditional management, including fire.

The controversy over fire use is not going to end soon but, in the absence of robust data, stakeholders' views, and policy, seem to be driven as much by personal politics as they are by the ecology of fire (Davies *et al.* 2016a; Edgeley and Paveglio 2016). Ultimately fire can and should continue to play a role in heathland management; these are fire-adapted systems where individual species exhibit evolutionary adaptations to fire and where ecosystem composition, diversity and services are a function of a history of fire use over millennia. Fire will continue to be a component of heathland ecosystems, whether humans will it or not. The onus is on managers to demonstrate they can use fire holistically, sustainably and sensitively. It is up to policy makers and campaigners to learn the lessons from regions where overly restrictive curtailment of

traditional prescribed fire use resulted in significant issues of both ecosystems and wildfire risk (e.g. Fernandes *et al.* 2013). It is worth remembering that current prescribed burning practice evolved in response to a very specific, and somewhat narrow, set of management goals relating to game and livestock production. Although there is much to be learned from traditional practice, whether these specific goals and traditions of management are appropriate in the 21st century is rightfully open to debate. We suggest that there are several significant challenges that will affect prescribed burning in the next few decades, including:

- climate change, which is likely to exacerbate the frequency and duration of high-risk and high-burn severity conditions
- divergent policies and views between intra- and international jurisdictions
- policy that increases the bureaucratic burden associated with using fire or that outright prohibits burning in certain situations
- changes in agricultural subsidy and environmental funding schemes after Brexit that reduce financial support for, and the economic viability of, traditional land management
- changes in economic goals for heathland management (e.g. re-wilding, afforestation, reduced livestock grazing, tourism and recreation) that lead to changes in fuels and fire risk
- changes in public opinion that undermine confidence in, and respect for, the ecological role of fire
- unsympathetic and intensive managed fire use that undermines public confidence in the validity of fire use
- a continued association between some managed fire users and wildlife crime, which undermines attitudes to the otherwise valuable habitat management work they do.

Our hope is that moving forward managers and policy makers can debate the trade-offs between the various environmental effects of prescribed burning on heathlands more effectively and dispassionately.

References

Alday JG, Santana VM, Lee H, Allen K, Marrs RH (2015) Above-ground biomass accumulation patterns in moorlands after prescribed burning and low-intensity grazing. *Perspectives in Plant Ecology, Evolution and Systematics* **17**, 388–396. doi:10.1016/j.ppees.2015.06.007

Allan T (1935) Birch brooms. *Journal of the Forestry Commission* **14**, 102–114.

Allen KA, Harris MPK, Marrs RH (2013) Matrix modelling of prescribed burning in *Calluna vulgaris*-dominated moorland: short burning rotations minimize carbon loss at increased wildfire frequencies. *Journal of Applied Ecology* **50**, 614–624. doi:10.1111/1365-2664.12075

Allen KA, Denelle P, Sánchez Ruiz FM, Santana VM, Marrs RH (2016) Prescribed moorland burning meets good practice guidelines: a monitoring case study using aerial photography in the Peak District, UK. *Ecological Indicators* **62**, 76–85. doi:10.1016/j.ecolind.2015.11.030

Amphlett A, Holden E, Allcorn R, Gurney M (2006) Effects of cutting and burning of heather *Calluna vulgaris* on fungal fruiting in Caledonian pine forest at Abernethy Forest RSPB Reserve, Inverness-shire, Scotland. *Conservation Evidence* **3**, 106–108.

Anderson SAJ, Anderson WR (2009) Predicting the elevated dead fine fuel moisture content in gorse (*Ulex europaeus* L.) shrub fuels. *Canadian Journal of Forest Research* **39**, 2355–2368. doi:10.1139/X09-142

Anderson P, Yalden DW (1981) Increased sheep numbers and the loss of heather moorland in the Peak District, England. *Biological Conservation* **20**, 195–213. doi:10.1016/0006-3207(81)90029-X

Ascoli D, Beghin R, Ceccato R, Gorlier A, Lombardi G, Lonati M, Marzano R, Bovio G, Cavallero A (2009) Developing an adaptive management approach to prescribed burning: a long-term heathland conservation experiment in north-west Italy. *International Journal of Wildland Fire* **18**, 727–735. doi:10.1071/WF07114

Ashby MA, Heinemeyer A (2020) Prescribed burning impacts on ecosystem services in the British uplands: a methodological critique of the EMBER project. *Journal of Applied Ecology* **57**, 2112–2120. doi:10.1111/1365-2664.13476

Baird AJ, Evans CD, Mills R, Morris PJ, Page SE, Peacock M, Reed M, Robroek BJM, Stoneman R, Swindles GT, *et al.* (2019) Validity of managing peatlands with fire. *Nature Geoscience* **12**, 884–885. doi:10.1038/s41561-019-0477-5

Bargmann T, Måren IE, Vandvik V (2014) Life after fire: smoke and ash as germination cues in ericads, herbs and graminoids of northern heathlands. *Applied Vegetation Science* **17**, 670–679. doi:10.1111/avsc.12106

Blundell A, Holden J (2015) Using palaeoecology to support blanket peatland management. *Ecological Indicators* **49**, 110–120. doi:10.1016/j.ecolind.2014.10.006

Brown T (1997) Clearances and clearings: deforestation in Mesolithic/Neolithic Britain. *Oxford Journal of Archaeology* **16**, 133–146. doi:10.1111/1468-0092.00030

Brown LE, Holden J (2020) Contextualizing UK moorland burning studies with geographical variables and sponsor identity. *Journal of Applied Ecology* **57**, 2121–2131. doi:10.1111/1365-2664.13708

Brown LE, Holden J, Palmer SM, Johnston K, Ramchunder SJ, Grayson R (2015) Effects of fire on the hydrology, biogeochemistry, and ecology of peatland river systems. *Freshwater Science* **34**, 1406–1425. doi:10.1086/683426

Bruce MB, Servant G (2003) Fire and pinewood ecology in Scotland: a summary of recent research at Glen Tanar Estate, Aberdeenshire. *Scottish Forestry* **57**, 33–38.

Bullock JM, Webb NR (1995) Responses to severe fires in heathland mosaics in Southern England. *Biological Conservation* **73**, 207–214. doi:10.1016/0006-3207(94)00110-C

Caporn JM, Emmett BA (2008) Threats from air pollution and climate change on upland systems-past, present and future. In *Drivers of Environmental Change in the Uplands*. (Eds A Bonn, T Allott, K Hubacek and J Stewart) pp. 34–58. Routledge, Abingdon.

Caseldine C, Hatton J (1993) The development of high moorland on Dartmoor: fire and the influence of Mesolithic activity on vegetation change. In *Climate Change and Human Impact on the Landscape*. (Ed FM Chambers) pp. 119–131. Springer, Dordrecht.

Chambers FM, Lageard JGA, Boswijk G, Thomas PA, Edwards KJ, Hillam J (1997) Dating prehistoric bog-fires in northern England to calendar years by long-distance cross-matching of pine chronologies. *Journal of Quaternary Science* **12**, 253–256. doi:10.1002/(SICI)1099-1417(199705/06)12:3<253::AID-JQS310>3.0.CO;2-I

Chambers FM, Cloutman EW, Daniell JRG, Mauquoy D, Jones PS (2013) Long-term ecological study (palaeoecology) to chronicle habitat degradation and inform conservation ecology: an exemplar from the Brecon Beacons, South Wales. *Biodiversity and Conservation* **22**, 719–736. doi:10.1007/s10531-013-0441-4

Charters H (1939) Forest fires. *Journal of the Forestry Commission* **18**, 138.

City & Guilds (2011) *Level 3 Diploma in Work-based Game and Wildlife Management*. City & Guilds Group, London, <https://www.cityandguilds.com/-/media/product documents/land_based_services/environment_country side_and_conservation/0069/0069_level_3/centre_ documents/0069_l3_qualification_handbook_v1-1-pdf. ashx>.

City & Guilds (2012) *Level 3 Certificate, Subsidiary Diploma, 90-Credit Diploma, Diploma, Extended Diploma in Countryside Management*. City & Guilds Group, London, <https://www.cityandguilds.com/-/media/productdocuments/land_based_services/environment_countryside_and_conservation/0076/0076_level_3/centre_documents/0076-03_l3_qualification_handbook_v4-pdf.ashx>.

Clay GD, Worrall F, Clark E, Fraser EDG (2009) Hydrological responses to managed burning and grazing in an upland blanket bog. *Journal of Hydrology* **376**, 486–495. doi:10.1016/j.jhydrol.2009.07.055

Department for Agriculture Food and the Marine (DAFM) (2018) *Prescribed Burning Code of Practice – Ireland*. DAFM, Dublin. <https://www.agriculture.gov.ie/media/migration/forestry/firemanagement/CofPPrescribedBurningFinal90212.pdf>.

Davies GM (2006) Fire behaviour and impact on heather moorlands. PhD thesis. University of Edinburgh, Scotland.

Davies AL (2016) Late Holocene regime shifts in moorland ecosystems: high resolution data from the Pennines, UK. *Vegetation History and Archaeobotany* **25**, 207–219. doi:10.1007/s00334-015-0544-9

Davies GM, Legg CJ (2008) The effect of traditional management burning on lichen diversity. *Applied Vegetation Science* **11**, 529–538. doi:10.3170/2008-7-18566

Davies GM, Legg CJ (2011) Fuel moisture thresholds in the flammability of *Calluna vulgaris*. *Fire Technology* **47**, 421–436. doi:10.1007/s10694-010-0162-0

Davies GM, Legg CJ (2016) Regional variation in fire weather controls the occurrence of Scottish wildfires. *PeerJ* **4**, e2649. doi:10.7717/peerj.2649

Davies GM, Legg CJ, Hamilton A, Smith AA (2008) Using visual obstruction to estimate heathland fuel load and structure. *International Journal of Wildland Fire* **17**, 380–389. doi:10.1071/WF07021

Davies GM, Legg CJ, Smith AA, McDonald AJ (2009a) Rate of spread of fires in *Calluna vulgaris*-dominated moorlands. *Journal of Applied Ecology* **46**, 1054–1063. doi:10.1111/j.1365-2664.2009.01681.x

Davies GM, Legg CJ, Rein G, Hadden R (2009b) The effect of moisture content on fire initiation from smouldering ignition sources. In *Proceedings of the Northwest Scientific Association 81st Annual Meeting*. 25–28 March, Seattle. (Eds K Glew, R Lesher, BR Barton, P Pringle, J Duda, K Troost, E Nesbitt, A Sullivan, S Rust and R Matheny) p. 15. Northwest Scientific Association, Mountlake Terrace, <https://www.northwestscience.org/Resources/Final%20Annual%20Meeting%20Abstracts%20and%20Programs/2009%20NWSA%20Program%20and%20Abstracts.pdf>.

Davies GM, Smith AA, McDonald AJ, Bakker JD, Legg CJ (2010a) Fire intensity, fire severity and ecosystem response in heathlands: factors affecting the regeneration of *Calluna vulgaris*. *Journal of Applied Ecology* **47**, 356–365. doi:10.1111/j.1365-2664.2010.01774.x

Davies GM, O'Hara R, Smith AA, MacDonald A, Legg CJ (2010b) Winter desiccation and rapid changes in the live fuel moisture content of *Calluna vulgaris*. *Plant Ecology & Diversity* **3**, 289–299. doi:10.1080/17550874.2010.544335

Davies GM, Gray A, Rein G, Legg CJ (2013) Peat consumption and carbon loss due to smouldering wildfire in a temperate peatland. *Forest Ecology and Management* **308**, 169–177. doi:10.1016/j.foreco.2013.07.051

Davies GM, Kettridge N, Stoof CR, Gray A, Ascoli D, Fernandes PM, Marrs R, Allen KA, Doerr SH, Clay GD, *et al.* (2016a) The role of fire in UK peatland and moorland management: the need for informed, unbiased debate. *Philosophical Transactions of the Royal Society of London. Series B, Biological Sciences* **371**, 20150342. doi:10.1098/rstb.2015.0342

Davies GM, Kettridge N, Stoof CR, Gray A, Ascoli D, Fernandes PM, Marrs R, Allen KA, Doerr SH, Clay GD, *et al.* (2016b) Informed debate on the use of fire for peatland management means acknowledging the complexity of socio-ecological systems. *Nature Conservation* **16**, 59–77. doi:10.3897/natureconservation.16.10739

Davies GM, Domènech R, Gray A, Johnson PCD (2016c) Vegetation structure and fire weather influence variation in burn severity and fuel consumption during peatland wildfires. *Biogeosciences* **13**, 389–398. doi:10.5194/bg-13-389-2016

Davies GM, Legg CJ, Smith AA, McDonald AJ (2019) Development and participatory evaluation of fireline intensity and flame property models for managed burns on *Calluna*-dominated heathlands. *Fire Ecology* **15**, 30. doi:10.1186/s42408-019-0046-8

de Hullu E, Gimingham CH (1984) Germination and establishment of seedlings in different phases of the *Calluna* life cycle in a Scottish heathland. *Vegetatio* **58**, 115–121. doi:10.1007/BF00044936

Department of Environment, Food and Agriculture (DEFA) (2010) *The Heath Burning Code*. Department of Environment, Food and Agriculture, St Johns, <https://www.gov.im/media/277566/heath_burning_code.pdf>.

Department for Environment, Food & Rural Affairs (DEFRA) (2007) *The Heather and Grass Burning Code*. DEFRA, London, <http://gfmc.online/programmes/natcon/UK-DEFRA–Heather-Grass-Burning-Code-2007.pdf>.

Department for Environment, Food & Rural Affairs (DEFRA) (2021) *England's 'National Rainforests' to be Protected by New Rules*. [Press release] DEFRA, London,

<https://www.gov.uk/government/news/englands-national-rainforests-to-be-protected-by-new-rules>.

Diemont WH, Heijman WJM, Siepel H, Webb NR (2013) *Economy and Ecology of Heathlands*. KNNV Publishing, Zeist.

Dodgshon RA, Olsson GA (2006) Heather moorland in the Scottish Highlands: the history of a cultural landscape, 1600–1880. *Journal of Historical Geography* **32**, 21–37. doi:10.1016/j.jhg.2005.01.002

Douglas DJT, Buchanan GM, Thompson P, Amar A, Fielding DA, Redpath SM, Wilson JD (2015) Vegetation burning for game management in the UK uplands is increasing and overlaps spatially with soil carbon and protected areas. *Biological Conservation* **191**, 243–250. doi:10.1016/j.biocon.2015.06.014

Douglas DJT, Buchanan GM, Thompson P, Wilson JD (2016) The role of fire in UK upland management: the need for informed challenge to conventional wisdoms: a comment on Davies *et al*. *Philosophical Transactions of the Royal Society of London. Series B, Biological Sciences* **371**, 20160433. doi:10.1098/rstb.2016.0433

Ecological Continuity Trust (2020) Moor House, Upper Teesdale: investigating the effects of vegetation management by grazing and long-term rotational burning on blanket bog vegetation since 1954. Ecological Continuity Trust, Abingdon, <https://www.ecologicalconti nuitytrust.org/moor-house>.

Edgeley CM, Paveglio TB (2016) Influences on stakeholder support for a wildfire early warning system in a UK protected area. *Environmental Hazards* **15**, 327–342.

Elkington T, Dayton N, Jackson DL, Strachan IM (2001) *National Vegetation Classification: Field Guide to Mires and Heaths*. Joint Nature Conservation Committee, Peterborough.

European Commission DG Environment (2013) *Interpretation Manual of European Union Habitats*. <https://ec.europa.eu/environment/nature/legislation/habitatsdirective/docs/Int_Manual_EU28.pdf>.

European Environment Agency (EEA) (2020) *EUNIS habitat classification*. <https://www.eea.europa.eu/data-and-maps/data/eunis-habitat-classification>.

Evans JO (1948) The preparation of ground. *Journal of the Forestry Commission* **19**, 62–63.

Evans CD, Baird AJ, Green SM, Page SE, Peacock M, Reed MS, Rose NL, Stoneman R, Thom TJ, Young DM, *et al*. (2019) Comment on: 'Peatland carbon stocks and burn history: Blanket bog peat core evidence highlights charcoal impacts on peat physical properties and long-term carbon storage,' by A. Heinemeyer, Q. Asena, W. L. Burn and A. L. Jones (*Geo: Geography and Environment* 2018; e00063). *Geo: Geography and Environment* **6**, e00075. doi:10.1002/geo2.75

Fagúndez J (2013) Heathlands confronting global change: drivers of biodiversity loss from past to future scenarios. *Annals of Botany* **111**, 151–172. doi:10.1093/aob/mcs257

Fernandes PM, Davies GM, Ascoli D, Fernández C, Moreira F, Rigolot E, Stoof CR, Vega JA, Molina D (2013) Prescribed burning in southern Europe: developing fire management in a dynamic landscape. *Frontiers in Ecology and the Environment* **11**, e4–e14. doi:10.1890/120298

Findlay TSL (1964) But whit's a muir? A puzzle for the lawyers. *Journal of the Forestry Commission* **33**, 186–188.

Frandsen WH (1997) Ignition probability of organic soils. *Canadian Journal of Forest Research* **27**, 1471–1477. doi:10.1139/x97-106

Froyd CA (2006) Holocene fire in the Scottish Highlands: evidence from macroscopic charcoal records. *The Holocene* **16**, 235–249. doi:10.1191/0959683606hl910rp

Gallego-Sala AV, Charman DJ, Harrison SP, Li G, Prentice IC (2016) Climate-driven expansion of blanket bogs in Britain during the Holocene. *Climate of the Past* **12**, 129–136. doi:10.5194/cp-12-129-2016

Gao J, Holden J, Kirkby M (2016) The impact of land-cover change on flood peaks in peatland basins. *Water Resources Research* **52**, 3477–3492. doi:10.1002/2015WR017667

Gimingham CH (1972) *Ecology of Heathlands*. Chapman & Hall, London.

Gimingham CH (1988) A reappraisal of cyclical processes in *Calluna* heath. *Vegetatio* **77**, 61–64. doi:10.1007/BF00045751

Gimingham CH (1992) *The Lowland Heathland Management Handbook*. English Nature, Peterborough, <http://publications.naturalengland.org.uk/publication/2267376>.

Graham A (1939) Fire protection and Glentress. *Journal of the Forestry Commission* **18**, 131–132.

Granath G, Moore P, Lukenbach M, Waddington JM (2016) Mitigating wildfire carbon loss in managed northern peatlands through restoration. *Scientific Reports* **6**, 28498. doi:10.1038/srep28498

Grandy JW, Stallman E, Macdonald DW (2003) The science and sociology of hunting: shifting practices and perceptions in the United States and Great Britain. In *The State of the Animals II*. (Eds DJ Salem and AN Rowan) pp. 107–130. Human Society Press, Washington, DC.

Grant MJ, Hughes PDM, Barber KE (2014) Climatic influence upon early to mid-Holocene fire regimes within temperate woodlands: a multi-proxy reconstruction from the New Forest, southern England. *Journal of Quaternary Science* **29**, 175–188. doi:10.1002/jqs.2692

Grau-Andrés R, Davies GM, Waldron S, Legg CJ (2015) Moisture codes of the Canadian Fire Weather Index System could be used to forecast the flammability of key moorland fuels. In *Wildfires 2015*. 10–11 November, Glasgow,

<https://www.firescotland.gov.uk/media/901438/
Grau_Canadian_FWI__Moisture_codes__moorland_
fuels_2015.pdf>

Grau-Andrés R, Davies GM, Waldron S, Scott EM, Gray
A (2017a) Leaving moss and litter layers undisturbed
reduces the short-term environmental consequences
of heathland managed burns. *Journal of Environmental
Management* **204**, 102–110. doi:10.1016/j.jenvman.2017.
08.017

Grau-Andrés R, Gray A, Davies GM (2017b) Sphagnum
abundance and photosynthetic capacity show rapid
short-term recovery following managed burning. *Plant
Ecology & Diversity* **10**, 353–359. doi:10.1080/17550874.20
17.1394394

Grau-Andrés R, Davies GM, Gray A, Scott EM, Waldron S
(2018) Fire severity is more sensitive to low fuel moisture content on *Calluna* heathlands than on peat bogs.
The Science of the Total Environment **616–617**, 1261–1269.
doi:10.1016/j.scitotenv.2017.10.192

Grau-Andrés R, Gray A, Davies GM, Scott EM, Waldron
S (2019a) Burning increases post-fire carbon emissions
in a heathland and a raised bog, but experimental
manipulation of fire severity has no effect. *Journal of
Environmental Management* **233**, 321–328. doi:10.1016/j.
jenvman.2018.12.036

Grau-Andrés R, Davies GM, Waldron S, Scott EM, Gray A
(2019b) Increased fire severity alters initial vegetation
regeneration across *Calluna*-dominated ecosystems.
Journal of Environmental Management **231**, 1004–1011.
doi:10.1016/j.jenvman.2018.10.113

Gray A, Davies GM, Domènech R, Taylor R, Levy P (2020)
Peatland wildfire severity and post-fire gaseous carbon
fluxes. *Ecosystems* doi:10.1007/s10021-020-00545-0.

Grishin AM, Golovanov AN, Sukov YV, Preis YI (2006)
Experimental study of peat ignition and combustion.
Journal of Engineering Physics and Thermophysics **79**,
563–568. doi:10.1007/s10891-006-0136-8

Groves JA, Waller MP, Grant MJ, Schofield JE (2012) Long-
term development of a cultural landscape: the origins and
dynamics of lowland heathland in southern England. *Vegetation History and Archaeobotany* **21**, 453–470. doi:10.1007/
s00334-012-0372-0

Halsall KM (2019) Image analysis of charcoal fragments to
explore Holocene fire – vegetation dynamics in northern
Europe. PhD thesis. University of Liverpool, England.

Halvorsen R, Bryn A, Erikstad L (2016) NiN systemkjerne –
teori, prinsipper og inndelingskriterier. Versjon 2.2, *Sys-
temdokumentasjon* 1, s 1–292. Artsdatabanken, Trondheim.

Hancock MH (2008) An exceptional *Calluna vulgaris* winter
die-back event, Abernethy Forest, Scottish Highlands. *Plant Ecology & Diversity* **1**, 89–103. doi:10.1080/
17550870802260772

Hancock M, Egan S, Summers R, Cowie N, Amphlett A,
Rao S, Hamilton A (2005) The effect of experimental
prescribed fire on the establishment of Scots pine *Pinus
sylvestris* seedlings on heather *Calluna vulgaris* moorland.
Forest Ecology and Management **212**, 199–213. doi:10.1016/
j.foreco.2005.03.039

Hancock MH, Amphlett A, Proctor R, Dugan D, Willi J,
Harvey P, Summers RW (2011) Burning and mowing as
habitat management for capercaillie *Tetrao urogallus*: an
experimental test. *Forest Ecology and Management* **262**,
509–521. doi:10.1016/j.foreco.2011.04.019

Harper AR, Doerr SH, Santin C, Froyd CA, Sinnadurai P
(2018) Prescribed fire and its impacts on ecosystem services in the UK. *The Science of the Total Environment* **624**,
691–703. doi:10.1016/j.scitotenv.2017.12.161

Heinemeyer A, Asena Q, Burn WL, Jones AL (2018) Peatland carbon stocks and burn history: blanket bog peat
core evidence highlights charcoal impacts on peat
physical properties and long-term carbon storage.
Geo: Geography and Environment **5**, e00063. doi:10.1002/
geo2.63

Hendry J (1964) Basic course on fire protection Northerwood
House. *Journal of the Forestry Commission* **33**, 166–170.

Hester AJ, Sydes C (1992) Changes in burning of Scottish
heather moorland since the 1940s from aerial photographs. *Biological Conservation* **60**, 25–30.

Hjelle KL, Halvorsen LS, Overland A (2010) Heathland
development and relationship between humans and
environment along the coast of western Norway
through time. *Quaternary International* **220**, 133–146.
doi:10.1016/j.quaint.2009.09.023

Hobbs RJ, Gimingham CH (1984) Studies on fire in Scottish
heathland communities: I. Fire characteristics. *Journal of
Ecology* **72**, 223–240. doi:10.2307/2260015

Holden J, Shotbolt L, Bonn A, Burt TP, Chapman PJ, Dougill
AJ, Fraser EDG, Hubacek K, Irvine B, Kirkby MJ, *et al.*
(2007) Environmental change in moorland landscapes.
Earth-Science Reviews **82**, 75–100. doi:10.1016/j.earscirev.
2007.01.003

Hovstad KA, Johansen L, Arnesen A, Svalheim E, Velle
LG (2018) *Kystlynghei, Semi-naturlig. Norsk rødliste for
naturtyper 2018*. Artsdatabanken, Trondheim. <https://
artsdatabanken.no/RLN2018/74>.

Huang X, Rein G (2015) Computational study of critical
moisture and depth of burn in peat fires. *International Journal of Wildland Fire* **24**, 798–808. doi:10.1071/
WF14178

Ingram RC, Moore PA, Wilkinson S, Petrone RM, Waddington JM (2019) Postfire soil carbon accumulation does
not recover boreal peatland combustion loss in some
hydrogeological settings. *Journal of Geophysical Research.
Biogeosciences* **124**, 775–788. doi:10.1029/2018JG004716

Innes JB, Blackford JJ (2003) The ecology of late Mesolithic woodland disturbances: model testing with fungal spore assemblage data. *Journal of Archaeological Science* **30**, 185–194. doi:10.1006/jasc.2002.0832

Innes J, Blackford J, Simmons I (2010) Woodland disturbance and possible land-use regimes during the Late Mesolithic in the English uplands: pollen, charcoal and non-pollen palynomorph evidence from Bluewath Beck, North York Moors, UK. *Vegetation History and Archaeobotany* **19**, 439–452. doi:10.1007/s00334-010-0266-y

Joint Nature Conservation Committee (JNCC) (2010) *Handbook for Phase 1 Habitat Survey: A Technique for Environmental Audit.* JNCC, Peterborough, <https://data.jncc.gov.uk/data/9578d07b-e018-4c66-9c1b-47110f14df2a/Handbook-Phase1-HabitatSurvey-Revised-2016.pdf>.

Joint Nature Conservation Committee (JNCC) (2019) *UK BAP Priority Habitats.* JNCC, Peterborough, <https://jncc.gov.uk/our-work/uk-bap-priority-habitats> (accessed 11 November 2020).

Jollands M, Morris J, Moffat AJ (2011) *Wildfires in Wales. Report to Forestry Commission Wales.* Forest Research, Farnham, <http://www.forestry.gov.uk/fr/wildfiresinwales#finalreport>.

Kaland PE (1979) Landskapsutvikling og bosetningshistorie i Nordhordlands lyngheiområde. In *På leiting etter den eldste garden.* (Eds R Fladby and J Sandnes) pp. 41–71. Universitetsfor-laget, Oslo.

Kaland PE (1986) The origin and management of Norwegian coastal heaths as reflected by pollen analysis. In *Anthropogenic Indicators in Pollen Diagrams.* (Ed. KE Behre) pp. 19–36. Balkema, Rotterdam.

Kaland PE (2014) Heathlands – land-use, ecology and vegetation history as a source for archaeological interpretations. In *Northern Worlds, Landscapes, Interpretations and Dynamics.* (Ed. HC Gulløv) pp. 19–47. National Museum of Denmark, Copenhagen.

Kaland PE, Kvamme M (2013) *Coastal Heathlands in Norway – Descriptions of 23 Reference Areas.* Miljodirektoratet, Trondheim.

Karg S (2008) Direct evidence of heathland management in the early Bronze Age (14th century B.C.) from the gravemound Skelhøj in western Denmark. *Vegetation History and Archaeobotany* **17**, 41–49. doi:10.1007/s00334-007-0109-7

Kvamme M, Kaland PE (2009) Prescribed burning of coastal heathlands in western Norway: history and present day experiences. *International Forest Fire News* **38**, 35–50.

Kvamme M, Kaland PE, Brekke NG (2004) *Conservation and Management of North European Coastal Heathlands Case study.* The Heathland Centre, Lygra.

Lageard JGA, Thomas PA, Chambers FM (2000) Using fire scars and growth release in subfossil Scots pine to reconstruct prehistoric fires. *Palaeogeography, Palaeoclimatology, Palaeoecology* **164**, 87–99. doi:10.1016/S0031-0182(00)00177-2

LANTRA (n.d.) *Basic Wildfire Fighting.* Lanta, Coventry, <https://www.lantra.co.uk/course/basic-wildfire-fighting>.

Lee H, Alday JG, Rose RJ, O'Reilly J, Marrs RH (2013) Long-term effects of rotational prescribed burning and low-intensity sheep grazing on blanket-bog plant communities. *Journal of Applied Ecology* **50**, 625–635. doi:10.1111/1365-2664.12078

Legg C (1995) Heathland dynamics: a matter of scale. In *Heaths and Moorlands: Cultural Landscapes.* (Eds DBA Thompson, AJ Hester and MB Usher) pp. 117–134. HMSO, Edinburgh.

Legg CJ, Maltby E, Proctor M (1992) The ecology of severe moorland fire on the North York Moors: seed distribution and seedling establishment of *Calluna vulgaris. Journal of Ecology* **80**, 737–752. doi:10.2307/2260863

Legg CJ, Davies GM, Kitchen K, Marno P (2007) *Developing a Fire Danger Rating System for the UK: FireBeaters Phase I Final Report. Report to the Scottish Wildfire Forum.* The University of Edinburgh, Edinburgh, <https://era.ed.ac.uk/handle/1842/3011. Accessed 11 Nov 2020>.

Log T (2020) Modeling drying of degenerated *Calluna vulgaris* for wildfire and prescribed burning risk assessment. *Forests* **11**, 759. doi:10.3390/f11070759

Log T, Thuestad G, Velle LG, Khattri SK, Kleppe G (2017) Unmanaged heathland – a fire risk in subzero temperatures? *Fire Safety Journal* **90**, 62–71. doi:10.1016/j.firesaf.2017.04.017

Log T, Vandvik V, Velle LG, Metallinou M-M (2020) Reducing wooden structure and wildland–urban interface fire disaster risk through dynamic risk assessment and management. *Applied System Innovation* **3**, 16. doi:10.3390/asi3010016

Lovat L (1911) *The Grouse in Health and Disease.* Smith, Elder & Co., London.

Lovegrove AT (2016) Management and Monitoring in Protected Areas: a case study in The New Forest National Park: the effects upon Valley Mire and Heathland Communities. PhD thesis. University of Bournemouth, England, <http://eprints.bournemouth.ac.uk/28718/1/LOVEGROVE%2C%20Alexander%20Thomas_Ph.D._2016.pdf>.

MacDonald AJ, Kirkpatrick AH, Hester AJ (1995) Regeneration by natural layering of heather (*Calluna vulgaris*): frequency and characteristics in upland Britain. *Journal of Applied Ecology* **32**, 85–90. doi:10.2307/2404418

Maltby E, Legg C, Proctor M (1990) The ecology of severe moorland mire on the North York Moors: effects of the

1976 fires, and subsequent surface and vegetation development. *Journal of Ecology* **78**, 490–518. doi:10.2307/2261126

Marrs RH, Marsland E, Lingard R, Appleby PG, Piliposyan GT, Rose RJ, O'Reilly J, Milligan G, Allen KA, Alday JA, *et al.* (2019) Experimental evidence for sustained carbon sequestration in fire-managed, peat moorlands. *Nature Geoscience* **12**, 108–112. doi:10.1038/s41561-018-0266-6

Mause R, Kraus D, Held A (2010) Use of prescribed fire for maintaining open *Calluna* heathlands in North Rhine-Westphalia, Germany. In *Best Practices of Fire Use – Prescribed Burning and Suppression Fire Programmes in Selected Case-Study Regions in Europe*. (Eds C Montiel and D Kraus). pp. 77–88. European Forest Institute, Joensuu.

McCarroll J, Chambers FM, Webb JC, Thom T (2016) Informing innovative peatland conservation in light of palaeoecological evidence for the demise of *Sphagnum imbricatum*: the case of Oxenhope Moor, Yorkshire, UK. *Mires and Peat* **18**, 1–24. doi:10.19189/MaP.2015.OMB.206

McNab C (1931) Heather burning. *Journal of the Forestry Commission* **10**, 62–63.

Metallinou MM (2020) Emergence of and learning processes in a civic group resuming prescribed burning in Norway. *Sustainability* **12**, 5668. doi:10.3390/su12145668

Metallinou MM, Log T (2017) Health impacts of climate change-induced subzero temperature fires. *International Journal of Environmental Research and Public Health* **14**, 814. doi:10.3390/ijerph14070814

Milligan G, Rose RJ, O'Reilly J, Marrs RH (2018) Effects of rotational prescribed burning and sheep grazing on moorland plant communities: results from a 60-year intervention experiment. *Land Degradation & Development* **29**, 1397–1412. doi:10.1002/ldr.2953

Milne JA, Pakeman RJ, Kirkham FW, Jones IP, Hossell JE (2002) Biomass production of upland vegetation types in England and Wales. *Grass and Forage Science* **57**, 373–388. doi:10.1046/j.1365-2494.2002.00339.x

Monbiot G (2016) Meet the conservationists who believe that burning is good for wildlife. *The Guardian*, <https://www.theguardian.com/environment/georgemonbiot/2016/jan/14/swaling-is-causing-an-environmental-disaster-on-britains-moors#comment-66745036>.

Moore J (2000) Forest fire and human interactions in the early Holocene woodlands of Britain. *Palaeogeography, Palaeoclimatology, Palaeoecology* **164**, 125–137. doi:10.1016/S0031-0182(00)00180-2

Murgatroyd IR (2002a) *Planning Controlled Burning Operations in Forestry. Technical Note.* Forestry Commission, Edinburgh, <https://www.forestresearch.gov.uk/documents/4762/fctn2.pdf>.

Murgatroyd IR (2002b) *Forest and Moorland Fire Suppression. Technical Note.* Forestry Commission, Edinburgh, <https://www.forestresearch.gov.uk/documents/4761/fctn3.pdf> (accessed 5 November 2020).

Murgatroyd I, Bruce M (2009) Fire suppression in heather and grass in upland Britain. *Scottish Forestry* **63**, 3–12.

Murray JM (1931) Clearing of fire rides. *Journal of the Forestry Commission* **10**, 5–6.

Natural England (2020) *Burning as a tool for the restoration of upland blanket bog: Position Statement from Natural England (UPS01).* Natural England, York, <http://publications.naturalengland.org.uk/publication/6647144950005760>.

Niemeyer T, Niemeyer M, Mohamed A, Fottner S, Härdtle W (2005) Impact of prescribed burning on the nutrient balance of heathlands with particular reference to nitrogen and phosphorus. *Applied Vegetation Science* **8**, 183–192. doi:10.1111/j.1654-109X.2005.tb00644.x

Noble A, O'Reilly J, Glaves DJ, Crowle A, Palmer SM, Holden J (2018a) Impacts of prescribed burning on *Sphagnum* mosses in a long-term peatland field experiment. *PLoS One* **13**, e0206320. doi:10.1371/journal.pone.0206320

Noble A, Palmer SM, Glaves DJ, Crowle A, Brown LE, Holden J (2018b) Prescribed burning, atmospheric pollution and grazing effects on peatland vegetation composition. *Journal of Applied Ecology* **55**, 559–569. doi:10.1111/1365-2664.12994

Noble A, Crowle A, Glaves DJ, Palmer SM, Holden J (2019a) Fire temperatures and *Sphagnum* damage during prescribed burning on peatlands. *Ecological Indicators* **103**, 471–478. doi:10.1016/j.ecolind.2019.04.044

Noble A, Palmer SM, Glaves DJ, Crowle A, Holden J (2019b) Peatland vegetation change and establishment of re-introduced *Sphagnum* moss after prescribed burning. *Biodiversity and Conservation* **28**, 939–952. doi:10.1007/s10531-019-01703-0

OECD (2002) Less-favoured area (LFA). *Glossary of Statistical Terms*, <https://stats.oecd.org/glossary/detail.asp?ID=1520>.

Palmer SCF, Bacon PJ (2001) The utilization of heather moorland by territorial red grouse *Lagopus lagopus scoticus*. *The Ibis* **143**, 222–232. doi:10.1111/j.1474-919X.2001.tb04478.x

Parry LE, Holden J, Chapman PJ (2014) Restoration of blanket peatlands. *Journal of Environmental Management* **133**, 193–205. doi:10.1016/j.jenvman.2013.11.033

Prat-Guitart N, Rein G, Hadden R, Belcher C, Yearsley J (2016) Effects of spatial heterogeneity in moisture content on the horizontal spread of peat fires. *The Science of the Total Environment* **572**, 1422–1430. doi:10.1016/j.scitotenv.2016.02.145

Prat-Guitart N, Belcher CM, Thompson DK, Burns P, Yearsley JM (2017) Fine-scale distribution of moisture in the surface of a degraded blanket bog and its effects on the potential spread of smouldering fire. *Ecohydrology* **10**, e1898. doi:10.1002/eco.1898

Prøsch-Danielsen L, Simonsen A (2000) Palaeoecological investigations towards the reconstruction of the history of forest clearances and coastal heathlands in south-western Norway. *Vegetation History and Archaeobotany* **9**, 189–204. doi:10.1007/BF01294634

Ramchunder SJ, Brown LE, Holden J (2013) Rotational vegetation burning effects on peatland stream ecosystems. *Journal of Applied Ecology* **50**, 636–648. doi:10.1111/1365-2664.12082

Rein G, Cleaver N, Ashton C, Pironi P, Torero JL (2008) The severity of smouldering peat fires and damage to the forest soil. *Catena* **74**, 304–309. doi:10.1016/j.catena.2008.05.008

Rural Payments Agency (2021) *The guide to cross compliance in England 2021*. London, UK Government, <https://www.gov.uk/guidance/guide-to-cross-compliance-in-england-2021>.

Ryan PA, Blackford JJ (2010) Late Mesolithic environmental change at Black Heath, south Pennines, UK: a test of Mesolithic woodland management models using pollen, charcoal and non-pollen palynomorph data. *Vegetation History and Archaeobotany* **19**, 545–558. doi:10.1007/s00334-010-0263-1

Sangar OJ (1928) Plantation fires. *Journal of the Forestry Commission* **7**, 84–89.

Santana VM, Marrs RH (2014) Flammability properties of British heathland and moorland vegetation: models for predicting fire ignition and spread. *Journal of Environmental Management* **139**, 88–96. doi:10.1016/j.jenvman.2014.02.027

Santana VM, Marrs RH (2016) Models for predicting fire ignition probability in graminoids from boreo-temperate moorland ecosystems. *International Journal of Wildland Fire* **25**, 679–684. doi:10.1071/WF15126

Scottish Government (2017a) *The Muirburn Code*. Scottish Natural Heritage, Inverness, <https://www.nature.scot/sites/default/files/2017-11/Guidance%20-%20Management%20of%20Moorland%20-%20Muirburn%20Code.pdf>.

Scottish Government (2017b) *The Muirburn Code: Supplementary Information*. Scottish Government, Edinburgh, <https://muirburncode.org.uk/wp-content/uploads/2019/08/180812SuppInfo-Complete.pdf>.

Scottish Qualifications Authority (SQA) (2020) *SVQ Game and Wildlife Management: Gamekeeping at SCQF Level 7*. SQA, Glasgow, <https://www.sqa.org.uk/sqa/65614.html>.

Sedláková I, Chytrý M (1999) Regeneration patterns in a Central European dry heathland: effects of burning, sod-cutting and cutting. *Plant Ecology* **143**, 77–87. doi:10.1023/A:1009807411654

Sernander R (1912) Die geologische Entwicklung des Nordens nach der Eiszeit in ihrem Verhältnis zu den archäologischen Perioden. Berichte über den balt. archäologischen Kongreß, Stockholm.

Sernander R (1929) The warm postglacial period and the post-glacial climatic deterioration on Northern Europe. *Proceedings of the International Congress of Plant Sciences* **I**, 663–666.

Simmons IG (2003) *The Moorlands of England and Wales: An Environmental History*. Edinburgh University Press, Edinburgh.

Skre O, Wielgolaski FE, Moe B (1998) Biomass and chemical composition of common forest plants in response to fire in western Norway. *Journal of Vegetation Science* **9**, 501–510. doi:10.2307/3237265

Stevenson AC, Thompson DBA (1993) Long-term changes in the extent of heather moorland in upland Britain and Ireland: palaeoecological evidence for the importance of grazing. *The Holocene* **3**, 70–76. doi:10.1177/095968369300300108

Stewart AJA, Lance AN (1983) Moor-draining – a review of impacts on land-use. *Journal of Environmental Management* **17**, 81–99.

Stewart AJA, Lance AN (1991) Effects of moor-draining on the hydrology and vegetation of northern Pennine blanket bog. *Journal of Applied Ecology* **28**, 1105–1117. doi:10.2307/2404228

Strachan IM (2017) 'Manual of terrestrial EUNIS habitats in Scotland, version 2'. Scottish Natural Heritage Commissioned Report No. 766, Scottish Natural Heritage, Inverness.

Sutherland WJ, Bailey MJ, Bainbridge IP, Brereton T, Dick JTA, Drewitt J, Dulvy NK, Dusic NR, Freckleton RP, Gaston KJ, *et al.* (2008) Future novel threats and opportunities facing UK biodiversity identified by horizon scanning. *Journal of Applied Ecology* **45**, 821–833. doi:10.1111/j.1365-2664.2008.01474.x

Taylor ES, Levy PE, Gray A (2017) The recovery of *Sphagnum capillifolium* following exposure to temperatures of simulated moorland fires: a glasshouse experiment. *Plant Ecology & Diversity* **10**, 77–88. doi:10.1080/17550874.2017.1302017

Thacker JI, Yallop, AR Clutterbuck B (2015) 'Burning in the English Uplands – a review, reconciliation and comparison of results of Natural England's burn monitoring: 2005–2014'. CS Conservation Survey Technical Report, IPENS 05, Natural England,

London <http://publications.naturalengland.org.uk/publication/5706963981697024>

Thomas PH (1963) The size of flames from natural fires. In *Proceedings of the 9th International Symposium on Combustion.* 27 August–1 September, Ithaca. (Eds WG Berl) pp. 844–859. Cornell University, The Combustion Institute, Ithaca.

Thomas PH (1971) Rates of spread of some wind-driven fires. *Forestry* **44**, 155–175. doi:10.1093/forestry/44.2.155

Thompson DBA, Hester AJ, Usher MB (1995a) *Heaths and Moorlands: Cultural Landscapes.* HMSO, Edinburgh.

Thompson DBA, MacDonald AJ, Marsden JH, Galbraith CA (1995b) Upland heather moorland in Great Britain: a review of international importance, vegetation change and some objectives for nature conservation. *Biological Conservation* **71**, 163–178. doi:10.1016/0006-3207(94)00043-P

Thorvaldsen P, Velle LG (2020) *Skjøtselsplan for kystlynghei på Valsøya i Ørland kommune, Trøndelag.* Norsk Institutt for Bioøkonomi, Ås, <https://nibio.brage.unit.no/nibio-xmlui/bitstream/handle/11250/2689724/NIBIO_RAPPORT_2020_6_146.pdf>.

Tipping R (2008) Blanket peat in the Scottish Highlands: timing, cause, spread and the myth of environmental determinism. *Biodiversity and Conservation* **17**, 2097–2113. doi:10.1007/s10531-007-9220-4

Tveraabak LU (2004) Atlantic heath vegetation at its northern fringe in central and northern Norway. *Phytocoenologia* **34**, 5–31. doi:10.1127/0340-269X/2004/0034-0005

Vacchiano G, Ascoli D (2015) An implementation of the Rothermel fire spread model in the R programming language. *Fire Technology* **51**, 523–535. doi:10.1007/s10694-014-0405-6

Van Wagner CE (1972) Duff consumption by fire in eastern pine stands. *Canadian Journal of Forest Research* **2**, 34–39. doi:10.1139/x72-006

Van Wagner CE (1987) 'Development and structure of the Canadian Forest Fire Weather Index System'. Forestry Technical Report 35, Canadian Forestry Service, Ottawa.

Vandvik V, Töpper JP, Cook Z, Daws MI, Heegaard E, Måren IE, Velle LG (2014) Management-driven evolution in a domesticated ecosystem. *Biology Letters* **10**, 20131082. doi:10.1098/rsbl.2013.1082

Velle LG, Vandvik V (2014) Succession after prescribed burning in coastal *Calluna* heathlands along a 340-km latitudinal gradient. *Journal of Vegetation Science* **25**, 546–558. doi:10.1111/jvs.12100

Velle LG, Norderhaug A, Øpstad SL (2008) Feral sheep in coastal heaths – developing sustainable agriculture in vulnerable cultural landscapes. In *Biodiversity and Animal Feed: Future Challenges for Grassland Production, Proceedings of the 22nd General Meeting of the European Grassland Federation.* 9–12 June, Uppsala. (Eds A Hopkins, T Gustafsson, J Bertilsson, G Dalin, N Nilsdotter-Linde and E Spörndly) pp. 949–951. European Grassland Federation, Uppsala.

Velle LG, Nilsen LS, Vandvik V (2012) The age of *Calluna* stands moderates post-fire regeneration rate and trends in northern *Calluna* heathlands. *Applied Vegetation Science* **15**, 119–128. doi:10.1111/j.1654-109X.2011.01144.x

Velle LG, Nilsen LS, Norderhaug A, Vandvik V (2014) Does prescribed burning result in biotic homogenization of coastal heathlands? *Global Change Biology* **20**, 1429–1440. doi:10.1111/gcb.12448

Velle LG, Egelkraut D, Davies MG, Kaland PE, Marrs RH, Vandvik V (2021) HeathlandCycle_Management.jpg. figshare. Figure. <https://doi.org/10.6084/m9.figshare.14207354.v2>

Warming E (1909) *Oecology of Plants.* Oxford University Press, Oxford.

Watson A, Miller GR, Green FHW (1966) Winter browning of heather (*Calluna vulgaris*) and other moorland plants. *Transactions of the Botanical Society of Edinburgh* **40**, 195–203. doi:10.1080/03746606608685143

Watt AS (1955) Bracken versus heather, a study in plant sociology. *Journal of Ecology* **43**, 490–506. doi:10.2307/2257009

Webb N (1998) The traditional management of European heathlands. *Journal of Applied Ecology* **35**, 987–990. doi:10.1111/j.1365-2664.1998.tb00020.x

Welsh Assembly Government (2008) *The Heather and Grass Burning Code for Wales.* Welsh Assembly Government, Cardiff, <https://gov.wales/sites/default/files/publications/2018-01/heather-and-grass-burning-code.pdf>.

Werritty A (2019) *Grouse Moor Management Group: Report.* Scottish Government, Edinburgh, <https://www.gov.scot/publications/grouse-moor-management-group-report-scottish-government>.

Wightman A (1996) *Who Owns Scotland?* Canongate, Edinburgh.

Wildlife and Countryside (2020) Government under increasing pressure to ban burning on England's peatlands. Wildlife and Countryside Link, London, <https://www.wcl.org.uk/ban-the-burn.asp>.

Wilkinson SL, Tekatch AM, Markle CE, Moore PA, Waddington JM (2020) Shallow peat is most vulnerable to high peat burn severity during wildfire. *Environmental Research Letters* **15**, 104032. doi:10.1088/1748-9326/aba7e8

Williams DN (1936) Forest protection in the Dean. *Journal of the Forestry Commission* **15**, 62–67.

Williams JM (2006) *Common Standards Monitoring for Designated Sites: First Six Year Report. Habitats.* Joint Nature Conservation Committee, Peterborough, <https://data.jncc.gov.uk/data/15967de5-9da5-4d1f-b067-a8e76549b-dca/CSM-4-Habitats-2006.pdf>.

Wiltshire J, Hekman J, Fernandez Milan B (2019) *Carbon Loss and Economic Impacts of a Peatland Wildfire in North-east Sutherland, Scotland, 12–17 May 2019. Report to WWF-UK.* Ricardo Energy & Environment, Didcot, <https://www.wwf.org.uk/sites/default/files/2019-11/Carbon%20loss%20and%20economic%20impacts%20of%20a%20peatland%20wildfire%20in%20north-east%20Sutherland.pdf>.

Worrall F, Clay GD, Marrs R, Reed MS (2010) Impacts of Burning Management on Peatlands. IUCN UK Peatland Programme, <https://www.iucn-uk-peatlandprogramme. org/sites/www.iucn-uk-peatlandprogramme.org/files/images/Review%20Impacts%20of%20Burning%20on%20Peatlands%2C%20June%202011%20Final.pdf>.

Yallop AR, Thacker JI, Thomas G, Stephens M, Clutterbuck B, Brewer T, Sannier CAD (2006) The extent and intensity of management burning in the English uplands. *Journal of Applied Ecology* **43**, 1138–1148. doi:10.1111/j.1365-2664.2006.01222.x

Yeloff DE, Labadz JC, Hunt CO (2006) Causes of degradation and erosion of a blanket mire in the southern Pennines, UK. *Mires and Peat* **1**, 4.

13

Prescribed burning in the European Mediterranean Basin

Paulo M. Fernandes, Carlos G. Rossa, Javier Madrigal, Eric Rigolot, Davide Ascoli, Carmen Hernando, Nuno G. Guiomar and Mercedes Guijarro

A historical introduction

Fire disturbance is an intrinsic and vital ecological process in the Mediterranean Basin wildlands (Pausas and Vallejo 1999). Fire use by humans has a long history and fire has been used in the region at least since approximately 1000–3000 BCE (Pyne 1997; Tinner *et al.* 2009; Gil-Romera *et al.* 2010; Connor *et al.* 2012). Initially used for land reclamation, fire has been key in maintaining ecosystem services related to grazing and agroforestry (Naveh 1975; Keeley *et al.* 2011), as well as a means of rural protest and resistance (Tedim *et al.* 2015; Da Ponte *et al.* 2019). However, depopulation of rural areas in recent decades following socioeconomic changes and fire use restrictions have led to the gradual loss of a 'fire culture' in the region, as well as the traditional knowledge of fire as a management tool (Di Pasquale *et al.* 2004; Ganteaume *et al.* 2013). Fire, in the form of the institutionalised practice of prescribed burning, is now being established as a technology serving fire hazard reduction and ecosystem maintenance and restoration goals (Fernandes *et al.* 2013). Only Portugal, Spain, France and Italy are considered in this chapter, because

prescribed burning is not practiced elsewhere in southern Europe, despite the late 1960s pioneering experimentation of Liacos (1974) in Greece.

Early 19th century descriptions reveal burning practices in maritime pine (*Pinus pinaster* Ait.) forests in southern France and Portugal consistent with the concept of prescribed burning (e.g. Alexandrian 1988). In France, burning was legislated and generalised among landowners in the Maures and Esterel regions (Alexandrian 1988). However, the practice was subsequently lost in both countries.

Silva (1987, 1997) gives an account of the inception and early development of prescribed fire in Portugal. The Forest Service trialled prescribed burning in the north-west pine stands between 1976 and 1981 after visits by Edwin Komarek of the Tall Timbers Research Station in Florida in the US. Starting in 1982, a fuel-reduction program with prescribed fire was implemented over 55% of the communal forest area in the region. More than simply being adopted, prescribed underburning was adapted to the local context and its development paralleled that of research. Analysis of data collected by the Forest Service revealed insufficient planning, but also effective hazard reduction without negative environmental effects (Fernandes and Botelho 2004). Prescribed burning became an occasional and very localised practice from 1994 to 2004. Increased political support following tragic wildfire seasons and improved and more extensive training subsequently revived prescribed fire in Portugal, the use of which has spread from the north-west region to include open vegetation types.

In 1980, foresters from France, Spain and Italy travelled to the US under the auspices of the Direction of Forest Resources of the Food and Agriculture Organization of the United Nations (FAO) and were introduced to prescribed fire as a safe, ecological and cost-effective technique (Alexandrian *et al.* 1980). After this visit to the US, the use of prescribed fire was introduced in France. The initial demonstrations in pine forests were fostered by the contemporary Portuguese experience and were conducted *à la portugaise* (Binggeli 1997). However, insufficient interest from forest managers limited initial initiatives to study the ecological effects of prescribed burning and compare them with the results of other fuel treatment methods (Rigolot 2000). The first prescribed fire programs in France were established in the early 1980s in shrubland in the Eastern Pyrenees and Maritime Alps and subsequently expanded to other regions. Prescribed burning is now actively and officially supported by the Mediterranean French agencies and organisations involved in fire management (Lambert 2010). Fuel reduction was the initial objective, with proven benefits to wildfire control operations (Rigolot 1997; Lambert *et al.* 1999). However, additional objectives were added as burn crews expanded their capacity, including habitat management for pastoral, hunting or nature conservation purposes.

The first prescribed fires in Spain were conducted in Galicia, in the north-west of the country, on small test plots in shrubland and eucalypt plantations in 1978 and, on a greater scale, in 1980 on a pine plantation of *P. pinaster* and *Pinus radiata* within the framework of a fuel management plan (Vélez 1981). This plan resulted from a collaboration between the Spanish National Forest Service (ICONA) and the National Institute of Agricultural Research (INIA), international exchange opportunities provided by the FAO/UNESCO Technical Consultation on Forest Fires and symposia and study trips organised by the US Department of Agriculture's (USDA) Forest Service (Vélez and Vega 1985). Prescribed fire research in pine stands continued throughout the 1980s–2000s (Vega *et al.* 1983, 2000; Rodríguez y Silva 2000), but there was scant translation of the research into the use of prescribed fire by managers.

The Spanish Forest Fire Service undertook two initiatives relevant to further develop prescribed fire. In 1998, it created Integral Wildfire Prevention Teams (EPRIF) to work directly with the rural population in areas where traditional agricultural practices contribute to high wildfire incidence. EPRIF teams work to reduce the impact of wildfires and support the rural economy, and include prescribed burning within their activities. The second initiative was the experimental burning program in forest, started in 2014 and developed by the Reinforcement Brigades against Forest Fire (BRIF) in cooperation with researchers. The main aim of this program was to improve knowledge of the techniques to decrease wildfire risk through fuel reduction and the avoidance of tree damage.

Group of Support to Forest Actions (GRAF) teams, specialised wildland firefighters from Catalonia, north-east Spain, started using fire to train personnel in 1998. This strategy was expanded and Catalonia was the first Spanish territory in which prescribed burning was used as a fire management tool. Other regions, namely Andalucía and Castilla-La-Mancha, are now replicating this model.

In Italy, interest in prescribed fire also arose in the late 1970s (Susmel 1977). The National Forest Service acknowledged the benefits of prescribed burning (Calabri 1981) and, in the 1980s, promoted experiments in pine forests (Toscana) and to maintain fuel breaks (Sardegna) under the supervision of the Istituto Sperimentale di Selvicoltura (Buresti and Sulli 1983). The experiments were abandoned despite 'promising' results (Calabri 1988). In Italy, unlike in France, Portugal and Spain, the interest in prescribed fire died off. Attention to prescribed fire returned in the early 21st century, and several scientific studies (e.g. Battipaglia *et al.* 2016; Giuditta *et al.* 2020), legislation initiatives, training and burn programs have been conducted throughout the country (Ascoli and Bovio 2013). However, the use of prescribed burning for management purposes is currently restricted to Campania, Piemonte, Toscana and Sardegna.

Since the 1990s, the Directorate-General for Research and Innovation of the European Commission has funded international cooperation on the use of prescribed burning (Vega *et al.* 1994; Valette *et al.* 1998; Botelho *et al.* 2000; Silva *et al.* 2010). These projects have produced a substantial body of knowledge (Fernandes *et al.* 2011, 2013; Fernandes 2018) from which several burn guidelines and manuals have been produced and helped with the implementation of prescribed burning in southern Europe.

Prescribed burning effort and objectives

As a consequence of its fragmented and intermittent history, prescribed fire activity in southern Europe is essentially local in scope and the area treated is modest (Figure 13.1). Prescribed fire implementation in Spain is limited to national or regional organisations, either forest services or fire management agencies. Users of prescribed fire in France, Portugal and Italy have more diverse backgrounds, and include private forest associations, pastoral associations, volunteer or professional fire brigades and municipalities. Still, the number of active teams is limited in all countries. In France, the number of active prescribed burning teams stabilised at 20–25, after a gradual increase between the 1980s and 2000s. In Portugal, although 150 technicians are currently certified to apply prescribed fire, only 24 have worked as a burn boss in more than 20 burn operations (2006–15). In Spain, there are currently 18 EPRIF distributed throughout the country, mainly in the north; each team consists of two to four technicians.

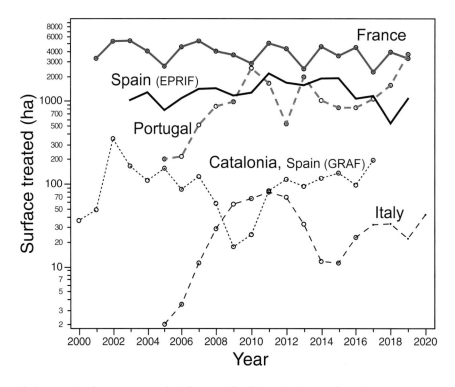

Figure 13.1: Temporal changes in the area treated with prescribed burning in southern Europe.

During 2006–15, a period for which data are available for France, Portugal and Spain, the number of burn operations in Portugal was exceeded by a factor of 1.9 in Spain (EPRIF plus GRAF) and by a factor of 2.4 in France. The leading position of France is confirmed by the amount of area treated, which is 3.6-fold higher than in Portugal and 2.4-fold higher than in Spain. Since 2010, France and Portugal have used prescribed burning on an average of 0.19% and 0.08% of their shrubland area every year respectively. Interannual variation is substantial, but no temporal patterns in the extent of prescribed fire activity are visible in Figure 13.1. Current area targets for Portugal are ambitious, as determined by its national prescribed burning plan, and in 2019 the area treated with prescribed fire in Portugal slightly exceeded that in France. The use of prescribed fire remains very limited in Italy (Ascoli and Bovio 2013), although there are prospects for its expansion, particularly in Toscana. Considering the recent upward trend in Portugal, we estimate that approximately 10 000 ha year^{-1} are now treated with prescribed fire in southern Europe.

More than 90% of prescribed fire activity in France occurs in the south of the country. The Maritime Alps and Eastern Pyrenees are particularly important and account for 31% and 20% of the total area treated respectively; in the Eastern Pyrenees, 14% of the total rangeland area has been treated with prescribed fire from 1987 to 2009 (Lambert

2010). Most burn operations in Portugal take place in the north, especially in the oceanic north-west quadrant (55% of the total area treated), with practically no prescribed fire operations in the south of the country. Coincidentally, 55% of the total area burned by the EPRIF is in north-western Spain; Navarra, in the north-east, accounts for 23% of the total surface treated (Ministerio de Agricultura Pesca y Alimentación 2019).

Prescribed burning objectives in southern Europe are variable, but fuel hazard reduction and pastoral burning prevail. Fuel reduction is particularly (and overwhelmingly) important in Portugal (Table 13.1), where the wildfire problem is considerably more severe.

Spain shows substantial regional variation in burn objectives. In the northern regions (Galicia, Asturias, Cantabria, Navarra, Aragón) and in Extremadura, prescribed fire is merely used to manage pastures and shrublands for grazing. Here, and in France, prescribed burning is largely a surrogate for traditional burning practices that are declining or are perceived as unsustainable or risky, given the current trends in fuel accumulation and landscape-scale fuel connectivity. In Castilla-La Mancha, Andalucía and the Canary Islands, fire management plans consider the use of fire to reduce fuels, manage habitats and for research and training purposes. Fuel reduction in wildlands and at wildland–urban interfaces and training are

Table 13.1. Distribution (%) of prescribed fire operations by treatment objective in France, Portugal and Spain

Data show the percentage of prescribed burns for each objective/the percentage of area burned. Data for France are mean values for 2002, 2007 and 2014. EPRIF, Integral Wildfire Prevention Teams of the Spanish Forest Fire Service; GRAF, Group of Support to Forest Actions

Burn objective	France	Portugal (2006–16)	Spain	
			EPRIF (2006–12)	GRAF (1998–2017)
Fuel reduction	33.0/–	80.9/83.6	23.6/13.1	67.1/39.9[D]
Silviculture	18.7/–[B]	4.5/4.6[C]	2.7/1.8	–
Pastoral	41.3/–	6.0/9.3	65.6/79.5	19.4/46.5
Habitat management[A]	7.0/–	1.5/0.7	8.1/5.6	2.9/5.8
Training		5.1/1.6		8.0/6.7
Research		2.0/0.1		2.5/1.1

[A] Wildlife management (including for hunting), nature conservation.
[B] Includes burning for agricultural purposes and other objectives (silviculture being a minority).
[C] Mostly slash burning after tree harvesting in eucalypt plantations.
[D] Includes silviculture.

evident in Castilla-La Mancha and Andalucía, as well as in Valencia (eastern Spain) and Castilla y León (central Spain).

Catalonia has the most complete set of objectives regarding the use of prescribed burning. There is an equilibrium between hazard reduction, essentially by treating specific areas in strategic locations, and pastoral and habitat management. However, consideration of Departamento de Medio Ambiente burn activity in Catalonian mountains (on average 747 ha year^{-1} from 1996 to 2002; Grillo Delgado 2002) strongly shifts burn objectives towards rangeland management.

In France, management objectives other than hazard reduction prevail. In Italy, prescribed burning is used mostly to reduce fuels and manage rangelands, with examples of habitat restoration programs (Ascoli *et al.* 2013).

Quantitative information on the distribution of prescribed fires by fuel type is scarce and is available for Portugal and Catalonia only (Table 13.2). Various shrubland communities are treated with fire, including: heathlands in the Iberian Peninsula, comprising *Pterospartium tridentatum* and species of the *Erica*, *Ulex* and *Cytisus* genera; mixed shrub–grass stands of *Cytisus oromediterraneus* in the French Pyrenees and *Calluna vulgaris* in Italy; and Mediterranean shrublands dominated by *Cistus* spp. or *Quercus coccifera* at various locations. Prescribed fire in forest is used in pine stands of *P. pinaster*, *Pinus nigra* and *Pinus canariensis* (Canary Islands, Spain), as well as to consume *Eucalyptus*

globulus slash after clearfelling; other species (e.g. *Pinus pinea*, *Pinus halepensis*, *Pinus sylvestris*, *Quercus pubescens*) are much less represented. In any case, forest understorey burning is a minor component of burn activity in southern Europe, except in Catalonia; again, consideration of high-elevation rangeland burning in the region would substantially decrease the relative weight of prescribed fire in forest. Although understorey burning has never been a significant component of prescribed burning in France, current figures for Portugal are in stark contrast with earlier (1980s–1990s) practice, which was essentially focused in maritime pine stands (Fernandes and Botelho 2004). Prescribed burning in forest requires more personnel per unit area because the need to maintain fire intensity within limits tolerable by trees implies conservative ignition patterns; this is more time consuming and probably contributes to the contemporary preference for prescribed fire in open vegetation.

Prescribed burning requirements and barriers

During the past two decades, despite increased studies into and communication regarding prescribed burning in southern Europe, its acceptance remains limited (Montiel and Kraus 2010; Fernandes *et al.* 2013). The policies, legislative framework and practices of prescribed burning in southern Europe and their evolution are well documented (Lázaro and Montiel 2010; Montiel and Kraus 2010), as are existing societal concerns and future perspectives and challenges (Fernandes *et al.* 2013).

Cultural and social issues with fire

Obstacles to prescribed burning expansion are varied and important, including public and institutional acceptance, policies adverse to risk, funding, training and available human resources, administrative constraints, land tenure and conservation status, conflicts with other land management activities and assets and weather or climate constraints (Cleaves *et al.* 2000; Fernandes *et al.* 2013). Cultural barriers to fire use and poor social acceptance have

Table 13.2. Prescribed fire distribution by fuel type

Data show the percentage of prescribed burns for each fuel type/the percentage of area burned. GRAF, Group of Support to Forest Actions

Fuel type	Portugal	Catalonia (GRAF)
Grassland	0.7/0.1	6.0/13.0
Shrubland	78.6/84.2	26.3/41.0
Forest		
Grass–litter	0.1/0.0	15.2/10.3
Shrub–litter	8.3/3.3	37.9/23.9
Litter	4.9/4.9	–
Slash	7.4/7.5	9.7/6.3
Cereal stubble	0.0/0.0	4.7/5.5

ancient roots, in some cases dating back to the 16th century (Pyne 1982).

The early 20th century need to increase vegetation cover to reduce soil erosion and desertification in the Mediterranean Basin outlawed traditional fire (Métailié 1981; Seijo and Gray 2012; Ascoli and Bovio 2013; Coughlan 2014). The use of fire, including prescribed burning, was limited and, in most cases, hampered by the increasing demand of forest ecosystem services requiring fire protection (e.g. wood production) and a disregard of fire ecology by classical forestry (Fernandes *et al.* 2013; Marino *et al.* 2014). Consequently, fire bans generated social conflicts throughout the 20th and early 21st centuries (Seijo and Gray 2012). Where rural burns have been prohibited or severely restricted, the surreptitious use of fire for range management on days of high fire danger increased. This contributed to wildfires with negative effects on ecosystem services and large socioeconomic impacts, thus strengthening opposition from environmentalists and the general public to the use of fire.

Laws and regulations governing prescribed burning

The legal framework for prescribed fire in southern Europe is quite variable. In France it first appears in the 1992 forestry law (*Loi n° 92-613 du 6 juillet 1992*), which allows land management agencies to conduct prescribed burning for wildfire prevention purposes. However, legislation considering prescribed fire in its full extent did not appear until 2001, although it was preceded by the definition of formal training processes in 1996 (a burn crew leader, 12 days of training) and 1998 (a burn crew element, 5 days of training). The regulation of training activities was completed in 2004, and these are located in two centres in Gardanne (Bouches-du-Rhône) and Bazas (Gironde) and are monitored and assessed by a national committee. In addition, burn certification requires significant operational experience. In France, the framework for prescribed fire is given by a general law (*Loi d'Orientation Forestière* 2001) and supplementary legal documents that address wildfire prevention

and the competencies and training of those involved in prescribed burning; prescribed burning can also be subjected to local regulations.

The use of prescribed burning in Portugal preceded formal regulation. Its practice, and the use of fire in fire management operations in general, has been regulated by dedicated legislation since 2006 (*Regulamento do Fogo Técnico*, with the most recent update in 2014), which abides by a 2006 decree (and its subsequent modifications) that established the National System of Forest Protection Against Wildfires.

Prescribed burning legislation and regulation are regional in Spain. Complexity is high, because each region has generated a plethora of legal frameworks and specific fire use and prescribed burning regulations. Some regions (Galicia, Asturias, Castilla y León, Valencia, Andalucía) have forest laws in which the use of fire follows specific annual regulations. Other regions base their regulations on specific ordinances or decrees. In any case, most of these regulations are oriented to control the use of fire and rarely to promote prescribed burning programs.

In Italy, prescribed fire legislation is also a regional responsibility (Bovio and Ascoli 2012). Both regional fire management plans (Italian law on wildfire No. 353/2000) and regional laws provide the legal framework for prescribed burning, mostly in the forestry sector, although some regions regulate prescribed burning in the fire management law. The Campania region enacted a specific prescribed burning law, but it is a unique case. To date, 70% of Italian regions regulate prescribed burning in either a fire management plan or in a regional law. Notably, these regions account for 95% of the area affected by wildfires in the past two decades. However, many regulatory documents still lack clear information on key issues such as liability and detailed authorisation procedures (Bovio and Ascoli 2012).

A positive outlook for prescribed fire development?

Traditional fire use regulation through prescribed burning has lessened conflicts in recent decades. In central–northern Spain and Portugal, regulations now allow the use of fire under conditions of low fire danger, although the demand for burn permits is higher than the administrative capacity to manage the burns requested by farmers. The traditional use of fire would benefit from rural extension to assist people in their practices, more than from administrative permits and awareness strategies.

The expansion of prescribed fire programs succeeded in changing wildfire regimes into planned burning regimes (e.g. in the French Pyrenees). Increased scientific knowledge (Fernandes 2018), scientific communication on climate change and fire-related issues and recent tragedies caused by fires have increased the acceptance of prescribed burning and pushed for its inclusion on the agenda of European policy makers. Understanding within groups of professionals linked to the forest and nature conservation sectors is evolving in the same direction, albeit slowly. A recent position paper coordinated by the Ministry of Agriculture of Spain (Comité de Lucha contra Incendios Forestales 2019) suggested, for the first time, a role for prescribed burning in forest management and fire hazard mitigation. This is one example of signs of a cultural change that sees prescribed fire as a key element of modern fire management systems throughout southern Europe (Faivre 2018; Moreira *et al.* 2020). However, most national or regional stakeholders in different countries remain far from this understanding, which is visible in the current narratives, particularly in the discourse in relation to actions that enhance or limit pyrodiversity.

Because prescribed burning can be the subject of high levels of controversy and scrutiny (e.g. Davies *et al.* 2016), burn programs should increasingly include systematic, after-the-fact assessment of results and long-term monitoring to document and improve the practice (Van Wagtendonk *et al.* 1982; Pyne *et al.* 1996). Methods and tools for such assessment and long-term monitoring, including from a scientific perspective, include user surveys (Sando 1969; Cleaves *et al.* 2000; Haines *et al.* 2001;

Quinn-Davidson and Varner 2012), operational data collection (Czuhai and Cushwa 1968; Fernandes and Botelho 2004), monitoring of permanent plots (Ewell and Nichols 1983; Keifer 1998; Waring *et al.* 2016) and remote sensing (Yallop *et al.* 2006; Allen *et al.* 2016).

Getting fire on the ground

Prescribed burning in southern Europe is a practice that varies substantially among and within countries. People with different backgrounds and from distinct organisations use fire to accomplish variable goals in specific ecosystems. However, the small scale of the operations is shared by all, and is a distinctive feature compared with the relatively large organisations that manage fire on public land and on broader scales in North America and Australia.

Burn seasonality and prescribed weather

Prescribed burning in southern Europe follows the Mediterranean climate seasonality. Thus, most activity takes place between October and May, before the summer wildfire season, when fire use of any kind is banned. However, regional specificities are possible, particularly in mountain regions where a winter fire season can occur. A certain amount of prescribed burning takes place in late spring, with the potential to increase soil heating and litter consumption (and hence soil erosion) in case of a dry spring (Stoof *et al.* 2013).

Prescribed fire operations in Portugal are conducted mostly from October to May, with an emphasis during the February–April period (Figure 13.2). In Catalonia, prescribed burning can be conducted in any month of the year, but February and March are the main months. In the rest of Spain, the prescribed fire season is from late autumn to spring. As in Portugal, burn operations conducted by the EPRIF crews occur mostly (76% of the total number) in February–April. Prescribed fire operations in France occur during winter and spring, but can also occur in the autumn months in the Maritime Alps, Haute-Garonne, Eastern

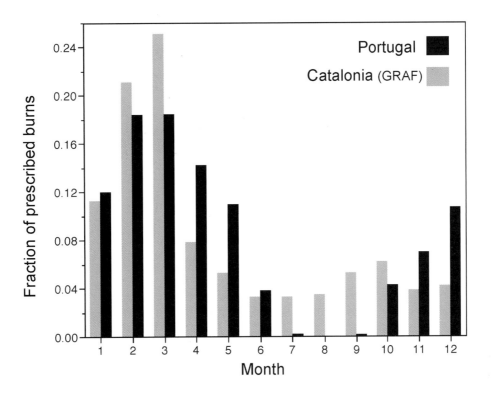

Figure 13.2: Monthly distribution of prescribed burning operations in Portugal (2006–19) and Catalonia (1998–2017).

Pyrenees, Corse and Landes de Gascogne. Finally, prescribed fire in Italy occurs from autumn to spring, except in Piemont (autumn–winter).

Burn prescriptions in Europe are variable, ranging from generic windows for broad objectives to site-specific windows for specific objectives. More often than not, prescribed fire users monitor local weather conditions, the fire danger rating and larger-scale forecasts and their effects on fuel moisture content to comply with generic burning windows.

A set of burn prescriptions for European ecosystems has been developed based on an analysis and compilation of existing burning guides and best practices, prescriptions from the agencies and individuals involved in burn management or research in Europe and the use of fire behaviour and effects models to help attain specific treatment goals (Fernandes and Loureiro 2010). Prescription windows vary markedly according to management goals and vegetation structure, but only approximately 10% of the prescriptions are lower or higher

than 25 (km h⁻¹ [wind speed], °C [ambient temperature], % [relative humidity] or the duff moisture code of the Canadian Fire Weather Index or FWI]; Figure 13.3). Thus, prescribed fire in Europe proceeds under mild weather conditions and, in general, shortly (up to 2–4 weeks) after rain. Optimum burn conditions typically combine an air temperature of 8–16°C and a relative humidity of 40–65% under steady surface wind speeds of 4–12 km h⁻¹.

Burn size and spatial patterns

Burn operations are relatively small and spatially scattered in the Mediterranean Basin. Approximately half the burns in both Portugal and Spain are smaller than 5 ha. In Spain (EPRIF), only 19% of burns exceed 10 ha; in Portugal, 10% of burns exceed 20 ha; and in Catalonia 10% of burns exceed 10 ha. Similarly, treatment units in Italy are <5 ha (Piemonte, Toscana) and <10 ha (Campania, Sardegna). Maximum recorded sizes of individual burn operations are 146 ha in Portugal, 128 ha in Spain (EPRIF) and 67 ha in Catalonia (GRAF), with

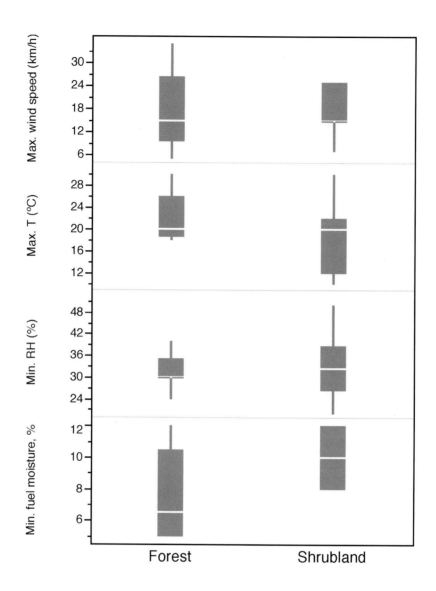

Figure 13.3: Box plots for weather-related variables in the compilation of European burning prescriptions of Fernandes and Loureiro (2010). Whiskers indicate the 10th and 90th percentiles, boxes indicate the 25th–75th percentiles and white horizontal lines indicate the 50th percentile. RH, relative humidity; T, temperature.

a maximum size of 179 ha mentioned by Lambert (2010) for the Eastern Pyrenees in France.

In Spain (EPRIF), the annual mean burn size is 6.8 ha with little interannual variation. In France, the annual mean burn size decreased by almost half within the period 2001–19, reaching approximately 10 ha, which is viewed as a refinement of prescribed fire implementation. Burn operations increase in size from Catalonia to Portugal and from Portugal to France, and those conducted in

shrubland and grassland are twice the size of the fires conducted for forest underburning (Table 13.3). Mean treatment size in Portugal is similar in shrubland, pine forest without an understorey (an hence lower potential fire intensity) and post-harvest slash fuels.

By way of comparison, the mean prescribed burn size on US federal land is 34.5 ha (Barnett *et al.* 2016), which is three- to sevenfold greater than that in the European Mediterranean Basin. In

Table 13.3. Mean prescribed fire size (ha) by fuel type

Fuel type	Portugal	Catalonia (GRAF)	France
Grassland	1.27	7.17	–
Shrubland	8.48	5.19	11.54
Forest	4.93	2.13	5.23
Grass–litter	–	2.25	
Shrub–litter	3.59	2.09	
Litter	9.18	–	
Slash	7.56	2.15	
Cereal stubble	–	3.92	

south-western Australia, the annual prescribed burning rate in public forest is 6.6% of the total area (vs 1.1% burned by wildfire; Burrows and McCaw 2013), exceeding that in the Eastern Pyrenees by a factor of 10. The small scale of prescribed burning in southern Europe, in terms of both the size of the treatment units and the treatment effort, implies that most burn units are dispersed in the landscape and account for a small fraction of the potentially treatable area. However, at subregional to local scales, the landscape imprint of prescribed fire history is noticeable. Such is the case of the Eastern Pyrenees in southern France, where prescribed burning is mostly used to maintain or restore rangelands. Long-term use of prescribed fire in the region produced a small-grained mosaic of vegetation patches, which is generally viewed as beneficial for both wildfire hazard reduction and biodiversity (Lambert 2010).

In Catalonia (GRAF), 47% of the total number of prescribed fires are designed as 'strategic management points' (i.e. the treatment is applied to specific locations that are expected to block or delay the spread of a subsequent wildfire; Madrigal *et al.* 2019). Most patches shown in Figure 13.4 reflect this strategy. In Portugal, burn units vary in shape in forests, but tend to be more linear in shrubland, corresponding to fuel breaks (up to 200 m wide).

Burn planning and evaluation

Management of prescribed fire activity varies widely across southern Europe. Managers can use different tools to help with decisions regarding where, when and how to burn. In particular,

plot-, stand- or landscape-level fire behaviour simulators are available, including those developed by the USDA Forest Service, based on Rothermel's fire spread model and the assignment of fuel models to typify fuel conditions (Finney 2006; Andrews 2014). Empirically based burning guides and applications developed in Europe, such as PiroPinus (Fernandes *et al.* 2012) and FireGlobulus (Pinto *et al.* 2014), allow site-specific development of prescriptions and simulation of fire behaviour and effects, unlike tools requiring fuel models. Prescribed fire planning in most of Spain makes use of fire behaviour modelling tools, and training on the use of such tools is standard in Portugal; however, French users of prescribed fire do not rely on fire behaviour simulation (Rigolot 1993). In Portugal, an online platform (CeaseFire) is available that maps whether or not, and to what extent, generic prescriptions are met over subsequent days and the whole country based on forecasts of the Canadian FWI (Fernandes 2018).

Spatial planning of prescribed burning based on fire modelling is useful for optimising treatment locations when the objective is fire hazard reduction. For example, FlamMap (Finney 2007) identifies major wildfire travel routes using a minimum travel time algorithm and proposes treatments for the locations that disrupt fire spread the most. This approach is customary in Catalonia (GRAF), but only occasionally used elsewhere in Europe.

Prescribed fire planning in the landscape occurs on an annual (France, Spain, Italy) to multi-annual (Portugal) scale. As in other countries around the world, an operational burn plan includes a map, the firing pattern, holding strategy, a contingency plan and a notification checklist; it may also include a complexity analysis. The degree to which these elements are developed depends on organisational structure, burn size and complexity and perceived risk.

Portugal and France have implemented systems to collect burn data and monitor practitioners' activity respectively through the Instituto da Conservação da Natureza e das Florestas (ICNF;

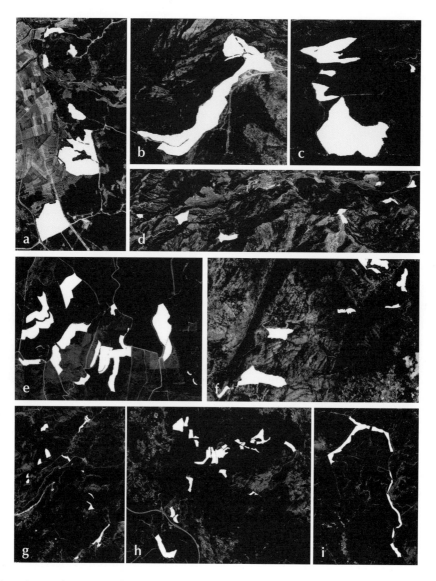

Figure 13.4: Examples of spatial patterns of prescribed fire in (a–d) Catalonia and (e–i) Portugal. The scale is variable and treatment units are overlaid on Google Earth imagery as white patches. Data were obtained from official databases (http://interior.gencat.cat/ca/arees_dactuacio/bombers/ for Catalonia; supplied by the Instituto da Conservação da Natureza e das Florestas [Forest Service] for Portugal).

Forest Service) and a national prescribed burning network that periodically gathers to share experiences. A knowledge-based system and a relational database are used in France to collect and organise information (Rigolot *et al.* 1998). The major challenge of meeting annual planning targets relates to the constraints imposed by scarce resources and weather opportunities. Statistics for France (2001–15) are illustrative of the existing difficulties, where the estimated number of annual

burn days for each burn team, based on normal climatology, varied between 20 and 83. However, on average, burn operations took place on just 58% of those days, with the mean annual number of burn days per team varying between 7 and 18 (averaging 10) and only half the target area burned (range 33–72%).

In Portugal, prescribed fire reporting includes an assessment of whether treatment objectives were met and, if so, to what extent. For the 2006–15 period, the accomplishment of burn objectives was overwhelmingly (93%) classified as very good or good. This is a far more optimistic assessment than previously found for the 1980s–1990s (Fernandes and Botelho 2004), and it should reflect improved procedures but probably suffers from self-assessment bias.

Costs are an important component of the evaluation of prescribed burning. In France, an important cost factor is whether the burn is a first entry or a maintenance operation, the former being costlier. Portuguese surrogate data for costs (personnel and equipment used; data on file at Universidade de Trás-os-Montes e Alto Douro [UTAD] from ICNF records) offer some insights into what drives burn costs. The amount of human resources and vehicles used in burn operations in Portugal is poorly correlated with burn size. This implies that increasingly larger burn units will be increasingly less costly to treat.

Burn operations

Burn units are delimited as much as possible by existing natural or man-made barriers to fire spread (e.g. rock outcrops, non-flammable vegetation, snow [common in the Pyrenees], fuel breaks, roads and tracks). However, additional work has to be undertaken to establish control lines, which is done manually or mechanically or by creating wet lines or blacklines. In Spain, preparation costs associated with control lines accounts for 41% of the total operational cost, followed by ignition costs (36%) and extinction costs (23%; González-Pan 2012). Control lines are at least 1 m wide and are wider in shrubland than in forest, often following a rule of thumb that the width of the control line should be at least twice the height of the vegetation.

The areas selected for treatment can be divided in small plots of 1–5 ha that are burned on different days according to the prescription window. The burn crew includes a burn boss and one or more people igniting the fire using drip torches, depending on burn size and subdivision. However, the overall organisation and the amount and type of equipment used vary and can be minimal. In Spain, all people involved in prescribed burns are professional specialised wildland firefighters following the Incident Command System and equipped with international standard individual security equipment; logistic and suppression sections are established to contain possible fire escape and at least one fire engine is available for possible contingencies.

In Portugal, different organisations often cooperate in a given burn, which allows scaling-up and provides learning and training opportunities. A complete burn team is composed of a burn boss, a holding boss and the corresponding holding crew(s), a lookout and several drip torch operators. However, in low-complexity operations and when available resources are scarce, a burn can be conducted with just one burn boss and a holding crew; in these situations, the burn boss performs all tasks other than holding the fire, although sometimes members of the holding crew operate the drip torches.

Figure 13.5 shows examples of prescribed burn operations in southern Europe. The firing patterns used in prescribed burning in Europe are very much a function of vegetation type and safety concerns. Conservative ignition techniques are used in forest (i.e. downslope and against the wind or strip-head firing at short distances between consecutive ignition lines). The same methods are used in open vegetation, but often are extended to include more aggressive ignition patterns, namely head firing and ring ignition, provided that the likelihood of fire escape is minimal. Fire behaviour characteristics follow these options and the inherent environmental conditions of wind speed, fuel moisture, fuel load and structure and slope. Although flame lengths of 0.2–1.2 m and spread rates of 20–60 m h^{-1} are preferred in pine stands, these variables can be higher by one order of magnitude in shrubland (Fernandes and Loureiro 2010). Lower fire intensities than in pine forest are advised for thin-barked broadleaved trees (e.g. in short-rotation eucalypt plantations; Pinto et al. 2014), but the routine use of prescribed fire in those

Figure 13.5: Examples of prescribed burning in Europe: (a) in a *Pinus pinaster* stand in Soria (Northern Plateau), Spain, conducted by the Lubia BRIF (Reinforcement Brigade against Forest Fire) to reduce fuels; (b) in *Cytisus oromediterraneus* shrubland in the Eastern Pyrenees for habitat management, and where the presence of snow often implies fire patchiness and circumvents the need to prepare firebreaks; (c) in grass–heather in the Apennine Mountains of Italy to preserve *Vaccinium myrtillus* for fruit production; (d) in a young *Pinus nigra* plantation in northern Portugal with dense dry heathland to establish a fuel break and where high tree mortality is expected due to stand age; and (e) *Pinus canariensis* after underburning in Gran Canaria, Spain. This species is highly resistant to fire due to its thick bark and resprouting traits. (f) Prescribed fire can be challenging in Mediterranean shrubland types, such as *Cistus ladanifer* in southern Portugal, given the lack of elevated dead fuel. Back burning was used in all cases shown, except in the *P. pinaster* stand in Soria (a), where strip headfiring was used. Photographs taken by the authors: J. Madrigal (a), P. M. Fernandes (b, d, e), D. Ascoli (c) and N. G. Guiomar (f).

settings and the recommended procedures are still emerging.

In recent years, there have been new opportunities to introduce or expand the use of fire to forest and fire management agencies in Spain and Portugal. As wildland fire fighting systems evolve, the ability to use fire in fire suppression settings becomes manifest, as does the need to train people for such purposes. This has the potential of increasing the acceptance of prescribed burning, and Catalonia is a good example of such a process. In Portugal, where certified burn personnel are being trained (since 2014) to support both prescribed fire and suppression fire technicians, there has been a rising trend in the use of burn operations to exercise the use of fire as a suppression tool. The introduction in Europe of Prescribed Fire Training Exchanges (TREX) training camps (in 2017 in Portugal and in 2019 in Spain), plus other international cooperation initiatives, has allowed for the exchange of experiences and facilitated the accreditation of professionals and organisations in the use of fire.

Future of prescribed burning in Mediterranean Europe

The fact that proper, 'complete' regulation frameworks for prescribed burning exist only in France and Portugal indicates that prescribed burning is better established in these countries and mirrors the current state of development and acceptance of the practice in southern Europe. The degree of implementation of prescribed burning is limited, as indicated by the size of the treatment units and, in particular, the extent of the areas treated. Nonetheless, prescribed burning in south-western Europe is a relevant practice at subregional to local scales.

If traditional burning (Figure 13.6) is accepted as a legitimate practice (i.e. complying with an acceptable prescription), then its effects could be

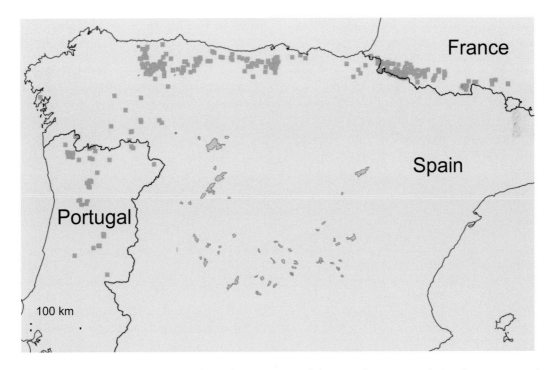

Figure 13.6: Fires larger than 20 ha in Portugal, northern Spain and the French Pyrenees during the autumn–winter of 2019–20 (from 1 October 2019 to 31 March 2020), mapped by the COPERNICUS Emergency Management System for the European Forest Fire Information System (EFFIS; https://effis.jrc.ec.europa.eu). Most fires correspond to pastoral burning, but prescribed fires are also shown.

assumed equivalent to formal prescribed burning practices and thus contribute to treated area statistics. For example, approximately 4000 ha of shrubland burns, on average, in Portugal every year under weather conditions consistent with prescribed burning (data on file at UTAD based on ICNF records). Portuguese legislation now allows unplanned fires to be treated as management fires if they occur under prescribed conditions. However, this requires more than a change in doctrine or legislation: it requires time for a change in defining the priorities established for fire fighters and to internalise that change, as well as training to support conscious decisions. In the Pyrenees, prescribed burning teams increasingly support traditional burning practices and limit their own activity to the most difficult burn operations (Fernandes et al. 2013). Integration of conventional prescribed fire technology with traditional ecological knowledge has the potential to decrease conflicts between local communities and resource managers (Ray et al. 2012).

Open vegetation types are the main burn targets in southern Europe due to the existing barriers to applying fire in forests, as well as because of the land cover and land management context. And yet, in fire-prone regions where hazard reduction is an important concern, forests are generally more valued than shrubland, and prescribed burning is expected to be more effective in the former (Fernandes 2015). More awareness and knowledge transfer are needed regarding prescribed burning in forest (Fernandes 2018).

The spatial features of prescribed burning indicate how the practice affects landscape structure and the potential for the spread of large fires. Where the prescribed burning effort is large enough to create a consistent fuel age mosaic (e.g. Eastern Pyrenees), wildfire spread should be substantially constrained. Otherwise, current spatial patterns of prescribed burning in Europe are not likely to be effective at disrupting the growth of large fires (Davim et al. 2021), even if fire behaviour and fire severity are mitigated (Fernandes 2015; Espinosa et al. 2019), because prescribed burning

projects are very localised and the effect of treatments in blocking or delaying wildfire spread is seldom replicated or supplemented by nearby treatments (Finney 2007). The Catalonian practice of treating 'strategic points' is suggestive of a low cost-to-benefit ratio, but this warrants further research, including determination of the leverage effect of prescribed burning on wildfire extent (Price et al. 2015).

Current management of prescribed burning operations is quite heterogeneous across Europe, but the procedures seem poorly developed compared with overseas practices. The need for better prescribed burning management will only increase if the practice expands, but further progress is desirable under the current situation, specifically through the increased use of decision-support tools. There is room for improvement in spatial planning, weather monitoring and forecasting, exploitation of burning opportunities, compliance with burn prescriptions and optimisation of costs. Costs are determined mostly by human resources management and would strongly benefit from larger prescribed burning units, which, in turn, would increase the effect on wildfire extent. The current inability to attain treatment area targets is a flagrant example of the need to improve planning: given the limited work force available for prescribed burning, it is crucial that burning opportunities (as defined by the prescribed weather conditions) are fully taken advantage of through close monitoring of forecasts and fire danger ratings, combined with flexibility (i.e. prescribed burning should be a top priority activity on suitable days).

Prescribed burning has attracted increased interest during the current decade, but so far this has not translated into substantially more area being treated. Such an increase in burn effort is unlikely as long as fire management policies are reactive and dominated by activities in the realm of pre-suppression and suppression (Moreira et al. 2020). Until then, societal concerns with smoke production and burn impacts on ecosystem services, namely biodiversity, carbon and water, will be minimal, with the potential side effect of neglecting improved planning and evaluation procedures. If prescribed fire monitoring is inadequate, then its shortcomings and opportunities for improvement will not be identified, and adaptive management informed by sound scientific evidence (Fernandes *et al.* 2013; Davies *et al.* 2016) will not be implemented. Wildfire threats under climate change are increasingly recognised in Europe, particularly after the marked effects of wildfires in Portugal in 2017 and in Greece in 2018, and unprecedented fire seasons in Siberia, South America, south-eastern Australia and California in 2019 and 2020. Media attention and public opinion on fire issues will increase attention on and expectations of prescribed burning, creating opportunities and challenges for its future development in Mediterranean Europe.

Acknowledgements

This chapter evolved from a deliverable of Global Change Impacts on Wildland Fire Behaviour and Uses in Mediterranean Forest Ecosystems (Med-WildFireLab), a networking action of FOREST-ERRA ERA-NET. Rui Almeida, Hugo Saturnino, Bernard Lambert, Jean-Luc Dupuy, Domingo Molina, Antonio López Santalla, Raul Quílez, Juan Ramón Molina, José Almodóvar, Federico Grillo, Giuseppe Delogu, Luca Tonarelli, Salvatore Cabiddu and Marcello Murino provided information or comments.

References

Alexandrian D (1988) Feu contrôlé et contre-feu dans les Maures et l'Estérel en 1869. *Forêt Méditerranéenne* **10**, 218–219.

Alexandrian D, Chaudrand L, Delabraze P (1980) Prescribed fire study tour (voyage d'études aux Etats-Unis d'Amérique sur le feu prescrit). *Forêt Méditerranéenne* **II**, 229–236.

Allen KA, Denelle P, Ruiz FMS, Santana VM, Marrs RH (2016) Prescribed moorland burning meets good practice guidelines: a monitoring case study using aerial photography in the Peak District, UK. *Ecological Indicators* **62**, 76–85. doi:10.1016/j.ecolind.2015.11.030

Andrews PL (2014) Current status and future needs of the BehavePlus Fire Modeling System. *International Journal of Wildland Fire* **23**, 21–33. doi:10.1071/WF12167

Ascoli D, Bovio G (2013) Prescribed burning in Italy: issues, advances and challenges. *iForest- Biogeosciences and Forestry* **6**, 79–89. doi:10.3832/ifor0803-006

Ascoli D, Lonati M, Marzano R, Bovio G, Cavallero A, Lombardi G (2013) Prescribed burning and browsing to control tree encroachment in southern European heathlands. *Forest Ecology and Management* **289**, 69–77. doi:10.1016/j.foreco.2012.09.041

Barnett K, Parks SA, Miller C, Naughton HT (2016) Beyond fuel treatment effectiveness: characterizing interactions between fire and treatments in the US. *Forests* **7**, 237. doi:10.3390/f7100237

Battipaglia G, Savi T, Ascoli D, Castagneri D, Esposito A, Mayr S, Nardini A (2016) Effects of prescribed burning on ecophysiological, anatomical and stem hydraulic properties in *Pinus pinea* L. *Tree Physiology* **36**, 1019–1031. doi:10.1093/treephys/tpw034

Binggeli F (1997) Dix ans de brûlage dirigé dans les forêts du Massif des Maures. *Forêt Méditerranéenne* **18**, 311–317.

Botelho H, Rigolot E, Rego F, Guarnieri F, Bingelli F, Vega J, Fernandes P, Prodon R, Molina D, *et al.* (2000) FIRE TORCH: an European project to improve prescribed burning knowledge and use. In *Proceedings of The Joint Fire Science Conference and Workshop – Crossing the Millenium: Integrating Spatial Technologies and Ecological Principles for a New Age in Fire Management*. 15–17 June, Boise. (Eds L Neuenschwander and KC Ryan) pp. 173–179. University of Idaho, Moscow.

Bovio G, Ascoli D (2012) Fuoco prescritto: stato dell'arte della normativa italiana. *L'Italia Forestale e Montana* **67**, 347–358. doi:10.4129/ifm.2012.4.04

Buresti E, Sulli M (1983) Il fuoco strumento colturale? *Annali dell'Istituto Sperimentale per la Selvicoltura* **16**, 355–385.

Burrows N, McCaw L (2013) Prescribed burning in southwestern Australian forests. *Frontiers in Ecology and the Environment* **11**(s1), e25–e34. doi:10.1890/120356

Calabri G (1981) Il fuoco prescritto, una discussa tecnica per la gestione dei boschi. *Monti e Boschi* **32**, 35–42.

Calabri G (1988) L'introduction du brûlage contrôlé en Italie. In *Proceedings of the Atelier sur le Brûlage Contrôlé*. 14–18 March, Avignon. pp. 45–52. INRA-FAO-IUFRO.

Cleaves DA, Martinez J, Haines TK (2000) 'Influences on prescribed burning activity and costs in the National Forest System'. General Technical Report SRS-37, USDA Forest Service, Southern Research Station, Asheville.

Comité de Lucha contra Incendios Forestales (CLIF) (2019) 'Orientaciones estratégicas para gestión de incendios forestales en España'. Ministerio de Agricultura Pesca y Alimentación, Madrid, <https://www.miteco.gob.es/fr/biodiversidad/temas/incendios-forestales/orient_estrategicas_gestion_iiff-2019_tcm36-512358.pdf>.

Connor SE, Araújo J, van der Knaap WO, van Leeuwen JFN (2012) A long-term perspective on biomass burning in the Serra da Estrela, Portugal. *Quaternary Science Reviews* **55**, 114–124. doi:10.1016/j.quascirev.2012.08.007

Coughlan MR (2014) Farmers, flames, and forests: historical ecology of pastoral fire use and landscape change in the French Western Pyrenees, 1830–2011. *Forest Ecology and Management* **312**, 55–66. doi:10.1016/j.foreco.2013.10.021

Czuhai E, Cushwa CT (1968) 'A resumé of prescribed burnings on the Piedmont National Wildlife Refuge'. Research Note SE-86, USDA Forest Service, Asheville.

Da Ponte E, Costafreda-Aumedes S, Vega-Garcia C (2019) Lessons learned from arson wildfire incidence in reforestations and natural stands in Spain. *Forests* **10**, 229. doi:10.3390/f10030229

Davies M, Kettridge N, Stoof CR, Gray A, Ascoli D, Fernandes PM, Marrs R, Allen KA, Doerr SH, *et al.* (2016) The role of fire in UK peatland and moorland management: the need for informed, unbiased debate. *Philosophical Transactions of the Royal Society of London. Series B, Biological Sciences* **371**, 20150342. doi:10.1098/rstb.2015.0342

Davim DA, Rossa CG, Fernandes PM (2021) Survival of prescribed burning treatments to wildfire in Portugal. *Forest Ecology and Management* **493**, 119250. doi:10.1016/j.foreco.2021.119250

Di Pasquale G, Di Martino P, Mazzoleni S (2004) Forest history in the Mediterranean region. In *Recent Dynamics of the Mediterranean Vegetation and Landscape*. (Eds S Mazzoleni, G Di Pasquale, M Mulligan, P Di Martino and F Rego) pp. 13–20. John Wiley and Sons, New York.

Espinosa J, Palheiro P, Loureiro C, Ascoli D, Esposito A, Fernandes PM (2019) Fire severity mitigation by prescribed burning assessed from fire-treatment encounters in maritime pine stands. *Canadian Journal of Forest Research* **49**, 205–211. doi:10.1139/cjfr-2018-0263

Ewell DM, Nichols HT (1983) Prescribed fire monitoring in Sequoia and Kings Canyon National Parks. In *Proceedings of the Symposium and Workshop on Wilderness Fire*. USDA Forest Service General Technical Report INT-182. (Eds J Lotan, BM Kilgore, WC Fischer and RW Mutch) pp. 15–18. USDA Forest Service, Ogden.

Faivre N (Ed.) (2018) Forest fires: sparking firesmart policies in the EU. European Commission, Brussels, <https://ec.europa.eu/info/publications/forest-fires-sparking-firesmart-policies-eu_ro>.

Fernandes PM (2015) Empirical support for the use of prescribed burning as a fuel treatment. *Current Forestry Reports* **1**, 118–127. doi:10.1007/s40725-015-0010-z

Fernandes PM (2018) Scientific support to prescribed underburning in southern Europe: what do we know? *The Science of the Total Environment* **630**, 340–348. doi:10.1016/j.scitotenv.2018.02.214

Fernandes PM, Botelho HS (2004) Analysis of the prescribed burning practice in the pine forest of northwestern Portugal. *Journal of Environmental Management* **70**, 15–26. doi:10.1016/j.jenvman.2003.10.001

Fernandes PM, Loureiro C (2010) *Handbook to Plan and Use Prescribed Burning in Europe.* Universidade de Trás-os-Montes e Alto Douro, Vila Real.

Fernandes PM, Rego FC, Rigolot E (2011) The FIRE PARADOX project: towards science-based fire management in Europe. *Forest Ecology and Management* **261**, 2177–2178. doi:10.1016/j.foreco.2010.12.024

Fernandes PM, Loureiro C, Botelho H (2012) PiroPinus: a spreadsheet application to guide prescribed burning operations in maritime pine forest. *Computers and Electronics in Agriculture* **81**, 58–61. doi:10.1016/j.compag.2011.11.005

Fernandes PM, Davies GM, Ascoli D, Fernández C, Moreira F, Rigolot E, Stoof K, Vega JA, Molina D (2013) Prescribed burning in southern Europe: developing fire management in a dynamic landscape. *Frontiers in Ecology and the Environment* **11**(s1), e4–e14. doi:10.1890/120298

Finney MA (2006) An overview of FlamMap fire modeling capabilities. In *Fuels Management – How to Measure Success: Conference Proceedings*. Proceedings RMRS-P-41. (Eds PL Andrews and BW Butler) pp. 213–220. U.S. Department of Agriculture, Forest Service, Rocky Mountain Research Station, Fort Collins.

Finney MA (2007) A computational method for optimising fuel treatment locations. *International Journal of Wildland Fire* **16**, 702–711. doi:10.1071/WF06063

Ganteaume A, Camia A, Jappiot M, San-Miguel-Ayanz J, Long-Fournel M, Lampin C (2013) A review of the main driving factors of forest fire ignition over Europe. *Environmental Management* **51**, 651–662. doi:10.1007/s00267-012-9961-z

Gil-Romera G, Carrión JS, Pausas JG, Sevilla-Callejo M, Lamb HF, Fernández S, Burjachs F (2010) Holocene fire activity and vegetation response in south-eastern Iberia. *Quaternary Science Reviews* **29**, 1082–1092. doi:10.1016/j.quascirev.2010.01.006

Giuditta E, Marzaioli R, Esposito A, Ascoli D, Stinca A, Mazzoleni S, Rutigliano F (2020) Soil microbial diversity, biomass, and activity in two pine plantations of southern Italy treated with prescribed burning. *Forests* **11**, 19. doi:10.3390/f11010019

González-Pan JR (Ed.) (2012) *Quemas prescritas realizadas por los EPRIF. Método y aplicación*. Organismo Autónomo de Parques Nacionales, MAGRAMA, Madrid.

Grillo Delgado F (2002) Manejo del fuego – quemas prescritas. In *Proceeding of the IX Jornadas Forestales de Gran Canaria*, Arucas, <https://jornadasforestalesdegrancanaria.com/wp-content/uploads/2019/10/Federico-Grillo-Delgado-Manejo-del-fuego-quemas-prescritas.pdf>.

Haines TK, Busby RL, Cleaves DA (2001) Prescribed burning in the South: trends, purpose, and barriers. *Southern Journal of Applied Forestry* **25**, 149–153. doi:10.1093/sjaf/25.4.149

Keeley JE, Bond WJ, Bradstock RA, Pausas JG, Rundel PW (2011) *Fire in Mediterranean Ecosystems: Ecology, Evolution and Management*. Cambridge University Press, New York.

Keifer M (1998) Fuel load and tree density changes following prescribed fire in the giant sequoia-mixed conifer forest: the first 14 years of fire effects monitoring. In *Fire in Ecosystem Management: Shifting the Paradigm from Suppression to Prescription*. Proceedings of the Tall Timbers Fire Ecology Conference, No. 20. (Eds L Brennan and T Pruden) pp. 306–309. Tall Timbers Research Station, Tallahassee.

Lambert B (2010) The French prescribed burning network and its professional team in Pyrénées Orientales: lessons drawn from 20 years of experience. In *Best Practices of Fire Use – Prescribed Burning and Suppression Fire Programmes in Selected Case-Study Regions in Europe*. EFI Research Report 24. (Eds C Montiel and D Kraus) pp. 90–106. European Forest Institute, Joensuu.

Lambert B, Casteignau D, Costa M, Étienne M, Guiton J, Rigolot E (1999) *Analyse Après Incendie de Six Coupures de Combustible*. Editions Cardère, Montfavet.

Lázaro A, Montiel C (2010) Overview of prescribed burning policies and practices in Europe and other countries. In *Towards Integrated Fire Management – Outcomes of the European Project Fire Paradox*. EFI Research Report 23. (Eds JS Silva, F Rego, P Fernandes and E Rigolot) pp. 137–150. European Forest Institute, Joensuu.

Liacos L (1974) Present studies of history of burning in Greece. In *Proceedings of the Annual Tall Timbers Fire Ecology Conference*, No. 13. (Ed. E Komarek) pp. 65–95. Tall Timbers Research Station, Tallahassee.

Madrigal J, Romero-Vivó M, Rodríguez y Silva F (Eds) (2019) 'Definición y recomendaciones técnicas en el diseño de puntos estratégicos de gestión. "Decálogo de Valencia" para la defensa integrada frente a los incendios en la gestión del mosaico agroforestal'. Sociedad Española de Ciencias Forestales. Generalitat Valenciana, Valencia, <http://secforestales.org/sites/default/files/archivos/documentopeg.pdf>.

Ministerio de Agricultura Pesca y Alimentación (MAPA) (2019) 'Los incendios forestales en España. Decenio 2006–2015'. MAPA, Madrid.

Marino E, Hernando C, Planelles R, Madrigal J, Guijarro M, Sebastián A (2014) Forest fuel management for wildfire prevention in Spain: a quantitative SWOT analysis. *International Journal of Wildland Fire* **23**, 373–384. doi:10.1071/WF12203

Métailié JP (1981) *Le Feu Pastoral dans les Pyrénées Centrales (Barousse, Oueil, Larboust)*. Editions du CNRS, Toulouse.

Montiel C, Kraus D (Eds) (2010) *Best Practices of Fire Use – Prescribed Burning and Suppression Fire Programmes in Selected Case-Study Regions in Europe*. EFI Research Report 24. European Forest Institute, Joensuu.

Moreira F, Ascoli D, Safford H, Adams MA, Moreno JM, Pereira JM, Catry FX, Armesto J, Bond W, González ME, *et al.* (2020) Wildfire management in Mediterranean-type regions: paradigm change needed. *Environmental Research Letters* **15**, 011001. doi:10.1088/1748-9326/ab541e

Naveh Z (1975) The evolutionary significance of fire in the Mediterranean Region. *Vegetatio* **29**, 199–208. doi:10.1007/BF02390011

Pausas JG, Vallejo VR (1999) The role of fire in European Mediterranean ecosystems. In *Remote Sensing of Large Wildfires*. (Ed. E Chuvieco) pp. 3–16. Springer, Berlin.

Pinto A, Fernandes PM, Loureiro C (2014) 'Prescribed burning guide for blue gum plantations'. GIFF SA/UTAD, Vila Real.

Price OF, Pausas JG, Govender N, Flannigan M, Fernandes PM, Brooks ML, Bird RB (2015) Global patterns in fire leverage: the response of annual area burnt to previous fire. *International Journal of Wildland Fire* **24**, 297–306. doi:10.1071/WF14034

Pyne SJ (1982) *Fire in America: A Cultural History of Wildland and Rural Fire*. Princeton University Press, Princeton.

Pyne SJ (1997) *Vestal Fire. An Environmental History, Told Through Fire, of Europe and Europe's Encounter with the World*. University of Washington Press, Seattle.

Pyne SJ, Andrews PL, Laven RD (1996) *Introduction to Wildland Fire*, 2nd edn. John Wiley and Sons, New York.

Quinn-Davidson LN, Varner JM (2012) Impediments to prescribed fire across agency, landscape and manager: an example from northern California. *International Journal of Wildland Fire* **21**, 210–218. doi:10.1071/WF11017

Ray L, Kolden C, Chapin F, III (2012) A case for developing place-based fire management strategies from traditional ecological knowledge. *Ecology and Society* **17**(3), 37. doi:10.5751/ES-05070-170337

Rigolot E (1993) Le brûlage dirigé en région méditerranéenne française. In *Rencontres forestiers-chercheurs en forêt méditerranéenne*. (Ed. H Oswald) pp. 223–250. INRA Editions, Versailles.

Rigolot E (1997) 'Etude sur la caractérisation des effects causés aux écosystèmes forestiers méditerranéens par les brulages dirigés et répétés, exercice 1996, Rapport final'. Ministère de l'Environnement, Direction de la prévention et des risques, sous-direction de la prévention des risques majeurs, Paris.

Rigolot E (2000) Le brûlage dirigé en France: outil de gestion et recherches associées. *Cuadernos de la Sociedad Española de Ciencias Forestales* **9**, 165–178.

Rigolot E, Grossiord R, Guarnieri F, Mathieu E, Napoli A (1998) 'Specifications of the prescribed burning TDSS. Fire Torch, prescribed burning as a tool for the Mediterranean region: a management approach'. CEE-ENV4-CT98-0715, INRA.

Rodríguez y Silva F (2000) Bases técnicas para la elaboración de un plan regional de quemas prescritas, aplicación a la comunidad autónoma de Andalucía. *Cuadernos de la Sociedad Española de Ciencias Forestales* **9**, 253–279.

Sando RW (1969) 'The current status of prescribed burning in the Lake States'. Research Note NC-61, North Central Forest Experimental Station, USDA Forest Service, St. Paul.

Seijo F, Gray R (2012) Pre-industrial anthropogenic fire regimes in transition: the case of Spain and its implications for fire governance in Mediterranean type biomes. *Human Ecology Review* **19**, 58–69.

Silva JM (1987) Fogo controlado. *Boletim da Sociedade de Geografia de Lisboa* **103**, 95–105.

Silva JM (1997) Historique des feux contrôlés au Portugal. *Forêt Méditerranéenne* **18**, 299–310.

Silva JS, Rego FC, Fernandes P, Rigolot E (Eds) (2010) *Towards Integrated Fire Management – Outcomes of the European Project Fire Paradox.* EFI Research Report 23. European Forest Institute, Joensuu.

Stoof CR, Moore D, Fernandes PM, Stoorvogel JJ, Fernandes R, Ferreira AJD, Ritsema CJ (2013) Hot fire, cool soil. *Geophysical Research Letters* **40**, 1534–1539. doi:10.1002/grl.50299

Susmel L (1977) Ecology of systems and fire management in the Italian Mediterranean region. In *Proceedings of the Symposium on Environmental Consequences of Fire and Fuel Management in Mediterranean Ecosystems.* 1–5 August, Palo Alto. USDA Forest Service General Technical Report WO-3. (Eds HA Mooney, C Conrad and C Eugene) pp. 307–317. USDA Forest Service, Washington, DC.

Tedim F, Xanthopoulos G, Leone V (2015) Forest fires in Europe: facts and challenges. In *Wildfire Hazards, Risks and Disasters.* (Ed. D Paton) pp. 77–99. Elsevier, Amsterdam.

Tinner W, van Leeuwen JFN, Colombaroli D, Vescovi E, van der Knaap WO, Henne PD, Pasta S, D'Angelo S, La Mantia T (2009) Holocene environmental and climatic changes at Gorgo Basso, a coastal lake in southern Sicily, Italy. *Quaternary Science Reviews* **28**, 1498–1510. doi:10.1016/j.quascirev.2009.02.001

Valette JC, Vega JA, Botelho H, Gillon D, Hernando C, Ventura J (1998) Forest fire prevention through prescribed burning. Prediction of effects on trees. In *Proceedings of the III International Conference on Forest Fire Research.* 16–20 November, Coimbra. (Ed. DX Viegas) pp, 1509–1510. Associação para o Desenvolvimento da Aerodinâmica Industrial, Coimbra.

Van Wagtendonk JW, Bancroft L, Ferry G, French D, Hance J, Hickman J, McCleese W, Mutch R, Zontek F, Butts D (1982) 'Prescribed fire monitoring and evaluation guide'. National Wildfire Coordinating Group (NWCG), Washington.

Vega JA, Bará S, Gil MC (1983) Prescribed burning in pine stands for fire prevention in the NW of Spain: some results and effects. *Freiburger Waldschutz Abhandlungen* **4**, 49–74.

Vega JA, Valette JC, Rego FC, Hernando C, Gillon D, Ventura JMP, Bará S, Botelho H, Guijarro M, Houssard C, *et al.* (1994) Forest fire prevention through prescribed burning: an international cooperative project carried out in the European STEP program. In *Proceedings of the 2nd International Conference on Forest Fire Research.* 21–24 November, Coimbra. (Ed. DX Viegas) pp 75–84. Associação para o Desenvolvimento da Aerodinâmica Industrial, Coimbra.

Vega JA, Landsberg J, Bará S, Paysen T, Fontúrbel MT, Alonso M (2000) Efectos del fuego prescrito bajo arbolado de *P. pinaster* en suelos forestales de Galicia y Andalucía. *Cuadernos de la Sociedad Española de Ciencias Forestales* **9**, 123–136.

Vélez R (1981) Fire effects and fuel management in Mediterranean ecosystems in Spain. In *Proceedings of the Symposium on Dynamics and Management of Mediterranean-Type Ecosystems.* June 22–26, San Diego. (Eds CE Conrad and WC Oechel) pp. 458–463. Pacific Southwest Forest and Range Experiment Station, Forest Service, U.S. Department of Agriculture, Berkeley.

Vélez R, Vega JA (1985) *Estudios sobre Prevención y Efectos Ecológicos de los Incendios Forestales.* MAPA-ICONA, Madrid.

Waring KM, Hansen KJ, Flatley WT (2016) Evaluating prescribed fire effectiveness using permanent monitoring plot data: a case study. *Fire Ecology* **12**(3), 2–25. doi:10.4996/fireecology.1203002

Yallop AR, Thacker JI, Thomas G, Stephens M, Clutterbuck B, Brewer T, Sannier CAD (2006) The extent and intensity of management burning in the English uplands. *Journal of Applied Ecology* **43**, 1138–1148. doi:10.1111/j.1365-2664.2006.01222.x

Possibility of introducing prescribed burning in Mongolian rangelands

Jamsran Undarmaa, Yu Yoshihara, Asuka Koyama and Toshiya Okuro

Introduction

Mongolia is one of the top 11 grassland-based countries in the world (Gibson 2009), with 110 million hectares of rangelands, or 70.5% of the total land area (National Statistical Office of Mongolia 2019). Mongolia is home to more than 70 million head of rangeland livestock, as well as the home to many unique wildlife species in Eurasia. Mongolians have used the rangelands for more than 5000 years (Tseveendorj 2004) to rear livestock, and the country remains one of the few places in the world where nomadic pastoralism is still practised. Pastoralists have had centuries to acquire knowledge of the ecosystems they inhabit and the animals they raise, as well as to develop management practices that are finely tuned to an ecosystem that experiences variable processes across both space and time (Fernandez-Gimenez 2000). Recent increases in livestock numbers, changes in socioeconomic systems and the collapse of traditional sustainable land use systems have resulted in serious rangeland degradation, which could affect both dryland and other areas across the region. Therefore, there is a strong need for the restoration of degraded rangelands and

sustainable land management (Okuro 2010). Among various measures, prescribed burning is regarded as an effective tool for the restoration of degraded vegetation in grasslands. However, the effectiveness of prescribed burning in Mongolian rangelands remains debatable. In order to understand the context of current prescribed burning research and questions, it is essential to understand the extensive history of Mongolian rangelands and the people who use them.

This chapter presents a brief history of rangeland use and management in Mongolia since 2000 BCE, what we know so far about the effects of fire on Mongolian rangeland ecosystems and Mongolian people's perception of and intention for fire use. We then discuss the social and technical issues relevant to the introduction of prescribed fire as a management tool.

Seasonal movement as a traditional rangeland management practice

Mongolian pastoralists have a rich heritage of traditional rangeland management practices that have evolved over thousands of years under an extremely harsh continental climate (Fernandez-Gimenez 2000). This knowledge has been transferred from generation to generation and has been adapted as a result of new experiences and observations, coming to represent an accumulation of local knowledge (Undarmaa 2010). The herders' perceptions of the spatial and temporal variability of rangelands have been applied to traditional rangeland management and to the main strategies entailing the seasonal movements of herds. Herders never move randomly across the landscape; rather, their movements are well organised and are regulated by complex social systems (Miller and Sheehy 2008). Patterns of movement vary widely across Mongolia, depending on variations in topography, soil, climate, vegetation and livestock types, and are divided into four types according to region (Bazargur 2005):

1. Altai mountainous region: in the regions of the Mongolian Altai and the western part of the Gobi–Altai Mountains, herders favour the upper and northern slopes of mountains at >2700 m a.s.l. in summer, move down to valleys with an elevation of 1500 m a.s.l. in autumn and then move to mid-elevation mountains with an elevation of 2200–2600 m a.s.l. during winter. In spring, herders move down to the southern slopes and pediments of mountains with an elevation of 1600–2000 m a.s.l.
2. Khangai–Khentii mountainous region: throughout the northern part of Mongolia, herders use several patterns of seasonal movements between mountains, river basins and valleys, depending on topography, but the distance between the seasonal rangelands is 10–20 km, which is shorter than in the other regions
3. Central and eastern plains region: in this region, with flat and rolling plains, herders stay with their livestock on the southern slopes of hummocks and on low-elevation mountains in winter–spring, move north in summer and then move to the southern plains in autumn

4. Eastern Gobi region: in the southern part of Mongolia, in the desert steppe, herders move frequently, with the total distance travelled reaching around 100 km each year, from lowlands or wide valleys in summer–autumn to the southern slopes of low-elevation mountains or hummocks in winter–spring.

History of institutional arrangements for rangeland management

The traditional rangeland management practices detailed above have been affected by socioeconomic and political changes during the history of Mongolia; as a result, institutional arrangements, such as rangeland use and land tenure regulations for allocating and managing resources and rangeland health, have also changed (Fernandez-Gimenez 1999).

During the Tribal Society Period (2000 BCE–3rd century CE), nomadic pastoralism became the main form of subsistence of the people inhabiting the territory we now know as Mongolia. Tribes, clans and chiefdoms governed the rangelands, and land possession and land ownership did not exist (Tseveendorj 2004). During that period, a kind of comanagement system offered people equal opportunities to use the land, ensured their rights to campsites, rangelands and livestock herding and regulated four-season mobility inside or outside their given territory.

The Xiongnu Empire, the first Mongolian state, from the 3rd century BCE to the 1st century CE, allowed nomads freedom of movement with their herds and the use of rangelands. Small groups of nomadic households or tribes, as main users of rangeland, owned livestock and decided on the daily use of the rangelands by themselves, while the powerful government ensured their safety (Tseveendorj 2004). This kind of governance and pattern of rangeland use was common for all the ancient empires in Mongolia until the 13th century CE.

Following the establishment of the Mongol Empire in 1206 CE, the state owned the rangelands, water sources and other natural resources, and offered herders equal opportunities to exercise their rights to use campsites and rangelands to rear livestock, and to share lands during droughts and harsh winters. Thus, the state recognised herders' traditional practices and customs, granting them informal control (Fernandez-Gimenez 1999), which entitled them to micromanage livestock production and rangeland use.

After the revolution in 1921 and the foundation of the Mongolian People's Republic, all herders had joined livestock cooperatives by 1959. During the socialist period, rangelands and livestock production were entirely controlled and managed by the cooperatives and state-owned farms on the basis of scientific knowledge coupled with traditional practices (Jagvaral 1987), and the basic tenets of traditional management practices at the micro- or herding group level were upheld and enforced.

Following the abrupt transition to a free-market economy and large-scale privatisation in the early 1990s, almost all the state-owned livestock were transferred to herders, and the state ceased to enforce customary rangeland use rules and norms. As a result, the number of livestock increased, with the largest number of livestock (70.969 million) in the past 100 years was registered in 2019 (National Statistical Office of Mongolia 2019). This rapid increase in the number of livestock has overwhelmed the carrying capacity of many rangelands. Under this situation, many herders returned to pre-collective ways, practising locally recognised land use rights and alternating campsites to maintain freedom of movement. Although these herders faced difficulties in implementing such customary practices, the long history of private livestock ownership and production in Mongolia supported the traditional practices.

With each political–economic regime in Mongolia, there is clear evidence that dual formal and informal regulation of rangeland use existed and was apparently successful in maintaining the sustainable use of rangelands. For the most part, formal regulation was enforced by the state or other governing institution that defined social and resource boundaries and controlled livestock production, whereas informal regulation was enforced within local herding communities (Fernandez-Gimenez 2006; Undargaa and McCarthy 2016).

To summarise, the main strategy of traditional rangeland management in Mongolia is seasonal movement, which can adapt to a highly variable environment, followed by knowledge of rangelands and livestock and strong regulation of rangeland use at different institutional levels. These strategies have kept the rangeland ecosystems intact until recently. However, a thorough examination of the historical evidence suggests that herders have never used fire as a tool for rangeland management or restoration.

Knowledge and experience of fire in Mongolian rangelands

Although there are no historical records of fire use and management by herders in Mongolia, wildfire itself is a common event and is recognised as essential to regulating both forest and rangeland ecosystems there.

The spring (main) wildfire season in Mongolia runs from late February to early June, with a peak in April–May, which accounts for 80% of all annual wildfires (Goldammer 2002; Chuluunbaatar 2012). The autumn fire season runs from September to late November or early December (Chuluunbaatar 2012; Ministry of Nature, Environment and Tourism (MNET) 2019). The *Forest Law* of Mongolia defines the fire hazard periods as 20 March–10 June and 20 September–10 November.

Low levels of precipitation, strong winds, highly flammable pine and larch forest and steppe vegetation increase the risk of wildfires. Steppe and forest fires in Mongolia tend to be large in extreme weather conditions and will often invade surrounding areas, causing massive damage. For example, 302 wildfires were recorded during the extremely dry period from the winter of 2017 to spring of 2018, during which 137 500 ha of forest and 1 018 600 ha of rangeland burned, at an estimated environmental and economic cost of 117.2 billion

Mongolian tugrik (≈US$41.1 million in October 2020; MNET 2019).

The fire regime in Mongolia varies considerably depending on ecosystem type, with burn intervals estimated to range from 10 to 175 years in forested systems and being, on average, 10 years in grassland systems (Johnson *et al.* 2009). In Mongolia, there are, on average, 50–60 forest fires and 80–100 steppe fires annually (Goldammer 2002). An increase in fire frequency in forested areas has been reported since the introduction of the market economy in the 1990s owing to a sharp rise in the number of people using forests (Tsogtbaatar 2004; Johnson *et al.* 2009). Recent deforestation in Mongolia has been attributed to the effect of forest fires, as well as to increases in the number of livestock and the demand for timber (Tsogtbaatar 2004). Therefore, there is growing concern that frequent fires could have a significant impact on regeneration processes and species composition (Otoda *et al.* 2013b).

The effects of smoke from wildfires on air quality are also of great concern in Mongolia. Greenhouse gas emissions from forest fires from 1988 to 1997 were estimated to be 2- to 10-fold the Mongolian marginal emissions (Chuluunbaatar 2012). Air pollution in Ulaanbaatar, the capital, with a population of 1.5 million, is a serious environmental issue. However, little research has been conducted on the effect of wildfires on suspended particulate matter in urban areas.

Conversely, appropriate fire intervals may promote the regeneration of species with disturbance-dependent traits and a short life cycle (Otoda *et al.* 2013a). Nevertheless, little is known about the positive and negative effects of changes in the fire disturbance regime in rangeland ecosystems.

Information and infrastructure for fire management were first introduced, for the purpose of fire suppression and prevention, by the Soviet Union in the 1920s (Johnson *et al.* 2009).

In 1969, the Mongolian Fire Protection and Aerial Patrol Service was established to provide early detection of and a rapid response to wildfires, and employed 'smoke jumpers' and helicopter abseilers. Smoke jumpers on routine aerial patrols detected a high percentage of the fires and handled approximately 90% of the suppression workload. Until recently, a division of the armed forces known as the Civil Defence centrally managed fires in Mongolia, and maintained all training regimes, equipment and personnel, with little support from local communities. Since the early 1990s, government departments have been restructured, with new departments created at all levels (national, provincial and district) with responsibility for disaster management, including fire suppression, thus significantly changing the fire management infrastructure in Mongolia (Johnson *et al.* 2009).

The main government body in charge of fires in Mongolia is the National Emergency Management Agency (NEMA), which was established in 2004. The main duties of NEMA are the implementation of laws, regulations and state policies on disaster protection, organising and managing disaster protection activities at all levels and providing professional management. The Fire Prevention Department of NEMA manages fire prevention, preparedness, risk reduction, rescue and fire suppression, and exercises government control over all types of fires. Its primary function is to provide early detection of and response to fires. Nowadays, moderate-resolution imaging spectroradiometer (MODIS) satellite imagery, obtained under contract from the Information and Computer Centre, National Remote Sensing Centre, is used to detect fires, with fire and rescue teams serving as ground crew in fire-fighting efforts. The MODIS data are received online at the central offices in Ulaanbaatar and then distributed to the provinces. The Meteorological Agency provides precipitation and temperature data used to determine fire danger ratings. The Ministry of Nature and Environment is responsible for issuing fire alerts and administering laws, policies and other matters, but does not fight fires.

Provincial emergency departments are responsible for fire management at the local level. They maintain fire teams (consisting of professional personnel) by contract, as well as equipment for fighting fires. In each soum (the smallest administrative unit), the governor, state inspector and chief of police, who make up the soum 'commission', are responsible for coordinating fire-fighting efforts. The soum may have fire-fighting units or citizen volunteers. One of the tasks of the commission is to ensure that all volunteers are local and have fire-fighting training and experience. In the event of severe fires, the soums request expert fire-fighting crews from the province and state. The budget for disaster management, including fire, is provided by the state and province.

The *Law on Fire Safety* of Mongolia requires citizens to report forest and steppe fires in a timely manner to the governor's office or provincial emergency department, and to work in fire-fighting volunteer units. Citizens are required to receive fire-fighting training, but not with special equipment such as fire trucks.

Scientific knowledge of rangeland management, including prescribed fire, has been used in Mongolia since the latter half of the 20th century. Some textbooks on rangeland management (Research Institute of Animal Husbandry 1983; Jadamba *et al.* 2005; Jigjidsuren 2005) state that prescribed burning can be used to improve forage value and yield by removing remnant litter and old stems, which significantly lower the quality of hay and prevent the full use of grass stands. Those books describe burning as promoting an increase in the density of the herbage and its productivity, improving plant consumption, increasing the development of rhizomatous and tufted grasses and decreasing wormwood (*Artemisia adamsii*), forbs and sedges. They also mention the importance of the timing of burning and site selection. For example, prescribed burning in late spring and autumn could cause the disappearance of valuable plants; burning in autumn makes it difficult to retain snow and thus accumulate moisture in the soil; and burning in late spring damages the regeneration buds of the plants. Thus, these books recommend that only shrub-free grasslands with high soil moisture content, such as wetlands, are suitable for prescribed burning, and recommend burning in early spring,

when the soil is still frozen, immediately after the snow melts, in calm weather.

Although there are no records of empirical studies of the effects of fire on rangeland vegetation during the socialist period, field experiments have been conducted since the beginning of the 21st century. Tuvshintogtokh and Urgamal (2007) reported that frequent fire, combined with grazing, may induce replacement of dominant species and decrease in productivity.

For the restoration of degraded rangelands, several fire trials have been conducted with the support of international organisations. For example, prescribed burning was performed in degraded rangelands in northern Mongolia (Bayangol Soum, Selenge Province) under the United Nations Development Programme project Sustainable Grassland Management to remove wormwood in 2004–05 (Jadamba *et al.* 2005). Other fire treatments were conducted in central (Yosonzuil Soum, Uvurkhangai Province) and southern (Guchin-Us Soum, Uvurkhangai Province) Mongolia to restore communities of *Achnatherum splendens*, a perennial tussock grass known as a key resource (*sensu* Scoones 1996), by burning litter and old culms under the Asian Development Bank project Water Point and Extension Station Establishment for Poor Herding Families (J. Undarmaa, unpubl. data). Although these projects did not provide any quantitative empirical data, because they were intended for training pastoralists rather than academic research, quick recovery and rejuvenation of degraded vegetation have been clearly observed (Figure 14.1).

More recently, detailed prescribed burning experiments were conducted in early spring in two types of degraded grasslands in Mongolia (Figure 14.2) by Japanese and Mongolian ecologists. Burning significantly reduced the seed bank density of both annual and perennial species and the seedling density of the palatable grass *Cleistogenes squarrosa*, although *C. squarrosa* showed significantly greater vegetative growth in burned plots (Figure 14.3). The floristic composition showed small changes after burning, depending on the preburning vegetation, but cover of the unpalatable

Figure 14.1: Prescribed burning of declining *Achnatherum splendens* community in Yosonzuil Soum, Uvurkhangai Province, Mongolia. (a) Before and (b) after burning in April 2010. (c) Regrowth of *A. splendens* after burning (August 2011) and (d) decline of *A. splendens* in the unburned control plot (August 2011).

sub-shrub *A. adamsii* decreased after burning. Thus, the reduced seed bank density caused by burning had less of an effect on vegetation composition due to vegetative regrowth of predominantly perennial species with less seed recruitment. However, burning suppressed the unpalatable *A. adamsii* and hastened growth of the palatable *C. squarrosa*, an attractive outcome for livestock production, especially in overgrazed areas with low forage palatability. These findings illustrate the possibility of using prescribed burning in spring as a restoration tool in degraded Mongolian steppe, and the importance of site-specific

conditions for understanding post-fire recovery (Yoshihara *et al.* 2015).

Another fire experiment was conducted in a degraded grassland to compare the effectiveness of prescribed burning in spring with that of seasonal mowing (spring, summer and summer+autumn) as tools to restore degraded grasslands. After the burning and mowing treatments, soil properties and total plant biomass did not differ among treatments. The biomass and number of flowering shoots of *A. adamsii* were decreased by spring burning and growing season mowing, due to the disappearance of woody shoots (Koyama *et al.*

Figure 14.2: Prescribed burning experiment conducted in degraded grasslands in the Hustai National Park, Töv Province, Mongolia (April 2012).

2016). Although the loss of woody shoots may increase a plant's investment in current-year shoots, prescribed burning in spring would reduce the biomass and reproduction of *A. adamsii* overall as a result of the loss of woody shoots (Drewa *et al.* 2006). Conversely, spring mowing had a less negative effect on the biomass of *A. adamsii* due to an increase in new shoots (Koyama *et al.* 2016). Thus, the results of the study suggest that spring burning

has the potential to control undesirable sub-shrubs due to the loss of woody shoots, but that spring mowing may not be a useful management tool in the Mongolian steppe (Koyama *et al.* 2016).

Scientific, technical and social issues regarding the introduction of prescribed fire

Care is needed in introducing prescribed burning into grasslands without a history of fire management, as in Mongolia. Recent studies have shown that prescribed burning could be an effective tool for the restoration of degraded Mongolian rangelands by reducing the dominance of undesirable (unpalatable) plants and accelerating the growth of desirable (palatable) plants for livestock production. However, the effectiveness of prescribed burning remains debatable because of its site dependency. For example, spring burning would accelerate the decline of plant production in sparsely vegetated grasslands by over-grazing (Yoshihara *et al.* 2015). Because the recovery pattern after burning differs markedly depending on the preburning vegetation communities, the existing community must be considered when using burning as a restoration tool in over-grazed Mongolian grassland.

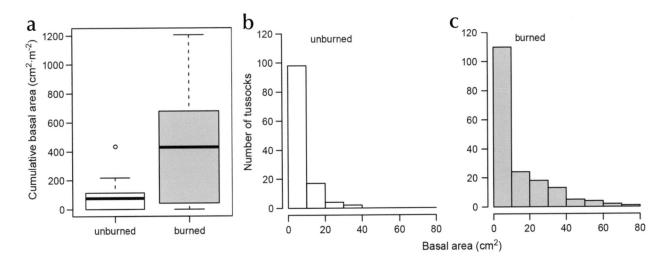

Figure 14.3: (a) Cumulative basal area of palatable *Cleistogenes squarrosa* tussocks in unburned and burned plots. The boxes indicate 75th, 50th and 25th percentiles, and whiskers indicate 90th and 10th percentiles. Circles show outliers. (b, c) Size class distribution of the basal area in unburned (b) and burned (c) areas (Yoshihara *et al.* 2015).

Vegetation responses to prescribed burning, as well as mowing treatments, likely change depending on external factors such as climatic variation and grazing impact. In addition, the introduction of prescribed burning into degraded rangelands has various potential risks (MacDougall and Turkington 2007; Valkó et al. 2014). A long-term evaluation of vegetation responses to grassland management is needed so as to better quantify the effectiveness of the introduction of this management tool for the restoration of degraded Mongolian rangelands.

Herders perceived fire negatively because they were unaware of any benefits resulting from it (e.g. rejuvenation of useful plants, improvement of pasture quality for livestock grazing; Johnson et al. 2009). The results of our informal interviews with local land managers also showed that they have little interest in introducing prescribed burning for rangeland restoration and improvement. Another reason for this, other than a lack of knowledge about the benefits of prescribed burning, is that local land managers do not have adequate technology and equipment to use and control fire. However, there is still a demand for environmentally friendly and economically affordable restoration technologies. In Hustai National Park, where the prescribed burning experiments were conducted, the land manager recognised the potential applicability of fire management as a restoration tool and permitted the experiments in accordance with the Law on Fire Safety and other legal regulations. Nevertheless, several steps must first be followed to establish appropriate fire management technologies.

In conclusion, to make prescribed burning an acceptable tool for rangeland management in Mongolia in the future, it is crucial to disseminate information on the ecological, economic and labour benefits of fire, based on scientific knowledge, to stakeholders and to support the transfer of essential technologies for fire control.

References

Bazargur (2005) Geography of Pastoral Animal Husbandry. [In Mongolian] Research Institute of Geoecology, Mongolian Academy of Sciences, Ulaanbaatar.

Chuluunbaatar T (2012) Protecting the Mongolian Forest From Fire. Bitpress Publishing, Ulaanbaatar.

Drewa P, Peters DC, Havstad K (2006) Population and clonal level responses of a perennial grass following fire in the northern Chihuahuan Desert. Oecologia 150, 29–39. doi:10.1007/s00442-006-0502-4

Fernandez-Gimenez M (1999) Sustaining the steppes: a geographical history of pastoral land use in Mongolia. Geographical Review 89, 315–342. doi:10.1111/j.1931-0846.1999.tb00222.x

Fernandez-Gimenez M (2000) The role of Mongolian nomadic pastoralist's ecological knowledge in rangeland management. Ecological Applications 10, 1318–1326. doi:10.1890/1051-0761(2000)010[1318:TROMNP]2.0.CO;2

Fernandez-Gimenez M (2006) Land use and land tenure in Mongolia: a brief history and current issues. Proceedings RMRS-P-39. In Rangelands of Central Asia: Proceedings of the Conference on Transformations, Issues, and Future Challenges. 27 January, Salt Lake City. (Eds DJ Bedunah, ED McArthur and M Fernandez-Gimenez) pp. 30–36. U.S. Department of Agriculture, Forest Service, Rocky Mountain Research Station, Fort Collins, <https://www.fs.usda.gov/treesearch/pubs/22866>.

Gibson JD (2009) Grasses and Grassland Ecology. Oxford University Press, New York.

Goldammer JG (2002) Fire situation in Mongolia. International Forest Fire News 26, 75–83.

Jadamba D, Altanzul T, Batjargal N (2005) Technique for Restoration of Degraded Rangelands. [In Mongolian] Munkhiin Useg, Ulanbaataar.

Jagvaral (1987) Some Economic Issues of Socialist Agriculture. [In Mongolian] State Publisher, Ulaanbaatar.

Jigjidsuren S (2005) Rangeland Management. [In Mongolian] Admon, Ulanbaataar.

Johnson D, Oyunsanaa B, Myers RL, Babler M (2009) 'Fire management assessment of the Eastern Steppe, Mongolia'. GFI Technical Report. The Nature Conservancy, Arlington.

Koyama A, Kubo D, Yoshihara Y, Undarmaa J, Okuro T (2016) Response of degraded vegetation to introduction of prescribed burning or mowing management in a Mongolian steppe. Grassland Science 62, 37–44. doi:10.1111/grs.12113

MacDougall AS, Turkington R (2007) Does the type of disturbance matter when restoring disturbance-dependent grasslands? Restoration Ecology 15, 263–272. doi:10.1111/j.1526-100X.2007.00209.x

Miller D, Sheehy D (2008) The relevance of Owen Lattimore's writing for nomadic research and development in inner Asia. Nomadic Peoples 12(2), 103–115. doi:10.3167/np.2008.120207

Ministry of Nature, Environment and Tourism (MNET) (2019) *Report on the State of the Environment of Mongolia, 2017–2018*. MNET, Ulaanbaatar.

National Statistical Office of Mongolia (2019) *Mongolian Statistical Yearbook*. National Statistical Office, Ulaanbaatar.

Okuro T (2010) Current status of desertification issues with special reference to sustainable provision of ecosystem services in northeast Asia. *Global Environmental Research* **14**, 3–10.

Otoda T, Sakamoto K, Hirobe M, Undarmaa J, Yoshikawa K (2013a) Influences of anthropogenic disturbances on the dynamics of white birch (*Betula platyphylla*) forests at the southern boundary of the Mongolian forest–steppe. *Journal of Forest Research* **18**, 82–92. doi:10.1007/s10310-011-0324-z

Otoda T, Doi T, Sakamoto K, Hirobe M, Nachin B, Yoshikawa K (2013b) Frequent fires may alter the future composition of the boreal forest in northern Mongolia. *Journal of Forest Research* **18**, 246–255. doi:10.1007/s10310-012-0345-2

Research Institute of Animal Husbandry (1983) *Manual for Improvement of Rangelands and Hay Making Lands*. [In Mongolian] State Publisher, Ulaanbaatar.

Scoones I (1996) New directions in pastoral development in Africa. In *Living With Uncertainty: New Directions in Pastoral Development in Africa*. (Ed. I Scoones) pp. 1–36. Intermediate Technology Publications, London.

Tseveendorj D (Ed.) (2004) *History of Mongolia*. Vol. 1. [In Mongolian] State Publisher, Ulaanabaatar.

Tsogtbaatar J (2004) Deforestation and reforestation needs in Mongolia. *Forest Ecology and Management* **201**, 57–63. doi:10.1016/j.foreco.2004.06.011

Tuvshintogtokh I, Urgamal M (2007) Fire effects on productivity and community dynamics of Mongolian grasslands. *International Forest Fire News* **36**, 67–75.

Undargaa S, McCarthy JF (2016) Beyond property: co-management and pastoral resource access in Mongolia. *World Development* **77**, 367–379. doi:10.1016/j.worlddev. 2015.08.012

Undarmaa J (2010) Involvement of local communities in restoration of ecosystem services in Mongolian rangeland. *Global Environmental Research* **14**, 79–86.

Valkó O, Török P, Deák B, Tóthmérész B (2014) Review: prospects and limitations of prescribed burning as a management tool in European grasslands. *Basic and Applied Ecology* **15**, 26–33. doi:10.1016/j.baae.2013. 11.002

Yoshihara Y, Koyama A, Undarmaa J, Okuro T (2015) Prescribed burning experiments for restoration of degraded semi-arid Mongolian steppe. *Plant Ecology* **216**, 1649–1658. doi:10.1007/s11258-015-0548-7

15

Prescribed fires of the future: technology and fire

Dirac Twidwell, Rheinhardt Scholtz and Victoria Donovan

The future of fire management depends on critical choices regarding societal visions for fire function in nature relative to advances in technology. Technology can be used to extend efforts that seek to control fire in nature, reduce its variability and attempt to make the system 'more predictable' (Figure 15.1a). Or, rather, technology can be used to embrace critical ranges of fire variability and its role as a driver of ecosystem structure and function (Figure 15.1b). Over the past century, the prevailing use of technology in fire management has been to reinforce policies and practices that seek to limit variability in fire's role as a driver of ecological function and biological organisation. This paradigm became the prevailing approach to fire management around the world following the displacement of indigenous peoples who thrived with fire (Twidwell *et al.* 2020). Although the pursuit to limit variability in fire clearly has a place in fire management today, relatively little effort has been made in comparison to expand technological applications into the mainstream prescribed fire sector to facilitate broader functioning of fire and promote critical ranges of variation for ecosystem function.

Arguably, global change in fire represents one of the greatest sources of anthropogenically driven global environmental change this century (Bowman *et al.* 2011; Archibald *et al.* 2013). In general, humanity's relationship with fire has shifted rapidly from fire promotion to fire extermination. Billions of dollars are now spent each year in an attempt to minimise or eliminate fire occurrence, control its spread and minimise extreme behaviours. In stark contrast, intentional fire ignitions for purposes of resource management were commonplace for several thousand years and gave rise to the world's expansive grassland, savannas and pyrophytic fire-tolerant forest ecosystems. Efforts to minimise fire follow the general tendencies of ecosystem management in the 20th century (Holling and Meffe 1996). The prevailing view was that ecosystems could be held at a desired equilibrium (Twidwell *et al.* 2013a), which better serve humanity's interests (Chapin *et al.* 2009). However, simplifying fire in nature has eroded the resilience of many pyric systems (Nowacki and Abrams 2008), leading to a suite of undesirable outcomes that have increased, not reduced, the vulnerability

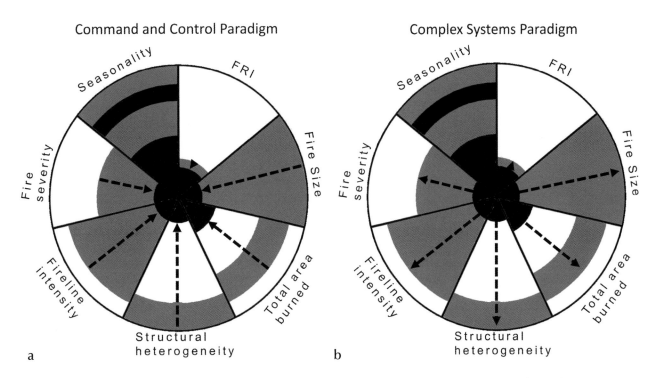

Figure 15.1: (a) Conceptual representation of how fire regime characteristics have changed due to the 20th century's 'command and control' paradigm in fire management and (b) a future vision of fire consistent with the complex systems paradigm informed by modern resilience theory. Each piece of the pie represents a characteristic of the fire regime adapted from Twidwell *et al.* (2020). Grey fill represents a pre-settlement era for the Great Plains grasslands of North America, where indigenous groups long coexisted with fire (Twidwell *et al.* 2020). Black fill represents contemporary ranges of variation imposed on the culture of prescribed fire (Twidwell *et al.* 2020). Arrows indicate how technology can be used to influence each fire regime characteristic based on the ideals of command and control (a) versus a complex systems approach (b). FRI, fire return interval.

of human lives and infrastructures to more extreme and large wildfire events.

The pitfalls of this global experiment with fire have led to various calls for change and, specifically, finding ways to coexist with the occurrence of fire in nature (Moritz *et al.* 2014). This calls for the fire management community to find innovative ways to coexist rather than continuing to assume humans can completely control fire as a force of nature (Moritz *et al.* 2014; Schoennagel *et al.* 2017). Coexistence requires a renewed focus on prescribed fire as central to managing ecosystems, but prescribed fire will also need to evolve to meet the broader sustainability challenges emerging in society. Given the increasing role of technology in everyday life, technological innovation holds considerable promise for prescribed fire management.

Yet, technology needs to be applied to support broader applications of fire in resource management (Figure 15.1b), resist attempts to overly control and minimise prescribed fire occurrence and behaviour, and promote greater complexity and heterogeneity in ecosystem structure and function. In this chapter we describe many ways in which technology can foster an era that embraces critical ranges of variation in the fire process and overcome tendencies to leverage technology only to command control over fire. Specifically, technological innovation is poised to help address three major issues that have plagued the prescribed fire community: (1) limited workforce capacity; (2) uncertainty in vegetation or habitat responses; and (3) the inability to scale-up prescribed fire to meet regional conservation goals.

Expanding workforce capacity

A lack of resources is commonly referenced as a major barrier for conducting prescribed fires and meeting resource objectives (Weir 2009). Even though funds allocated to wildfire response and suppression are growing, the same investments are not expected for the prescribed fire sector (Moritz *et al.* 2014; Topik 2015). Given workforce limitations, unmanned aerial vehicles (UAVs) represent one of the only existing transformative technologies to expand prescribed fire operational capabilities. The integration of UAVs in wildfire management is already underway and includes multiple benefits, such as supporting incidence awareness, earlier spot fire detection that allows more rapid suppression capabilities, improved allocation of personnel, continuous updating of fire size and behaviour and better visibility during dense smoke or low light levels (Twidwell *et al.* 2020). These same benefits have the potential to be transferred to the prescribed fire sector. Prescribed fire operations have always relied on on-the-ground crews for all aspects of a prescribed fire, including monitoring, ignition and spot fire suppression. Innovations using UAVs could revolutionise all these practices.

The lead author of this chapter (DT) was part of a team that pioneered UAV technology for fire ignitions (Beachly *et al.* 2016; Twidwell *et al.* 2016a), downscaling technologies used for helicopter-based aerial ignitions. At present, UAV technology is operationalised using the same approach as manned aircraft. One operator controls one UAV, which greatly limits applications. The true promise of UAV technology for prescribed fire applications lies in the ability to control a cooperative swarm of UAVs with a single operator (Twidwell *et al.* 2016a). UAVs can already be programmed to control multiple UAVs to operate as a coordinated unit. Distance-based constraints can be programmed to fly multiple UAVs in close proximity to each other while avoiding collisions. These programs also allow UAVs to be semiautonomous, equipped with sensors that determine where it is safe to fly, when conditions are optimal to drop delayed aerial ignition devices and when to reconfigure the UAV swarm to optimise the ignition pattern (Twidwell *et al.* 2016a). A cooperative swarm of UAVs for ignition purposes can also replace the need to position personnel within burn units for the purpose of conducting interior ignitions. This can help reduce common causes of serious prescribed fire injuries, which are not usually the result of the fire itself but rather due to accidents involving all-terrain vehicles or heavy machinery (Twidwell *et al.* 2015). All of this technology brings unprecedented capacity, particularly aerial ignition capacity, to prescribed burners. This accelerates operational capacity because helicopter-based ignitions are expensive, cannot be conducted by most prescribed burners and are relatively risky (manned aviation-related fatalities account for 26% of all firefighter deaths in the US since 2000; Butler *et al.* 2015).

Reducing uncertainty

Moving towards a future where prescribed fires manage for critical ranges of variability (Figure 15.1b) requires a better understanding of the complexity of fire. This has been oversimplified in rangelands. The current narrative focuses on areas that were burned and then comparisons are made to areas that were not burned. In addition, fire is often discussed as a single, discrete event or treatment rather than a critical ecological process that is part of a long-term disturbance regime (or long-term management strategy). Both viewpoints ignore many important aspects of rangeland fire regimes and how those factors interact to drive ecological structure and function (Twidwell *et al.* 2020). Ultimately, more awareness is needed within the prescribed fire community on how the modern prescribed fire culture has greatly changed fire regimes, which fire regime components have been changed and how those changes are going to affect desired resource management goals. Changing long-held fire regimes is fundamentally no different than changes in the climate system, and we should fundamentally expect major shifts in ecological function in rangelands given that fire has been a dominant structuring force in the Earth system for millennia (Bowman *et al.* 2009).

Managing for greater variability in fire processes brings greater complexity, but also uncertainty, to rangelands. Higher-quality data are needed to advance fire and meet societal information demands (Kolden 2020). More timely information on post-fire vegetation responses could greatly reduce uncertainty among fire practitioners and concerns within the general public. Uncertainty leads to misinformation and ultimately limits prescribed fire adoption.

Addressing misinformation with technology

As technology continues to advance, more timely tracking of vegetation and other important ecological indicators has become possible. One such example is the availability of remotely sensed imagery, which has revolutionised how we study global ecological processes and made it possible to track vegetation changes in closed ecosystems such as forests. In contrast, this remains a challenge in open ecosystems, such as rangelands, savannas and grasslands, which usually recover shortly after a fire has passed. As a result, many fires, especially smaller fires, often go undetected. Therefore, metrics such as burned area can be underestimated from satellite-derived data alone (Scholtz *et al.* 2020). Data platforms like the Rangeland Analysis Platform (https://rangelands.app/) can bridge this tracking gap and now afford opportunities to track trends in rangeland vegetation over time anywhere in the western US. When combined with geospatial information of fire occurrence data (e.g. LAND-FIRE (Rollins 2009) or moderate-resolution imaging spectroradiometer (MODIS; Justice *et al.* 2002; Giglio *et al.* 2018)) or local knowledge where prescribed fires have been implemented, it is now possible, for the first time, to track vegetation responses for any prescribed fire or wildfire.

Misinformation on the effects of fire in rangelands is rampant within the general public and needs to be addressed if prescribed fire is to play a large role in the future. Despite decades of fire research in grasslands showing relatively rapid rates of recovery following wildfire, a persistent belief exists in the Great Plains that fires during drought will cause desertification and a persistent, large-scale bare ground state (Neary 2009; Tanaka *et al.* 2011). To mitigate erosion concerns, reseeding, deferred grazing or other rehabilitation treatments are often incentivised following wildfire and prioritised over other treatments to alleviate potential societal or landowner concerns (Gates *et al.* 2017; Donovan *et al.* 2020). An analysis of 1390 large wildfires in the Great Plains of North America from 2000 to 2018 showed no such evidence, even for wildfires occurring during more severe drought conditions (Donovan *et al.* 2020). Instead, grasses and forbs recovered relatively rapidly at the scale of wildfires, and persistent increases in bare ground were only observed as a localised phenomenon. We showcase this analysis as an example of the computational power that is becoming available. Annual tracking of vegetation response following fire is now possible (e.g. Figure 15.2) and readily available for prescribed fire practitioners to self-monitor vegetation trends over time and adapt accordingly.

Misinformation on fire effects is also due to fundamental misunderstandings on how fire functions in rangelands. Again, innovations in technology and spatial analysis make it possible to better capture this complexity and address misunderstandings or misinformation. Prescribed fire is often viewed as a homogeneous process, giving the impression that a uniform treatment was applied. This never occurs for any sizeable fire. Heterogeneity in the system before the fire drives variability in many fire regime components, and variability in the fire process subsequently drives heterogeneity in post-fire responses. Failing to account for this type of spatial complexity leads to heightened uncertainty in prescribed fire managers' expectations of the post-fire response environment. Although we recognise that assumptions of homogeneity stem from a long history of homogeneity-based training within the rangeland ecology discipline (Fuhlendorf *et al.* 2017), spatial imaging is advanced enough to capture information on

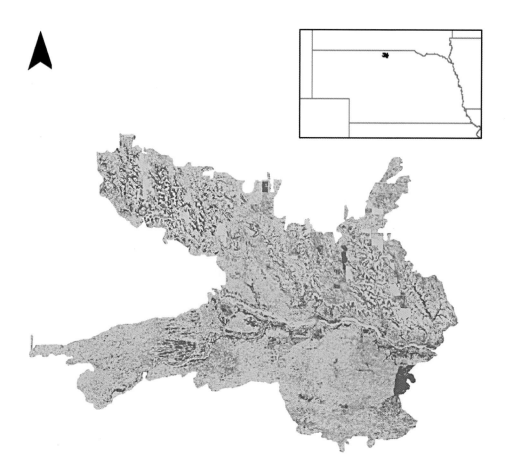

Figure 15.2: Advanced spatial imaging of vegetation change revealed rapid recovery of perennial forb and grass cover for the Region 24 Complex wildfire that burned in a record-drought year (2012) within the Nebraska Sandhills. Lighter areas depict locations with no change in perennial grass and forb cover between 2011 and 2017. Darker areas indicate locations where perennial grass and forb cover changed, which largely occurred due to widespread tree mortality and forest stand collapse along a northern riparian corridor (Uden *et al.* 2019). These types of comprehensive spatial imaging products capture greater complexity in fire and were used in combination with smaller-scale field-based assessments (Arterburn *et al.* 2018) to address concerns over potential fire-induced destabilisation and erosion in Sandhills prairie. The inset shows the location of the Region 24 Complex wildfire within the state of Nebraska.

many fire regime components at highly detailed resolutions. Fire intensity, fire severity and temporal aspects such as fire return interval all have spatial context and are not actually independent metrics (Figure 15.3).

To illustrate, fire return interval is usually described as a temporal metric of a fire regime and depicts how often a particular location burned over a specified period of time; however, it is best depicted as a metric capable of capturing spatial heterogeneity resulting from patterns of burned and unburned patches over the course of multiple

fire events (Figure 15.3). We recently used spatial imaging technology to quantify fine-scale spatial complexity in fire within long-standing treatments at the Konza Prairie Long-term Ecological Research Station in Kansas (USA; Plate 16; D. Twidwell, unpubl. data). The customary practice is to assume fire behaviour is homogeneous both within and across treatment units, as well as consistent over time; yet, spatial heterogeneity in both fire occurrence and fire intensity is known to contribute to variation in rangeland vegetation response that goes unaccounted for when assuming uniform fire

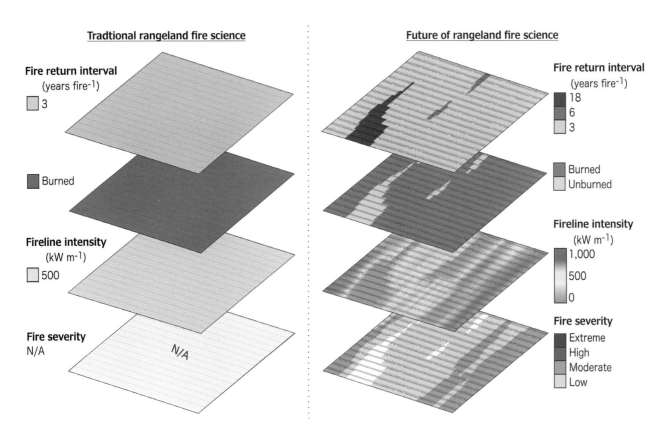

Figure 15.3: Comparison of traditional viewpoints of the fire process in rangelands versus a more realistic portrayal of the complexity of fire that drives rangeland structure and function. Illustrations by Christine Bielski.

behaviour (Twidwell *et al.* 2009; Fuhlendorf *et al.* 2018). This is the problem of making this assumption for users of prescribed fire. Fire is fundamentally different than other treatments used to manage rangelands (e.g. herbicides), and heterogeneity in the fire process needs to be considered to reduce self-imposed uncertainty in post-fire ecological responses. This is a simple example, but such approaches could be expanded beyond this field-scale example to incorporate future advances in satellite-based technology (e.g. using MODIS or other technologies to capture more than fire presence or absence) into the prescribed fire sector.

Scaling-up prescribed fire

Coexisting with fire and smoke

If prescribed fire is going to be used to manage critical ranges of variation in nature and occur at large scales, increased literacy is needed to more realistically communicate how multiple fire regime components interact to affect air quality. Air quality during the fire season is a growing concern around prescribed fire today, and pressure is increasing to minimise smoke impacts. This is particularly evident for regions where the occurrence of prescribed fire still persists at large scales and where fire regimes are relatively intact. This leads to an obvious question: how much smoke should be expected, especially if regional fire regimes were still intact?

Consider, for example, the Flint Hills region of Kansas. The Flint Hills is the most intact prescribed fire culture remaining at large scales within the grassland biome of North America and represents the last remaining tallgrass prairie region. On average, approximately 0.8 million hectares burn each year in the Flint Hills (Scholtz *et al.* 2020). Although fire is considered essential to the sustainability of the Flint Hills, numerous questions have emerged in recent years about the smoke produced from the region, including: (1) how much have fire and smoke increased (compared with pre-settlement); and (2) are fire and smoke operating in novel ways (e.g. outside of historical reference points)? These questions remain unanswered but are fundamental to regional and national policy discussions. Of course, historical data do not exist to answer these types of question directly; nevertheless, changes in smoke can be well understood by leveraging

modern fire occurrence data (Scholtz *et al.* 2020) as a proxy within a simple framework (Twidwell *et al.* 2020) for understanding how fire regimes have changed in contemporary times compared with previous cultural eras.

Many fire regime components have been altered considerably in the Flint Hills compared with pre-settlement estimates, despite having one of the most intact fire frequency regimes within US rangelands today (Figure 15.4). At a regional scale, less area has burned in the Flint Hills in recent

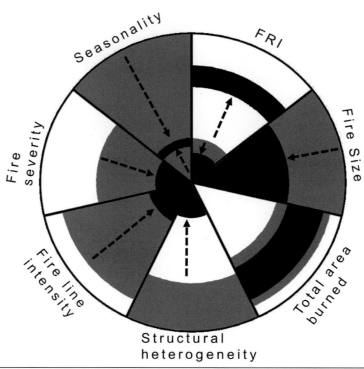

Fire Regime Characteristic	Pre-settlement condition	Contemporary Condition
Seasonality	Year round	Spring only (dormant season)
Fire return interval (FRI)	Every 3 years or less	Polarized region dominated by annual burning or infrequent burning
Maximum fire size	100,000+ to 1,000,000+ acres	75 000+ acres
Total burned area	1/3 of the entire ecoregion (approx. 2 million acres)	Ranges between 800 000 acres and 2.6 million acres per annum (2000-2019)
Structural heterogeneity	Heterogeneous	Homogeneous
Fire line intensity	Varied	Low
Fire severity	Mixed	Low

Figure 15.4: Fire regime change for one of the most intact prescribed fire cultures remaining in grasslands of North America (Flint Hills, USA) using a framework to compare pre-settlement and contemporary fire cultures (Twidwell *et al.* 2020). Grey fill, indigenous (pre-settlement) culture; black fill, contemporary (prescribed fire) culture. Arrows show the direction of change for the region. FRI, fire return interval.

decades compared with pre-settlement. In general, between 12% and 38% of the Flint Hills ecoregion burns each year (Scholtz *et al.* 2020), whereas one-third was estimated to have burned pre-settlement (Kansas Department of Health and Environment 2010). The frequency of fire is polarised within the region. Locations either burn frequently or rarely (Figs 15.4, 15.5). Some locales have increased the occurrence of fire compared with pre-settlement expectations and burn annually, but this is offset by a higher number of locations that have reduced the frequency of fire (having burned only once or twice over the past two decades; Figure 15.5). Although fire size remains relatively large compared with the rest of the Great Plains, fire severity, intensity and structural heterogeneity are substantially constricted. Based on this information, and assuming relative constancy in other factors contributing to smoke production, the annual fire and smoke production from the Flint Hills is relatively consistent or even slightly less than pre-settlement expectations. We know of no communication of this fact to the general public and no consideration of annual smoke budgets in regional policy.

Instead, concerns over smoke and air quality (specifically particulate matter and ozone) stem from changes in an alternative fire regime component: fire season. Current standards of daily particulate matter are set at 150 μg m^{-3}, whereas the 8-h standard of ozone may range between 0.06 and 0.07 ppm. Although the overall amount of fire has decreased in the Flint Hills, the timing of burning has also changed as the burning season has been constricted to a shorter period of time in the dormant season (from mid-February to late-April). Importantly though, pre-settlement, growing season fires were likely to also have been common (Twidwell *et al.* 2020). Changes in fire season present a more serious complication for regional prescribed fire cultures because air quality is regulated based on hourly and daily exceedances, not annual smoke budgets (Kansas Department of Health and Environment 2010; Baker *et al.* 2019). This problem is not unique to the Flint Hills. Other flammable regions battle with constricted air quality concerns in some areas of Australia (Keywood *et al.* 2015), where particulate matter exceeded 200 μg m^{-3}, and South America (Mataveli *et al.* 2019), where the highest monthly particulate matter emissions were observed at the end of the dry season (0.224 and 0.386 Tg month^{-1} in August and September respectively).

This is an example of how one simple change in the fire regime can trigger complications to prescribed burning cultures, even if the total amount of smoke produced from a region is less than how the system functioned in the past. Innovations in monitoring, if coupled with more ecologically informed scenarios of ecosystem function, could provide new insights into how to better manage smoke from prescribed fires, avoid well-intended policy guidance that focuses on only one characteristic of the fire system and pave pathways forward to enhance the benefit of regional prescribed fire cultures while mitigating for trade-offs. Contrast this approach with the more traditional use of monitoring data and communication of air quality impacts. Monitoring data are often presented in a simplistic manner to communicate air quality

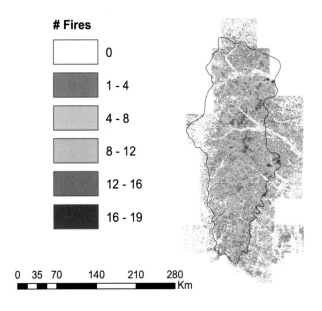

 # Fires

0

1 - 4

4 - 8

8 - 12

12 - 16

16 - 19

0 35 70   140   210   280
Km

Figure 15.5: Number of fires recorded between 2001 and 2018 within the Flint Hills ecoregion (USA). Adapted from Scholtz *et al.* (2020).

impacts for days that had smoke versus those days that did not. This is a classical burned versus unburned (control) comparison that lacks any realistic standard of reference in nature (Twidwell *et al.* 2020). Not implementing prescribed fires promotes a wildfire-driven system in the Flint Hills, which has occurred elsewhere in the Great Plains of North America (Donovan *et al.* 2017), and changes the context for how smoke will be produced from the region into the future. In neither case, however, is the system able to persist in an unburned state long term. Rather, it should be assumed that pyric systems will burn with some degree of regularity, either as a result of prescribed fires, which are highly predictable and used for resource management objectives, or from the more stochastic, unpredictable and extreme conditions typical of wildfires.

Moving forward, more realistic standards of reference that explore these plausible future scenarios are needed to better manage and regulate air quality. These standards should be ecologically informed, reflect the historical occurrences of fire for a region's dominant vegetation and account for sources of novelty that could alter vegetation–fire–smoke relationships and their impacts in modern society. Clearly, this is an example of how technological advances could be used to avoid tendencies to oversimplify the role of fire in nature and the classical tendency to attempt to minimise or overly control fire, often to the detriment of society at large.

Moving past 'the failure of safe prescribed burning'

Prescribed fire conditions are so tightly controlled (and with good intent: to ensure safety and containment) that they often fail to create sufficient differences in fire intensity, fire severity and corresponding spatial heterogeneity required for numerous floral and faunal specialists (Smucker *et al.* 2005; Hutto *et al.* 2008; van Wilgen 2013; Donovan *et al.* 2019; Roberts *et al.* 2019). This has been referred to as the 'failure of safe prescribed burning' (van Wilgen 2013) and fundamentally reflects the

command-and-control philosophy of the modern prescribed fire era (Figure 15.1a).

Many 'rules of thumb' exist to dictate what is considered safe and acceptable, including long-standing constraints in rangelands imposed on the ranges of temperature, relative humidity (RH) and wind speed conditions (Wright and Bailey 1982). These include the 30°C/20% RH/30 kph wind speed rule in South Africa, the 80°F (27°C)/20% RH/20 mph (32 kph) rule of Texas in the US and the 60°F (16°C)/40% RH/15 mph (24 kph) rule of the central Great Plains of North America. Each rule describes a maximum temperature limit, a minimum RH limit and a maximum wind speed that defines acceptable prescribed burning parameters (Bidwell *et al.* 2011). However, these simple rules of thumb mostly reflect information that was readily available and could be easily monitored, they assume a particular type of prescribed fire design and they do not reflect the physical process of fire behaviour, ember transport or other factors affecting the probability of ignition once an ember lands on a receptive fuel source. Many critical ecological responses were associated with greater variability in fire regimes that occurred pre-settlement (e.g. Figure 15.1) and lie outside what is considered, in contemporary times, to be typical 'safe' fire prescriptions. Concerns over containment also reinforce a culture where prescribed fires are applied on smaller-sized parcels of land instead of larger landscapes, and this makes large-scale prescribed fire management impossible given the limited number of burn days that meet long-held rules of thumb. This is not to overemphasise that rules of thumb are not important or useful; rather, it showcases a need to rethink our vision of prescribed fire and begin to incorporate broader-scale thinking into planning, management and implementation.

Mathematical models of fire behaviour and ember transport have been around for decades to aid fire planning (Rothermel 1972; Andrews and Rothermel 1982; Andrews and Bradshaw 1990). Most have seen limited use in rangeland prescribed fires, but these types of models provide an opportunity to rethink large-scale fire planning. For example, considerable time and effort is spent monitoring for the occurrence of spot fires that result from embers produced by a prescribed fire. Ember transport models are readily available to compute the maximum spot fire distance that can be expected from a fire source, one of the most useful pieces of information available for prescribed fire planning. Ember transport models were used to establish experimental infrastructure for the Extreme Fire Trials in Texas (Twidwell *et al.*

2013b, 2016b, 2020) and to expand fire conditions for purposes of scientific inquiry. Fires were conducted far beyond traditional temperature and RH constraints while burning at low wind speeds (due to wind's disproportionate impact on ember transport distances; Twidwell *et al.* 2013b). In a similar manner, calculation of maximum spot fire distance can identify instances where prescribed fires can be scaled-up by burning into non-receptive fuel sources within the surrounding landscape matrix (Figure 15.6). Non-receptive fuels include

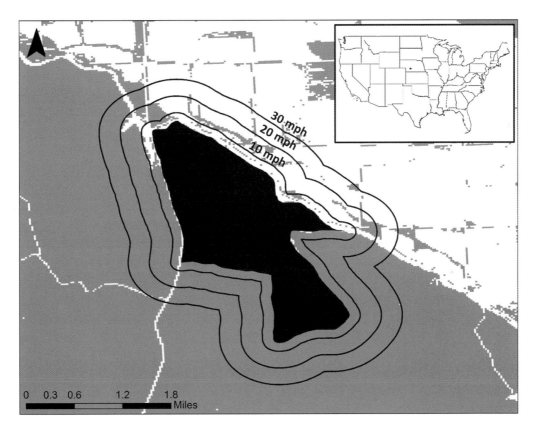

Figure 15.6: Prescribed fire planning based on models of maximum spot fire distance. The distribution of potential receptive fuels (grey) within the maximum spot fire distance from the perimeter of an actual prescribed fire (black) conducted in the Loess Canyons Experimental Fire Landscape in Nebraska. Calculations are based on flame sources at the perimeter of the burn unit for 10, 20 and 30 mph (16, 32 and 48 kph respectively) wind speed scenarios (black lines). Non-receptive fuels are represented in white. Maximum spot fire distance was computed using SPOT within the BehavePlus modelling software environment (Andrews *et al.* 2005) and parameterised using local data. Receptive fuels were categorised based on standard fuel models in Anderson (1982) using LANDFIRE's 2014 geospatial layer. Variation in the spatial distribution of receptive fuels reveals locations with minimal probability of spot fire occurrence to the northeast of the burn unit compared to the south. The distribution of receptive fuels within the maximum spot fire distance perimeter can be used to plan ignition techniques to scale-up prescribed fires, where to focus spot fire monitoring efforts and how to more efficiently allocate personnel on burn units. The inset shows the location of the Loess Canyons Experimental Fire Landscape in Nebraska within the US.

many types of agricultural lands, large water sources, snow and ice, barren areas or previous fire management units that consumed receptive fuel sources.

Ignition plans that send embers into non-burnable fuel sources minimise spot fire ignition potential compared with traditional prescribed fire designs in rangelands, which are surrounded by burnable and easily ignitable herbaceous-dominated fuel sources. This, in turn, reduces the risk of prescribed fire escape (or prescribed fire turned wildfire). In cases where this has been applied, less time has been needed using back fires to secure the downwind side of the burn unit because there was already sufficient space to capture ember transport from the headfire. This enables practitioners to effectively scale-up the size of prescribed fire units while broadening the range of conditions used to ignite prescribed fires to meet key resource management objectives.

Summary

Humanity's relationship with fire has changed substantially in recent centuries, representing one of the largest signatures of anthropogenically induced global environmental change (Archibald *et al.* 2013). The future of fire management depends on a critical choice over how to leverage fire and technology for the benefit of future generations. In this chapter we show opportunities to align technological innovations with modern ecological theory and move towards a paradigm better able to manage complex systems of people and nature. We provide examples of how a complex systems viewpoint, supported by technology, can overcome three challenges that have limited prescribed fire: limited workforce capacity, uncertainty in ecological responses and the inability to scale-up prescribed fires to manage regional conservation goals. Our hope is that this chapter inspires a broader vision for the use of technology and prescribed fire in the future and ultimately fosters more sustainable management within Earth's pyric systems.

References

Anderson HE (1982) 'Aids to determining fuel models for estimating fire behavior'. USDA Forest Service, General Technical Report INT 122:22, Intermountain Forest and Range Experiment Station, Ogden.

Andrews PL, Bradshaw LS (1990) 'RXWINDOW, defining windows of acceptable burning conditions based on desired fire behavior'. USDA Forest Service, General Technical Report INT-GTR-273, Intermountain Research Station, Ogden.

Andrews P, Rothermel R (1982) 'Charts for interpreting wildland fire behavior characteristics'. USDA Forest Service, General Technical Report INT-131, Intermountain Forest and Range Experiment Station, Ogden.

Andrews PL, Bevins CD, Seli RC (2005) 'BehavePlus fire modeling system, version 4.0: user's guide'. USDA Forest Service, General Technical Report RMRS-GTR-106 Revised, Rocky Mountain Research Station, Ogden.

Archibald S, Lehmann CE, Gómez-Dans GL, Bradstock RA (2013) Defining pyromes and global syndromes of fire regimes. *Proceedings of the National Academy of Sciences of the United States of America* **110**, 6442–6447. doi:10.1073/pnas.1211466110

Arterburn JR, Twidwell D, Schacht WH, Wonkka CL, Wedin DA (2018) Resilience of Sandhills grassland to wildfire during drought. *Rangeland Ecology and Management* **71**, 53–57. doi:10.1016/j.rama.2017.07.010

Baker KR, Koplitz SN, Foley KM, Avey L, Hawkins A (2019) Characterizing grassland fire activity in the Flint Hills region and air quality using satellite and routine surface monitor data. *The Science of the Total Environment* **659**, 1555–1566. doi:10.1016/j.scitotenv.2018.12.427

Beachly E, Higgins J, Laney C, Elbaum S, Detweiler C, Allen C, Twidwell D (2016) A micro-UAS to start prescribed fires. In *International Symposium on Experimental Robotics*. (Eds D Kulić, Y Nakamura, O Khatib and G Venture) pp. 12–24. Springer, Cham.

Bidwell TG, Weir JR, Masters RE, Carlson J, Engle DM (2011) *Fire Prescriptions for Maintenance and Restoration of Native Plant Communities*. Oklahoma Cooperative Extension Service, Oklahoma State University.

Bowman DM, Balch JK, Artaxo P, Bond WJ, Carlson JM, Cochrane MA, D'Antonio CM, DeFries RS, Doyle JC, Harrison SP (2009) Fire in the Earth system. *Science* **324**, 481–484. doi:10.1126/science.1163886

Bowman DM, Balch J, Artaxo P, Bond WJ, Cochrane MA, D'Antonio CM, DeFries R, Johnston FH, Keeley JE, Krawchuk MA (2011) The human dimension of fire regimes on Earth. *Journal of Biogeography* **38**, 2223–2236. doi:10.1111/j.1365-2699.2011.02595.x

Butler CR, O'Connor MB, Lincoln JM (2015) Aviation-related wildland firefighter fatalities – United States,

2000–2013. *MMWR. Morbidity and Mortality Weekly Report* **64**, 793. doi:10.15585/mmwr.mm6429a4

Chapin FS, III, Kofinas GP, Folke C, Chapin MC (2009) *Principles of Ecosystem Stewardship: Resilience-Based Natural Resource Management in a Changing World.* Springer Verlag, New York.

Donovan VM, Wonkka CL, Twidwell D (2017) Surging wildfire activity in a grassland biome. *Geophysical Research Letters* **44**, 5986–5993. doi:10.1002/2017GL072901

Donovan VM, Roberts CP, Wonkka CL, Wedin DA, Twidwell D (2019) Ponderosa pine regeneration, wildland fuels management, and habitat conservation: identifying trade-offs following wildfire. *Forests* **10**, 286. doi:10.3390/f10030286

Donovan VM, Twidwell D, Uden DR, Tadesse T, Wardlow BD, Bielski CH, Jones MO, Allred BW, Naugle DE, Allen CR (2020) Resilience to large, 'catastrophic' wildfires in North America's grassland biome. *Earth's Future* **8**, e2020EF001487. doi:10.1029/2020EF001487

Fuhlendorf SD, Fynn RW, McGranahan DA, Twidwell D (2017) Heterogeneity as the basis for rangeland management. In: *Rangeland Systems.* (Ed. D Briske) pp. 169–196. Springer, Cham.

Fuhlendorf SD, Davis CA, Elmore RD, Goodman LE, Hamilton RG (2018) Perspectives on grassland conservation efforts: should we rewild to the past or conserve for the future? *Philosphical Transactions of the Royal Society B* **373**, 20170438. doi:10.1098/rstb.2017.0438

Gates EA, Vermeire LT, Marlow CB, Waterman RC (2017) Reconsidering rest following fire: northern mixed-grass prairie is resilient to grazing following spring wildfire. *Agriculture, Ecosystems & Environment* **237**, 258–264. doi:10.1016/j.agee.2017.01.001

Giglio L, Boschetti L, Roy DP, Humber ML, Justice CO (2018) The Collection 6 MODIS burned area mapping algorithm and product. *Remote Sensing of Environment* **217**, 72–85. doi:10.1016/j.rse.2018.08.005

Holling CS, Meffe GK (1996) Command and control and the pathology of natural resource management. *Conservation Biology* **10**, 328–337. doi:10.1046/j.1523-1739.1996.10020328.x

Hutto RL, Conway CJ, Saab VA, Walters JR (2008) What constitutes a natural fire regime? Insight from the ecology and distribution of coniferous forest birds in North America. *Fire Ecology* **4**, 115–132. doi:10.4996/fireecology.0402115

Justice CO, Giglio L, Korontzi S, Owens J, Morisette JT, Roy D, Descloitres J, Alleaume S, Petitcolin F, Kaufman Y (2002) The MODIS fire products. *Remote Sensing of Environment* **83**, 244–262. doi:10.1016/S0034-4257(02)00076-7

Kansas Department of Health and Environment (2010) Flint Hills smoke management plan. Kansas Department of Health and Environment, Division of Environment, Bureau of Air, Topeka, <https://www.ksfire.org/docs/regulations/Flint_Hills_SMP_v10FINAL.pdf>.

Keywood M, Cope M, Meyer CPM, Iinuma Y, Emmerson K (2015) When smoke comes to town: the impact of biomass burning smoke on air quality. *Atmospheric Environment* **121**, 13–21. doi:10.1016/j.atmosenv.2015.03.050

Kolden C (2020) Wildfires: count lives and homes, not hectares burnt. *Nature* **586**, 9. doi:10.1038/d41586-020-02740-4

Mataveli GAV, Silva MES, França DDA, Brunsell NA, de Oliveira G, Cardozo FDS, Bertani G, Pereira G (2019) Characterization and trends of fine particulate matter (PM2.5) fire emissions in the Brazilian Cerrado during 2002–2017. *Remote Sensing* **11**, 2254. doi:10.3390/rs11192254

Moritz MA, Batllori E, Bradstock RA, Gill AM, Handmer J, Hessburg PF, Leonard J, McCaffrey S, Odion DC, Schoennagel T (2014) Learning to coexist with wildfire. *Nature* **515**, 58–66. doi:10.1038/nature13946

Neary DG (2009) Post-wildland fire desertification: can rehabilitation treatments make a difference? *Fire Ecology* **5**, 129–144. doi:10.4996/fireecology.0501129

Nowacki GJ, Abrams MD (2008) The demise of fire and 'mesophication' of forests in the eastern United States. *Bioscience* **58**, 123–138. doi:10.1641/B580207

Roberts CP, Donovan VM, Wonkka CL, Powell LA, Allen CR, Angeler DG, Wedin DA, Twidwell D (2019) Fire legacies in eastern ponderosa pine forests. *Ecology and Evolution* **9**, 1869–1879. doi:10.1002/ece3.4879

Rollins MG (2009) LANDFIRE: a nationally consistent vegetation, wildland fire, and fuel assessment. *International Journal of Wildland Fire* **18**, 235–249. doi:10.1071/WF08088

Rothermel RC (1972) 'A mathematical model for predicting fire spread in wildland fuels'. USDA Forest Service, Research Paper INT-115, US Department of Agriculture, Intermountain Forest and Range Experiment Station, Ogden.

Schoennagel T, Balch JK, Brenkert-Smith H, Dennison PE, Harvey BJ, Krawchuk MA, Mietkiewicz N, Morgan P, Moritz MA, Rasker R (2017) Adapt to more wildfire in western North American forests as climate changes. *Proceedings of the National Academy of Sciences of the United States of America* **114**, 4582–4590. doi:10.1073/pnas.1617464114

Scholtz R, Prentice J, Tang Y, Twidwell D (2020) Improving on MODIS MCD64A1 burned area estimates in grassland systems: a case study in Kansas Flint Hills Tall Grass Prairie. *Remote Sensing* **12**, 2168. doi:10.3390/rs12132168

Smucker KM, Hutto RL, Steele BM (2005) Changes in bird abundance after wildfire: importance of fire severity and time since fire. *Ecological Applications* **15**, 1535–1549. doi:10.1890/04-1353

Tanaka J, Brunson M, Torell L (2011) A social and economic assessment of rangeland conservation practices. In *Conservation Benefits of Rangeland Practices: Assessment, Recommendations, and Knowledge Gaps.* (Ed. DD Briske) pp. 371–422. United States Department of Agriculture, Natural Resources Conservation Service, Lawrence.

Topik C (2015) Wildfires burn science capacity. *Science* **349**, 1263. doi:10.1126/science.aad4202

Twidwell D, Fuhlendorf SD, Engle DM, Taylor CD, Jr (2009) Surface fuel sampling strategies: linking fuel measurements and fire effects. *Rangeland Ecology and Management* **62**, 223–229. doi:10.2111/08-124R2.1

Twidwell D, Allred BW, Fuhlendorf SD (2013a) National-scale assessment of ecological content in the world's largest land management framework. *Ecosphere* **4**, 1–27. doi:10.1890/ES13-00124.1

Twidwell D, Fuhlendorf SD, Taylor CA, Rogers WE (2013b) Refining thresholds in coupled fire–vegetation models to improve management of encroaching woody plants in grasslands. *Journal of Applied Ecology* **50**, 603–613. doi:10.1111/1365-2664.12063

Twidwell D, Wonkka CL, Sindelar MT, Weir JR (2015) First approximations of prescribed fire risks relative to other management techniques used on private lands. *PLoS One* **10**, e0140410. doi:10.1371/journal.pone.0140410

Twidwell D, Allen CR, Detweiler C, Higgins J, Laney C, Elbaum S (2016a) Smokey comes of age: unmanned aerial systems for fire management. *Frontiers in Ecology and the Environment* **14**, 333–339. doi:10.1002/fee.1299

Twidwell D, Rogers WE, Wonkka CL, Taylor CA, Jr, Kreuter UP (2016b) Extreme prescribed fire during drought reduces survival and density of woody resprouters. *Journal of Applied Ecology* **53**, 1585–1596. doi:10.1111/1365-2664.12674

Twidwell D, Bielski CH, Scholtz R, Fuhlendorf SD (2020) Advancing fire ecology in 21st century rangelands. *Rangeland Ecology and Management.* doi:10.1016/j.rama.2020.01.008

Uden DR, Twidwell D, Allen CR, Jones MO, Naugle DE, Maestas JD, Allred BW (2019) Spatial imaging and screening for regime shifts. *Frontiers in Ecology and Evolution* **7**, 407. doi:10.3389/fevo.2019.00407

van Wilgen BW (2013) Fire management in species-rich Cape fynbos shrublands. *Frontiers in Ecology and the Environment* **11**, e35–e44. doi:10.1890/120137

Weir JR (2009) *Conducting Prescribed Fires: A Comprehensive Manual.* Texas A&M University Press, College Station.

Wright HA, Bailey AW (1982) *Fire Ecology: United States and Southern Canada.* John Wiley & Sons, New York.

16

Epilogue

John R. Weir and John Derek Scasta

The public is becoming more and more aware of the increase in tragic wildfires around the globe. These wildfires are seemingly burning more area than ever before, causing more damage to property, and are becoming ever more costly to control. Central to the mitigation of these devastating events is the practice and culture of prescribed fire management needed to reduce the fuel load caused by altered fire regimes and to modify the spatial continuity of areas receptive to active wildfires.

In the western US during 2020, wildfires were one of the main news headlines, with some states experiencing some of the biggest fire in recent recorded history. For example, California was the hardest hit, with 9639 reported wildfires burning nearly 1.9 million hectares, causing 33 fatalities and damaging or destroying over 10 400 structures (CalFire 2021). The magnitude of this fire year cannot be overemphasised, because the number of hectares burned in the 2020 wildfire season in California doubled the previous record for most hectares burned in a single year (Wigglesworth and Serna 2020). Similarly, other countries around the globe have been hit hard by wildfires in recent

years. Australia's worst wildfire season on record was 2019–20, with ~18 million hectares burned. For perspective, this is approximately 15% of Australia's surface land area, or an area equal in size to France, Spain and Portugal combined (https://en.wikipedia.org/wiki/List_of_Australian_bushfire_seasons).

Although the biophysical evidence suggests that prescribed burning is an effective, yet underutilised tool for combatting catastrophic wildfires (Kolden 2019; Miller *et al.* 2020), and the sociological evidence suggests that society is more accepting of prescribed fire after serious wildfires (Australasian Fire and Emergency Service Authorities Council and Forest Fire Management Group 2015), one persistent question has emerged from the ashes of those wildfires: why are the areas most affected by these wildfires not using prescribed burning more to reduce wildfires? That question has sparked numerous answers and debates around the world. In the US, these events and question have prompted legislators in Washington, DC to draft a national prescribed burning bill to pump money into prescribed fire, rather than fire suppression. Currently, prescribed fire is at the forefront of the wildfire issue, but can it stay that way or will the wildfire industry push it aside to continue their multibillion dollar per annum attempt to 'control' wildfires? Similar conversations are going on in other countries, with Australian (Reality Check Team 2020) and South African (Evans 2020) governments struggling with ways to combat the devastating effects of wildfires.

This book has come at a time when prescribed fire is being talked about more and more around the globe as a proactive strategy, especially as wildfires continue to dramatically affect people's lives, homes and businesses. This book offers the reader several case studies on the challenges of implementing and the successes of applying prescribed fires not only for wildfire mitigation, but also for the conservation of biodiversity and agricultural and traditional reasons. It is our hope that this book can be a starting point for people who want to reintroduce or increase the amount of fire on the ground. Fire is a common thread that occurs around the world, and a society's need or desire for fire is often complex, and not simply because of the ecological and agricultural benefits, but also because of the need to protect human lives and property. There are years of experience and a vast wealth of knowledge about the use of prescribed fire in these pages just waiting for readers to discover this knowledge and to apply it. The book serves as a modern avenue for knowledge sharing and transfer across large spatial boundaries and offers up the wisdom and experiences of authors from around the world. Examples range from why fire is not being used to places where fire may be used to the extreme. There are chapters on how fire is used in its most simplest and most primitive form, to complex and difficult planning processes that seem to be written to limit fire more than to aid it. This book highlights the leading edge of prescribed fire knowledge as it applies to policy, governance and organisation. Finally, the integration of technology with the use of unmanned aerial vehicles and global positioning systems to ignite fires seemingly without the need of humans, along with thermal imaging to understand fire complexity, is just the beginning for technological innovation for prescribed fire.

In many cases, it is easiest to choose not to burn rather than to understand the guiding policies and the preparation and planning steps necessary to successfully implement a prescribed fire. However, as this book illustrates, prescribed fire can be embraced and used in a highly professional manner to obtain the ecological benefits that are as important as sunlight, soils and rainfall. Moreover, we need to remember that prescribed fire can be limited by governmental policies, outlawed by legislation or feared and shunned by society. However, no matter how prescribed fire is perceived or used around the globe, we know one thing will always remain constant: fire is going to occur, with or without a plan! So take the time to read and re-read this book and absorb the knowledge within, not only for the good of the land, but also for the good of society.

References

Australasian Fire and Emergency Service Authorities Council, Forest Fire Management Group (2015) *Overview of Prescribed Burning in Australasia: Report for National Burning Project: Sub-Project 1.* Australasian Fire and Emergency Service Authorities Council, Melbourne, <https://knowledge.aidr.org.au/media/4893/overview-of-prescribed-burning-in-australasia.pdf>.
CalFire (2021) *2020 Incident Archive.* State of California, Sacramento, <https://www.fire.ca.gov/incidents/2020/>.
Evans M (2020) Prescribed burning in dry ecosystems to reduce emissions: fighting fire with fire (to restore ecosystem health). *Forest News,* <https://forestsnews.cifor.org/70066/prescribed-burning-in-dry-ecosystems-to-reduce-emissions?fnl=en>.
Kolden CA (2019) We're not doing enough prescribed fire in the western United States to mitigate wildfire risk. *Fire* **2**(2), 30.
Miller RK, Field CB, Mach KJ (2020) Barriers and enablers for prescribed burns for wildfire management in California. *Nature Sustainability* **3**(2), 101–109.
Reality Check Team (2020) Australia fires: does controlled burning really work? *BBC News* <https://www.bbc.com/news/world-australia-51020384>.
Wigglesworth A, Serna J (2020) California fire season shatters record with more than 4 million acres burned. *Los Angeles Times,* <https://www.latimes.com/california/story/2020-10-04/california-fire-season-record-4-million-acres-burned>.

GLOSSARY

abiotic   non-living chemical and physical features of the environment

afforestation   establishment of trees in an area where there were no prior trees present

agricultural burning   human use of fire for clearing crop land, preparing seedbed, enhancing forage for livestock grazing, enhancing forestry or other production of a commodity

Anthropocene   current geological period in which human activity is a dominant influence on environmental and climatic features

anthropogenic   referring to an activity that is human induced (e.g. anthropogenic fire)

anti-fire   referring to a position or policy that discourages burning

arson   criminal act of wilful or malicious burning property or structures for many types of nefarious purposes, including to collect insurance or harm another

back-burn   fire that burns into the wind typically lit off of a firebreak or fire line; the opposite of a headfire due to slower spread and intensity; similar to a back fire

back fire   fire that burns into the wind typically lit off of a firebreak or fire line; the opposite of a headfire due to slower spread and intensity; similar to a back-burn

backpack pump sprayer   a portable sprayer that includes a tank and nozzle that is pressurised with a hand pump

berg wind   katabatic wind; hot, dry wind blowing down an escarpment; mountain wind (South Africa)

biomass   total volume of organic matter; in the context of fire, the volume available for burning

biomass burning   fire consumption of organic matter

biome   natural and extensive ecological community with characteristic flora, fauna, climate and geology

biotic   living organisms

block burning   referring to homogeneous application of fire with no unburned patches left

boreal   forest ecosystem of northern North America and Eurasia; characterised by spruce, fir and pine trees

brigade   a formation of people who work to suppress fire; term originally used to refer to a military tactical formation

Bronze Age   prehistoric period of time that followed the Stone Age but preceded the Iron Age; approximately 3000–1200 BC

bryophyte   non-vascular and flowerless plants typically small in size and stature and including mosses and liverworts

burn boss   person with the responsibility to make decisions about how, when and where to ignite a prescribed fire; more common in the US

burn chief   person with the responsibility to make decisions about how, when and where to ignite a prescribed fire; more common in Europe

burn crew   group of individuals conducting a prescribed burn with specific assigned tasks

burn severity   relative amount of fire-induced alteration, disruption or damage a site experiences, as indicated qualitatively by soil heating, fuel consumption and mortality; similar to fire severity

burn unit   specifically delineated area of land to be burned with a prescribed fire

burn window   time period when weather conditions are appropriate for a safe and effective prescribed fire

bushfire   Australian term for wildfire

Campos Sulinos   grassland ecoregion in Brazil

canopy   referring to the elevated portion of a plant, typically the branches and leaves elevated by the trunk of a tree

capercaillie a very large grouse in Europe inhabiting areas dominated by hills and coniferous trees

Cerrado savanna ecoregion in Brazil

charcoal carbon residue produced by slow pyrolysis of organic material

circumboreal referring to the boreal region that circumvents the northern portion of the globe

combustion process of rapid oxidation and production of heat and flame; four stages include preignition, flaming, smouldering and glowing

controlled burn fire that is intentionally and lawfully ignited, and includes measures to prevent its escape; often used synonymously with prescribed fire

controlled fire fire that is intentionally and lawfully ignited, and includes measures to prevent its escape; often used synonymously with prescribed fire

crown fire fire that is moving through the elevated crowns of trees and/or shrubs independent of the fire moving along the surface of the ground; different than ground or surface fire

Crown Land public land in commonwealth countries such as Canada and Australia that is under the purview of the monarchy

crowning process of a fire moving into the elevated crowns of trees and/or shrubs; often rapid and very hot

cultural burning burning practices developed by Indigenous people to care for the land; commonly used in Australia; analogous to firestick farming

cured referring to the drying process of vegetation fuels such that fuels are receptive to ignition and flaming

deciduous trees or shrubs that drop leaves annually (in contrast to evergreen coniferous trees)

desiccation extreme drying or a state of extreme dryness

diurnal daily rhythms

drip torch device for igniting prescribed fires; hand-held canister with a wick that drips flaming liquid fuel that typically consists of a mix of diesel and petrol (gasoline)

driver in the context of prescribed fire, referring to ecological drivers

dry season predictable periods of the year when precipitation is not common (in contrast to the wet season)

duff organic layer above the soil that consists of decomposing twigs, needles and leaves

ecological process referring to the biological, chemical and physical processes that influence ecosystems; includes the water cycle, nutrient cycle, energy flow and community dynamics

ecological restoration intentional activities that initiate or accelerate the recovery of an ecosystem that has been damaged or degraded with respect to its health, integrity and sustainability

ecosystem community of living organisms that interact with non-living characteristics linked together through energy flow and nutrient cycles

emissions the production or discharge of something; in the context of fire, suggests the production of smoke and other particulate matter

energy flux rate of flow of a property through a unit of area; in the context of fire, referring to heat transfer

ericaceous denoting shrubs or trees from the Ericaceae (heather) family

erosion process of soil, rock and/or organic matter physically moving due to water and/or wind; suggests a degrading state

escape in the context of prescribed fire, fire that moves beyond the intended burn area

ethnographic study of individual cultures that explores a cultural phenomenon from the subject's point of view

experiential learning instructional activities that include hands-on opportunities to actually perform the activity of study

expropriation   the act of an authority taking private property

external fire protection   maintaining a fire break around the perimeter of a property

fauna   animals

fine fuels   fuels that respond to environmental humidity fluctuations rapidly and ignite readily; generally grasses, leaves and needles

fire adapted   an ecosystem or community that readily coexists with regular fire via mechanisms to recover after a fire

fire beater   a fire suppression tool, sometimes called a flapper or swatter, that is a long pole with a sturdy piece of rubber at the end

fire behaviour   how fire responds to weather and fuels; includes flame length, height and depth, residual flame time, fire intensity and rate of spread

firebreak   features of a burn unit, often linear, where vegetation was reduced or removed prior to igniting a prescribed fire so that fire cannot leave the intended area; synonymous with fireguard or fire line

fire culture   denoting a social tendency to use fire on the land regularly by a group of people for a variety of purposes

fire dependent   referring to species or ecosystems where fire is essential to their structure and function; species will have evolved adaptations allowing them to respond to fire and facilitate fire spread

fire ecology   the interaction of fire with abiotic and biotic features of an ecosystem, and the associated fire behaviour, fire regime and responses to fire by abiotic and biotic features; a scientific discipline

fire evader   species with persistent propagules either stored in the soil or a reliable outside seed source that evade exposure to fire

fire exclusion   policies or mandates to attempt to eliminate fires from the landscape using fire suppression strategies and techniques

fire fighting   attempts to suppress and/or extinguish unwanted fires from damaging property or lives

fire frequency   indication of the frequency through time that fires occurred; there are many ways to calculate fire frequency, including fire rotation, mean fire interval, mean fire return interval and annual probability of fire

fireguard   features of a burn unit, often linear, where vegetation was reduced or removed prior to igniting a prescribed fire so that the fire cannot leave the intended area; synonymous with fire line or firebreak

fire hazard reduction   proactive strategies to reduce hazardous fuels that may ignite and burn causing damage; similar to fuel hazard reduction

fire history   quantitative and qualitative details about fire regimes in the past, and often prior to European settlement; measured in many ways, including historical records, tree rings/dendrochronology, charcoal and pollen studies

fire intensity   the rate at which fire produces thermal energy; fire line intensity as calculated by Byram's equation ($I = HWR$, where I is fire line intensity, H is heat yield, W is the amount of fuel consumed and R is the rate of spread)

fire line   features of a burn unit, often linear, where vegetation was reduced or removed prior to igniting a prescribed fire so that fire cannot leave the intended area; synonymous with fireguard or firebreak

fire management   comprehensive approach to managing any type of fire (planned or unplanned); includes proactive and reactive strategies

fire prone   species or areas that have a tendency to burn

fire regime   fire patterns that include seasonality, frequency, size, continuity, intensity, type and severity; generalised over long periods due to repetition and predictability

fire return interval   the mean time period between fire events under some assumed historical conditions

fire seasonality   indication of periods during a year when fires are more frequent or prevalent;

regional patterns are often driven by seasonal patterns

fire sensitive species that have a high probability of mortality after a fire

fire severity relative amount of fire-induced alteration, disruption or damage a site experiences; similar to burn severity

fire spatial continuity horizontal continuity and completeness of fire spread and fuel consumption

fire spread movement or transmission of active flames through an arrangement of fuel particles

firestick farming referring to Aboriginal cultural burning in Australia or burning practices developed by Indigenous people to care for the land

fire temperature how hot a fire is; often used as a proxy for fire intensity

fire tolerant species that have a high probability of surviving a fire

fire type how the fire moves across the landscape; three types: crown fire, surface fire and ground fire

First Nations Indigenous people groups in Canada

first-order fire effects direct or immediate consequences of a fire due to heat-induced processes; include fuel consumption, smoke production, soil heating, plant injury and heating; drivers of second-order fire effects

flame depth distance behind the fire front that is continuously covered with flames; horizontal measurement

flame height perpendicular distance from the ground to the top of the main body of flames; vertical measurement

flame length length of the flame from the lowest point where active burning is occurring to the top of the main body of flames; measured at an angle on wind-driven fires; used as a proxy for intensity

flammability capacity of a fuel to ignite and combust; four components, namely ignitability, sustainability, combustibility and consumability; similar to flammable

flammable capacity of a fuel to ignite and combust; four components, namely including ignitability, sustainability, combustibility, and consumability; similar to flammability

flank fire ignition technique and a fire type where a fire is set so that it burns outwards at right angles to the wind; fire perimeter that is approximately parallel to the main direction of fire spread

flora plants

foam an artificial chemical product comprised of a stable mass of small air-filled bubbles used for suppressing fires; in combination, foam cools, separates the flame or ignition source from a surface, suppresses vapours and smothers

fogging referring to a nozzle for a sprayer that breaks the water stream into small droplets producing a very fine spray; increases water use efficiency

föhn-like wind rain shadow winds (South Africa)

forest ecosystem natural or planted; plant communities dominated by trees

fuel in the context of prescribed fire this refers to either naturally occurring vegetation fuels or petroleum-based fuels used in an ignition device to intentionally set fires

fuel accumulation the aggregation of dead vegetation material over many years

fuel availability indication of adequate fuel in terms of amount and receptivity for burning

fuel bed the collective fuel characteristics, including the horizontal and vertical continuity, representing a unique fire environment and associated fire spread; sometimes fuelbed

fuel consumption amount of natural vegetation fuels consumed by fire, and thus removed from an area

fuel hazard fuels that can rapidly ignite and burn, often explosively, and burn causing damage

fuel hazard reduction proactive strategies to reduce hazardous fuels that may ignite and burn causing damage; similar to fire hazard reduction

fuel load   naturally occurring vegetation fuels that are a measure of the potential energy that could be released by a fire; total amount of flammable fuel for the surface area of the burn unit

fuel moisture   amount of water in a fuel particle that is available to fire; generally expressed on a dry weight basis

fuel reduction   treatments to reduce the amount of vegetative fuel and likelihood of ignition; can include mechanical treatment (mowing, cutting etc.), grazing, spraying herbicide and/or prescribed fire; similar to fuel treatment

fuel treatment   treatments to reduce the amount of vegetative fuel and likelihood of ignition; can include mechanical treatment (mowing, cutting etc.), grazing, spraying herbicide and/or prescribed fire; similar to fuel reduction

fuel type   description of fuel features, including species, size and structure relative to predictable fire behaviours and flammability

fuels management   intentional alteration of the amount or arrangement of natural vegetative fuels; strategies include prescribed burning, mowing, grazing, logging etc.

fynbos   natural shrubland and heathland vegetation in the Eastern and Western Cape provinces of South Africa

game   in the context of wildlife, species that are valued for hunting

geomorphology   the study of the Earth's physical features and association with geology

gorse   thorny evergreen shrubs in the genus *Ules*; native to western Europe and northern Africa

graminoids   grass-like plants; grasses, sedges and rushes

grassland ecosystem   system where vegetation is dominated by grasses and may include sedges and rushes; often fire is a regulating disturbance

gross negligence   negligence that was so careless that it showed a complete lack of concern for the safety of others; more than simple careless action

ground fire   type of fire that is burning the organic matter beneath the surface litter of the ground, such as the peat layer; different from surface fire or crown fire

guide outfitter   person and/or businesses that provide services for clients in remote areas for hunting, fishing or other recreation endeavours

Harmattan   season characterised by dry dusty trade winds; West Africa

headfire   a fire type that spreads with the wind; often intense and fast

heathland   similar to moorlands but drier; shrubland habitats occurring on barren and infertile lands and dominated by shrubs including heather; historic and 'seminatural' landscapes facilitated by anthropogenic management, particularly prescribed burning

herbaceous   vascular plants with no persistent woody stems

herbivory   consumption of plant material by animals, particularly herbivores

heterogeneity   indicating a diversity or variation of features; in the context of prescribed fire, indicates variability in time since fire

heterogeneity-based management   applying fire in a variable manner across space and time such that some areas have been burned recently and others areas are unburned

heterogeneous   indicating a diversity or variation of features; in the context of prescribed fire, indicates variability in time since fire; see heterogeneity

Holocene   current global epoch; the second epoch of the Quaternary period following the Pleistocene

human ignitions   fires lit by humans

humidity   amount of water vapour present in the air; important for predicting the probability a natural fuel particle will ignite

humus   organic component of the soil; formed as microorganisms decompose plant material

hydrophobicity   soil water repellency; forms relative to fire temperature, organic matter, soil texture and soil water content

Ice Age   period of cold temperatures and glacial activity during the Pleistocene

ignition   process of setting a fuel particle on fire or starting to burn

ignition chief   person with the responsibility of directing the ignition of a prescribed fire

ignition crew   group of people with the responsibility of directing the ignition of a prescribed fire

ignition pattern   manner by which a fire is ignited; includes distance between ignition points and the sequence of ignitions as determined by topography, fuel, weather and burn unit features

incendiary   suggesting a device or an effort to cause fires

internal fire protection   division of a property into burn blocks; African

Iron Age   prehistoric period of time that followed the Bronze Age; noted for weapons and tools being made from iron

land reclamation   process and strategies to improve lands to make them more suitable for other uses, such as conservation

land tenure   legal or cultural demarcation of ownership and use of land; synonymous with land holder

layering   plant reproduction strategy where vertical stems droop horizontally and produce adventitious roots upon contacting the soil

legislation   multiple laws; society formally and collectively addressing an issue; may refer to proposed laws that are being considered but not yet enacted

liability   the state or condition of being responsible for something; may be a legal determination

litter   layer of dead plant material on the soil surface

Mediterranean Basin   the region of lands around the Mediterranean Sea that have a Mediterranean climate

Medieval   also known as the Middle Ages; started at the fall of the Roman empire and lasted until the Renaissance

meristem   plant tissue that consists of actively dividing cells; important for plant growth; located at the tips of roots and shoots and in the cambium

mesic   an environment or habitat that receives a moderate amount of moisture; as opposed to arid

Mesolithic   archaeological period occurring between the Palaeolithic and Neolithic; 15 000–5000 BP

mineral soil   in the context of fire, exposed soil horizons formed by initial parent material (i.e. rock) and devoid of upper organic layers because of burning; also referring to installation of fire lines where vegetation is mechanically (or otherwise) removed down to this layer

monitoring   systematic measurements of soil, plants and animals; relative to fire

monoculture   agricultural practice of growing a single crop; areas dominated by a single feature; in contrast to polyculture

moorland   similar to heathlands but more upland and wetter; shrubland habitats occurring on barren and infertile lands and dominated by shrubs, including heather; includes blanket bogs and valley fens; historic and 'seminatural' landscapes facilitated by anthropogenic management, particularly prescribed burning

moribund   referring to vegetation that is lacking vitality or vigour

morphology   study of the structural form of organisms

mosaic   physical features comprised of diverse elements; in the context of fire, an area with a diversity of burned and unburned areas; similar to heterogeneity

muirburn   Scottish practice of burning old heather growth to encourage new growth for grazing and wildlife; sometimes moorburn

natural fire   in the context of prescribed fire, fires that are not ignited by humans but rather by natural ignition sources, such as lightning or volcanic activity

negligence   failure by a person or entity to use reasonable care that results in damage or injury

Neolithic   prehistoric period of time during the later part of the Stone Age when stone weapons and tools dominated

objectives   a goal or metric that is aimed for with action; in the context of prescribed fire, could include reducing fuel loads, enhancing habitat or improving forage for grazing

operations   in the context of prescribed fire, referring to the active process of conducting a prescribed burn including ignitions, suppression, communications etc.

particle emissions   the release of ash, soot or other constituents into the atmosphere by combustion

pastoral   agricultural practices that involve the keeping and/or grazing of livestock, particularly cattle, sheep and horses, but other species also

patch   in the context of prescribed fire, an area that is set apart from the surrounding area based on its treatment (e.g. a burned patch within a larger unburned pasture)

patch burning   the practice of only burning small patches within a larger management units, such as a pasture

patch burn grazing   the practice of burning a small patch within a larger management unit such as a pasture combined with grazing or browsing by animals that have full access to and can choose to use burned or unburned areas

patch mosaic burning   the practice of burning a small patch within a larger management unit such as a pasture combined with grazing or browsing by animals that have full access to and can choose to use burned or unburned areas; has the objective of creating a mosaic on the landscape; similar to patch burn grazing

peat   ground deposit of wet and partially decomposed organic matter; occurring in acidic bogs and fens

plant injury   direct damage to a plant caused by fire; often specified for the root, cambium and/ or crown

plant mortality   death of a plant caused directly or indirectly by fire

plant phenology   cyclical growth events of a plant as influenced by seasonal temperature and precipitation patterns; timing of emergence, foliage production, stem elongation and flowering

plant reseeding   natural reproductive strategy that relies on the production and dispersal of seeds for recruitment of new plants after a disturbance

plant resprouting   natural reproductive strategy that relies on new plant growth originating from below- or aboveground plant parts after a disturbance

plant species composition   relative richness and diversity of plant species

plant structure   physical features of plant communities

plastic ignition spheres   aerial ignition devices in which glycol has been injected into plastic spheres that contain potassium permanganate and are subsequently dropped from a helicopter; also referred to as delayed aerial ignition devices (DAID) or plastic sphere dispenser (PSD); similar in size and shape to a ping pong ball

pleurocarpus   in reference to mosses that bear fructifications on the main stem or lateral branches

point ignition   referring to the igniting of a fire from a single discrete point in space; as opposed to a line of fire

policy   standard, guideline or action principle established by a government or other party

political geography   subdiscipline of geography that addresses the spatial outcomes and impacts of political structures and processes

portable blower   hand-held equipment that focuses forced air blown in a direction; the device is mobile and can be used for ignition and suppression activities

prescribed burn   fire that is intentionally and lawfully ignited, and includes measures to prevent its escape; often used synonymously with prescribed fire and/or controlled burn

prescribed burn associations   groups of landowners and other interested people who organise to conduct prescribed burns; equipment and knowledge are shared to enhance the safety and effectiveness of burns

prescribed fire   fire that is intentionally and lawfully ignited, and includes measures to prevent its escape; often used synonymously with prescribed burn and/or controlled burn

prescription   a set of parameters, dosages and/or guidelines that are established authoritatively; instructions written by a professional authorising specific actions

propagule   vegetative structure distinct from the parent plant that can develop into a new plant (e.g. buds or other tissues)

propane torch   hand-held tool for the direct application of flame; propane is a natural hydrocarbon gas

pyric   relating to burning

pyric herbivory   grazing and/or browsing by animals as focused due to the attraction to burned areas and new plant growth

pyrodiversity   diversity of spatial and temporal patterns of fire on a landscape; variable fire regimes and associated biodiversity patterns and ecological processes

pyrogenic   caused or produced by combustion or fire; fire prone

range tenure holder   Canadian term referring to the individual or group that has access to a set amount of Crown Land for grazing as administered by the Ministry of Forests and Range

rangeland   land type that is unsuitable for crop agriculture; includes deserts, shrublands, grasslands, wetlands and forested lands; grazing and browsing by domestic and wild herbivores is a key feature

reforestation   natural or human planting of new tree stands

regulation   rules or directions established by an authority; often governmental

residence time   amount of time that active flaming occupies a single point in space

resilience   ability or capacity to return to predisturbance conditions

resistance   ability or capacity for conditions to remain unchanged relative to disturbance

restoration   process of returning something to a former pre-existing state or condition

riparian   interface area between uplands and water; includes unique plant communities and hydrological features

risk   probability of, or exposure to, danger, loss and/or harm

Rocky Mountains   mountain range and region in western North America

Rothermel's fire spread model   quasi-empirical model developed in the 1960s and 1970s predicting the spread of fire based on data obtained from artificial fuel beds in a wind tunnel and heat balance models

rural incendiarism   use of fire to protest against authorities

sanctioned fire   fire intentionally set and managed under any cultural or political authority, regardless of whether it occurs outside of, or even counter to, national legislation

savanna ecosystem   open grassland with scattered trees; common in tropical and subtropical regions

scale   concept in landscape ecology that includes the spatial and temporal measures of features and disturbances

second-order fire effects   indirect effects of a fire that occur over long time frames, including soil, plant and animal responses to fire after the direct effects (first-order effects) are over

semi-arid   a dry region or climate often dominated by grasses and/or shrubs; characterised by mean annual precipitation between 200 and 700 mm

serotinous   an ecological adaptation where seed release is triggered by an environmental trigger such as fire removing external resin from a seed and seeds being released for growth

shifting mosaic   concept of landscape disturbances that are variable through space and time and facilitate the development of a mosaic of vegetation patterns

shrubland   plant community that is dominated and characterised by short statured woody plants referred to as shrubs or bushes

silviculture   forestry practice that includes the management of the growth, species composition, physical structure and quality of vegetation

slash and burn   agricultural practice that involves the cutting and then burning of vegetation to clear the land and prepare it for the planting of a crop

smoulder   a stage of ignition characterised by slow burning with no flaming but including smoke production

social license   realisation or perception of the right or legitimacy to act

strict liability   when an activity is not so unreasonable to prohibit it altogether, but is sufficiently dangerous that it provides unusual risks

stump sprouts   resprouting stems from the base of a tree or woody plant

subalpine   referring to a topographical position on higher slopes of mountains that is below the timberline

suckering   asexual reproduction strategy where vegetation forms a new stem from an extensive root system, specifically from an adventitious bud

suppression   stopping or reducing an activity or process; the process of putting out a fire or limiting fire activity

surface fire   fire type that burns the litter and vegetation on the surface of the ground; different from ground fire or crown fire

svæla   Old Norse term meaning to smoke out or a thick smoke

swaling   burning for grazing; derived from the traditional practice and linked to the Low German *swelan*, meaning to singe grass

sward   stand of grass; grassy surface of land

swidden agriculture   slash and burn approach to agriculture but using a shifting pattern where plots of land are cultivated only temporarily and then abandoned for revegetation

tanker truck   motor vehicle that is designed to carry a large volume of liquid; specific to prescribed fire, trucks with a large volume of water available for suppression activities

temperate   regions and/or climates with mild temperatures; occur at middle latitudes between the tropics and polar regions of the globe

terrestrial   referring to the land; not aquatic or aerial

time since fire   the time elapsed since an area burned

tracer lines   mowed or sprayed narrow strips of vegetation to create a cured fuel bed surrounded by live vegetation; for ease of burning

traditional ecological knowledge   knowledge of the environment that has been acquired over long periods by Indigenous or Native people

underburning   burning practice that seeks to only burn surface fuels while leaving the overstorey of trees unburned

unsanctioned fire   arson and undesired natural or accidental ignitions requiring suppression

vapour pressure deficit   difference between the amount of moisture in the air and the amount of moisture the air can hold when saturated

veld   land type characterised by grasslands; commonly stratified by altitude such as highveld, middleveld and lowveld; common in southern Africa

water table   upper surface of the zone of soil or ground saturation by water

weather monitoring   systematic evaluation of weather conditions; often includes both on-site measurements and remote measurements of wind speed, wind direction, relative humidity, temperature, precipitation etc.

wet season   period during a year when the majority of precipitation is received in a region; also called the rainy season

wetland   ecosystem characterised by flooding either seasonally or permanently and where oxygen-free processes and characteristic vegetation subsequently occur

wildfire   uncontrolled and unplanned fire burning in natural vegetation

wildfire mitigation   practices to prevent or reduce the negative effects of wildfire; often include modifying the natural fuels

wildland fire   fire in extensive natural landscapes; refers to both planned (prescribed or controlled fires) and unplanned fires (wildfires)

wildland–urban interface   transition zone between extensive natural areas and urban areas; these areas are particularly vulnerable to the negative effects of wildfires

wind speed   atmospheric feature of air moving from high to low pressure; often due to changes in temperature

INDEX